THE TORY LEADERS

Nigel Fisher

THE TORY LEADERS

THEIR STRUGGLE FOR POWER

WEIDENFELD AND NICOLSON
LONDON

To my step-father, Sir Geoffrey Shakespeare,
who first interested me in
the endless adventure of politics

CONTENTS

	List of Illustrations	*vi*
	Acknowledgements	*vii*
	Preface	*ix*
1	Choosing a Leader	*1*
2	Disraeli to Chamberlain	*15*
3	Winston Churchill	*32*
4	Anthony Eden	*56*
5	Harold Macmillan	*83*
6	Alec Douglas-Home	*101*
7	Edward Heath	*124*
8	Margaret Thatcher	*145*
	Appendix 1	*187*
	Appendix 2	*194*
	Appendix 3	*198*
	Index	*201*

ILLUSTRATIONS

1 Benjamin Disraeli at Osborne
2 Robert Cecil, Marquess of Salisbury
3 Lord Balfour with David Lloyd George
4 A. Bonar Law in 1911
5 J. H. Thomas, Stanley Baldwin and Neville Chamberlain
6 Sir Anthony Eden
7 Sir Winston Churchill with Harold Macmillan
8 Iain Macleod with Duncan Sandys
9 Reginald Maudling, Lord Hailsham and R. A. Butler
10 A Man For All Seasons
11 Sir Alec Douglas-Home, Margaret Thatcher, Harold Macmillan
   and Edward Heath
12 Edward Heath
13 Margaret Thatcher

ACKNOWLEDGEMENTS

I am very grateful to my wife and to Lord Fraser of Kilmorack for the time they gave and the trouble and care they both took to read and correct the manuscript of this book.

My thanks are also due to Dennis Kavanagh, who researched the first two chapters, and to Christopher Barnett, who researched the next five, without whose help my own research work would have been greatly prolonged.

I owe special gratitude to Mrs R. Kloegman for her accuracy and speed in typing the manuscript and to my secretary, Caroline Borg, for the considerable extra work which the book entailed.

The following friends and colleagues were very kind in finding the time in their busy lives to discuss the people and events described in this book and to refresh my memory from their own knowledge and experience. Without their help and advice my recollections would have resulted in a far less accurate account of what took place and why:

Lord Aldington, Humphrey Atkins, the late Earl of Avon and the Countess of Avon, Kenneth Baker, Lord Barber, Sir Frederic Bennett, Lord Boothby, Sir Harry Boyne, Miss Ursula Branston, Sir Paul Bryan, Lord and Lady Butler, Lord Carr of Hadley, Lord Carrington, Sir Robin Chichester-Clark, William Clark, Kenneth Clarke, Sir John Colville, Lord Colyton, Brian Connell, Viscountess Davidson, John Devine, Edward du Cann, Lord Duncan-Sandys, Peter Emery, Sir Edward Ford, Hugh Fraser, Lord Geoffrey-Lloyd, Lady Hailes, Miss Joan Hall, Sir Charles Harris, Kenneth Harris, Lady Hartwell, Lord Home, Sir Geoffrey Howe, David Howell, George Hutchinson, Michael Jopling, Sir Keith Joseph, Anthony Kershaw, Sir Timothy Kitson, Harold Macmillan, James Margach,

ACKNOWLEGDEMENTS

Neil Marten, Michael Mates, Reginald Maudling, Fergus Montgomery, Airey Neave, John Peyton, James Prior, Lord Selwyn-Lloyd, William Shelton, Earl St Aldwyn, Sir John Taylor, Mr Denis Thatcher, Mrs Margaret Thatcher, Christopher Tugendhat, Peter Walker, Ian Waller, Sir Brian Warren, Bernard Wetherill, William Whitelaw, the late Michael Wolff, Richard Wood.

The illustrations are reproduced by kind permission of Radio Times Hulton Picture Library (1, 2, 3, 5), Keystone (4, 6–9), *Morning Star* (cartoon by Eccles), *The Times* (11), *Daily Telegraph* (12), and Press Association (13).

PREFACE

This book is not a study of the Conservative Party or even of its leaders, most of whom have already been the subject of many biographies. I have concentrated on the evolution or election of each of the leaders I have known personally from Sir Winston Churchill to Margaret Thatcher and I have tried to assess why others, notably Lord Butler, who were strong candidates for the leadership, never attained it.

In the introductory chapter I have outlined the powers of the leader and the consultative, and later elective process, by which he or she has emerged. I have also shown the change in the composition of the Parliamentary Party in recent years and thus in the type of leader it has chosen. In the second chapter I have dealt briefly with the leadership from Disraeli to Neville Chamberlain and in the later chapters I have described in detail the rise and fall of each leader since 1940.

As I have been a Member of Parliament for over twenty-seven years, I have had the opportunity to see at first hand (and sometimes to play a small part in) the making and breaking of all the post-war leaders of the Party. This gives this account the advantage of authenticity but the disadvantage of some almost inevitable loss of objectivity.

I

CHOOSING A LEADER

The Conservative Party has always entrusted its leader with great authority. He is free to choose his Cabinet or Shadow Cabinet and he appoints the chairman and officers of the Party. After consultation with his colleagues, he is authorized to decide on policy and to issue the Party manifesto for general elections.

The membership of the Party in the country is represented on the constituency executive committees, the area organizations and ultimately on the National Union of Conservative and Unionist Associations. At its annual council and Conference meetings the National Union passes policy resolutions, reflecting opinion in the constituencies, but these are advisory, not mandatory, and do not bind the leader. Arthur Balfour once said that he would as soon consult his valet on policy as the Party Conference; and, until Edward Heath set a precedent in 1965, the leader did not listen to the debates or even attend the Conference until the last day when he arrived to make the final key-note speech. One of the few occasions on which the Conference has had any decisive influence on policy was in 1950 when a resolution was passed against the advice of the platform committing a future Conservative Government to build 300,000 houses a year.

It was not until 1965 that a democratic procedure was adopted for the election of the leader and only in 1975 that provision was made for his re-election or rejection. The process now follows the same lines as the system already in use by the Labour Party.

In contrast to his Conservative counterpart, the Labour leader controls only the Parliamentary Party; he is subject to more restraints and his responsibilities are shared with other elements in the Party. Since its inception in 1900 the Labour Party has had a written constitution which lays down the powers and duties of its different

1

sections. The bureaucracy at Transport House is under the formal control of the National Executive, the members of which are elected by the annual Conference; and responsibility for policy and even for the election manifesto is shared between the Executive, the Conference and the Parliamentary leaders. In opposition, most members of the Shadow Cabinet, as well as the leader and his deputy, are elected by the Labour Members of Parliament.

These formal differences between the powers of the leaders of the two Parties are not, however, as great in practice as they may seem in theory. When the Labour Party is in office, its Prime Ministers have shown as much independence as Conservative leaders and in recent years Harold Wilson was usually able to ignore the views of the Conference and of the National Executive when he was in power. It is a curious irony that the Labour Party devised a most democratic constitution, which has since been adjusted in various ways to make it more workable in practice, whereas the Conservative Party began with a theoretically autocratic constitution, which has since been modified to make it more democratic.

A Party's choice of leader is of great electoral importance. He influences, sometimes decisively, the image of the Party and its appeal to the public. In the mid-60s many people saw Harold Wilson, then aged fifty, as a more modern figure than his Conservative opponents, Macmillan and Douglas-Home, who were respectively twenty and ten years older. He was an electoral asset in 1964 and 1966, as Harold Macmillan had been in 1959, but Edward Heath, who was never a vote-winner, had become an actual liability by 1974.

The leader is a potential Prime Minister and his choice of colleagues and decisions on policy can shape the fortunes of the Party and of the nation. Over a period of time he can also influence the type of candidate chosen by the constituency Parties. In recent years the Conservative Central Office list of approved candidates has reflected the meritocratic background of Edward Heath and most of his leading colleagues.

It is worth noting, however, that individual candidates can no longer be imposed on constituency associations. After the Conservative defeat in 1945, when many of the Party's leaders lost their seats, Winston Churchill suggested that Central Office should influence associations, where by-elections were likely or pending, to choose Harold Macmillan, Brendan Bracken, Richard Law (now Lord Coleraine) and Peter (now Lord) Thorneycroft, in order to strengthen his front bench in the House of Commons. The constituencies conformed but they resented the restriction on their freedom of choice and no Party leader would venture such interference today. Even Churchill failed in his first attempt to get Sir Walter Monckton adopted.

It is clear from the historical record that Conservative leaders have rather less security of tenure than Labour leaders. The Conservative Party has had eight leaders in the last forty years, serving for an average of five years, compared with an average of ten years each for Labour's last four leaders until James Callaghan, and in nearly every case the Conservative leader was under some pressure to retire before he actually did so. In spite of the difficulties which Labour leaders have often experienced in managing their Party, it is the Tories who have the more ruthless record. A Conservative leader can command much greater day-to-day loyalty than a Labour leader; but, once under serious criticism, his fall is more likely and is usually swifter. This combination of total loyalty up to a point and then dismissal in the event of failure is usually an advantage to the Party. Winston Churchill summed it up in vol. II of *The Second World War*:

> The loyalties which centre upon number one are enormous. If he trips he must be sustained. If he makes mistakes they must be covered. If he sleeps he must not be wantonly disturbed. If he is no good, he must be pole-axed.

It is true, however, that a Prime Minister who is in good health and enjoys the support of his Cabinet colleagues is virtually irremovable. During this century Lord Salisbury in 1902, Bonar Law in 1921 and 1923, Baldwin in 1937, Churchill in 1955, Eden in 1957, and Macmillan in 1963, all retired voluntarily, though in some cases reluctantly, owing to age or serious illness. Neville Chamberlain retained the leadership for some months after losing the premiership and Balfour and Alec Douglas-Home relinquished their positions because both felt they had lost the confidence of a section of the Parliamentary Party. Austen Chamberlain and Edward Heath were explicitly rejected by their followers in the House of Commons.

Conservative leaders have lost the confidence of their supporters for a number of reasons, the most usual of which has been defeat in the last general election or the prospect of defeat at the next. Conservatives like and are accustomed to office. Since 1886 the Party has been in government for over sixty years out of ninety, including several periods of almost unbroken Conservative rule, notably from 1886 to 1906, during most of the inter-war years, and from 1951 to 1964. For the last century Conservatives have looked upon themselves as the natural Party of government and for much of that time the leader has also been the Prime Minister, which has strengthened his authority in the Party. The poor electoral records of Arthur Balfour and Edward Heath, who each lost three elections, certainly weakened their positions and, although Alec Douglas-Home did well to run Labour so close in 1964, the view was widely held in the Party that he was not an electoral asset.

A second factor in weakening a leader's security has been disagreement over policy. The Conservative Party has never been as monolithic as its critics allege. Because Conservatives have held strong views about Britain's place in the world, many of their disputes have been over foreign and imperial questions such as Home Rule for Ireland, Dominion status for India, the appeasement of Hitler and the seizure of the Suez Canal. Of the domestic issues, Balfour's critics wanted a more wholehearted commitment to tariffs and more vigorous opposition to the Liberal attacks on the House of Lords; Austen Chamberlain's downfall was due to the disagreement over continued Conservative support for the Lloyd George coalition; and some of Edward Heath's critics believed that his incomes policy eroded true Conservative principles. In most of these cases disagreement over policy coincided with criticism of the leader's style and his general performance. The most decisive reason for Heath's loss of support was his own personality.

The leader is expected to unite his own Party and to inspire his followers to electoral victory. But the qualities he requires vary according to the circumstances – for instance, Winston Churchill's single-minded opposition to Nazism and his belligerent reputation were a handicap to his career in the 1930s, but a great asset in 1940.

It is not essential for the leader to be sociable. Both Salisbury and Bonar Law were shy and Heath has little or no small talk; but contemporary leaders have to pay much more attention to their back benchers than was once the case and nowadays an unwillingness or inability to communicate is less easily overlooked than it used to be. Among his Parliamentary colleagues and indeed the electorate as a whole, a leader's personality and the way in which he attracts or alienates support is often of greater significance than the policies he proposes. The newspapers and television tend to personalize politics

4

and people are more interested in the man than in the message. They are interested in his eloquence, his ability and above all in his sincerity. By reacting as they eventually did against Lloyd George's style of leadership, both Bonar Law and Baldwin made a virtue of their soundness and comparative lack of brilliance. Character is usually as important as brains.

Some leaders have been heirs-apparent. The office of Vice-President of the United States provides for an uncontroversial succession if a President dies. By contrast, the British constitution does not recognize the position of deputy Prime Minister. There was no doubt about the succession of Balfour, Neville Chamberlain or Eden; but both Curzon in 1923 and Butler in 1957 and again in 1963 saw their legitimate expectations disappointed. The argument for the established heir-apparent is that he is experienced and well-known and, presumably, acceptable to the Party. A potential disadvantage is that he may be blamed for past policies if the Party is seeking a new direction.

Luck is important. It is virtually certain that Winston Churchill would never have become Prime Minister but for the tragedy of war. On the other hand, Austen Chamberlain was ill-served by circumstances in 1922. Bonar Law owed his position to a deadlock between two better supported candidates. Baldwin only emerged because of the collapse of the Lloyd George coalition, the resignation of Austen Chamberlain and the death of Bonar Law, all of which occurred within the space of eighteen months. Only six years before he became leader of the Party his ministerial position was among the most modest in the coalition Government; yet Curzon, who was to be passed over in his favour in 1923, had been ranked next to the Prime Minister in a War Cabinet of five.

The leader's personal and political presentation is important. His debating ability in the House of Commons must be high enough to evoke the enthusiasm of his back benchers and to command their confidence; nowadays his television technique must be attractive to the electorate. Since the economy became the central issue in contemporary politics, he should also have a sound knowledge of economics. Alec Douglas-Home's lack of confidence in this era was a handicap which his opponents were quick to exploit.

This century has seen two major changes affecting the emergence of Conservative leaders. In the first place the leader of the Party in the House of Commons has become the leader of the whole Party in

Parliament and in the country. The second and more recent development has been the choice of a new leader by formal election.

During the nineteenth century, whenever the Party was in opposition, the leadership went into commission between the leaders in the two Houses. Indeed, the leader in the House of Commons was often the junior partner. This was the case when Granby was chosen in 1846, Disraeli in 1849, Northcote in 1876, Hicks-Beach in 1885, Lord Randolph Churchill in 1886, W. H. Smith in 1887 and Balfour in 1891. But in the twentieth century it gradually became clear that the leader of the Party must be a member of the elected House where the main political battle is fought. This change was underlined in 1923, when Baldwin was preferred to Curzon, and in 1940 when Churchill instead of Halifax succeeded Chamberlain. Even then it was not conclusive for, in each case, the two peers were at least seriously considered. In 1963 Alec Home's decision to relinquish his peerage before becoming Prime Minister seemed further to confirm this new principle.

Until 1965 there was no democratic election procedure. When the Conservative Party was in office it was usual for the sovereign, after consultation with senior figures in the Party or on the advice of the retiring Prime Minister, to invite someone to form an administration. This sounding of views arose because the crown was anxious to appoint somebody who would be acceptable to the Party. The new Prime Minister was then formally elected as leader at a meeting attended by Members of Parliament and peers. Under these circumstances the Parliamentary Party was merely confirming the choice made by the monarch. This method was defended by Captain Pretyman at the meeting of Conservative MPs to elect Austen Chamberlain as leader in 1921:

> Great leaders of parties are not elected, they are evolved. Our leader [Bonar Law] who has just laid down his sword for the moment was never elected formally leader of the party at all; he was evolved, and I venture to hope it will not be necessary – and I think it will be a bad day for this or any party – to have solemnly to meet to elect a leader. The leader is there and we all know it when he is there.
>
> There is no necessity either now or at any future time to hold a competition for the leadership of the whole Party.

This consensus system favoured the man who encountered least opposition among his Cabinet and Parliamentary colleagues.

By 1957, and especially in 1963, the prior discussions had become more exhaustive. In 1957 the Members of Parliament as well as the Cabinet were included informally in the consultative process and in 1963 the Conservative peers, the National Union, and the Young Conservatives were also permitted to express a view. But despite these more extensive soundings there was still criticism that the leader was effectively chosen by a 'magic circle' of senior figures in the Party.

Circumstances had conspired to make the 1963 succession an awkward and anxious one: Harold Macmillan's illness coincided with the annual Party Conference and his decision to resign was announced deliberately to that body. This was a major political mistake which created an electioneering atmosphere at the Conference. Another unusual factor was the number of possible contenders for the post including Hailsham and Home, who had both become eligible as a result of the recent legislation which made it possible for members of the House of Lords to renounce their peerages.

The controversy surrounding Alec Home's emergence and the refusal of two of his colleagues to serve under him made the private soundings system seem ill-attuned to the age and the intense coverage by the newspapers and television did the Party some harm in the short term. Explanations of the consultative process did not reassure the critics, especially in the light of an admission by the then Chief Whip that he had given more weight to the preferences of some MPs than to those of others.

In view of these criticisms it seemed best to adopt a formal and more democratic procedure for future elections to the leadership. The new rules still favoured the emergence of a consensus leader and attempted to minimize the possibility of a divisive result. The names of the proposers and seconders remained confidential; a winner would emerge on the first ballot only if he gained a majority over the runner-up plus fifteen per cent of the total vote; on a second ballot the winning candidate needed an overall majority and if a third ballot was required MPs could indicate their first and second preferences as between the top three candidates left in the contest after the second ballot. A revision of the rules in 1975 provided for the re-election or dismissal of the leader. This was a logical development of the 1965 system and ensured that what Members of Parliament had given they could also take away.

Since 1965 the adoption of the formal election process has established the supremacy of the Parliamentary Party's choice beyond any doubt. In the last volume of his memoirs, *At the End of the Day*, Harold Macmillan recalled a conversation with the Queen on 20 September 1963:

> She feels the great importance of maintaining the prerogative intact, and ... I was determined at all costs to preserve the prerogative, which had been so useful in the past and which might be so useful in the future.

In fact it was never exercised again, because it could only be preserved, even theoretically, as long as the consultative procedure for electing a new leader still prevailed. The Parliamentary Labour Party had long since elected its own leader by secret ballot and, once Alec Douglas-Home had introduced the same method for the Conservative Party, the Queen was obliged to accept as Prime Minister whoever had been chosen by the majority Party as its leader.

The effect of a leadership election in eliminating the royal prerogative was at first not obvious, because the successive elections of Hugh Gaitskell and Harold Wilson to lead the Labour Party and of Edward Heath and Margaret Thatcher to lead the Conservatives all occurred when their respective Parties were in opposition and when the sovereign was not, therefore, in any way involved.

It was not until Harold Wilson retired as Prime Minister in 1976 that the prerogative was effectively terminated by the Labour Party's choice, when in government, of Jim Callaghan as its new leader. This left the Queen no discretion. She was obliged to send for Callaghan and invite him to form a Government.

It may be argued that, even under the consultative method, the Queen had to accept the advice offered her and it is certainly true that the prerogative had been eroded in 1940, 1957, and 1963, but private advice is less mandatory than a public *fait accompli* and, by resigning as Prime Minister, Harold Wilson finally removed the constitutional right of the sovereign to choose her Prime Minister.

In examining the careers of the Conservative leaders in this century a number of features emerge. To be eligible the candidate must be a Member of the House of Commons and will usually have served for some time in the Cabinet or Shadow Cabinet.

Conservative leaders have been Members of Parliament for an average of twenty-five years before being elected to the leadership. The exceptions were Bonar Law and Baldwin, who entered Parliament as middle-aged businessmen and reached the summit owing to a series of accidents, and Edward Heath and Margaret Thatcher, who first became Members at the age of thirty-four and who both served relatively short apprenticeships of fifteen years.

The great offices of state, such as that of Foreign Secretary, Chancellor of the Exchequer and Home Secretary, have usually been the last rung on the ladder to the top. In this century only Bonar Law, Edward Heath and Margaret Thatcher have not held at least one of these posts before becoming leader and, until Heath's accession in 1965, all the leaders in the last fifty years had served as Chancellors of the Exchequer except Eden and Home, who had both held office as Foreign Secretary.

These two qualifying conditions – a lengthy spell in Parliament and considerable Cabinet experience – make it unlikely that in future anyone will become leader of the Party at a young age. There will be no more William Pitts. The average age of election to the leadership in this century is fifty-seven and Chamberlain, Churchill, Macmillan and Home were sixty or over. The last two leaders, both elected at forty-nine, have been the youngest.

In the past twenty-five years there has been a marked change in the type of Conservative entering Parliament and this is now being reflected in the type of leader. Until the present century the leaders (except for Disraeli, who is *sui generis*) were almost all drawn from the aristocratic and land-owning class. They came from political families like the Cecils, Churchills and Stanleys, were educated at the major public schools and traditional universities and entered Parliament almost as a matter of course. They mixed easily at court, in London clubs and in the great country houses. This social background provided ties of kinship, friendship and mutual interests apart from the political views they shared. There was a tradition of service in their families and they regarded public life as both a duty and a pleasure, which they could afford and enjoy.

As W. L. Guttsman wrote in *The British Political Elite*:

> One is struck again and again by the extent and intimacy of these personal contacts. They are inevitably related to the greater freedom and ease of intercourse which stems from a considerable degree of independence.

A century ago, of the 111 owners of 50,000 acres each, or more, fifty-nine sat in the House of Commons.

Money was the key. The change in the composition and character of the Parliamentary Party, especially since the Second World War, has been due to the social and economic changes in the country as a whole. Between the two wars only fifty or sixty ambitious young men entered politics with the motivation of Ministerial office and the exercise of power.

There was another section of about the same number of older men who had made a success in business or in the professions. Some of them had virtually bought their seats and were described by Baldwin as 'hard-faced men . . . who look as if they had done very well out of the war'. They regarded Parliament as a suitable culmination of their careers, but they had no wish or prospect of becoming Ministers.

The majority of the Parliamentary Party during the first half of the twentieth century were country land-owners, ex-officers retired from the armed forces, or the sons of aristocratic families. As Lord Geoffrey-Lloyd expressed it to me, 'Many were on their way from the Brigade of Guards to the House of Lords.' Almost all were drawn from the upper or upper middle class, enjoyed private incomes and could afford politics as an interesting part-time occupation. Few of them aspired to office or fame, but they appreciated the amenities and companionship of what was still regarded as the best club in the world. They came to Parliament, as their fathers and grandfathers had done (and often representing the same seats), out of a sense of service and duty. None were in public life for a living. They were amateurs – independent financially and often independent in their views. They were loyal and could be persuaded to support the Government's policies. They could not be ordered or compelled to do so.

Jaspar Moore, who sits for Ludlow, is typical of this disappearing category of the Conservative membership. He is a country gentleman who entered Parliament 'from family habit' and was in fact the sixth member of his family to represent a Shropshire seat. Never ennobled, he and his forbears have served their country faithfully for 400 years without expectation of office or reward.

People with this sort of background did not suddenly disappear from the Conservative hierarchy. Indeed, some of Edward Heath's most senior colleagues, Sir Alec Douglas-Home, Lord Hailsham, William Whitelaw and Lord Carrington were from this class. But by 1970 they were becoming the exceptions rather than the rule. There were seven Old Etonians in Churchill's post-war Cabinet, eight in Eden's and eleven in Douglas-Home's, but only three in Heath's. On the back benches, too, the number of business and professional men was increasing and the proportion of Etonians fell from twenty-four per cent in 1951 to eighteen per cent in 1970 and must be much lower today.

Even towards the end of Macmillan's premiership an Eton education was becoming almost a political disadvantage. I remember when a young back bencher of promise was recommended for a junior Ministerial vacancy, the Chief Whip replying, 'I am afraid the administration is over-subscribed with Etonians. You had better suggest someone else.' It is agreeable to be able to record that the young man who was rejected on this occasion got his chance later and did well in Heath's government.

It so chanced that I played a small part in the democratization of the Tory Party. I had returned from Germany in 1945 to contest the Chislehurst division of north Kent. After six years of war the association had few members and no funds and its chairman and I had to defray all the election expenses between us. When the election was over, J. P. L. Thomas (later Lord Cilcennin), who was then vice-chairman of the Party, asked me to form and become first area chairman of the new Young Conservative movement in the south-east of England. I agreed to do so, but suggested that there was little point in encouraging these young men and women to work for the Party if we could not open the financial door for the more able amongst them to enter Parliament in the years ahead. Jim Thomas agreed wholeheartedly and invited me to move a resolution at the next Party Conference, limiting the amount of money which any candidate or Member of Parliament might subscribe annually to his local association and obliging the association itself to raise the money for general elections. The resolution was passed and thereafter a Party committee, on which I served, was set up under the chairmanship of Sir David Maxwell-Fyfe, later Lord Kilmuir, to work out the proposals in detail. Its recommendations were adopted by the next Conference and the Party rules were changed accordingly. This prevented rich men buying seats and enabled poorer ones to stand for Parliament.

The long-term effect was significant in altering the type of Tory representation in the House of Commons, but at first the reform was ill-received in some constituencies which disliked the prospect of having to raise their own funds locally. In 1947 I submitted my application for the Conservative candidature in the Hitchin division

11

of north Hertfordshire, which was then vacant and in which my mother and stepfather happened to have a weekend farmhouse. The first question I was asked at the selection committee interview was, 'How much will you subscribe to the local association?' I took a deep breath and replied, 'That is a question I am not prepared to answer and which you should not have asked.' There was a leaden silence, broken, to his credit and my gratitude, by the late Guy Kindersley, then chairman of the association, who said he agreed with me and that the committee should be choosing their candidate on his merits, not on the power of his purse. In the end I was adopted and won the seat from the socialists in 1950.

At that election several young men, who could not have afforded to go into politics before the war, entered the House of Commons for the first time. Some of them had started their political careers in the Conservative Research Department. Others, then and later, came in from the legal professions, publishing, journalism, insurance companies, the merchant banks, investment trusts, advertising and public relations firms. It was a far more varied intake than ever before and was described by Aneurin Bevan as 'the finest Tory vintage in political history'. This and subsequent entries of the meritocracy have resulted in the replacement of the aristocratic attribute of *noblesse oblige* by a pragmatic, indeed technocratic, concern for economic growth and efficiency. Although undoubtedly more in accord with the age, it is at least questionable whether this has in fact led to better and more effective government.

Although the financial easement has increased the diversity of the younger Conservative recruits, their quality owes more to the progressive policies promulgated by Eden, Macmillan, Butler and, later, Macleod, as a result of which the Party has been able to attract into its ranks many idealists and former Liberals. This has not only strengthened it intellectually and numerically, but has kept it in tune with the social changes which have come about in the second half of the century. As Harold Macmillan pointed out in *The Past Masters*:

A successful Party of the Right must continue to recruit from the Centre and even from the Left Centre. Once it begins to shrink into itself like a snail, it will be doomed.

Even before the war, by assimilating the Liberal Nationals, the Tory Party had been influenced by Liberal philosophy. And certainly many, possibly even a majority, of its Members in the present House of

Commons would not be Conservatives at all if the Party had not re-assessed its attitudes and policies after 1945.

Before the last war one could live comfortably on an income of £2000 or £3000 a year. Even as late as 1950, when I entered the House of Commons, it was still possible to do so on a small private income, supplemented by the Parliamentary salary we then received. But it was already becoming more difficult. For my first few years in the House I was considerably out of pocket after paying for a secretary, postage, telephone, travelling and obligatory entertaining. There were no secretarial or living allowances of any kind. A Member's salary was then £1000 and, even as late as 1962 when I joined the Government, junior Ministers only earned £2500 for a more than full-time job with considerable responsibility.

I remember Harold Macmillan addressing the new Ministers after the 'July massacre' that summer. 'I do not ask of you gentlemen great oratorical brilliance in the House of Commons,' he told us, 'or great administrative ability in your departments. All I ask of you is sheer physical endurance.' I saw what he meant after over two years at the Colonial Office, where I worked on an average seventeen or eighteen hours a day during the week and nine or ten hours a day at the weekends and had one week's holiday a year.

Even back benchers work much longer hours since the war than before it. More time is taken up by Government business both up-stairs in committees and in the chamber, and, as the Parties are often evenly divided, this entails constant attendance. In their constituencies MPs are treated as glorified welfare workers and their mail and 'surgery' cases have increased immeasurably. My stepfather, Sir Geoffrey Shakespeare, who was Member for Norwich and a Minister for many years between the wars, has told me that he received fewer letters from constituents in a week than I receive in a day.

The contrast in the work-load of Members of Parliament, when one compares the first decade and the second half of the twentieth century, is even more marked. Before the First World War the House of Commons only sat from February until August. An autumn session was unusual in the second half of the nineteenth century, so there was ample time to shoot grouse, partridges and pheasants and to enjoy at least half a season's fox-hunting.

Politics is no longer a spare-time pursuit and people cannot nowa-days afford to work long hours for relatively low pay, so Members' salaries will increase and their independence will diminish. The transformation of a Parliamentary career from a money-spending to a money-making occupation is an inevitable, though not necessarily a desirable development, which is certain to continue.

The world has changed and, with it, the House of Commons. The leisurely, dilettante approach to politics which characterized its Conservative component has virtually vanished. The Labour Party is changing too. The solid nucleus of elderly trade unionists, moderate in their views, stemming from and genuinely representative of the pre-war working class, is disappearing from the socialist benches and being replaced by university-educated professional men and women. I believe that ex-teachers now form the largest single block in the Parliamentary Labour Party. Looking down from the gallery, the two sides of the House are almost indistinguishable. Gone are the black coats and striped trousers which used to be almost a uniform for Conservative MPs and, whatever their politics, most of the Members now dress alike and look alike, as well they may because in all Parties they are drawn mainly from the graduate middle class.

2

DISRAELI TO CHAMBERLAIN

The Conservative Party can trace its origins to the late seventeenth century, but for much of the period before 1832 the Whigs and Tories were informal groupings in Parliament. The name 'Conservative' was first used in the *Quarterly Review Journal* in 1830 and it is usual to date the Tory transition to Conservatism from the passage of the 1832 Reform Act. Historians have regarded the Duke of Wellington, who rejected any extension of the franchise, as the last Tory Prime Minister and Sir Robert Peel, who accepted the Reform Bill, as the first Conservative Prime Minister in 1835.

The moves towards adult male suffrage wrought many changes including lessening the corruption which had hitherto characterized public life. Two hundred and fifty years ago the constituents of Anthony Henry MP wrote asking him to vote against the budget. He replied:

Gentlemen,
I have received your letter about the excise and I am surprised at your insolence in writing to me at all.

You know, and I know, that I bought this constituency. You know, and I know, that I am now determined to sell it, and you know, what you think I don't know, that you are now looking out for another buyer, and I know, what you certainly don't know, that I have now found another constituency to buy.

About what you said about the excise: May God's curse light on you all, and may it make your homes as open and as free to the excise officers as your wives and daughters have always been to me while I have represented your rascally constituency . . .

Even as late as the nineteenth century, election to the House of Commons was expensive. No limit was placed upon the cost of an election and the candidate was expected to 'treat' the voters, as well as paying for the returning officer. Members themselves received no salaries until 1912, when they were given £400 a year, which was not increased (and then only to £600 a year) until 1937.

Peel's decision to repeal the Corn Laws in 1846 split the Conservative Party. The protectionists led by Lord Stanley (later Lord Derby) and Disraeli broke away, and the Peelites, including Gladstone, drifted to the Whigs, soon to become the Liberal Party. It was only after 1867 that there developed the great Liberal/Conservative duel – so dramatically personified in the contrasting styles and personalities of Gladstone and Disraeli – which was to dominate the political scene for the next twenty years.

Benjamin Disraeli is a romantic, rather bizarre figure. He was the son of an affluent Jewish man of letters and himself wrote several clever novels, but he was not sent to a public school or university and had no formal education after the age of fifteen. Although proud of his Jewish birth, he was converted to Christianity when he was thirteen years old and baptized into the Church of England. This was important because, for most of his life, non-Christians were unable to sit in Parliament. In spite of his background he became the leader of the Conservative establishment, mainly due to the help and support of Lord George and Lord Henry Cavendish-Bentinck, the younger sons of the then Duke of Portland. Many years later Disraeli, by then Earl of Beaconsfield and Prime Minister of Britain, invited the young Duke of Portland, who had just succeeded to the title, to dine at Hughenden. No one else was present and throughout the meal no word was spoken. At the end of dinner, Disraeli rose and said:

My Lord Duke, I belong to a race which never forgives an injury or forgets a benefit. Without the assistance of your uncles, Lord George and Lord Henry Cavendish-Bentinck, who enabled me to enter public life, I could never have attained the position which I hold today of the Queen's first Minister.

These were the only words spoken during the evening. They referred to a conversation between the Cavendish-Bentincks and their father, when one of the brothers had declared:

'There is only one man in England clever enough to lead the Tory Party. He is a Jew, who wears his hair in ringlets and rings outside his gloves.'
The Duke of Portland: 'Is he a country gentleman?'
Answer: 'No.'
Long pause.

The Duke: 'No one who is not a country gentleman can lead the Tory Party.'

Long pause.

The Duke: 'So we must make him one.'

And they did. They bought him Hughenden and 1000 acres, and held the deeds of the property until 1878, when Lord Rothschild bought them and gave them to Disraeli.

Some of the observations of this remarkable man are worth quoting 100 years later. A nation is 'a work of art and a work of time', he said; 'with us it has been the growth of ages and brooding centuries have watched over and tended its perilous birth and feeble infancy'. He saw that the real wealth of England lies in the character of her people and that to impair it is national suicide. 'The national character,' he declared, 'is more important than the Magna Carta or trial by jury.' And again, 'In place of the paper perfection of abstract uniformity, let us turn rather to the pride of a living patriotism based not on official forms and figures but on the realities of human nature.'

In defence of the crown, the House of Lords and the independence of the judiciary, Disraeli saw clearly that

the House of Commons by itself could never preserve liberty. Alone, it might easily become a weapon of despotism and one against which there would be no appeal. . . . I will allow for the freedom of the press; I will allow for the spirit of the age; I will allow for the march of intellect. But I cannot force from my mind the conviction that a House of Commons, concentrating in itself the whole power of the state, might establish in this country a despotism of the most formidable and dangerous character. . . . The throne embodies a conception of perpetual trusteeship . . . it rests upon a firm and sure foundation; it rests upon the hearts of the people. . . . It is not difficult to conceive an occasion when, supported by the sympathies of a loyal people, the royal prerogative might defeat an unconstitutional government and a corrupt Parliament.

Disraeli inspired in the Conservative Party a romantic imperialism which characterized it for the next seventy-five years. He acquired for Queen Victoria the title of Empress of India, which flattered and pleased her, and he bought a forty-four per cent share in the Suez Canal by raising a loan from the banking house of Rothschild. His greatest diplomatic triumph was achieved at the Congress of Berlin in 1878, when he obtained Cyprus from the Turks and from which he returned with 'peace with honour' to a Knighthood of the Garter. But his foreign and imperial successes did not dwarf his domestic policies and he did much to establish the identity of modern Conservatism. In a famous speech at the Crystal Palace in 1872, he proclaimed the Party's guiding principles as the maintenance of our institutions, the defence of the Empire and the improvement of the conditions of the people, only the second of which has ceased to be relevant a century later. Nor did he neglect the Party organization. In the changing era of household suffrage and larger constituencies, he was the first to see the need to organize the voluntary workers and he established successively the Conservative Central Office, the National Union and the Primrose League.

In spite of these notable contributions to the country and to the Conservative cause, Disraeli had to contend throughout his career with deep distrust, not least from within his own Party. His bitter attacks on Peel over the repeal of the Corn Laws in 1846 had given him fame as a young man, but they divided the Tories, lost the support of the Peelites and helped to keep the Conservative Party out of office, except for three short spells of minority government, until 1874. For this reason he did not rise to the top of 'the greasy pole', in the sense of attaining real power, until he was sixty-nine years old. He died seiven years later in 1881.

Followng the extension of the franchise in 1867, there was clearly an important electoral prize to be won by appealing to the working-class vote. The Liberal Party was dominated by the industrialists and inhibited by its *laissez-faire* philosophy from bringing in much-needed social reforms, but the legislative achievements of Disraeli's last administration in its Factory Act, trade union law, housing and public health measures showed a genuine concern for the manual workers. He was said to have done more for the working man in six years than the Liberals had done in fifty. The remarkable electoral record of the Conservative Party owes much to this source of support. Indeed, about a quarter of the working class has habitually voted Conservative ever since.

The Conservatives lost office in the general election of 1880 and, when Disraeli died, Lord Salisbury became leader of the Party in the House of Lords and Sir Stafford Northcote continued to lead it in the House of Commons. There was as yet no recognized leader of the Conservative Party as such. But Northcote, who had at one time served as Private Secretary to Gladstone, was too deferential to the Liberal Prime Minister to be an effective leader of the Opposition and his timid direction gave ample scope for Lord Randolph

Churchill's greater vigour and more formidable debating ability. Churchill was the leader of the so-called Fourth Party,* a combative group of progressive young Tories who waged unrelenting war on the Liberal administration. With his slogan 'trust the people', he appealed to the working-class electorate in much the same spirit as Disraeli some years earlier, and he tried to strengthen the influence of the National Union as a vehicle for his own ambitions. But his impulsive resignation from Salisbury's Cabinet in 1886 was misjudged and spelled the end of his influence. Like Joseph Chamberlain, the other great figure in contemporary radical politics, his hopes were to be posthumously fulfilled by his son.

In 1885 the Liberals resigned after their defeat on the budget and Queen Victoria invited Lord Salisbury to form a government. In theory she could have sent for either Northcote or Salisbury, because neither had been Prime Minister before and there was no established hierarchy between them.

Except for a short period of Liberal rule between 1892 and 1895, the Conservative Party was in office for the next twenty years and Salisbury was unchallenged as Prime Minister. This long Tory ascendancy was due to the split in the Liberal Party following Gladstone's commitment to Home Rule for Ireland, as a result of which nearly one third of the Liberal MPs and half the Liberal peers left their Party to join the Conservatives as Liberal-Unionists.

Robert Cecil, third Marquess of Salisbury, had a remarkable career. He was a Member of the House of Commons for fifteen years before succeeding his father in 1868 at the age of thirty-eight and was Secretary of State for India, Foreign Secretary for a total of thirteen years and Prime Minister for fourteen. By nature a pessimist, he was by conviction a high Tory, who believed democracy to be 'a dangerous and irrational creed'. His sustained, almost venomous disloyalty to Disraeli was generously overlooked in 1866 when he was invited to join the Cabinet as Secretary of State for India – only to leave it within the year in protest against his leader's Reform Bill of 1867. He shared with Gladstone a 'reverence for the Church of England and a common dislike of Disraeli'. In the end a mutual respect gradually developed between the two men, but it had taken twenty-five years, despite the magnanimity which Disraeli always displayed. Although the least flexible of Tory leaders, he held the great office of Prime Minister for longer than anyone since Lord Liverpool.

* The Irish Members formed the Third Party.

It was no surprise when he was succeeded by his nephew, Arthur Balfour, in 1902. Balfour had been heir-apparent for some years and had taken charge of the Government when Salisbury was ill. Between 1881 and 1911 the House of Cecil dominated the Conservative Party. Two days after the King had invited Balfour to form an administration, he was unanimously elected Party leader at a meeting of members of both Houses of Parliament. Joseph Chamberlain was the other major figure in the Unionist Party, but some MPs still doubted his claims to be a true Conservative; the vigorous anti-Tory attacks which he had made twenty years earlier still rankled with them, as Winston Churchill's did later, and the Liberal-Unionists were a separate, though allied Party, backed by their own organization and funds. There was no controversy about the succession. Chamberlain was turning his mind to a preferential tariff for the colonies and was quite prepared to serve under Balfour, as long as he was given scope to develop this policy.

Balfour's rise had been meteoric. He was born with the proverbial silver spoon and could trace his lineage back to Robert the Bruce. He was educated at Eton and Trinity College, Cambridge, and was given an early entrée to politics by working as Private Secretary to his uncle at the Congress of Berlin in 1878. He had first come to notice through his association with the Fourth Party, and his reputation was enhanced by his success as Chief Secretary for Ireland after 1887. When W. H. Smith, the leader of the Party in the House of Commons, died in 1891, Lord Salisbuty appointed Balfour to succeed him.

Arthur Balfour was a brilliant, cultured intellectual of considerable courage and great personal charm. He was an elegant, courteous, unambitious man, remarkably detached from the turmoil of everyday politics. With his many other interests he gave the impression of being a dilettante and Lady Salisbury once referred to his 'unfortunate love of music'. He could always see both sides of a question, so that he usually felt it best not to come down too firmly on either side. His critics considered that this showed an indecisive mind and a lack of conviction. It is not surprising that his hobby was philosophy and that his first treatise was entitled *A Defence of Philosophic Doubt*.

Balfour's nine years as leader were unfortunate for his Party. Chamberlain's advocacy of a preferential tariff for colonial products had much to commend it; but it meant dearer food and this damaged the Party's electoral prospects. Moreover, the Cabinet contained a number of firm free traders who were opposed to the tariff policy. Balfour never committed himself to a precise position, either for or against tariff reform. 'Was I a protectionist or a free trader in 1903?' he once asked his niece. As Prime Minister, he knew that a clear decision either way would split his Cabinet and he did not regard tariff reform as either the most important issue in politics or as the surest road to electoral success. In view of the difficulties which this policy brought his Party over the next twenty years, his caution was perceptive and wise, but he was too aloof and indifferent to political realities to make a good Party leader.

In December 1905 Balfour resigned, hoping that the divided Liberals would be unable to form a government and that he would regain the initiative. The gamble failed. After nearly twenty years in the wilderness the Liberal leader, Campbell-Bannerman, became Prime Minister, dissolved Parliament and gained a great victory at the polls in January 1906. The Conservative Parliamentary Party was reduced to 157 seats in the House of Commons.

Balfour's misfortunes continued in opposition. He found, like other leaders after him, that though the Party gives its leader great authority, his influence is much less in opposition than in government. This is particularly so when he has voluntarily relinquished office and led the Party to a damaging election defeat, as Edward Heath was to discover nearly seventy years later. Under these circumstances the leader is inevitably the victim of retrospective wisdom.

The real trouble for Balfour began later when the large Conservative majority in the House of Lords decisively rejected Lloyd George's budget. This was constitutionally unacceptable to the Liberals, because the House of Commons was generally acknowledged to be supreme in money matters, and in 1910 two general elections were fought on the issue of 'the Lords versus the People'. Although the Conservatives recovered much ground in these elections and almost achieved parity with the Liberals, the Prime Minister – now Herbert Asquith – could rely on the Irish Nationalist and Labour votes. The Opposition was further embittered because the Irish Members were able to demand Home Rule as the price of their support for the Government.

The Conservatives were divided over the lengths to which their resistance should be carried. Balfour believed that, as the Liberals had won a second general election and the King had promised

Asquith that he would create enough peers to pass the Parliament Bill, the Opposition should give way. But the large die-hard element in the Party were not so inclined and their continued resistance was an implied defiance of Balfour's leadership.

When he resigned in November 1911, Balfour gave ill-health as the reason; but he was only sixty-three and he continued to play a prominent part in public life until his death in 1930. The real reason was his boredom with the task of holding his restless Party together and his resentment that his advice had been ignored by a minority of his colleagues. Perhaps Harold Wilson's resignation in 1976 had much the same motivation. Balfour wrote at the time:

I confess to feeling that I have been badly treated. I have no wish to lead a Party under these humiliating conditions. . . . If they think that somebody else is better able to discharge the duties of leadership, I am quite willing to adopt that view.

Both in the dignified manner of his retirement and his continued public service thereafter, he foreshadowed the role played later by Sir Alec Douglas-Home.

Not since 1846 had the Party in the House of Commons elected its own leader and in its search for a successor to Balfour a new situation arose. As in 1881, the leadership again had to go into commission and in 1911 there was also the prospect of a contested election, a situation for which the Party had no rules.

The two candidates were Austen Chamberlain, son of Joseph and a former Chancellor of the Exchequer, and Walter Long, who had been Chief Secretary for Ireland. A bitter struggle seemed certain, for support was evenly divided between the two men and they themselves were not on good terms. There is a story that they met by accident in the House of Commons and, in the course of a heated argument (Chamberlain recollected later), 'I made a step towards him and had it on my lips to tell him he was a cad and to slap him across the face.' They accepted that the election of one or other of them would prove divisive, but neither would agree to withdraw unless a third candidate emerged who had substantial support and was acceptable to their supporters.

There was pressure to settle the leadership issue quickly and a meeting was arranged at the Carlton Club for 13 November, five days after Balfour had resigned. The major concern of the Chief

Whip, Balcarres, was to avoid an election that was certain to divide the Party. He hoped to ascertain the amount of support for each man and to persuade the less favoured to withdraw, but the intervention of the relatively unknown Bonar Law upset these calculations.

Anticipating a deadlock, Austen Chamberlain made it clear that he would withdraw if Long would do so. Long agreed to this proposal and Austen Chamberlain approached Bonar Law. Law showed some surprise, indeed reluctance, claiming that he had only entered his name as a marker for the future. Many MPs at the Carlton Club meeting were disappointed that the private arrangements made by the principal contenders left them with Bonar Law as the only candidate. He now became leader of the Party in the House of Commons while Lord Lansdowne remained its leader in the Lords. Lloyd George commented on hearing the news of the election, 'The fools have stumbled on their best man by accident.'

Law was a modest and very private man with a rather narrow mind and a positive aversion to the arts. His official biographer, Robert Blake, has called him *The Unknown Prime Minister*. He was also a different type of leader to those the Conservatives had chosen in the past. A Presbyterian, born in New Brunswick, he was a taciturn lowland Scot, a Glasgow iron merchant who had never been to university, and the first industrialist to lead the Conservative Party. At the time of his election he had not risen higher in politics than a junior ministerial appointment as Parliamentary Secretary at the Board of Trade in Balfour's administration. He was a sombre, melancholy personality who made a virtue of seeming ordinary, as Baldwin and Attlee did after him. He was a good listener and relied on his common sense and his ability to get to the heart of a matter quickly. On the eve of his election, Beaverbrook told him that he would now have to display more self-confidence and regard himself as a great man; to which Bonar Law replied, 'If I am a great man, then a good many great men must have been frauds.' He filled admirably the same role in the First World War, as a loyal second-in-command to Lloyd George, as Attlee did under Churchill a quarter of a century later. Their qualities were alike and made them perfect foils for their more dynamic leaders.

Law's personality was in sharp contrast to Balfour's. He was direct and blunt where Balfour had been sensitive and subtle; he was dour and partisan where Balfour had been humorous and open-minded. Politically, he was wholehearted in his advocacy of protection, the traditional prerogatives of the House of Lords and support for Ulster against the Government's plan for Home Rule. Indeed, his stand on Ulster strained the fabric of the constitution to its limits and under his leadership the Party displayed its most reactionary mood for a century.

In March 1921 Bonar Law resigned, owing to ill-health, from the Lloyd George coalition in which he was serving as Lord Privy Seal and leader of the House of Commons. Within a few days the Conservative MPs elected Austen Chamberlain as their leader in the House of Commons. He had long been regarded as heir-apparent and his own withdrawal from the previous leadership contest in 1911 had only increased his standing in the Party. But he was unlucky. He had great difficulty in keeping the Party united over the settlement with Ireland and his loyalty to Lloyd George proved in the end his undoing.

The coalition had won a great victory in the 1918 general election. But the Liberals were split between the Asquith and Lloyd George factions and Labour, fighting for the first time as an independent Party, was able to become the official Opposition, though the Party had only sixty-three MPs in the House of Commons. As the sense of unity and purpose engendered by the war evaporated, the coalition lost its momentum. Lloyd George was a formidable figure, the man who had won the war; but he was also a leader with few followers and it is impossible to survive for long in British politics without a Party base. His rise to power in 1916 had split the Liberals and he was now dependent on the support of the Conservatives, who held 335 of the 478 coalition seats. With Bonar Law to complement his genius, he had achieved what Baldwin described later as 'the most perfect partnership in political history'. But Lloyd George's arbitrary leadership, the lavish sale of honours, the negotiations with Sinn Fein for an Irish settlement and the Chanak crisis made many Conservatives fear that the coalition would collapse, and, with it, the Conservative Party, thus leaving the way open for Bolshevism. It is not now realized how much the Russian example was feared in Britain at that time. My own father, an able and level-headed man, went to the lengths of buying an estate in Kenya as a bolt-hole for his family in the event of revolution.

In spite of mounting criticism of the coalition among Conservative back benchers, the Party leaders remained loyal to the Government. This is usually the difficulty with coalitions; they coalesce more easily at the top than lower down. One possible development, a genuine fusion between Conservatives and Liberals to form a new Centre Party against Labour, had not come about, although in March 1920, ninety-five Conservative back benchers sent a petition to Lloyd George and Bonar Law requesting this new alignment. Most of the old issues like Home Rule, House of Lords reform and an extension of the suffrage had been settled, and many of the Conservative leaders, including Bonar Law, were favourably disposed towards the Centre Party concept. Unfortunately, most of the Liberal and Conservative Members were too jealous of their separate Party identities to agree to such an arrangement.

Another possibility was that the Conservatives, as the majority Party in the coalition, would form a purely Conservative Government. Chamberlain, deeply committed to Lloyd George and to the coalition as a vehicle for putting the country before the Party, refused this opportunity of the premiership. Within nine months his Party had repudiated the coalition and a Conservative Government was formed, though not under his leadership. As Winston Churchill is reported to have commented on Austen's high sense of honour and loyalty, 'He always played the game and always lost.'

The coalition leaders decided to soldier on and fight an election in the autumn, but Austen Chamberlain ran into immediate opposition from the Party organizers and many Conservative Members. Sir George Younger, chairman of the National Union and of the Party organization, condemned the proposal in a circular to MPs. Such insubordination was without precedent and there was a great danger that the Party would split. Chamberlain, Balfour and Birkenhead thought the Conservatives could not win without Lloyd George; Baldwin and many of the junior ministers believed they could not win with him.

Chamberlain was prevailed upon to consult the Parliamentary Party on whether to fight the election independently or as part of the coalition and a meeting was convened at the Carlton Club on 19 October 1922. All Conservative MPs and peers who were members of the Government were invited to attend. The real issue was Austen Chamberlain's leadership and the continuation of the coalition Government. Chamberlain was torn between his personal loyalty to Lloyd George and his wish to keep the Party together. Meanwhile Bonar Law, now given a clean bill of health by his doctor, had become unhappy with the coalition and its effect on the morale of the

Conservative Party. He told Austen Chamberlain that he would stay away from the meeting because, if he attended it, he would have to oppose him. Chamberlain acknowledged that any speech by Law would be decisive and Law replied, 'Well, it's a hateful position; I expect that if I had remained in your place, I should have acted like you.'

On the night before the meeting Lord Beaverbrook visited Bonar Law. Law produced a letter to the chairman of his Glasgow constituency declining to stand at the next general election. Beaverbrook managed to dissuade him from posting this and, after much persuasion, Law reluctantly agreed to attend the Carlton Club meeting. His presence there made it clear that there was an alternative leader. Arthur Balfour, a member of the coalition Government, supported Chamberlain. No doubt with his own experience in mind, he observed drily: 'It has never been a Conservative principle to stab a leader in the back, though I concede it has sometimes been a Conservative practice.' Joan Davidson (now Viscountess Davidson and Baroness Northchurch) was with Mrs Baldwin when they saw Sir Philip Sassoon, Lloyd George's Parliamentary Private Secretary, with a grim and dejected expression as he left the meeting. 'Look at Philip,' she cried, 'we've won.' Chamberlain had lost the vote by 185 to eighty-eight and within the hour he and the other Conservative Ministers resigned from the Government. That same afternoon Lloyd George tendered his resignation to the King. The great war-time coalition was at an end.

Bonar Law declined to accept the King's commission to form a government until he had been elected as leader of the Party, but he was duly confirmed in the leadership at a meeting consisting of members of both Houses and prospective candidates. He dissolved Parliament immediately and was returned with a majority of eighty-eight in the election which followed; but his premiership was to be shortlived. His health deteriorated rapidly and in May 1923 he was forced to resign. He was found to be suffering from an incurable cancer of the throat and died within five months. He had played a significant part in the making and breaking of every government between 1915 and 1922.

Stanley Baldwin was Bonar Law's successor, but his appointment by King George v is still a subject of controversy among constitutional commentators. Curzon, whose hopes of preferment had been dashed, is reported to have reacted bitterly that Baldwin was 'a person of the utmost insignificance'. Yet he remained leader of the Party for fourteen years which, apart from Churchill's tenure, was the longest in this century. Churchill described him later as 'the greatest Party manager the Conservatives ever had', and as 'the most formidable politician I have ever known in public life'. He spoke with feeling after being outmanoeuvred by Baldwin over India and the abdication crisis. Yet, by keeping Churchill out of office in the 1930s, Baldwin in fact aided his rise to power in 1940.

Stanley Baldwin was the son of a Worcester ironmaster. Educated at Harrow and Cambridge University, he joined the family business and succeeded his father as MP for Bewdley in 1908 at the age of forty-one. He served as Parliamentary Private Secretary to Bonar Law in 1916, as Financial Secretary to the Treasury from 1917 and as President of the Board of Trade in 1921, but at the age of fifty-four he had still not attained Cabinet rank and had done little to attract attention. No one would have wagered on his becoming leader of the Party, yet in less than eighteen months he was Prime Minister.

The Carlton Club meeting in 1922, which had resulted in the fall of the coalition, had also led to the emergence of Stanley Baldwin. The other Conservative leaders, with the exception of Curzon, remained committed to Lloyd George. Baldwin had voiced the views of many Members in speaking against the coalition. He feared that Lloyd George would divide the Conservatives as he had the Liberals. He was also concerned about the tone of politics – the sale of honours, the influence of the press barons and what he regarded as 'the morally disintegrating effect of Lloyd George'.

He had gained high office as Chancellor of the Exchequer in Law's government, and owed this mainly to the fact that the Party was still denuded of its top talent after the break up of the coalition. As Chancellor he arranged a settlement of Britain's war debts with the United States on terms that Law regarded as disadvantageous and would have liked to repudiate.

When Bonar Law resigned in May 1923 many commentators regarded Curzon as his obvious successor. He was the only figure of weight in the Cabinet. He had served as Viceroy of India and as a member of the War Cabinet and had been Foreign Secretary since 1919. That he had acted as deputy Prime Minister when Law was absent further encouraged his expectations.

Law said he was too ill to tender advice to the King. In fact he

27

would have preferred Austen Chamberlain to succeed him. In April 1923 he had invited Chamberlain to join the Government with the prospect of following him as Prime Minister, but Chamberlain refused. He had therefore turned down the opportunity of the succession twice in little over a year, in February 1922 and in April 1923. Law's resignation meant there was no chance of a third offer to Chamberlain; there were still too many scars from the Carlton Club meeting only seven months earlier. As between Baldwin and Curzon, Bonar Law preferred the former though he did not say so. A memorandum favouring Baldwin was prepared by his former secretary, J. C. C. Davidson (later Viscount Davidson), and presented to the King. The soundings taken by the King's Private Secretary, Lord Stamfordham, were not decisive as between the two men. But a new factor now influenced the choice. Since the Parliament Act of 1911, power had passed increasingly to the elected House. Moreover, the main opposition Party, now Labour, was not even represented in the Lords. There were thus solid constitutional grounds for overlooking a peer's claims to the premiership. It was also clear that Baldwin was more acceptable to most of the Conservative MPs. In the end King George v exercised the prerogative and sent for Baldwin.

Unlike Bonar Law, Baldwin accepted the King's commission to form a government without waiting to be elected as leader of the Party. This followed six days later, when a joint meeting of Conservative members of both Houses ratified the King's choice. Baldwin was the first to acknowledge that he was fortunate, in that so many of the leading Conservatives like Austen Chamberlain, Balfour and Birkenhead were still estranged from the Party. Within eighteen months he had persuaded Chamberlain, and then the others including Winston Churchill, to join his government.

Assessments of Baldwin have varied greatly since his death. In 1937 he retired to universal praise, a man almost above Party who had served the nation well. But within a few years he was being criticized for indolence and complacency and condemned as the leader who had failed to prepare the nation for war. There was little truth in these charges. He saw through Hitler at an early stage, encouraged rearmament, showed himself perceptive about the changing nature of the Empire, and handled the troubles over tariff reform with skill. It was largely due to his wisdom and restraint that the General Strike of 1926 left little lasting bitterness and, by his handling of the abdication crisis ten years later, he performed a great service to the crown and to the people. His reputation was marred by the pamphlet, 'Guilty Men', written by Cato, and by an unsympathetic first biographer. General Smuts said of him that the world rated him too high when he was in power, too low after he retired. There is now a more balanced appreciation of his career and the considerable contribution he made to the public life of Britain between the wars.

Stanley Baldwin, who was loved in his family business and was always called 'Master Stan' by his employees, has been described as the first 'modern' Conservative Prime Minister. He did much to educate the Tory Party for its role in the second half of the twentieth century and to ensure that the Labour Party would be a safe and responsible alternative government. Politically, he was shrewd, tolerant, progressive, liberal-minded, and he understood the English people very well. His policies were designed to attract the widest possible support from men of goodwill in all Parties and this ensured that the social revolution after the Second World War took place with general consent and without violence. 'I want to be a healer,' he once said. He was a cultivated man, musical, well-read, but by no means intellectual, and his appeal was to the heart rather than to the head; yet he attracted the young by his idealism and his sincerity. He was a lovable, though not a dynamic personality and his speeches lacked the poetry and the force of Lloyd George's oratory and the power of Churchill's, but the simplicity and directness of his language evoked warmth and sympathy from his audience. His abdication speech is remembered by those who heard it as a superb example of House of Commons oratory at its best and most sophisticated.

Harold Macmillan has described him in *The Past Masters* as 'a great Peace Minister, in many ways comparable to Walpole', and Smuts thought him 'a good Englishman, a bad European' – by which he meant that Baldwin was skilful in dealing with domestic issues, weaker on foreign affairs, in which he was less interested. He was rather shy and was taken, somewhat reluctantly, into the smoking room of the House of Commons by his close friend, J. C. C. Davidson; but he went there frequently and came to know most of the Members, not only of his own Party. Unlike Neville Chamberlain, he was popular with his Labour Parliamentary colleagues, who trusted and respected him. He also sat in the Chamber more than any other Prime Minister before or since and he always dined – early, at about 7 p.m. – in the Members' dining room. He was a modest man, who did not enter public life with any exalted ambitions:

29

The position of leader came to me when I was inexperienced, before I was really fitted for it, by a succession of chances which could not have been foreseen. I had never expected it.

Above all, he was a patriot, deeply devoted to his country and with an instinctive appreciation of the character of its people.

It is remarkable that such a self-effacing man held high office for so long. He made it clear in 1923 that he was quite prepared to serve under Lord Curzon and between 1931 and 1935 he was content to act as Lord President of the Council with MacDonald as Prime Minister of the National Government, despite the fact that the Conservative Party provided over eighty per cent of the Government's back bench support and he was himself under some pressure to demand the office of Prime Minister.

Other Ministers have paid tribute to his management of the Cabinet, his willingness to promote frank discussion and to defer to others. He was a good House of Commons man and his sensitivity to its moods and atmosphere was the secret of his mastery of the chamber. He was also trusted by the trade-union leaders and did much to lower the tensions between the social classes in the inter-war years. He realized the importance of encouraging the Labour Party to follow constitutional and Parliamentary practice. 'When the Labour Party sits on these benches,' he said, 'we shall all wish them well in their efforts to govern the country.'

By helping to unseat Lloyd George in 1922 and by successfully defying the attempts of the press barons to dictate his policies and his choice of Ministers, he did much to improve the tone of public life.

Baldwin was followed as Prime Minister by Neville Chamberlain, a man of limited imagination and little charm, who succeeded where his father and elder brother, both perhaps more talented, had failed. Chamberlain's career is now seen through the perspective of the years of appeasement and he is regarded as a man who, at the nation's supreme test, was found wanting and replaced by the heroic Churchill. But he had earlier proved himself an outstanding administrator and reformer. As Minister of Health and Housing, he had laid before the Cabinet a list of twenty-five measures which he wanted to enact. Of these, twenty-one became law before he left office and the remainder were passed later. He had been chairman of the Party organization and had served as Chancellor of the Exchequer in Baldwin's final administration. Increasingly, he became the key figure in the National Government.

On 28 May 1937, when Baldwin resigned, the King sent at once for Chamberlain. He was then sixty-eight years old. He commented in his diary, 'It [the leadership] has come to me without my raising a finger to obtain it, because there is no one else.' Three days later he was elected leader of the Party at a meeting of Conservative MPs, peers, prospective candidates and, for the first time, members of the Executive Committee of the National Union. Like Balfour and Eden, he had a smooth succession. But, like them also, he had a relatively short premiership and much of it was stormy and controversial. He was a man of ability and great integrity who would have been an effective and successful Prime Minister in time of peace, but whose qualities were not those to inspire a nation soon to be committed to a great war against a formidable and ruthless adversary.

3

WINSTON CHURCHILL

As long ago as 1931, Harold Nicolson wrote of Churchill, 'He is a man who leads forlorn hopes and when the hopes of England become forlorn, he will once again be summoned to leadership.' It was a prescient observation nine years before the event.

On 31 March 1939, the British Government had given a public pledge that, if Poland was attacked, we would at once give her all the support in our power. Five months later, at dawn on 1 September, German mechanized troops invaded Poland.

In a debate in the House of Commons next day, the Prime Minister's statement sounded equivocal and was a disappointment to those who expected an immediate ultimatum to Germany. There were fears of another Munich and when Arthur Greenwood rose for the Opposition, Leo Amery and Bob Boothby called from the Conservative benches, 'Speak for England, Arthur.' In fact, Neville Chamberlain had already made the fateful decision and the delay was due to an attempt to synchronize his announcement with that of the French. Britain's ultimatum to the German Government was despatched next morning. There was no reply and at 11 a.m. on Sunday 3 September, the Prime Minister told the House that we were at war with Germany. Amery described Chamberlain's statement on this occasion as 'good, but not the speech of a war leader' and he added, 'I think I see Winston emerging as PM out of it all by the end of the year.'

Winston Leonard Spencer Churchill had had an extraordinary career. The son of Lord Randolph Churchill, Chancellor of the Exchequer in the government of Lord Salisbury, and a grandson of the seventh Duke of Marlborough, he was born at Blenheim Palace on 30 November 1874 and educated at Harrow and at the Royal

Military College, Sandhurst. He joined the 4th Hussars in 1895, saw active service on the north-west frontier in India, took part in the last cavalry charge of the British Army at Omdurman and escaped dramatically after being taken prisoner in the Boer War. Later in life he became an amateur artist of talent and over the years he was the author of many books of great distinction and historical importance.

In 1900 he was elected to Parliament as a Conservative but soon crossed the floor and first held office in 1905 as Under-Secretary of State for the Colonies in Campbell-Bannerman's Liberal government. He was successively President of the Board of Trade in 1908, Home Secretary in 1910 at the age of thirty-six, First Lord of the Admiralty in 1911 and Minister of Munitions in 1917.

After rejoining the Conservative Party in 1924, he was Chancellor of the Exchequer until 1929, but throughout the next decade he sat 'below the gangway' in the House of Commons, vigorously opposing the National Government over India and the abdication, and warning the country of the danger of German aggression. His passionate pleas for British rearmament were ridiculed as alarmist and largely ignored until they were shown to have been justified when war broke out in September 1939. His strong advocacy of unpopular policies had kept him out of office for ten years and many people thought that, at the age of sixty-five, his Ministerial career was over. In fact, he was about to reap the reward for being right, but it is certain that he would never have led the nation but for the tragedy of war.

It was questionable whether it would be more troublesome to have Churchill in the Government or outside it, but at length, on 2 September 1939, he was invited to join the War Cabinet as First Lord of the Admiralty. He had occupied the same position twenty-five years earlier at the outbreak of the First World War. Anthony Eden also rejoined the Government as Secretary of State for the Dominions. He had been reluctant to do so, but was persuaded by Churchill that together they could effect more from within the administration than from outside it. This was no doubt true once war was declared, but until then the policies of the two men had not been the same. Eden was a strong supporter of the League of Nations and of the concept of collective security. Since the late 1920s Churchill had not been much interested in these principles and he did not oppose Japan in Manchuria or Italy in Abyssinia. He recognized that the threat to Britain, which was his main concern, came from Germany. His preoccupation, therefore, was to rearm earlier and on a much greater scale in order to discourage and if necessary confront German aggression.

Churchill and Chamberlain could not have been more different in background, character, and personality. Chamberlain represented a relatively new element in the Conservative Party – the well-to-do middle class. Like Galsworthy's Forsytes, his family were 'men of property' (as Iain Macleod wrote in his biography, *Neville Chamberlain*, 'solid as their silver'). As a speaker, Chamberlain was clear, logical, effective, but uninspiring. He was intellectually arrogant; always sure that he was right. But he lacked warmth and friendliness outside his immediate family circle, so that he did not engender personal loyalty or affection among his followers. As a Prime Minister he had many of the qualities and defects which Edward Heath was to display over thirty years later.

Appeasement has become a term of reproach, but Chamberlain's policy in the years before the war, and especially at the time of Munich, undoubtedly reflected the hopes and wishes of the British Parliament and people, by whom it was fully supported and endorsed. He was a man of peace, sincere and dedicated in his efforts to preserve it. Sorrowfully, he summed up his personal tragedy to the House of Commons on the day the war began, 'Everything that I have worked for, everything that I have hoped for, everything that I have believed in during my public life has crashed in ruins.' It was a sad valediction to the years of toil.

No doubt he should have resigned as Prime Minister on the outbreak of hostilities. He did not possess the qualities required to lead a nation at war and just as Asquith, for the same reason, had to give place to Lloyd George, so it was inevitable that Churchill should soon succeed Chamberlain.

Throughout the war Winston Churchill's working day was a long one. He woke early and went through the mass of material awaiting decisions, which were made clearly and quickly. He dictated his instructions or annotated the documents in red ink, attaching his famous pink 'Action this Day' tabs to every urgent memorandum and some that were not. His great war-time speeches were dictated in his own incomparable English, usually without preparatory notes or even headlines, often to a succession of typists straight on to a silent typewriter, as he paced up and down the room, a cigar projecting from his mouth. These were powerful speeches, superbly delivered, but they were tied to the text and lacked the mercurial mobility of Lloyd

George's oratory (or Aneurin Bevan's). The Celts, more than the English, have the power to command and persuade people through the spoken word.

After lunch or before dinner Churchill would retire to bed for a short sleep. This refreshment, unshared by his staff, enabled him to resume work an hour later, fully revived, and he would often call conferences with his officials lasting until two or three in the morning and frequently finishing with a visit to the War Room to check the little flags which denoted the positions of Britain's warships on the oceans of the world. He once said to Lord Ponsonby, then a Labour MP, 'I like things to happen and, if they don't, I like to make them happen.'

Within a few weeks of his appointment, Churchill had absorbed the important areas of responsibility and much of the detail of the Admiralty work. He was full of ideas, such as the construction, from old converted merchant ships, of a dummy fleet to confuse the Germans as to the strength and whereabouts of Britain's capital ships.

He had boundless energy, inflexible purpose and an empirical approach to every problem. Some of his proposals were impractical, but, if one experiment was unsuccessful, his fertile imagination quickly suggested another. These were by no means confined to his naval responsibilities. He peppered the Prime Minister with almost daily letters and memoranda about every aspect of the war; but their relations, based on mutual trust, were easy and often cordial and Chamberlain recorded, 'To me personally Winston is absolutely loyal.'

In December, British morale was boosted by the dramatic action off the River Plate, when the heavily armed German pocket battleship, *Graf Spee*, was humiliated by our light cruisers, *Ajax*, *Achilles* and *Exeter*, and scuttled by her own crew. In April 1940, Churchill assumed the chairmanship of the Military Co-ordination Committee, which superintended the general conduct of the war. This gave him responsibility but without the power to make policy. He really wanted to become Minister of Defence.

During the autumn of 1939, while Churchill was busy with the war at sea, no military action was undertaken by France and Britain on the western front, despite Hitler's initial preoccupation in Poland and the fact that seventy-six Anglo-French divisions confronted only thirty-two German divisions behind the Siegfried line. It is fair to add that only four of the divisions were British, but the allied inactivity was of no help to Poland, on whose behalf the war had ostensibly been launched. As Hugh Dalton observed, 'We were letting them down and letting them die, while we did nothing to help them.' Geographically, there was in fact no effective aid Britain could ever have given to Poland. But the half-hearted and unenterprising conduct of the war was giving rise to renewed criticism of Chamberlain at home, as much from within the Conservative Parliamentary Party as from the Opposition side of the House of Commons.

This was not the earliest evidence of Tory discontent. It had first become apparent when Anthony Eden resigned as Foreign Secretary in February 1938. For some time the clash of personalities between Chamberlain and Eden had been evident. The Prime Minister's instinctive approach to any problem was coldly analytical; Eden's was warmer and more emotional. The break came following a disagreement over British policy towards Italy and, more immediately, over our relations with the United States. Eden had worked for a closer understanding with the American administration; Chamberlain was unenthusiastic, almost hostile. Matters came to a head when the Foreign Secretary was away in France and the Prime Minister, in temporary charge of the Foreign Office, sent a discouraging reply to a constructive suggestion made by President Roosevelt for an international conference. This, though belated, should have been accepted, if only for psychological reasons. Eden was neither consulted nor even informed until he returned to London three days later. Chamberlain's action in going behind the back of his own Foreign Secretary was reprehensible and the reason for it, though no doubt well-intentioned, was ill-advised. He thought he could trust the dictators and do business with them. His own upright character was such that he did not realize they would cheat. Eden was less sanguine. He deplored the Prime Minister's negative reaction to the President's initiative – described by Sumner Wells as a 'douche of cold water' – and felt obliged to resign. His Under-Secretary, Lord Cranborne, followed him to the back benches.

Eden was succeeded at the Foreign Office by the more pliable Lord Halifax, a much respected former Viceroy of India. Rab Butler followed Cranborne as Under-Secretary of State, a position of some importance on the political ladder because his chief was in the House of Lords; but his Parliamentary Private Secretary, Chips Channon, observed in his diaries that the Prime Minister always went over all the Foreign Office Parliamentary questions personally, correcting any answers he did not care for. 'He was really his own Foreign Minister,' Channon added, and this was certainly true after Eden's resignation.

The two ex-Ministers now formed the nucleus of what became known as the Eden group, sometimes derisively described by the Government whips as 'the glamour boys'. Eden took the chair at their meetings and, although small at first, the group gradually grew, especially after the fall of Prague in the spring of 1939. It eventually comprised between twenty and thirty Conservative Members of Parliament, including Leo Amery, Duff Cooper, Lord Wolmer, Harold Macmillan, Dick Law, Jim Thomas, Edward (Louis) Spears, Mark Patrick, Ronnie Tree, Sydney Herbert, Hubert Duggan, Derrick Gunston, Robert Bower, Paul Emrys-Evans, and Anthony Crossley and Ronnie Cartland, who were both soon to be killed in action. A National Labour Member, Harold Nicolson, also joined the group and Mark Patrick became its secretary. They met once a week when Parliament was sitting, at the houses in Westminster of Ronnie Tree, Jim Thomas or Mark Patrick. The purpose of these gatherings was to discuss the menacing international scene and to consider what could be done to avert its dangers. The much smaller Churchill group, which shared many of the same objectives, consisted of Churchill, Brendan Bracken, Bob Boothby and Duncan Sandys.

Churchill and Eden were on good terms and they and their followers often combined forces for debates of mutual concern in the House of Commons. In retrospect, it is strange that the two groups remained distant and had little contact with each other. This may have been due partly to Eden's reluctance to be overshadowed by a more powerful and colourful figure, but Churchill's strong opposition to the India Bill and his support for King Edward VIII at the time of the abdication had alienated his Parliamentary colleagues, including many of Eden's friends. They did not altogether trust Churchill and preferred to align themselves with Eden, who was not a natural rebel and who had no wish to antagonize the majority of Conservative Members to any greater extent than was necessary. There was still a feeling that more could be achieved by privately expressed pressure on the Government than by open opposition to it in Parliament. Nevertheless, after Eden's resignation, about twenty Conservatives abstained when a division was called on an Opposition censure motion and as many as thirty after the Munich debate eight months later, despite a moving speech on the second occasion by Neville Chamberlain.

After Churchill and Eden joined the Government, the dissident Conservative Members continued to meet, usually under the chairmanship of Leo Amery; and an all-Party group was also formed by Clement Davies, who later became leader of the Liberal Party. This group, for which Bob Boothby acted as secretary, was important as a bridge to the Labour leadership.

In April 1940, yet another committee came into existence. This consisted of Conservative members of both Houses, presided over by Lord Salisbury, a senior ex-Minister, with Emrys Evans as secretary. It was known as the Watching Committee and met at Salisbury's London house in Arlington Street. The peers included Lord Hailsham (a former Lord Chancellor), Lord Lloyd, Lord Londonderry, Lord Astor (the owner of the *Observer*), Lord Swinton, Lord Trenchard and Salisbury's younger brother, Lord Cecil of Chelwood. The House of Commons membership overlapped with that of the other disaffected groups, with Amery, Duff Cooper, Lord Cranborne, Lord Wolmer, Harold Macmillan, Harold Nicolson, Louis Spears, Dick Law and Patrick Spens as its most prominent participants. The committee was concerned mainly with inadequacies in the war effort and made private representations on these matters direct to the Prime Minister. One of its recommendations asking for a smaller War Cabinet, whose members should not be burdened with departmental duties, was brusquely dismissed by Chamberlain, and after a later meeting with Lord Halifax, Salisbury told the Foreign Secretary bluntly that his committee was 'not satisfied'.

These groups met frequently between 25 April and 8 May and were in touch with each other throughout this critical fortnight. It is not suggested that they effectively influenced Government policy. Their importance lay in the organized criticism from within the Party, which laid the foundation for the Conservative defections in the important debate on Norway in May and thus led directly to Chamberlain's downfall.

Since the autumn of 1939 Churchill had been urging a British initiative in Scandinavia. Germany's supplies of iron ore came from the Swedish mines and were shipped from the Norwegian port of Narvik through the Leads, a deep-water channel within the safety of Norway's territorial waters. Churchill wished to mine this channel, but his plan was vetoed by Chamberlain and Halifax because it involved the violation of Norway's neutrality.

On 30 November 1939, Russia's invasion of Finland gave rise to the possibility of a new form of allied intervention in Norway. A project was put forward, and was much discussed, for despatching a joint Anglo-French expeditionary force of 100,000 men to go to the aid of Finland. These troops would have had to cross Norway and Sweden and in the process could have seized Narvik and destroyed the Swedish iron mines. Such, at any rate, was Churchill's intention.

This plan to attack Russia's flank when we were already at war with Germany seems to have been remarkably reckless and was in any case abandoned, partly because the Swedish and Norwegian Governments refused to allow our troops passage to Finland and secondly, and decisively, because Finland made peace with Russia on 12 March 1940. The collapse of Finnish resistance had the effect, however, of reviving Churchill's idea of mining the Norwegian waters and, after considerable discussion and indecision, the project was at length approved.

It was at this point that Chamberlain, in a speech to the Central Council of the Conservative Party on 4 April, made the ill-advised assertion that Hitler had 'missed the bus' by not using the initial advantage of his greater military preparedness to attack Britain and France before they were ready. On 9 April 1940 the Germans invaded Norway and Denmark. The twilight war was over and Hitler had pre-empted our intervention in Scandinavia.

In anticipation of a German response to the mining of the Leads, five British territorial battalions embarked on cruisers on 6 and 7 April, unaware that the German forces were already at sea on their way to Norway. The enemy's invasion plans had been prepared with meticulous care; our own were improvised and continually altered. The Joint Planning Committee recommended an attack on the port of Trondheim. Churchill and his Military Co-ordination Committee preferred to move against Narvik and when the British expedition sailed it was, at first, to that destination; but the Norwegians then appealed to us for help at Trondheim and, under pressure, Churchill agreed to attacks on both these ports. On his instructions, part of the Narvik force was diverted to Namsos with disastrous results, and the naval assault upon Trondheim was postponed and finally abandoned at the beginning of May.

Churchill's friends feared that he would be blamed for these reverses and his prospects of the premiership prejudiced. They claimed that he was bedevilled by committees and had responsibility rather than power in the Norwegian enterprise; but Halifax was more critical, especially of Churchill's change of mind about the attack on Trondheim – a decision he had made after consulting the Prime Minister but, owing to lack of time, without reference to the Cabinet.

Churchill was probably right not to risk his ships in the face of German command of the air, and there was the added consideration that, when Sir Roger Keyes offered to lead the Trondheim assault with old ships, whose loss would not greatly have mattered, the First Sea Lord threatened to resign if this was allowed. The situation was too reminiscent of Lord Fisher's resignation over Gallipoli in the First World War for Churchill to court such a repetition of history.

The British troops in Norway fared ill, partly because they had no skis and were badly equipped in this and in other respects for Norwegian conditions, but mainly because they lacked naval and air support and the Navy had been unable to prevent the landing of German tanks. On 26 April, on the recommendation of the Chiefs of Staff, the War Cabinet agreed to the evacuation of central Norway and, although Narvik was eventually captured on 28 May, we had to withdraw from it in a final evacuation on 8 June.

Severe damage to the German Navy, which may have prejudiced Hitler's plans for the invasion of Britain, and the experience of evacuation, which was no doubt of value at Dunkirk, were gains from the Norwegian fiasco, but in fact we had been forestalled and outwitted and the failure of our intervention was a shock to public opinion which provoked a political crisis at home.

Ironically, although Churchill was more directly involved than Chamberlain, it was the Prime Minister whose reputation suffered most and Churchill emerged almost unscathed in the public estimation. The *Graf Spee* success and the boarding of the *Altmark* were remembered to his credit and he seemed to personify the drive and energy which the people were now looking to their leaders to supply.

From a military standpoint the Scandinavian setback was not a major disaster and did not damage our prospects of ultimate victory. Its significance lay in the apparent lack of efficiency and foresight with which the war was being waged.

The Opposition asked for a debate, ostensibly on the Norwegian reverse, in practice on the general conduct of the war. This was arranged for 7 and 8 May, on a motion for the Whitsun adjournment. In the days before this debate, newspaper comment did not predict important political changes as a result of it; indeed, on the morning it began the *Manchester Guardian* asserted that 'no experienced politician looks to this week's debates to produce dramatic consequences'. The Ministers were just as optimistic. On 4 May Chamberlain recorded, 'I don't think my enemies will get me down this time,' and on 6 May Halifax, while admitting 'considerable political clamour', doubted whether it would amount to much in the end. The Chief Whip was confident that he could keep the Party in line, and no one seriously imagined that the Government was in jeopardy. But the House was crowded and its mood critical when the Prime Minister came in at question time and he was greeted from the Labour benches with cries of 'resign' and 'the man who missed the bus'.

Chamberlain opened the debate with an appeal for unity and for the support and co-operation of all Parties, but he rejected suggestions for a re-organization of the War Cabinet and, although partly successful in lowering the temperature in the House, he failed to allay the anxieties and growing hostility of his critics.

Clement Attlee followed him from the Labour front bench. 'I am not in the least satisfied,' he declared, 'that the present War Cabinet is an efficient instrument for conducting the war. . . . We cannot afford to have our destinies in the hands of failures or men who need a rest.'

Sir Archibald Sinclair, for the Liberals, called for a smaller War Cabinet and a more vigorous prosecution of the war. Sir Roger Keyes, usually a poor speaker, appeared bemedalled and resplendent in the uniform of an Admiral of the Fleet and on this occasion spoke shortly, simply and with great effect. Although critical of the Government as a whole, he expressed confidence in Churchill and his contribution made a considerable impact on the House.

The strongest and most damaging condemnation of Chamberlain was yet to come. Leo Amery, small, combative and tenacious, did more than anyone to destroy the Government in the best speech of his career. The Prime Minister had said nothing, he declared,

which suggested that the Government either foresaw what Germany meant to do or came to a clear decision when it knew what Germany had done or acted swiftly or consistently throughout this whole lamentable affair.

He rounded upon the Ministers with Cromwell's words to Hampden,

Your troops are most of them old, decayed serving men and tapsters and such kind of fellows. .... You must get men of spirit . . . or you will be beaten still.

And, in his peroration, he quoted Cromwell again, using the Protector's savage attack on the Long Parliament,

You have sat here too long for any good you have been doing. Depart, I say, and let us have done with you. In the name of God, go.

As Churchill was to comment in *The Gathering Storm*, 'These were terrible words coming from a friend and colleague of many years, a fellow Birmingham Member and a Privy Councillor of distinction and experience.'

That evening Chamberlain saw the King. He explained that he had not come to offer his resignation and was still hopeful of being able to reconstruct his government by bringing the Labour leaders into a national coalition. The King offered to talk to Attlee in this sense, but Chamberlain thought it wiser to defer any such approach until after the Labour Party Conference, which was assembling that weekend at Bournemouth. George VI, who had a close relationship with his Prime Minister, felt the same loyalty to him as his father, King George V, had shown to Asquith in 1916. Neither he nor Chamberlain yet realized the degree of personal hostility which existed in the Labour ranks towards the Conservative leader. They would have served under Baldwin, but would not do so under his successor. It is of interest that Baldwin had himself suggested that Chamberlain should try to form a National Government after Munich, but Chamberlain had rejected the idea at that time.

In the third volume of his autobiography, *My Political Life*, Leo Amery records an important conversation between Attlee and Brendan Bracken on the evening of 7 May, when Attlee expressed the view that, in any change of government, his Party would favour Halifax as Prime Minister, with Churchill as Minister of Defence. On his own responsibility, Bracken argued that Churchill could not accept a situation in which he would have no real control but would be blamed if things went wrong. He persuaded Attlee not to refuse to serve under Churchill if a coalition government was formed. This would certainly have been reported to Churchill and no doubt strengthened his hand when the issue, as between Halifax and himself, developed two days later. Perhaps even more influential with Attlee was an intervention on the same lines by Clem Davies, who telephoned him at Bournemouth from Bob Boothby's flat in London.

It is surprising that some Labour opinion at that time was more favourably disposed towards a national leader from the House of Lords than towards any Conservative in the House of Commons. On 8 May, Clem Davies told Amery that Arthur Greenwood and some of the other socialist leaders would sooner serve under him than under Churchill. If this was so, it was perhaps attributable to the euphoric effect of Amery's speech two days earlier. He was normally a dull speaker, difficult to listen to, and he could never have inspired the nation as Churchill did in the war years. He had notable qualities of courage and sincerity and was liked and respected in all Parties, but, as he himself realized, the succession, if there was to be a change, lay between Churchill and Halifax.

Herbert Morrison opened for the Opposition on the second day of the debate and announced that his Party would force a division at the end of it. This decision was of great importance. It is unusual to vote on the adjournment and for this reason some Conservatives had felt less inhibited in their criticisms of the Government than would have been the case had it been clear from the outset that the Labour Party would carry their challenge into the lobbies. The Conservative rebels would not, on their own, have divided the House.

Chamberlain made an unprepared and injudicious intervention in reply to Morrison's attack.

I do not seek to evade criticism, but I say this to my friends in the House – and I have friends in the House – no government can prosecute a war efficiently unless it has public and Parliamentary support. I accept the challenge. I welcome it indeed. At least we shall see who is with us and who is against us, and I call on my friends to support us in the lobby tonight.

The reference to his friends was ill-advised. It seemed to personalize a great issue in which the national interest was at stake, and many Members felt that the appeal for loyalty to the Party and to himself fell below the level of the occasion.

Morrison, who was anxious to show that the challenge to Chamberlain extended beyond the ranks of the Labour Party, had been working behind the scenes to persuade Lloyd George, 'the energetic leader of the First World War, to make a vigorous speech against the feeble leader of the Second'. Lloyd George was reluctant to take part, but the combined pressures of his daughter, Megan, the chairman of the Welsh group of MPs, of Jim Griffiths, their secretary, and of

Clement Davies eventually prevailed and he consented to speak from the Opposition front bench. Such was his dislike of Chamberlain that he could scarcely have resisted the temptation to contribute to his downfall. It was the last great speech Lloyd George was to make in the House of Commons.

It is not a question of who are the Prime Minister's friends, it is a far bigger issue. . . . He is not in a position to appeal on the ground of friendship. He has appealed for sacrifice. . . . I say solemnly that the Prime Minister should give an example of sacrifice, because there is nothing which can contribute more to victory in this war than that he should sacrifice the seals of office.

His target was Chamberlain and he warned Churchill, who was to wind up the debate, not to allow himself 'to be converted into an air-raid shelter to keep the splinters from hitting his colleagues'.

Duff Cooper took the same line and accurately forecast

an eloquent and powerful speech by the First Lord of the Admiralty . . . who will be defending with his eloquence those who have so long refused to listen to his counsel . . . and those who so often trembled before his sword will be only too glad to shrink behind his buckler.

As the debate progressed, the whips became anxious about the number of dissident Conservatives who might abstain or even vote against the Government and were busy in the smoking room and corridors trying to persuade the doubtfuls not to join the incipient revolt. Alec Dunglass (later Lord Home), the Prime Minister's Parliamentary Private Secretary, was equally active, and he successfully cajoled a number of colleagues into staying their hand; but Emrys Evans rejected his pleas on behalf of the Amery group and at an emergency meeting of Conservative MPs of all groups held later that evening, Evans's action was endorsed by his associates, who agreed unanimously to vote against the motion. This decision proved fatal for Chamberlain's chances of weathering the storm.

Winston Churchill wound up the two-day debate for the Government. He did his best to regain control of the House, accepted his full share of responsibility for the failure to sustain Norway and loyally defended the Prime Minister and the conduct of the war in the face of continuous interruption from the Labour benches. The moral and intellectual position of the socialists, who had voted solidly against conscription and the pre-war Service Estimates, was not a strong one, but their anger, now, was uninhibited and it was directed less against

Churchill than against Chamberlain. As Amery observed, the speech 'strengthened Churchill's position with the defenders of the Government without weakening it in the eyes of those of us who saw in him the obvious successor to Chamberlain'.

At 11 o'clock the House divided. Conservative Members in uniform mixed with Labour pacifists in the 'No' lobby and the Amery group were joined by Clement Davies, Leslie Hore-Belisha, Lady Astor, Lord Winterton, Quintin Hogg, Bill Anstruther-Gray and John Profumo. In addition to the thirty-three Conservatives who voted against the Government, a further sixty abstained and, when the figures were announced, the normal majority of about two hundred had fallen to eighty-one. The Prime Minister had lost the confidence of a substantial section of his own Party in the House of Commons.

With his usual frosty smile to some of his supporters Chamberlain rose and walked slowly to his room, where he asked Churchill to join him. He said he could not go on and that someone must form a national coalition in which all Parties would serve. Churchill advised him to strengthen the Government and encouraged him to continue at its head, but Chamberlain remained uncomforted and unconvinced. Although not actually defeated in the House of Commons, such a large fall in his majority was almost the equivalent of a defeat, especially in war time when a dissolution of Parliament was unthinkable. He knew that he must resign.

As often happens at Westminster after a controversial debate and a dramatic division, many groups of Members met the next day to discuss the situation and decide what line to follow. Lord Salisbury's Watching Committee was not in doubt that Chamberlain should go, though there was some disagreement as to whether Churchill or Halifax should succeed him. Meanwhile, Clem Davies's group resolved that its members could only support an all-Party Government and this decision was conveyed to Chamberlain. Davies himself acted as a liaison between the Conservative critics and the Labour leadership. That afternoon Amery's group also agreed upon a National Government with an effective War Cabinet, chosen on merit, and issued a public statement to that effect.

It was clear that the Chamberlain administration could not continue in its existing form and that he was himself an obstacle to any reconstruction on an all-Party basis. The real question now crystallizing was whether Churchill or Halifax should succeed him. Halifax, though a man of the highest character, would not have made an inspiring leader in time of war. He had been a liberal-minded Viceroy for six years and his negotiations with Gandhi made independence for India inevitable. Churchill had condemned 'the nauseating and humiliating spectacle of this ... seditious fakir, striding half naked up the steps of the Viceroy's Palace, there to negotiate and to parley on equal terms with the representative of the King-Emperor'. Now these two very different men were the alternative successors to Chamberlain.

On the morning of 9 May, Halifax had received an interesting letter from Rab Butler, his Under-Secretary at the Foreign Office:

Dalton called to see me at dinner time yesterday evening and told me that his Party would come into the Government under you, but not under the PM. ... After the debate I saw Herbert Morrison, who said that the idea of Labour joining the Government was 'coming along well'. But he made it clear that the conditions were the same as Dalton had outlined. ... Dalton said there was no other choice but you. 'Churchill must stick to the war.' ... He saw no objection in the Lords difficulty.

Halifax, though gratified, was unenthusiastic. He thought, rightly, that he did not possess the qualities required in a war leader and that Churchill's drive and determination made him the obvious choice. 'If I was Prime Minister,' Halifax told Butler, 'Winston would run it. He might consult me, but he would be in charge.'

The Prime Minister asked Halifax to call and see him at ten o'clock. They agreed that confidence could only be restored on the basis of an all-Party Government and that the prospects of forming one under Chamberlain's leadership were negligible. The Prime Minister favoured Halifax as his successor, but this proposal was so unattractive to the Foreign Secretary that, as Lord Birkenhead wrote in his book, *Halifax*, he 'experienced a feeling of physical sickness in the pit of his stomach', even in discussing the suggestion. He argued that the position of a Prime Minister in the House of Lords, especially in war time, would be an impossible one. Their talk was adjourned for a meeting of the Cabinet at noon, but they agreed to continue it later that afternoon and to invite Churchill to join them.

In the meantime, Sir Kingsley Wood, then Secretary of State for Air, had informed Churchill of Chamberlain's view that a National Government was essential and that if it could not be formed under him, he would give way to anyone else who was more acceptable to the Labour Party. Kingsley Wood was one of the Prime Minister's closest political friends, so it was significant that he had made this personal approach and Churchill realized he might be called upon to take over the leadership. 'The prospect neither excited nor alarmed me,' he wrote characteristically in *The Gathering Storm*. 'I thought it would be by far the best plan. I was content to let events unfold.' They were soon to do so.

Anthony Eden lunched with Churchill, Bracken and Kingsley Wood and was surprised when the latter warned Churchill that Chamberlain wanted Halifax to succeed him and would like Churchill to agree to this solution. 'Don't agree,' was Kingsley Wood's advice, 'and don't say anything.' Eden was shocked that such a close associate of the Prime Minister's should be talking in this way, but it was good advice and he supported it. Kingsley Wood was, in a sense, the Judas in this situation, but perhaps his motives were patriotic as well as personal and no doubt he genuinely believed that the nation's interests would be best served if Churchill became Prime Minister. Brendan Bracken had also counselled Churchill to say nothing if and when his views were invited.

At 4.30 that afternoon Chamberlain saw Churchill and Halifax at Downing Street, where they were joined by David Margesson, the Government Chief Whip, who warned the Prime Minister that he could no longer rely upon the support of the Parliamentary Party. Chamberlain recapitulated his decision to retire from the premiership and added that he would be willing to serve under either Halifax or Churchill.

Acting on the advice he had received from Bracken and Kingsley Wood, Churchill said nothing and a long and crucial silence ensued. This was eventually broken by Halifax, who argued against himself, re-stating his opinion that, quite apart from Churchill's outstanding qualities, it was out of the question for the Prime Minister not to be a Member of the House of Commons. Winston then intervened briefly to say he had reached the same conclusion. It was now clear that the responsibility would fall upon him – a situation accepted regretfully by Chamberlain and evidently with much less reluctance by his probable successor. The most important interview of Churchill's life, and perhaps the most momentous for the nation in the whole course of the war, was now over and the Prime Minister left to keep another appointment. It was a warm, sunny afternoon and his two collegues remained together in the garden of No 10.

47

At 6.15 p.m. Attlee and Greenwood arrived at Downing Street. By this time Chamberlain had returned. He stressed the need for a National Government and asked if the Labour leaders would serve either under him or under someone else. They replied that they could not commit themselves without consulting their Party Executive, but that they would telephone their decision the following day. The conversation was courteous, but there was little doubt that they were disinclined to join a Government under Chamberlain's leadership.

That evening Anthony Eden dined with Churchill, who recounted what had transpired and said he thought it now certain that Chamberlain would advise the King to send for him. In this event he would act as Minister of Defence as well as Prime Minister and he hoped Chamberlain would lead the House of Commons and continue as leader of the Conservative Party. He wished Eden to become Secretary of State for War.

The early morning of 10 May brought with it the awesome news of Hitler's invasion of the Low Countries. The German armies had violated the frontiers of Belgium, Holland and Luxembourg. A Cabinet was called for 8 a.m. After it had taken place, Kingsley Wood called again to see Churchill and reported Chamberlain's initial reaction that the crisis which had now arisen made it necessary for the Government changes to be postponed. Kingsley Wood had, however, taken the opposite view and had advised the Prime Minister that the immediate formation of a National Government was more than ever essential in order to contend with the threatening new situation.

At a second meeting of the Cabinet at 11.30 a.m. Chamberlain told his colleagues of his original intention to resign, but indicated that the German attack meant a temporary deferment of this decision. He had asked Attlee to issue a statement expressing support for the Government under the grave new circumstances; when this came through on the tape, it was found to contain no more than vague general support for the war effort, which was not at all the same thing.

A third meeting of the Cabinet was held at 4.30 that afternoon. Before it broke up, Chamberlain's private secretary telephoned Attlee at Bournemouth to enquire if he could answer the two questions the Prime Minister had put to him the previous day. To the first he replied that his Party would not join the Government under Chamberlain; to the second that they would do so under another Conservative leader. No stipulation was made as to who this should be.

The message that the Labour leaders would not serve under him was decisive and shortly after receiving it Neville Chamberlain drove to Buckingham Palace to tender his resignation. The King accepted it with genuine regret, as he thought the Prime Minister had been unfairly treated. They then discussed the succession. George vi's preference was for Halifax and he hoped the peerage difficulty could be resolved by an arrangement, which would have required legislation, enabling Halifax to speak in the House of Commons. Chamberlain explained the Foreign Secretary's lack of enthusiasm for the task and advised the King to send for Churchill.

At 6 p.m. Winston Spencer Churchill was summoned to the Palace and invited to form a Government. He at once accepted and told the King he would send for the leaders of the Labour and Liberal Parties and would submit his first list of five or six Ministers before midnight.

Lord Boothby considers that three men played the major part in bringing Churchill to power – Leo Amery, who became Secretary of State for India, Kingsley Wood, who was made Chancellor of the Exchequer, and Clement Davies, who received no reward. Winston's closest personal associate, Brendan Bracken, became his Parliamentary Private Secretary and, unusually in that position, was given a Privy Councillorship. Beaverbrook and Rothermere were also helpful to Churchill during these critical days and, once it was clear that Chamberlain had to go, David Margesson played an important part in rallying Conservative back bench support for the new leader.

Attlee and Greenwood were on their way to London to discuss the situation with, as they thought, Neville Chamberlain; but by the time they arrived Churchill was Prime Minister and they accepted his offer to join a coalition government.

There is some doubt as to whether the Labour leadership would have preferred Halifax. The National Executive Committee had not expressed an opinion. On the evidence of his talk with Rab Butler, Dalton no doubt favoured Halifax and perhaps Morrison shared this view, but Attlee is on record in an article in the *Observer* in 1965:

I was certainly not among those Labour leaders who would have preferred Lord Halifax. To my mind, at that juncture, one requirement was imperative and over-rode every consideration: we had to win the war. I was convinced that Winston Churchill stood head and shoulders above any other possible Prime Minister.

At any rate, no effort was made to substitute Halifax, nor would the Labour Party have had any right to attempt a stratagem of his kind. The Conservatives had a large majority in Parliament and their leader had recommended to the King that Churchill should succeed him. The only option open to the Labour leaders was to decline the new Prime Minister's invitation to serve. There was never any question of such a refusal.

Chamberlain broadcast to the nation at nine o'clock that evening. He announced his resignation and urged support for his successor:

In the afternoon of today, it was apparent that the essential unity could be secured under another Prime Minister, though not myself. In these circumstances my duty was plain. . . . And you and I must rally behind our new leader and with our united strength and with unshakeable courage, fight and work until this wild beast, that has sprung out of his lair upon us, has been finally disarmed and overthrown.

He accepted Churchill's invitation to remain in the War Cabinet as Lord President of the Council, an offer which was at first coupled with the post of leader of the House of Commons, but the Labour Party objected to the second of these appointments and Chamberlain willingly withdrew from it. He behaved throughout with dignity and magnanimity.

Churchill responded with equal generosity. His first action after returning from the Palace was to write to his predecessor of

the long and dangerous defile through which we must march for many months. With your help and counsel and with the support of the great Party of which you are the leader, I trust we shall succeed. The example which you have set of self-forgetting dignity and public spirit will govern the action of many and be an inspiration to all. . . . To a very large extent I am in your hands – and I feel no fear of that. . . .

It was important that Chamberlain had agreed to remain a member of the Government. As the *Sunday Times* commented on 12 May:

Mr Chamberlain is leader of the Conservative Party and his policy has had such large support in Parliament and in the country that if he had not taken office, the Government would have been weakened on one side as it has been strengthened on another. . . .

50

Owing to the Labour Party's attitude towards Chamberlain, Churchill thought it wisest to retain the leadership of the House of Commons in his own hands, with Attlee as his deputy and *de facto* leader.

For the next five years, Clement Attlee, as leader of the Labour Party, was to fill the same role as a loyal second-in-command to Churchill as had Bonar Law, the Conservative leader, in Lloyd George's First World War coalition. The qualities of these two men, which were not unlike, made them admirable deputies for their more dynamic masters.

By 10 p.m. Churchill had sent the list of his key Ministerial appointments to the King and their names were announced next morning. In addition to Chamberlain as Lord President, Attlee became Lord Privy Seal, Greenwood Minister without Portfolio, Anthony Eden Secretary of State for War, A. V. Alexander First Lord of the Admiralty and Sir Archibald Sinclair Secretary of State for Air. Lord Halifax continued as Foreign Secretary. The new Ministers were sworn in at the Palace at noon on 12 May. The War Cabinet consisted initially of Churchill, Chamberlain, Attlee, Greenwood and Halifax.

On the following day Churchill faced Parliament for the first time as Prime Minister. As he entered the House of Commons, the cheers which greeted him came mainly from the Labour and Liberal benches. His own Party reserved theirs for Chamberlain, who was still their leader and remained so until he retired from public life the following October.

Churchill's relations with the Conservative Party had been stormy or uneasy, and at best ambivalent, for the whole forty years of his public life. The periods of amity and agreement had been far exceeded by those of friction or actual strife. Only the war and his warnings of Nazi aggression before its outbreak had restored his authority and his reputation and even in 1940 it was the will of Parliament and of the nation, rather than that of the Conservative majority in the House of Commons, which brought about his assumption of supreme power. 'The Conservatives have never liked or trusted me,' he once wrote, and this feeling was no doubt mutual.

In the decade proceeding the Second World War, Winston Churchill appeared to be a politician with a past but no future and, if he had died in the 1930s, he would have gone down in history as brilliant but unstable – a man of courage, eloquence and bad judgement. The hour had, however, produced the leader and, in opening the debate on 13 May, Churchill made the first of his famous war-time speeches:

I have nothing to offer but blood, toil, tears and sweat. We have before us an ordeal of the most grievous kind. We have before us many many long months of struggle and of suffering. You ask, what is our policy? I will say it is to wage war, by sea, land and air, with all our might and with all the strength that God can give us; to wage war against a monstrous tyranny, never surpassed in the dark, lamentable catalogue of human crime. That is our policy. You ask, what is our aim? I can answer in one word: it is victory, victory at all costs, victory in spite of all terror, victory however long and hard the road may be; for, without victory, there is no survival. . . .

Party affiliations and loyalties no longer mattered. Churchill personified the nation at war and achieved a unity at this moment of crisis more complete, perhaps, than ever before in our long island story. Now none were for the Party and all were for the state.

The formation of his government might well have occasioned Churchill greater difficulty than it did. There were many able Conservative Ministers in Chamberlain's administration who, in a coalition, had to sacrifice their positions and in some cases cut short their careers to make room for the Labour and Liberal leaders. For the most part they accepted the situation philosophically and with selfless patriotism. On the other hand, there were demands for a purge of the 'guilty men' held responsible for Munich and for Britain's unpreparedness when war came. Apart from Neville Chamberlain himself, Sir John Simon, Sir Samuel Hoare, Sir Kingsley Wood and the Chief Whip, David Margesson, were particular targets for these attacks and, if the critics had had their way, up to a third of Chamberlain's Ministers might have been dismissed. Nothing would have been more disruptive of the spirit of national unity which Churchill knew to be essential and he firmly resisted the pressures to penalize those with whom he had formerly disagreed. Unlike most of his Cabinet colleagues, Churchill had a clean sheet in pre-war terms and he appealed to them to suspend their antipathy towards members of the previous Government.

Neville Chamberlain remained leader of the Conservative Party and this, for the time being, was certainly the best arrangement. Churchill wrote to him on 16 May to say that, as the Prime Minister of a National Government comprising all three Parties, he felt it would be better not to undertake the leadership of one of them. 'I therefore express the hope,' he went on, 'that your own leadership of our Party will remain undisturbed. . . . The relations of perfect confidence which have grown up between us make this division of duties and responsibilities very agreeable to me.' And so matters continued for the next four months. Chamberlain was as loyal to his successor as Churchill had been to him in the early days of the war.

On 16 June Neville Chamberlain suffered considerable abdominal pain and, following X-rays a month later, an exploratory operation was ordered. It revealed an incurable cancerous growth. By September his health had deteriorated so gravely that he felt obliged to offer his resignation from the Government. Churchill at first refused to accept this, but was constrained to do so on 30 September. Chamberlain declined offers of an Earldom and of the Garter, preferring 'to die plain Mr Chamberlain like my father before me', and he accepted the prospect of his early death with stoicism.

His retirement from public life left vacant the position of leader of the Conservative Party. The Prime Minister was the natural and obvious successor, but some believed that, as the leader of the whole nation, he should remain above Party. Beaverbrook argued strongly for the opposite view. He pointed out the danger of divided loyalties, of possible complaints against Churchill by Conservative back benchers, of differing views about appointments and promotions and of the Prime Minister being removed from direct contact with the Conservative Chief Whip. These were powerful arguments and Churchill decided to accept the leadership.

A Party meeting was held at the Caxton Hall on 9 October to confirm Churchill's election. It was attended by MPs, peers in receipt of the Conservative whip, adopted candidates, and members of the Executive Committee of the National Union of Conservative Associations. Lord Halifax, who would no doubt have been the Party's choice had Churchill declined, presided over the meeting. He had also taken the chair for Chamberlain's election as leader three years earlier and on that occasion the resolution, proposed by Lord Derby, had been seconded by Winston Churchill.

Halifax put forward two resolutions: the first was to thank Chamberlain for his eminent services and to record his qualities of selflessness and unfaltering courage and tenacity. The second recommended Churchill to the meeting, recalling his unique experience in peace and war and his strength in the face of the disasters of Dunkirk and the collapse of France. These propositions were seconded by a senior back bencher, Sir George Courthorpe, and supported by Sir Eugene Ramsden, as chairman of the Executive Committee of the National Union. They were carried *nemine contradicente*. Churchill then arrived to what *The Times* described as 'a tumultuous reception, the meeting rising to its feet and cheering enthusiastically'.

After a tribute to Neville Chamberlain, the Prime Minister posed the problem as to whether the leadership of the Party was compatible with his position as head of an all-Party administration. He weighed the arguments, concluding that the balance of advantage lay in a formal relationship with the majority of Members of the House of Commons, if that was their wish. The second question which he had to put to himself, he said, was more personal: was he by temperament and conviction able to identify himself with the historical conceptions of Toryism and do justice to them? Very varying opinions had been entertained about his public life, he acknowledged amid laughter, 'but I shall attempt no justification. . . . I have always served two public causes – the maintenance of the enduring greatness of Britain and her Empire and the continuity of our island life.' He referred to the 'grand human causes which we, in our generation, have the honour to defend' and concluded that 'it is because I feel that these deep conceptions have always been yours and have always been mine that I accept solemnly, but also buoyantly, the trust and duty you now wish to confide in me'.

The *Daily Telegraph* commented next morning:

The names of Churchill and Chamberlain were linked long ago in our political history. To the sons of each of the Victorian statesmen has come higher honour than the fathers won and far sterner trials. Mr Churchill takes the torch from Mr Chamberlain's hand with the strength which will carry it on to victory.

Neville Chamberlain died on 9 November. He was a kind man, though shy, ungracious and without personal charm. In politics, he was effective and distinguished in his work for social reform, but he lacked the drive and decision to lead his country in time of war. All his work and hopes for peace had been frustrated, but they had won a respite, at least, in which to build our strength. And, as Churchill stated in his valedictory tribute, they had shown to the world that 'we were guiltless of the bloodshed, terror and misery which have engulfed so many lands and peoples. . . . Long and hard hazardous years lie before us, but at least we entered upon them united and with clean hearts.' To Chamberlain Britain owed the moral basis of victory, to Churchill the courage, the eloquence and the endurance which inspired and secured it.

For over five years of world war, Winston Churchill carried the immense burden of the leadership of Britain and the cause of freedom, 'at the end of which time,' in his own words, 'all our enemies having surrendered unconditionally, or being about to do so, I was immediately dismissed by the British electorate from all further conduct of their affairs'.

4

ANTHONY EDEN

In his memoirs, *The Art of the Possible*, Lord Butler describes the disservice Churchill did to Anthony Eden in making him wait so long for the premiership. 'This did not suit Anthony any more than it suited Edward VII,' Rab Butler wrote, 'the latter took it out in life and licence, the former in a controlled impatience. There is little doubt which of these is better for the nerves.' This was certainly true. The position of heir-apparent, if prolonged, is never an easy one and leads to frustrations which may prejudice his future performance in different ways, according to the character of the successor-in-waiting.

Randolph Churchill was less than fair when he wrote in *The Rise and Fall of Sir Anthony Eden*, 'It is curious that Eden was so impatient. In the spring of 1955 Eden was fifty-eight years old. Churchill had not become Prime Minister until he was sixty-five.' Age has nothing to do with it. Eden had been Churchill's acknowledged heir for fifteen years and the nervous strain of waiting so long for the authority to direct affairs in his own way would have been severe for anyone but must have been especially so for someone of Eden's temperament and background.

Robert Anthony Eden was the third son of Sir William Eden, the seventh baronet of West Auckland, whose family had owned estates in County Durham since the fourteenth century. He was born with the proverbial silver spoon, but his early years, though cushioned in a material sense, can have provided little emotional security for a sensitive, somewhat neglected child. His sister, Marjorie, was Sir William's favourite and his beautiful mother preferred her eldest and youngest sons and showed it, so that he felt unloved. His father, rich, handsome and gifted, was eclectic in his tastes – a sportsman, amateur boxer and master of hounds, he was also a talented artist and a discerning collector of French Impressionist paintings. But he was afflicted with a tempestuous temperament and was a complex, idiosyncratic and irrational eccentric, of whom his children stood in understandable awe. Anthony Eden inherited Sir William's quick temper and his efforts to control it led to nervous tension in times of stress or irritation. There was, however, another side of his character derived from his mother, who was a great-niece of Lord Grey of the Reform Bill, and his father once said to him, 'You are a typical Grey.'

Sir William Eden was not a fit companion for children and he realized this himself. His second son, Timothy, recalled in *Tribulations of a Baronet* that Sir William could not endure the presence of his children for any length of time and was 'incapable of placing his intellect on a level with theirs'. They got on his nerves and he terrified and sometimes humiliated them in front of other people, as for instance when he said to one of the boys, already fifteen years old, 'I suppose the governess still gives you your bath.' When Anthony won a divinity prize at Eton, he was embarrassed to be introduced to his father's friends throughout the next holidays as 'my son, who is going in to the Church'. In his own sensitive account of his early life, *Another World*, Eden gives a softer picture of his father, but in common with most children of his generation and background, he saw little of his parents and his relationship with them was relatively remote.

Anthony Eden left Eton in 1915, as soon as he was eighteen years old, to volunteer for the Army. He was awarded a Military Cross for rescuing his wounded platoon sergeant under heavy fire and at nineteen he became the youngest battalion adjutant in the British Army. By the time he was twenty, he was a brigade major. His eldest and youngest brothers were both killed in the war. When he was demobilized in 1919, he responded rather reluctantly to family pressure to complete his education by going to the university. It must have seemed a somewhat humdrum return to an almost school existence after his war service, but he spent three years at Christ Church, Oxford, and gained a first class honours degree in oriental languages. With a few friends, he formed a small club to discuss paintings and painters, but took no apparent interest in politics and did not join the Union. Nevertheless, a few months after coming down in 1922, he stood unsuccessfully as Conservative candidate for a mining seat near his home in Durham and two years later was elected for Warwick and Leamington, which he represented in Parliament for the next thirty-three years.

Eden soon became Parliamentary Private Secretary to a junior minister, Oliver Locker Lampson, and then to the Foreign Secretary, Austen Chamberlain, and this early initiation in foreign affairs set the pattern for his future career. In 1931 he was made Under-Secretary of State at the Foreign Office. It had been a smooth ascent to the first rung of the political ladder. In January 1934 he was promoted to Lord Privy Seal, with special responsibility for League of Nations affairs. He was becoming a well-known and attractive public figure and was referred to in the foreign press as the best looking and best dressed politician in Britain. Of greater importance was his rising reputation as a skilful diplomat and negotiator. When Baldwin became Prime Minister in succession to Ramsay MacDonald, Eden entered the Cabinet and in December 1935 he was made Secretary of State for Foreign Affairs. He was still only thirty-eight years of age.

A little over two years later growing differences of opinion with Neville Chamberlain (who by then had followed Baldwin as Prime Minister) about the conduct of foreign policy, especially in relation to Italy, culminated in his resignation; but this enhanced his reputation as a man of principle and integrity and on the outbreak of war he returned to the Government as Secretary of State for the Dominions and later Secretary of State for War.

When Lord Lothian, who had been British Ambassador to the United States, died in 1940, Halifax gave up the Foreign Office to go to Washington and Eden became Foreign Secretary for the second time. Churchill, who had in fact engineered this, wrote later:

I had no doubt who should fill the vacancy at the Foreign Office. On all the great issues of the past four years I had dwelt in close agreement with Anthony Eden. . . . We had been united in thought and sentiment at the outbreak of war and as colleagues during its progress. The greater part of Eden's public life had been devoted to the study of foreign affairs. He had held the splendid office of Foreign Secretary with distinction and had resigned from it when only forty-two years of age for reasons which are, in retrospect, viewed with the approval of all Parties in the state.

By this appointment, Churchill had virtually designated his eventual successor and this was soon to be formalized in a letter to the King which must be unique in British constitutional history. In June 1942 the Prime Minister, on the eve of flying to the United

States for a meeting with President Roosevelt, offered George VI formal advice, tendered at the King's request:

> In case of my death on this journey I am about to undertake, I avail myself of Your Majesty's gracious permission to advise that you should entrust the formation of a new Government to Mr Anthony Eden, the Secretary of State for Foreign Affairs, who is in my mind the outstanding Minister in the largest political Party in the House of Commons and in the National Government over which I have the honour to preside, and who, I am sure, will be found capable of conducting Your Majesty's affairs with the resolution, experience and capacity which these grievous times require.

No one, then, would have supposed that thirteen years were to elapse before Eden would be called upon to do so.

The post of Secretary of State for War had not carried a seat in the War Cabinet and it was perhaps because of Churchill's determination that Eden should succeed him that he was anxious to bring him in as Foreign Secretary. Eden himself was rather reluctant to leave the War Office. He enjoyed his work with the Army and felt that his role as a bridge between the Prime Minister and the generals was an important one. As he wrote in *Full Circle*, 'For once the Foreign Office had little appeal at a time when we had only exiled Governments as allies and little opportunity for diplomacy.'

This was soon to change. By 1942 the tide of war had turned and the next two years were fully occupied with a series of important and exacting international conferences, held not only to plan the allied victory but to lay the foundations for peace. In March 1943 Eden was in the United States for talks with Roosevelt and in May he visited Algiers. There followed in quick succession conferences at Quebec, Moscow, Cairo and Teheran and in February 1945 the last of the allied war-time meetings at Yalta.

On 7 May 1945 Germany signed the unconditional surrender of her forces. The Second World War in Europe was over.

After representing Britain at San Francisco for the drafting of the United Nations Charter, Eden fell ill with a duodenal ulcer. This was probably caused by overwork. In addition to his responsibilities as Foreign Secretary and as a member of the Defence Committee of the War Cabinet, he had been leader of the House of Commons from November 1942 until the end of the war. He was a success in this post, which he had been reluctant to accept, but it inevitably imposed an additional strain. The illness kept him out of most of the

1945 election campaign. He retained his seat at Warwick and Leamington, but the Conservative Party was decisively defeated and Attlee led the new Government with a massive majority of 194 in the House of Commons. This landslide to Labour had been unforeseen and Harold Macmillan, a year before the event, was one of the few to forecast the Tory disaster.

In the House of Commons the Conservative aristocrats – Churchill, Eden, Stanley and Lyttelton – confronted the 'revolutionaries' (as some die-hards considered the socialist Members) almost as though the tumbrils were about to roll up to the Palace of Westminster. It was an intriguing situation, which would have delighted a modern Trollope. The fallen Tory grandees had no option but to endure the impotence of opposition as best they could.

Eden accepted his new role with more grace than many of the Conservative rank and file. This was no doubt easier for him than it seemed, because his task was mainly to support and sustain Ernest Bevin, the new Foreign Secretary, against the pressures from the left wing of the Labour Party. As Ursula Branston, Eden's loyal and very able assistant at the Research Department, has observed, the overriding objective of both Government and Opposition was to strengthen Britain's influence abroad by demonstrating the continuity of her foreign policy. This purpose would certainly not have been as easy to achieve if, as at one moment seemed likely, Attlee had appointed Hugh Dalton instead of Bevin as Foreign Secretary.

Eden and Bevin were on easy and informal personal terms and together they developed a bi-partisan approach to most international issues. Oliver Stanley, widely renowned for his wit, congratulated Ernest Bevin in the House of Commons on his handling of foreign policy with the comment, 'It shows the importance of being ... [pause] Anthony.'

The trust and confidence which had grown during the war-time coalition between these two men of widely different background stood them both, and the nation, in good stead in the post-war years.

It was as well that their views coincided because this was a far from easy period in east-west relations: the trials in Eastern Europe, the death of Masaryk, the growth of the Cominform, the division of Germany, the Berlin air-lift, the Atlantic alliance, and later the Korean War and spreading unrest in the Middle East all created tensions and problems in which Britain was much more directly involved than she would be today.

Throughout this period, Eden's personal standing with the Labour Party and his reputation as a 'moderate' were invaluable. He sought always to lower the temperature, to avoid provocation and to advocate negotiation. His speeches contributed a balance and stability which offset Churchill's brilliantly ebullient and sometimes unpredictable interventions. This was a useful service, often discharged at some cost to his nervous system. But close co-operation could not survive Bevin's retirement and his successor, Herbert Morrison, incurred Eden's passionate condemnation for his unskilful handling of the Abadan crisis. Indeed, the years of collaboration with Bevin had masked the strong strain of impatience, even imperiousness, in Eden's temperament.

His method of work was very personal. He did not like others to press their ideas upon him unless he had invited them to do so and he confided his own views only to a small circle of intimate friends, among whom were the two Olivers (Stanley and Lyttelton), Bobbety Salisbury and sometimes Toby Low (later Lord Aldington). He disliked being questioned about the line he proposed adopting until the speech had taken shape in his own mind and he showed the draft to a very few chosen colleagues and even then only in the final stages of its preparation. On the other hand, he was always ready to accept suggestions if he had asked for them.

He was meticulous in sending Churchill an advance copy of what he intended to say, but he much resented any attempt to intercept it en route. On one occasion he had passed a speech up the table at a meeting of the Shadow Cabinet (then called the Consultative Committee) for Churchill to see and was outraged when Duncan Sandys began to read it in transit. He regarded this as an impertinence and stormed angrily into his own room after the meeting with the comment to Ursula Branston, 'One day, Duncan; not yet.'

Although, in matters of this kind, he was insistent upon the strict observance of protocol, he was never in the least stiff or pompous with his own staff and invariably expressed his gratitude for work well done, either personally at the time or in a letter in his own hand afterwards and always with great charm and generosity; so that, despite often long hours, those closest to him loved working for him. He did not find it easy to trust people, but once, they had earned his confidence, the relationship was rewarding and enduring.

Eden's relations with the lobby were excellent. Although Churchill described himself as a journalist, he never talked to newspaper correspondents if he could avoid it and James Margach recalls that as Prime Minister he only once held a press conference, which was unprofitable because he told his audience nothing! In contrast, Eden's diplomatic experience had accustomed him to dealing with journalists of many different nationalities and he understood that they appreciate being trusted and seldom betray a confidence. His charm was proverbial and he was probably the first Prime Minister to entertain the lobby journalists and their wives at 10 Downing Street. His thought in doing so is remembered to this day by senior lobby correspondents.

Eden's accord with the Young Conservatives was just as close. He insisted, after the war, that they should be given equal status with the seniors in the Party, and he was honorary Life Patron of the Y.C. movement until he died.

The six long years of opposition did little either to enhance or detract from Eden's standing in public life. He was essentially a man of government and had little liking for the cut and thrust of Party politics in the House of Commons or on the hustings. He had an attractive and often persuasive style of speaking and the content of his contributions was sensible and sound, but he had little aptitude for the dynamic, witty or memorable phrase and found it difficult to rouse a large audience to enthusiasm. Nevertheless, he exercised considerable influence both in the Shadow Cabinet and in the country as a whole during this period.

The fact that almost his entire official life had been spent at the Foreign Office was both an asset and a liability. He was the only British statesman, apart from Churchill, who could, even in opposition, still command an international audience; but in the changing post-war world it was a disadvantage that he knew little of industry, economics or the social services. Experience in a domestic department would have been a benefit to him and to the Party. It was noticeable that his leadership was diffident in areas where his knowledge was incomplete. The philosophy was constructive but its exposition lacked confidence and precision.

Nevertheless, he was far the best known and most popular of Churchill's lieutenants and his position as heir was undisputed. When Churchill took three months holiday in the United States at the end of 1945, it was announced that Eden would act as leader of the Opposition during his absence.

The modernization of the Tory Party and the renewal of its appeal to face the problems of the second half of the twentieth century would naturally have fallen to Eden as its future leader, but he took relatively little part in the work this entailed. The reconstruction of the Party machine and its finances was left in the able hands of Lord Woolton and the new Conservative policies were initiated in the Research Department at Old Queen Street under the direction of Rab Butler, who presided over and co-ordinated the work of an exceptionally brilliant team of young men, which included Iain Macleod, Reginald Maudling and Enoch Powell.

It is fair to add, however, that Eden at once saw the need for day-to-day research to facilitate the work of the Party committees, of the Conservative members of standing committees on public Bills, and of the front bench, now deprived of the civil service briefs to which the former Ministers had become accustomed. To meet this need, Eden and Ralph Assheton (later Lord Clitheroe), who was then chairman of the Party, organized the Parliamentary Secretariat, which was established at 24 Wilton Street in the autumn of 1945. This was, indeed, Eden's idea and he put the new department in the charge of Henry Hopkinson (later Lord Colyton), who was a close friend and who had resigned from the diplomatic service early in 1946 in order to enter politics. Hopkinson reported direct to Eden and it was not until 1948 that the Secretariat was merged with the Research Department under Rab Butler.

In an important speech to the Party Conference at Blackpool in 1946, Eden made a significant personal contribution to Conservative thinking when he proclaimed the new Tory slogan – a nation-wide, property-owning democracy – as the main post-war Conservative aim. He contrasted this with the socialist objective of State ownership. 'Whereas the socialist purpose is the concentration of ownership in the hands of the state,' he declared, 'ours is the distribution of ownership over the widest practicable number of individuals.' He was genuinely interested in this concept, which in his mind included profit sharing, co-partnership and joint consultation, as well as home ownership.

Eden's first speech on the subject had been made as long ago as 1929 when he advocated the 'spread of private ownership ... to enable every worker to become a capitalist'. It was at the heart of his political philosophy and he believed that its development was the only viable Tory alternative to a steady drift towards state socialism. Other Party leaders used the theme from time to time for tactical political purposes. To Eden it was the strategic centre of home policy, to which he would certainly have given far greater practical application had his tenure of power at Downing Street not been so grievously curtailed. His approach to the major domestic issues followed that of Stanley Baldwin, who had given him his first opportunity in public life and whom he greatly admired.

Churchill was mainly concerned with the great post-war international issues and took little part in home affairs or in the day-to-day work of the House of Commons. He gave the Party prestige and was loved by the people, who regarded him as the saviour of the nation. But he seldom attended Parliament except to make an important speech on a great occasion and scarcely ever addressed the 1922 Committee.* By 1947 Members were becoming restive at this lack of leadership and eventually Churchill was prevailed upon to appear before the Committee. He met the criticism head on but with subtlety. He said, in effect, 'I am writing my war books, which I hope will be a contribution to history. But if you think I am failing in my responsibilities to the Party, I am very ready to retire from the leadership.' Then he went on, 'But in that event I should remain in Parliament and resume my corner seat below the gangway.'

The vision of Churchill mounting great attacks, as he had done before the war, as much against his own side as against the socialists, so alarmed the Parliamentary Party that no more was heard of his resignation. Throughout the years of Opposition Eden acted as *de facto* Conservative leader in the House of Commons and held weekly meetings with his principal colleagues in order to co-ordinate the Party's work in Parliament. He had the help of a strong front bench team, which included Rab Butler, Harold Macmillan, Oliver Stanley, Oliver Lyttelton (later Lord Chandos), David Maxwell-Fyfe (later Lord Kilmuir), W. S. ('Shakes') Morrison (later Speaker), Walter Elliot and Harry Crookshank, who all looked to Eden as their leader. His influence on domestic policy was perhaps greater than any of his words or actions might suggest.

In the general election held in February 1950, the huge Government majority was reduced to seven, and eighteen months later

* The 1922 Committee is so called because of the date of its origin, when a meeting of Conservative Members at the Carlton Club decided to withdraw from the Lloyd George coalition. It consists, when the Party is in opposition, of all Conservative MPS and, when in government, of all back bench MPS, Ministers attending it only when invited to do so. It meets in room 14 at the House of Commons at 6 p.m. on every Thursday when Parliament is in session.

Attlee again went to the country. Churchill campaigned with the challenging pledge that he would 'set the people free' after six years of socialist austerity and restrictions – a slogan that is almost as apposite today – and the Conservative Party regained office with the slender majority of sixteen.

Some people thought that, in order to give him greater experience of home affairs, Eden might take a senior domestic department or a sinecure position, such as Lord President of the Council, which would have left him free to direct the home front while Churchill concentrated on the international problems of the post-war world. It was recalled that every Conservative leader for the past fifty years had served as Chancellor of the Exchequer before becoming Prime Minister. Presumably Churchill would not have denied him the wider experience of this or some other home department, so it must be assumed that Eden himself wished to return to the Foreign Office.

Churchill and Eden worked closely together and Rab Butler records in his memoirs that when the Prime Minister appointed him as Chancellor of the Exchequer, he said, 'I have thought much about this offer and in the end Anthony and I agreed that you would be best at handling the Commons.' Oliver Lyttelton was the alternative possibility.

Churchill's memoranda to his Ministers were famous. I remember one of them with special pleasure when I was working for Gwilym Lloyd George (later Lord Tenby), who had decided to discontinue the Christmas bonuses hitherto given to old-age pensioners. When this was announced, the following message arrived from Downing Street:

Minister of Food,
   Pray explain on one sheet of paper why we cannot give the Christmas bonuses.   SCROOGE!
                    WSC

But the Prime Minister seldom interfered in departmental matters of this kind. He was the umbrella, an Olympian figure above the Party battle and virtually unassailable. He was thought to be failing (and was), but his second administration was a success.

In the spring of 1953, Eden became seriously ill and it was announced that he would have to undergo major surgery. Two operations, both unsuccessful, were performed in London before an American surgeon, Dr Cattell, offered to operate if Eden could go to

Boston. He agreed to do so and an obstruction to the bile duct was safely removed, but the operations had weakened him and a long period of convalescence in the United States and later in the Mediterranean was necessary. He did not return to Westminster until October.

In the meantime, at the end of June, Churchill suffered a severe stroke. A bulletin understating the gravity of his condition was issued, but the situation was most difficult. Eden was still in the Boston clinic and the country was without both a Prime Minister and a Foreign Secretary. If Eden had been in good health, Churchill might have resigned at once, but it seemed wrong to do so in circumstances which would have made it impossible for Eden to succeed him. Nor did Churchill want to go. The diary of his doctor, Lord Moran, records that 4 July was a good day. When his retirement was mentioned, Churchill said, 'I shall do what is best for the country.'

Lady Churchill: 'Of course, dear. I know you will.'

The PM (with a whimsical smile): 'Circumstances may convince me of my indispensability.'

A compromise was agreed upon which put Salisbury in temporary charge of the Foreign Office while Rab Butler acted as head of the Government. It was the first of many occasions on which he was to fill this role. But such an arrangement could clearly not continue for long. Fortunately the House of Commons was soon to rise for the summer recess.

Churchill had two options: to remain at Downing Street until Parliament re-assembled in October and then hand over to Eden; or, if he himself was sufficiently recovered by then, to resume the reins of Government. His own remarkable resilience resolved the matter. By September his speech was restored and, although still unsteady on his feet, he felt able to face the physical ordeal of the Party Conference and thereafter to resume the full duties of Prime Minister.

The last thing Churchill wanted to do was to retire and he was soon behaving as though nothing had happened. In December he told his son-in-law, Christopher Soames, that he would go in May 1954, when the Queen was due back from a visit to Australia. 'You will wait until the Queen returns,' commented Soames prophetically, 'and then you will find a reason why you must carry on. . . .' 'Oh,' said the Prime Minister with a smile, 'I don't know why you should say that.' When May came he told Lord Moran, ' I shall go in July – unless of course more unexpected developments occur. . . .'

So matters continued. As the different dates drew nearer, there were reasons, or excuses, for remaining in office, as there always are, and no doubt Churchill genuinely believed them to be valid; but the uncertainty led inevitably to speculation in the press and to an uneasy atmosphere in the Parliamentary Party. It was also unfair to Eden. Just as Chamberlain had seized upon Hitler's invasion of the Low Countries as an excuse to delay his own resignation, so Churchill now tried to remain in office until the last possible moment.

Harold Macmillan wrote in the third volume of his memoirs, *The Tides of Fortune*:

> The Government had ceased to function with full efficiency; many of the Ministers were unsuited to their posts; no one co-ordinated policy; Cabinets were becoming long and wearisome as well as too frequent. The Parliamentary Party, already discontented, might soon break into groups and cabals; the whole Party machine was losing grip. All this was due to the continual uncertainty, discussed openly in the press, as to Churchill's intentions.

In March 1954, Rab Butler records a conversation over dinner in which the Prime Minister observed that he felt 'like an aeroplane at the end of its flight, in the dusk, with the petrol running out, in search of a safe landing'. It was a little over a year before he found it. In September Lord Woolton reported, after a survey in the areas and the constituencies, that an election either at that time or in the following year would be a disaster unless there was 'a complete change in the structure of the Government and a new PM'. This was the general view of most members of the Cabinet. But such was Churchill's authority and prestige that no one could challenge his continued leadership. Following a talk with the Prime Minister on 1 October, Macmillan recorded that he 'is absolutely determined to go on and is not willing to contemplate any definite retirement date'.

Meanwhile, after a flurry of diplomatic activity, including visits to Washington and many European capitals, Eden convened a nine-power Foreign Ministers' Conference in London in September 1954, during the course of which he committed Britain to maintain four divisions and a tactical Air Force on the European mainland as long as the Brussels Treaty Powers wished them to remain there. This was at the time a sensational new departure in our foreign policy, as a result of which Britain became a full member of the European military alliance and Germany a full member of NATO. Paul-Henri Spaak described the negotiations as

certainement parmi les plus heureuses de sa carrière. Il l'a conduite du début jusqu'à la fin avec maîtrise, tour à tour conciliant et ferme, enfin, pour enlever la décision finale, imaginatif et audacieux. . . . Il a, en 1954 et en 1955, sauvé l'Alliance Atlantique.

The conference was regarded as a triumph for Anthony Eden and a month later the Queen conferred upon him a Knighthood of the Garter.

It would have been unusual for a Parliament elected in the autumn of 1951 to continue beyond the end of the year 1955 and as Churchill would clearly not lead the Party into another general election, it seemed right to give his successor the choice of the election date. This meant in practice that Eden must take over the leadership not later than the spring of 1955, which would give him the chance of going to the country either in the early summer or the autumn of that year. Eventually 5 April was decided upon as the most convenient date for Churchill's retirement and at the end of March he invited Eden and Butler to the Cabinet room. It was a short meeting. Butler recalls in his memoirs that Churchill said simply, 'I am going and Anthony will succeed me. We can discuss details later.'

On 4 April the Prime Minister gave a farewell dinner party at Downing Street, attended by the Queen and the most senior members of the Cabinet, and at 4.30 p.m. on 5 April Churchill went to Buckingham Palace. The Queen did not ask for his advice about the succession and Churchill therefore offered none. Unless specifically invited to do so, he felt strongly that it would have been constitution-ally improper for him to express an opinion. He asked his Private Secretary, Sir John Colville, to make a note of this view for the official record and Colville at once did so. It was the last instruction he received from the Prime Minister.

Sir Winston Churchill retained his seat in the House of Commons for a further nine years. He died at the age of ninety on 25 January 1965. He has been variously described as a selfish egotist who had little regard for the feelings of others and as a man of great charm, irascible but very lovable. He was certainly erratic and self-centred and in his long career he espoused some mistaken causes. Jock

Colville, who knew him well and served him faithfully, has described him as a 'wayward, romantic, expansive and explosive genius, with the inspirational qualities of an Old Testament Prophet'.* Colville thought his outstanding qualities were his total courage, moral and physical, his imagination, his unique ability to inspire others and his unfailing magnanimity. Without question, he was the greatest man of his time and one of the greatest of all time.

At noon, on 5 April 1955, the Queen sent for Anthony Eden, who agreed to form a government. He had been deputy Prime Minister for the last three and a half years and there was never any doubt as to his right or qualifications to succeed to the premiership. Throughout the fifteen years of Churchill's leadership Eden had been acknowledged as his eventual successor by Churchill himself, by the Parliamentary Party and by the public at large. No rival candidate existed, so there was no discussion or controversy of any kind. In his memoirs, *Full Circle*, Eden quotes Sir Winston's words, 'No two men ever changed guard more smoothly.'

Only the formality of the usual Party meeting to confirm him in the Conservative leadership remained. This was held on 21 April. It was attended by the 320 Conservative Members of the House of Commons, about 280 Unionist peers in receipt of the Party whip, 250 adopted Parliamentary candidates and the 150 members of the Executive Committee of the National Union. Lord Salisbury presided and proposed Eden as leader. The resolution was carried unanimously. The main supporting speech was made by Butler, who was the most senior of Eden's Cabinet colleagues and was regarded as his probable successor. Thereafter he deputized for the Prime Minister whenever he was away or unable to attend the Cabinet.

Owing to a national newspaper strike which coincided with Churchill's retirement, the tributes which would have been paid to him, and no doubt to Eden, could only be printed in the provincial press. The *Yorkshire Post* commented, 'It is fortunate that there exists to succeed Sir Winston a leader who is a world statesman in his own right. . . . The prestige and fortunes of Britain remain in safe hands.' So it must have seemed at the time. Although he had no practical experience of home affairs, Eden had held the post of Foreign Secretary for a total of eleven years and it is ironical that the collapse of his government came about through the failure of an international initiative for which he was himself largely responsible.

* *Footprints in Time.*

The new Prime Minister appointed Harold Macmillan to succeed him at the Foreign Office, but made no other major changes. Butler continued as Chancellor of the Exchequer. Within a week, Eden announced the dissolution of Parliament on 6 May, and a general election on 26 May. His timing and conduct of the quiet and un-eventful campaign were skilful and resulted in a Conservative majority of sixty-one in the House of Commons. But the new reign, which had begun so auspiciously, was to end in disaster.

Eden took over in an atmosphere of optimism and goodwill. He was trusted and respected in the country and was identified, with Butler and Macmillan, as representing the new post-war Conserva-tism. He pictured the Party as 'a national Party, both in the source of its strength and in the objects of its policy'. He was a Conservative in the Baldwin tradition, who understood the Party and was skilful in assessing its reactions – more a Conservative than Churchill, more conscientious and hard-working than Baldwin. He was an empiricist; honest, courteous, courageous and a brilliant negotiator. His weak-nesses, partly hereditary and partly due to ill-health, were a dislike of criticism, a streak of obstinacy, impatience and a strong temper. He lived on his nerves and tended to fuss his Ministers with telephone calls and messages enquiring how their particular problems were progressing. David Kilmuir, who was his Lord Chancellor, refers in *Political Adventure* to this 'chronic restlessness which affected all his colleagues' and to 'his habit of interference in departmental affairs'.

Eden's inheritance appeared to be a good one. Abroad, there was a welcome thaw in east-west relations; at home Butler had talked with confidence of doubling the standard of living in twenty-five years. But as the year wore on, inflationary pressures increased and difficulties began to develop over the balance of payments. Wages, prices and Government expenditure were all beginning to rise too rapidly and by the end of August Eden had become convinced that 'we must put the battle of inflation before anything else'. In the autumn Butler was obliged to bring in a deflationary second budget, which was inevitably much attacked by the Opposition after the tax reductions of only seven months earlier.

On 22 December 1955, Eden announced a Christmas re-shuffle of his government. Butler became Lord Privy Seal and leader of the House of Commons, Macmillan succeeded him at the Treasury and Selwyn Lloyd was made Foreign Secretary. This re-arrangement of offices suited both Macmillan and the Prime Minister. It widened

Macmillan's experience and gave Eden a more direct control of foreign policy, which he naturally wished to exert but which had hitherto been difficult because Macmillan was not the sort of Minister to tolerate interference in a department of which he was in charge. The relatively junior Selwyn Lloyd was more ready to accept guidance from Eden on major issues of policy. Of the younger men, Edward Heath became Chief Whip and Iain Macleod was the first of the famous 1950 entry to enter the Cabinet, as Minister of Labour.

Eden was anxious about inflation, though its scale was of course minimal as compared with that of the late 1960s and 1970s. Macmillan, assisted by Macleod, held a series of private meetings with industrialists and trade union leaders to urge upon both sides the need for restraint, but there was no question at that time of the wage freezes and incomes policies which became a feature of economic policy under later governments.

Much depended on the 1956 budget. The Federation of British Industries was critical of Government expenditure, which entailed a correspondingly high level of taxation, and argued that a reduction in spending would be the biggest single contribution the Government could make to curb inflation. The Trade Union Congress considered that the rise in prices made wage restraint impossible and recommended that the budget should make its contribution towards lowering the price of necessities wherever possible.

The Chancellor of the Exchequer promised a reduction of £100 million in Government spending and persuaded the boards of the nationalized industries not to increase the prices of their goods and services. The FBI urged a corresponding restraint upon its members. But there was no response from the unions. In September the TUC rejected restraint by an overwhelming majority and wage rates continued to rise.

Although Eden's task in dealing with the economy seemed difficult at the time, in retrospect it did not compare with that of Edward Heath fifteen years later. Eden was negotiating with moderate union leaders like Sir Thomas (later Lord) Williamson, who at least understood his problems, as he understood theirs. I remember him telling me that during talks at Downing Street one of them had said, 'Prime Minister, we have our constituents too and if you give us nothing to take back to them, we shan't be here next year; we shall have been replaced by others who won't understand, or even want to understand, the difficulties you have been explaining to us.' Many of the men Heath had to argue with were of this much more militant turn of mind.

The new Prime Minister's honeymoon period was short-lived. By the turn of the year the Government's popularity was already on the wane and in a by-election at Tonbridge the Tory majority fell from 10,000 to scarcely more than 1000. After a poor speech by Eden in the House of Commons in March 1956, the experienced political commentator, Ian Waller, wrote, 'If the year goes on as it has begun, it will not be Sir Anthony Eden but Mr Harold Macmillan who reigns in Downing Street in 1957.' This prescient observation was remarkable not only for its prophetic warning of Eden's downfall, but because it was the first public prediction that Macmillan, rather than Butler, might be his successor.

The problems of the economy, though worrying, were soon to be over-shadowed by Colonel Nasser's seizure of the Suez Canal and the momentous events flowing from it, which in the end destroyed Eden's government.

The seeds of the Suez conflict, ironically in view of his subsequent attitude, were sown by the American Secretary of State, Foster Dulles. This gifted but obstinate statesman had brusquely, and with minimal tact and finesse, withdrawn his offer of a large loan to Egypt for the Aswan Dam. Whereupon, and as a direct retaliation, Nasser took control of the Canal on 26 July 1956 and gave notice that he would use its revenues to finance the dam. This was in defiance of international agreements going back to 1888 and confirmed by Egypt as recently as October 1954.

British public and Parliamentary opinion was strongly opposed to this arbitrary action. The pressures on Eden to take a firm line were not confined to the right-wing Suez group in the Conservative Party and they synchronized with his own instinctive reaction. His first concern was the need to safeguard our oil supplies, but the pre-war military adventures of the dictators in Abyssinia and Albania, in the Rhineland, Austria and Czechoslovakia were also much in his mind and he was not alone in regarding Nasser as a latter-day Hitler or Mussolini. 'We were determined that the like should not come again,' he wrote in *Full Circle*; 'there might be other mistakes, there would not be that one.'

On 27 July he established a special Cabinet committee under his own chairmanship to deal with the situation. It consisted of the Foreign Secretary, Selwyn Lloyd, the Chancellor of the Exchequer,

Harold Macmillan, the Commonwealth Secretary, Alec Home, the Minister of Defence, Walter Monckton, and Lord Salisbury, who was the Lord President of the Council. In addition, the Colonial Secretary was present at more than half the meetings and the Lord Chancellor from time to time. Perhaps significantly Rab Butler was not included as a member of this important committee, although he attended many of its meetings. For the first time Macmillan looked like the second-in-command in the Cabinet, and throughout the Suez crisis Butler was not in Eden's confidence and his position as the Prime Minister's probable successor was gradually eroded in the eyes of his colleagues, though not as a result of any wish or design on Eden's part.

The Prime Minister stated his position in the House of Commons on 30 July. 'No arrangements for the future of this great international waterway,' he declared, 'could be acceptable to Her Majesty's Government which would leave it in the unfettered control of a single power which could, as recent events have shown, exploit it purely for purposes of national policy.' No one dissented from this proposition and at this stage even the Opposition front bench gave Eden almost unqualified support. *The Times* leading article of 1 August affirmed that there could be 'no stability or confidence in the world so long as agreements can be scrapped with impunity'.

Early in August, the full Cabinet took the basic decision that, while a negotiated settlement should be sought, force would be used if negotiations failed within a measurable time. This guided all the Government's subsequent actions. But throughout the whole Suez affair there were two strands of opinion in the Cabinet. Both of them supported the Prime Minister's policy, but the aims of each were different. One section concurred with Eden's anti-dictator line against Nasser. The other, led by Butler, was anxious only to save the Canal and to internationalize it. At first these divergent attitudes were unobtrusive; it was only after the launching of hostilities that they became embarrassing.

The French reaction to the crisis was the same as the British, except that France was conscious of her close ties with Israel, whereas we had to consider our treaty engagements with Jordan. It was agreed, therefore, to treat the Arab/Israeli problem as quite distinct from the future of the canal.

From the outset Foster Dulles was more cautious than the French Foreign Minister, Pineau, but at first even Dulles considered it 'intolerable' that the Canal should be under the control of any single country and that a way had to be found to make Nasser 'disgorge'. At this stage the United States Government did not exclude the use of force for this purpose if all other methods failed. But Eden made the mistake of ignoring the Presidential election, due in November, which inevitably influenced Eisenhower's attitude.

It was decided to convene an international conference of the twenty-four countries concerned, including Russia, on 16 August. Within a week proposals acceptable to Britain were agreed by eighteen of the twenty-four delegations and Robert Menzies, the Prime Minister of Australia, was invited to convey them to the Egyptian Government, which refused them. Meanwhile Foster Dulles had suggested the formation of a Users' Association which would hire pilots, collect dues and manage the Canal. Eden accepted this idea, but Nasser in an intemperate speech again rejected it. A second international conference was held in London on 19 September to establish the Users' Association and decide upon its powers and duties.

On 26 September Eden and Selwyn Lloyd flew to Paris for consultations with the French Government. Although discouraged by the Americans from doing so, we had determined to take our case against Egypt to the Security Council of the United Nations; and, after presiding over the inaugural meeting of the Users' Association on 1 October, Selwyn Lloyd left with Pineau for New York. Ten days of discussion on the Anglo-French resolution followed, at the end of which – although agreed by all the other members of the Council except Yugoslavia – it was vetoed by Russia.

On 16 October Eden and Lloyd again visited Paris. Owing to mounting *fedayeen* raids and violent Egyptian propaganda against Israel, a difficult situation had arisen: Israel was not prepared quietly to await destruction when it suited the Arab states to attack her. There was a danger that she might become embroiled with Jordan, whom we were pledged to support, whereas France would go to the help of Israel. The French Ministers agreed to warn the Israelis that an attack on Jordan would mean British intervention and that, if they planned any retaliation against the Arabs, it would therefore be wiser to direct this against Egypt rather than against Jordan.

Israel mobilized on 25 October and a few days later attacked Egyptian forces in Sinai. The British and French Governments, wrote Eden in *Full Circle*, thereupon intervened 'to localize the dispute . . . to separate the belligerents and to guarantee freedom of transit through the Canal by the ships of all nations'. Notes were sent in identical terms to Egypt and Israel, demanding their withdrawal to ten miles on either side of the Canal. Nasser declined to comply.

When the Security Council met on 30 October, the American spokesman condemned the Israeli aggression and urged all members of the United Nations to refrain from force or the threat of force. This resolution received seven votes, with abstentions by Australia and Belgium. Britain and France voted against it, and we used our veto for the first time in the history of the UN. The rift between the United States and the United Kingdom was complete.

When the House of Commons re-assembled after the summer recess, Opposition approval turned to growing hostility and, as the Government's support for the Israeli attack on Egypt became obvious, the anger of the Labour Party mounted and the scenes in the House of Commons grew more bitter and more violent. Hugh Gaitskell, the leader of the Opposition, who had been helpful and conciliatory in July, was genuinely furious by October and his supporters 'below the gangway' were so noisy and unruly that on one occasion the Speaker was obliged to suspend the sitting for tempers to cool. As events unfolded and Cabinet meetings became more and more frequent, the Government sometimes seemed to be only an hour or two ahead of the House of Commons.

Throughout the Suez operation, the Cabinet was used more as a rubber stamp to endorse decisions already taken than as an executive; and senior officials in the Foreign Office were not consulted or even informed about what was happening. Lord Gore-Booth has recorded in his memoirs, *With Great Truth and Respect*, 'Just as Mr Chamberlain did not choose to have full advice from the Foreign Office in 1938, so did Sir Anthony Eden tragically avoid it in 1956 . . . [he] did not so much reject advice as decline to hear it.' There are probably no official papers on Suez in existence in Britain except those in Lord Selwyn Lloyd's private files and he is almost certainly the only British statesman alive today who knows exactly what happened.

On 31 October, with the rejection by Egypt of the Anglo-French note, the Cabinet authorized operation 'Musketeer', the plan prepared at the outset of the Suez crisis for armed intervention against

Egypt should this prove necessary. Air bombing attacks against military targets were launched from our bases in Cyprus, Malta and Aden and within twenty-four hours the Egyptian Air Force had been virtually destroyed. But the nearest deep-water port from which to embark our ground troops was Malta, 900 miles and six days steaming from Port Said. During the whole of this time international opinion was mounting against us.

Anthony Eden suggested that a UN force should be associated with the Anglo-French action at a later stage and this idea was taken up and developed by Lester Pearson, the Foreign Minister of Canada; but it did nothing to allay American indignation and the General Assembly of the UN, which met on 2 November, endorsed by sixty-four votes to five a hostile resolution moved by Foster Dulles. This was opposed by Britain, France, Israel, Australia and New Zealand. Canada, South Africa, Belgium, Laos, the Netherlands and Portugal abstained.

Meanwhile, the Israelis had won a brilliant series of victories in Sinai against better equipped Egyptian troops and had gained all their main objectives. On 5 November British and French parachutists occupied the Gamil airfield and Port Fuad and next day the assault forces arrived from Malta. They took Port Said without difficulty and advanced twenty-three miles south to El Cap. The Commander-in-Chief estimated that he could have occupied Ismailia by 8 November and Suez by 12 November; but fighting between Israel and Egypt had just ended and the Cabinet ordered a cease-fire at midnight on 6 November.

The official explanation put forward by Eden was, 'We had intervened to divide and, above all, to contain the conflict. The occasion for our intervention was over, the fire was out. Once the fighting had ceased, justification for intervention ceased with it.'

In fact the external pressures had become too intense to withstand. Some people feared a pro-Egyptian intervention by Russia; but the run on sterling was the decisive factor. This had developed with increasing momentum over the previous three months, culminating in a fall in the reserves of $279 million in November alone. Rab Butler recalls in *The Art of the Possible* the profound effect this had on Harold Macmillan, the Chancellor of the Exchequer, 'who switched almost overnight from being the foremost protagonist of intervention to being the leading influence for disengagement'. As Randolph Churchill wrote at the time, 'What was the difference between Rab Butler, who never wanted to go in, and Harold Macmillan, who took the Cabinet out?' The difference was to be one of the reasons for the Party's choice of a successor when Eden was forced to retire through ill-health two months later.

I remember the excited meeting of the 1922 Committee in December when the patriotic line taken by Macmillan was so much more in tune with the mood of the Parliamentary Party than Butler's more moderate attitude. 'I held the Tory Party for the weekend. It was all I intended to do,' Macmillan told Gwilym Lloyd George, then Home Secretary, and myself immediately after this meeting. It sounded to me a somewhat cynical remark. Disarmingly, in the fourth volume of his autobiography, *Riding The Storm*, Macmillan acknowledged:

I have often been reproached for having been at the same time one of the most keen supporters of strong action in the Middle East and one of the most rapid to withdraw when that policy met a serious check.

'First in, first out' was to be the elegant criticism of one of my chief Labour critics on many subsequent occasions.

This criticism was not confined to members of the Labour Party.

Macmillan had in fact struck the right note at the right moment in his speech to the 1922 Committee. I remember saying to my wife that evening that the Members desperately wanted a touch of Palmerstonian language, if only to restore their pride and self-confidence. Timing is the essence of politics, as of so many other things in life, and Macmillan had the intuition to sense the need to restore the morale of the Party.

There is no doubt that Butler was out of sympathy with the Suez adventure. Gil Lloyd George, one of the Prime Minister's most fervent supporters, remarked to me one day at the height of the crisis, 'I wish the Lord Privy Seal would stop hawking his conscience round the Cabinet room.' It was a harsh and somewhat unfair comment because Butler was sincere in his doubts about the wisdom of the policy, but he had antagonized many of his colleagues by his lukewarm acceptance of their decisions. He would have received support from others, like Iain Macleod, who shared his anxieties, had he given a clear lead against Eden's policy, but his position was always equivocal and therefore unconvincing.

The Parliamentary Party was loyal to the Prime Minister throughout the crisis. There were some opponents of the policy, like Nigel

77

Nicolson, who never wanted to go in to the Canal zone, and there were many more who did not want to come out; but only eight Conservatives abstained when the House divided on 8 November and there were only two resignations from the Government – those of Anthony Nutting, Minister of State at the Foreign Office, and Sir Edward Boyle, the Economic Secretary to the Treasury.

Criticism of the Anglo-French enterprise by the United Nations and the Commonwealth was predictable, but Eden did not expect the degree of hostility displayed by the United States. He hoped they would at least be neutral, if only because of their identity of interest with ourselves in maintaining stability in the Middle East and protecting the flank which the Communists were always anxious to turn. Instead, Foster Dulles seemed more anxious to vie with the Russians in supporting the views of the Afro-Asian bloc and he was disingenuous, at least initially, in failing to make his opposition clear to the British Cabinet.

One of the reasons for his critical attitude was no doubt the strength of his views on colonialism, of which he appeared to think the Anglo-French intervention at Suez was a form. But, as Eden pointed out in his memoirs, the dispute was between sovereign nations about the violation of a treaty. 'If the United States had to defend their treaty rights in the Panama Canal,' he wrote, 'they would not regard such action as colonialism; neither would I.'

Another and more personal reason for this low ebb in Anglo-American relations was the antipathy which had existed between Anthony Eden and Foster Dulles since their disagreements over Indo-China in 1954. On Eden's part this was not surprising. Foster Dulles was a devious man and never more so than throughout the Suez crisis. Again and again he misled Eden with expressions of agreement or promises of support which never materialized. No reliance could be placed on his word. Nevertheless, if the two men had been friends, the mutual misunderstandings might not have arisen and the Suez story might have ended differently. As it was, the alliance was shaken to its foundations and it took Macmillan many months of patient diplomacy to repair the damage.

On 5 October, when preparations for the invasion were in progress, Eden suffered a severe attack of fever with a temperature of 105°. It was a period of immense strain and he was not a good delegator, so that he was overworked and short of sleep. As the crisis developed, he became mentally and physically exhausted. Clarissa Eden told friends that she felt as though the Suez Canal was flowing through her drawing-room at Downing Street. But Eden's health did not have a decisive influence on his policy and it is probable that he would not have acted differently even if he had been well. It cannot be denied that, mainly due to the attitude of the United States Government, the Suez enterprise, though a tactical success, had proved a strategic failure. Control of the Canal reverted to Nasser, who soon refused passage to Israeli ships and cargoes, and the Arab/Israeli problem remained unsolved. It is worth recalling, however, that eighteen months later, after the murder of the King, the Crown Prince and Nuri es-Said in Iraq, the Goverments of Lebanon and Jordan, threatened by Nasser in their own countries, invited help from the west. The United States sent a force to the aid of Lebanon while Britain flew troops to Jordan.

The lesson is clear that, even in co-operation with a country the size of France, we can no longer take a major military initiative unless we have the support or at least the neutral goodwill of the United States.

There remains the charge of collusion. The dictionary definition of this word is 'a secret agreement to deceive'. In his last speech in the House of Commons, Eden denied 'a dishonourable conspiracy' or any foreknowledge of Israel's attack on Egypt. But the Government realized, he said, the risk of such an attack and he acknowledged that there had been contingency planning in case it should materialize. It was not a very complete or candid comment on this controversial question.

The autobiography of Moshe Dayan, the legendary figure who was Israeli Minister of Defence during both the six-day war and the Yom Kippur war, was published in 1976. At the time of Suez he was Chief-of-Staff of the Israeli defence forces and in this capacity was involved in the planning of the Suez campaign. His version of the events leading up to it cannot therefore be disregarded. It is clear from his account that collusion between France and Israel was complete. Britain and France were closely and openly allied in their Suez policy from the first day to the last. To what extent did our overt co-operation with the French involve us in France's covert co-operation with Israel?

Dayan writes in his book that an Anglo-French meeting took place in Paris on 22 October, at which the British handed the French Ministers a memorandum signed by Anthony Eden and intended for the Israelis, which stated that, after the commencement of hostilities, Britain and France would demand the retirement of both Egypt and Israel from the Canal area. If one side refused, the Anglo-French forces would intervene to restore the free operation of the Canal. This would provide the legal and moral justification for the invasion of the Canal zone by Britain and France. Britain would only join the enterprise if she could appear as an intermediary to restore peace in the area.

A separate Israeli-French meeting was taking place at the same time and was later joined – Dayan continues – by Selwyn Lloyd. After further negotiations on 24 October, at which Britain was represented by officials, the final plans for the invasion were agreed.

That there was an element of collusion, the degree of which is still unknown, seems certain. But I do not myself regard collusion as necessarily reprehensible if, as in this case, the perpetrators of it were acting in what they genuinely believed to be the national interest. Eden had tried to reverse an act of aggression inimical to Britain. Dean Acheson commented later, 'The British were pilloried for defending their rights under international law. . . . No wonder that this doctrine has led to the general breakdown of whatever respect for law survived the nineteenth century.'

Perhaps the real criticism of Eden's policy is not that it was immoral but that it was out of date. His thinking was conditioned by the events of the 1930s and he did not take fully into account the decline in Britain's economic, military and political power which followed the Second World War. Eden's motives were patriotic and his actions were courageous, but they were also an anachronism by the 1950s.

The strain of Suez took a heavy toll of Eden's health. His doctors decided that he could no longer live on a diet of stimulants and tranquillizers and persuaded him to take a complete rest in order to recuperate. He and his wife flew to Jamaica on 23 November, leaving Butler in charge of the Government. It was a difficult assignment. The troops had to be withdrawn, the pound stabilized and our international relations restored. These tasks were not made easier by the need to obtain Eden's authority for any major decision. The only method of communication was through the Governor, who had to transmit messages by road to Ian Fleming's house, Golden Eye, where the Edens were staying, at the other end of the island.

The atmosphere in the House of Commons was uneasy during the Prime Minister's absence, and his return on 14 December was greeted with sullen silence by the Opposition and the most perfunctory of cheers from the Conservative benches. Lord Kilmuir paid tribute in his autobiography to the skill shown by the Chief Whip, Edward Heath, in his handling of the Parliamentary Party during this and the earlier Suez period, and no doubt the morale of Members, instinctively loyal to the leadership, would gradually have been restored under Eden if he had been able to continue as Prime Minister.

His health was the hazard. He was sleeping badly and after Christmas he suffered another bout of fever, which lingered on into the New Year. These attacks were debilitating and made it impossible for him to undertake a full day's work and the responsibility of running the Government and making important decisions. He was advised by his doctors that the fevers were likely to recur and with increasing intensity. In view of this he felt he had no choice and must resign at once, so that his successor could form a Government and be ready to face Parliament when it re-assembled after the Christmas recess.

On 8 January the Prime Minister telephoned Butler to tell him of this decision and then proceeded at once to Sandringham to inform the Queen. No announcement was made to the newspapers, which regarded it as a routine visit. The next day the Queen returned to Buckingham Palace and Eden called there that evening to tender his resignation. Before doing so, he invited Macmillan to see him at Downing Street and a Cabinet was called for 5 p.m. to inform his other colleagues. Most of them were unprepared for this grievous news. Eden made known his decision briefly and with dignity, and Salisbury spoke with some emotion of their long friendship. Butler and Macmillan followed and the short meeting ended with the Prime Minister bidding farewell to each of his Ministers individually.

Over twenty years before, Stanley Baldwin, who was then Prime Minister, had predicted to Duncan Sandys, 'Chamberlain will be your leader for a short time. Then Anthony will have a long reign.' In fact, he was Prime Minister for one year and nine months.

After so long an apprenticeship and so short a tenure of power, the failure of the Suez policy and his breakdown in health were tragic for Anthony Eden and a source of sincere sorrow to his friends. He had had a long and, until the end, exceptionally successful career in guiding the international relations of Britain and his political influence was greater than is generally supposed. He died on 14 January 1977. Although his whole life had been devoted to politics, it was by no means his only interest. He was a man of culture, well read and a delightful companion. He had beautiful manners and was the most courteous and considerate of men. Many who worked closely with him were struck by his concern for other people's feelings, and by his remarkable capacity for remembering names and faces, often long after the incident with which they were associated in his mind. Those who knew him best loved him deeply.

Although uneventful and marred by ill-health, the last twenty years were not unhappy because he had come to terms with life, had accepted its vicissitudes and had refused to be soured by its misfortunes. Rab Butler described him to me as 'a gallant gentleman' and no one who knew him would quarrel with that tribute.

5

HAROLD MACMILLAN

The succession lay between Rab Butler and Harold Macmillan. There were no other contenders. The issue was swiftly resolved by the initiative of Lord Salisbury and Lord Kilmuir, on which they had agreed before the meeting of Eden's last Cabinet.

When Butler and Macmillan had withdrawn, the Lord President of the Council and the Lord Chancellor invited the other members of the Cabinet to wait behind for short individual interviews. This seemed an appropriate procedure for ascertaining the view of their colleagues, since both were senior members of the Government and neither was a candidate for the premiership. Their concern was to obtain a speedy decision on which to base the Cabinet's advice to the Queen, without prejudicing the exercise of her prerogative by allowing a Party meeting to elect a new leader (and therefore, in effect, the new Prime Minister) before she had taken soundings and made her decision.

It has been argued, on the one hand, that leaving the choice to the Queen meant bringing the crown into Party politics; on the other hand, that electing a Party leader first would have infringed the prerogative.

The two peers took the latter view and most people would agree that they acted with perfect propriety in seeking the opinions of their colleagues and then reporting the Cabinet's collective advice to the Queen.

Discretion was maintained by choosing Salisbury's room in the Privy Council offices as the venue, since this could be reached without leaving the building. Lord Kilmuir recounts in his memoirs that almost every member of the Cabinet observed, as he entered the room, that it was 'like coming to the headmaster's study'. But no attempt was made to influence anyone's opinion.

The procedure was as simple as it was neutral. Lord Salisbury found it difficult to pronounce the letter 'r', so his question to each Minister in turn was, 'Well, which is it to be, Wab or Hawold?' A large majority of the Cabinet favoured Macmillan.

Before reporting this view to the Queen, the two peers saw Edward Heath, the Chief Whip, and Oliver Poole (later Lord Poole), the chairman of the Conservative Party organization, in order to test the feeling in the Parliamentary Party and in the country. John Morrison (later Lord Margadale), the chairman of the 1922 Committee, telephoned his assessment from the Isle of Islay next morning. Back bench opinion, as reported by Heath and Morrison, endorsed that of the Cabinet, and I have no doubt that it was representative even of those whose personal preference was neither volunteered nor canvassed.

One of the younger members, Tom Iremonger (then MP for Ilford, North), wrote to the *Daily Telegraph* on 12 January complaining that soundings were not taken among Conservative back benchers – or, if they were taken, that it must have been on a selective and oligarchal basis since he himself had not been approached. This letter provoked an immediate reply from that redoubtable lady, Dame (later Baroness) Irene Ward, who pointed out that Iremonger need only have informed the whips of his opinion, as she had done, and Sir Martin Lindsay, MP for Solihull, wrote to the paper on the same lines. I remember sending my own views on the succession to the Chief Whip and there was certainly no inhibition about doing so. I have no doubt that Edward Heath had ample information on which to base his advice.

R. A. Butler was, perhaps understandably, a little critical of the procedure which had been adopted. He wrote in *The Art of the Possible* that 'Cabinet Ministers were "corralled" to give an immediate judgement . . .', and mentions that 'Selwyn Lloyd objected to this procedure being carried out by two peers'. It is not obvious who else could have discharged the task.

While the Cabinet interviews were taking place, Eden was at the Palace and thereafter his doctor, Sir Horace Evans, issued a bulletin expressing the opinion that 'his health will no longer enable him to sustain the heavy burdens inseparable from the office of Prime Minister'. The Queen's acceptance of his resignation was announced at the same time.

At 11 o'clock next morning Salisbury called at Buckingham Palace to convey to the Queen the collective advice of the Cabinet and, as reported to him, of the Parliamentary Party. The Queen also consulted both Sir Winston Churchill and Sir Anthony Eden before coming to a decision. Churchill was pleased to be summoned and advised the Queen to send for Macmillan. He told Rab afterwards, 'I supported the older man.' This was no doubt one of the reasons, but it would have been surprising if there were not others, including the fact that the two had been closely associated in friendship and policy since before the war. When Macmillan was a Churchill disciple, Butler was defending Chamberlain against Churchill's oratory; and whereas Churchill had inherited Butler as Under-Secretary at the Foreign Office, he himself gave Macmillan his first appointment as a junior minister and soon afterwards promoted him to Cabinet rank as Minister resident in North Africa.

Although Parliament was in recess at the time of Eden's resignation, anyone in close touch with Conservative opinion in the House of Commons should have known that Macmillan was the Party's probable choice as his successor. It is therefore surprising that on the morning of 10 January most of the newspapers made the wrong assessment. The *Daily Express*, the *Mail*, the *Herald*, the *Mirror* and the *News Chronicle* all predicted that Butler would become Prime Minister; only Randolph Churchill in the *Evening Standard* suggested that Macmillan had the better prospects, and this was due to Beaverbrook's sources of information rather than to Churchill's prescience. Beaverbrook had telephoned to ask the result of his researches. 'I think it's going to be Butler,' was the reply, to which Beaverbrook retorted, 'You said Macmillan, didn't you? That's right,' and rang off. Randolph Churchill took the tip and altered his article. *The Times* was ambivalent: its political correspondent doubted if Butler would be acceptable to the right-wing element in the Party, but the leading article considered that as 'the hope and leader of the younger Conservatives', he was the most likely choice. The *Manchester Guardian*, after weighing the pros and cons objectively, came to the conclusion that 'Suez apart, it would be astounding if in present circumstances Mr Butler was not given the first invitation to form a Government'.

There is no doubt that his attitude over Suez depreciated Butler's standing both in the Cabinet and in the Parliamentary Party. This was particularly true of the so-called Suez group, who criticized his assumed opposition to the military intervention in Egypt and his reputedly lukewarm support of action after it had been taken. Even those MPs who agreed with him were, though to a lesser extent, critical of his apparent lack of resolution. They thought he should have carried his disapproval to the point of resignation. But Butler believes in the need for compromise in politics and would not have divided the Cabinet at so crucial a time. Unlike some others, he is not always sure that he is right and his temperament is not that of a man ready, rashly or dramatically, to resign if his counsel in Cabinet does not prevail.

Those best qualified to decide between two rival claimants to the premiership are undoubtedly their colleagues who have worked closely with them both for several years, and it is possible that Macmillan would have been the Cabinet's choice even if the Suez affair had never happened. But Suez was certainly a weight in the scales against Butler and this was not only due to his ambiguous and non-committal support for Eden's policy.

The Conservative Party was distressed and embarrassed by the Suez failure. One of the factors, therefore, in the choice of leader was the need to select the man most likely to be able to heal the Party's wounded pride, to resore its self-confidence and to re-unite its members. As the *Daily Telegraph* put it, with hindsight, once the issue has been decided, 'Mr Macmillan is undoubtedly the best available choice when the first essential duty of the Party is to close its ranks.'

It would have been more difficult to reconcile the right wing of the Party to Butler than for the left wing to accept Macmillan, the author of *The Middle Way*. 'Butskellism', though agreeable to some of us, was much disliked by others as an erosion of Conservative principles.

In fact, as his premiership developed, Macmillan led the Party from a position well to the left of centre, but he knew instinctively when to make right-wing speeches. Butler was far more suspect to traditional Tory thinking and, certainly at the time of Suez, would have found it harder to hold the Party together.

Lord Kilmuir was no doubt correct in *Political Adventure* when he wrote that Conservative feeling in the House of Commons was running strongly against Butler at that time. But there was another consideration:

For this sharp decline in his personal fortunes, Rab had no one to blame but himself. Many considered that his habit of publicly hedging his political bets was too great a weakness and this had accordingly damaged his position both in the Conservative hierarchy and in the Parliamentary Party. I have no doubt that a straight vote between the two, either in the Cabinet or in the Party, would have left Rab in a very small minority.

From conversations with colleagues at the time I am sure that David Kilmuir, whose political judgements were not always impeccable, was right, if a little harsh, in this assessment. Rab Butler's prospects of becoming Prime Minister would certainly have been higher but for the Suez crisis, which had crystallized criticism among those already suspicious of his political ambivalence. But his unfortunate tendency in private conversation to please colleagues holding different opinions by giving each the answer he hoped for had become well known. I remember one occasion, at a dinner party of eighteen in the House of Commons, when he changed the emphasis of his remarks three times in reply to widely divergent views on immigration. He had a facility for conciliation, born of long experience, which he tended to over-play. He was entirely straightforward in talking to any one individual, but he often thought aloud, sometimes with rather curious results. Michael Fraser (now Lord Fraser of Kilmorack) tells a characteristic story to illustrate this. In conversation with a colleague Rab was heard to remark 'I see you are wearing the CUCA tie. Of course I designed it [egotistical]. It is practically unwearable [true]. But it looks rather good on you [agreeable flattery.'

No one accused him of insincerity, still less of dishonesty. They simply did not know, after talking to him, what his own opinions on some controversial subjects really were. This inevitably undermined their confidence in his leadership and made them reluctant to support his claims to the premiership. But no one interested in the 'endless adventure' of politics could fail to be fascinated by his intellectual distinction and by his quality of forward vision, rare in even the most distinguished of the political leaders of any Party.

It was a difficult time for Rab Butler. His first wife, Sydney, had died two years before and he only married Mollie Courtauld two years later. He was lonely and a little isolated. In a biography by Ralph Harris, called *Politics Without Prejudice*, published in 1956, a colleague is quoted as having commented that many Conservative Members regarded him as 'aloof, remote and impersonal' and another as saying, 'When you break the ice with Rab, you find the ice-water underneath.' The first description had validity so far as outward appearance was concerned. The second is the opposite of my own experience. Rab Butler is not the easiest man to get to know; but once a personal relationship has been established, his warmth, kindness and friendliness are endearingly evident and most generously accorded.

It has always surprised me that the Tory Party has never acknowledged the immense debt it owes to this gifted and forward-looking statesman. The list of senior offices he has held with distinction must be the longest in any reference book since Churchill died and there can be no doubt that it was under his influence, as chairman of the Conservative Research Department, that the whole outlook and attitude of the Party changed and developed after the war. Yet the only formal recognition he has ever received from a Conservative Government was the Companion of Honour for which Churchill recommended him in 1954. His life peerage was bestowed under a Labour Government and his Knighthood of the Garter was the personal gift of the sovereign.

While Macmillan's fate was being decided by his colleagues in the Privy Council offices, he is on record as passing the time by re-reading *Pride and Prejudice*. The next morning he thought it wise not to go to the Treasury, so remained in his room at 11 Downing Street until invited to the Palace at 2 o'clock on 10 January 1957. Lady Dorothy was so worried about the ill-health of one of her grandchildren that she did not immediately appreciate the significance of the summons and, on being informed of it, her first comment was 'What do *they* want?'

Despite the Conservative majority of fifty-eight in the House of Commons, some people wondered if, faced with the serious post-Suez situation, the new Government could last for very long; and Harold Macmillan, only half in jest, warned the Queen that he could not guarantee that it would survive for more than six weeks. She reminded him of this remark at an audience six years later. In fact, the degree of the Conservative depression was an advantage to the new leader. Things could hardly get worse and the state of disarray was itself a unifying influence in the Parliamentary Party.

The choice of Harold Macmillan was on three counts a break with recent precedent: Butler had always presided over the Cabinet in Eden's absence and so could have been (and by many people was) considered deputy Prime Minister; secondly, this was the first time that members of the Cabinet had been invited, separately and individually, to express their preference between two candidates; and thirdly, as *The Times* leading article pointed out on 11 January, this was the first occasion since Baldwin's appointment when the royal prerogative was no empty formality. There was a real choice to be made between two well-qualified men, either of whom, in the absence of the other, could confidently have expected to gain the prize.

Butler wrote later that he was not surprised at the decision, but he must have been bitterly disappointed. It was characteristically kind of Clarissa Eden to write at once from Chequers:

Dear Rab,
Just a line to say what a beastly profession I think politics are – and how greatly I admire your dignity and good humour.

Harold Macmillan well understood how Butler must feel and he realized how important it was that they should co-operate closely to unite the Party. In his own account of the formation of his government, he wrote that Rab had 'the right to whatever post he might choose, in addition to the leadership of the House of Commons'. Butler's own memoirs differ. He would have liked to go to the Foreign Office, where he thought he could be useful in mending 'the many ruptured friendships' in the aftermath of the Suez adventure. Understandably, Macmillan did not feel able to replace Selwyn Lloyd, since to have done so would have given the impression that the whole Eden/Lloyd policy had been a mistake. Instead, he offered Butler the Home Office and was relieved when Rab accepted it.

The *Daily Telegraph* reported on 11 January:

When he was asked how Mr Macmillan's appointment would affect his own future, Mr Butler's only answer was to smile. At fifty-four he can look forward to at least fifteen years of active political life. His chance of supreme office may come again. . . .

It did, when Harold Macmillan was forced by ill-health to resign six years later, but for the second time he failed to reach the top of the greasy pole.

On the evening of his appointment, the new Prime Minister took his Chief Whip, Edward Heath, out to dinner at the Turf Club, where they ate game pie and drank a bottle of champagne. In recounting the story, Macmillan wrote, 'Some of the critics suggested that a fatal choice had been made between the rival candidates. In Smith Square – the Butler home – there would have been plain living and high thinking.'

Following his accession as Prime Minister, the ritual Party meeting to elect the new leader was arranged for noon on 22 January in

Church Hall, Westminster. It was attended by the Conservative hierarchy of about 1000 people drawn from the Party membership in the Lords, Commons and National Union and from the adopted Conservative candidates. Lord Salisbury presided and moved a resolution to accept with regret Anthony Eden's resignation. This motion was seconded by Walter Elliot, the most senior Privy Councillor present in the absence of Winston Churchill. Salisbury then proposed the election as leader of Harold Macmillan, which was seconded by Butler and supported by Sir Eric Errington, the chairman of the Executive Committee of the National Union. This was passed unanimously.

Macmillan then addressed the meeting. After a tribute to Eden's courage and integrity, he claimed that social reform had begun long before the socialist Government of 1945; it had been built up over centuries of Conservative and Liberal thought and action. He added that 'unless we give opportunity to the strong and able, we shall never have the means to provide real protection for the weak and the old ... we have never been, and I trust that while I am your leader we never will be, a Party of any class or sectional interest'. Most people would acknowledge that he kept this pledge throughout his premiership.

Macmillan was fond of recalling that his forbears were Scottish crofters in the island of Arran; but at the age of eighteen his grandfather moved to Glasgow, where he obtained employment as a bookseller, and subsequently to Cambridge. He and his younger brother, Alexander, established the publishing firm of Macmillan and Harold's father, Maurice, developed the business so successfully that by the time of the future Prime Minister's birth in 1894 his parents were living in comfort at Cadogan Place in London and a few years later they were also able to buy a property in Sussex.

As happens so often and so easily in England, the family had advanced in two generations from its peasant origins into the upper middle class. Harold himself was educated at Eton and Balliol and in the war he served with distinction and gallantry in the Grenadier Guards. In 1920 he married Dorothy Cavendish, a daughter of the ninth Duke of Devonshire.

Although first elected to Parliament in 1924, political success came later to Macmillan than his abilities justified. Owing to his independence of mind in the pre-war years, he did not obtain junior office until he was forty-six years old, when Churchill appointed him

Parliamentary Secretary to the Ministry of Supply and two years later to his first important responsibility as Minister resident in North Africa. In the 1951 Conservative Government he gained fame as Minister of Housing by achieving the target of 300,000 new houses a year, and he subsequently occupied, albeit briefly, the high offices of Minister of Defence, Foreign Secretary and Chancellor of the Exchequer. He was an ambitious man and by the time of his accession as Prime Minister he had become the most skilful and the most decisive member of the Cabinet. He also had style and confidence, two qualities much needed by the Party in order to restore its own self-esteem.

The after-effects of Suez were not as serious or as lasting as had at first appeared probable. The Anglo-French intervention had prevented the possibility of a general war in the Middle East and American and British policy soon began to converge again even in that area. The alliance survived the shock of Suez mainly because of Macmillan's success in rebuilding his personal relations with President Eisenhower.

The new Prime Minister not only mended Britain's fences with the United States. His unruffled calm and sophisticated style did much to encourage and soothe the nerves of his colleagues; and in their weekend speeches Conservative Members of Parliament were soon singing his praises and talking enthusiastically of his leadership. Wisely, he maintained excellent social and political relations with the lobby correspondents, in which he was ably assisted by his press secretary, Sir Harold Evans. Not many Prime Ministers have taken office at such a low ebb in their Party's fortunes. Yet by the time of the 1959 general election twenty-one months later, the reputation of few peace-time Prime Ministers has stood higher. It was a remarkable achievement.

Following Suez, sterling was still under pressure and Macmillan was anxious to avoid any crisis at home which might worsen our credit overseas. But within two months of forming a Government, he was faced with serious disputes in the vital railway, engineering and ship-building industries. Strikes on this scale would have been most damaging to the economy. Fortunately the trouble on the railways was averted, but on 7 March 1957 the Confederation of Ship-Building and Engineering Unions called a national strike of their members from 16 March. A Court of Enquiry was appointed, but by 1 April more than 780,000 men were idle. It was the largest stoppage in Britain since the General Strike in 1926. The Government was in no position to force a trial of strength with the unions in a key sector of the economy and a compromise was eventually accepted by both sides.

As the year wore on, inflationary wage rises continued and in September Peter Thorneycroft, the new Chancellor of the Exchequer, decided on a credit squeeze, including a sharp rise in the bank rate. The Government's own expenditure was an important contributor to inflation and Thorneycroft asked the spending departments for cuts of £150 million, which they were reluctant to accept. After discussions in Cabinet, the difference between the Chancellor's demands and the concessions his colleagues were prepared to make was narrowed to £50 million, which seems a minimal amount twenty years later, but Macmillan commented in his diary, 'The Chancellor wants some swingeing cuts in Welfare State expenditure – more, I fear, than are feasible politically.' The Treasury Ministers were adamant and, when the Cabinet decided against them, Thorneycroft, Enoch Powell and Nigel Birch resigned *en bloc* on January 6 1958.

The Prime Minister, about to set off on an important tour of the Commonwealth, was unperturbed. He referred to the matter as 'a little local difficulty', which amused rather than annoyed the public. The Commonwealth tour was an immense success and added greatly to Macmillan's stature and self-confidence both at home and abroad. In the year since his accession he had already established his authority and was rapidly becoming a popular as well as a successful Prime Minister.

There was another major strike in 1958, following a dispute with the Transport and General Workers' Union over the pay of the London bus workers. This strike, though fully supported by the Labour Party in Parliament, was a good issue on which to confront the growing power of organized labour. A busmen's strike does not harm production or disrupt the economy, but it does much to annoy and inconvenience the public, who tend, therefore, to support the Government. Moreover, the new secretary of the union, Frank Cousins, was a left-wing militant who was already anathema to most Conservative supporters. The strike proved unsuccessful and Cousins suffered an humiliating personal defeat at the hands of Iain Macleod, the Minister of Labour.

The outcome of the dispute was a contributory factor in the

Conservative victory at the 1959 general election; but the main reason for this success was the reflation of the economy. Hire purchase controls were removed in the autumn of 1958 and in the 1959 budget the Chancellor was able to reduce taxation by £350 million, including 9d off the income tax and 2d off the beer tax. Although it was quoted out of context, and later used as a reproach, Macmillan's remark, 'You have never had it so good,' was true. The Conservatives were able to claim the credit for the unusually lucky combination of full employment, stable prices and a strong balance of payments all at the same time and they won the election by an overall majority of 100 seats.

I remember commenting to my wife at the time that Labour would be out for another decade and we should have to provide our own opposition in the House of Commons. Politics are unpredictable and the prophesy was to be falsified within half that period. Nevertheless, for at least two years after this election, Macmillan was at the height of his power and prestige. The cartoonist, Vicky, portrayed him as 'Supermac' and there were accusations that he was 'being sold to the country as though he were a detergent'. Even after the collapse of the 1960 summit meeting, which he had organized, he had a seventy-nine per cent popularity rating in the country.

During 1959 and 1960 Macmillan was much absorbed with foreign and Commonwealth affairs and made many overseas tours, including the first visit to Russia by a British Prime Minister in peace time. In his absence Butler presided over the Cabinet, as on previous occasions under Churchill and Eden, and he seemed at this period to be Macmillan's most likely successor.

Perhaps the most important feature of Macmillan's premiership was the deliberate acceleration of decolonization, especially in Africa. After two world wars Britain no longer had the military or economic power to hold down her colonies by force, even had she wished to do so. If de Gaulle could not contain Algeria, we could hardly impose our will upon a third of the continent. This was not in any case our intention. British policy had always been to lead her dependent territories to self-government within the Commonwealth and once independence had been granted to the Indian sub-continent, Africa was bound to follow. Ghana began the process in 1957, Nigeria came next in 1960 and the trend, although complicated by their white settler communities, was soon to continue in the East and Central African colonies.

By appointing Iain Macleod as Colonial Secretary after the 1959 election, Macmillan was in effect issuing a directive to speed up our withdrawal from Africa. Theoretically, Government policy remained unaltered, but the change in timing was so radical that it amounted in practice to a change of policy. Independence could have been postponed, but only by the rule of the gun and at the risk of bloodshed. Macleod, with the Prime Minister's full support, took the view that, although it was dangerous to go too fast, it would be still more dangerous to go too slow. It was the doctrine of the lesser risk. We devolved power too quickly but with goodwill and this policy at least ensured that our African territories remained members of the Commonwealth.

Harold Macmillan spent a month in Africa in January 1960, culminating in a major speech at Cape Town on 3 February:

In the twentieth century . . . we have seen the awakening of national consciousness in peoples who have for centuries lived in dependence upon some other power. Fifteen years ago this movement spread through Asia. . . . Today the same thing is happening in Africa. . . . The wind of change is blowing through the continent and, whether we like it or not . . . we must all accept it . . . and our national policies must take account of it.

The right wing of the Conservative Party in Parliament and many Europeans in Africa were shocked by this speech. They reacted as though Macmillan was inventing nationalism, whereas he was simply stating a fact. It was already a powerful movement and there was nothing, short of force, which could have stopped it.

The next major development in foreign policy came with the Government's application, on 31 July 1961, to join the European Economic Community. From the outset Macmillan regarded this as primarily a political issue. He believed it was 'both our duty and our interest' to contribute towards the unity and therefore the strength of Europe 'in the struggle for freedom and progress throughout the world'. The British team was led by Edward Heath, who had done well as Chief Whip but whose reputation and standing in the Party were now to be greatly enhanced by his dedicated work and able grasp of the complexities of these negotiations.

By the end of 1961 the tide of popularity for Macmillan's government was on the turn. After a decade of increasing prosperity, the economy was faltering. With imports rising faster than exports, the balance of payments looked vulnerable. Real growth was slowing down and wage increases were outpacing productivity. Selwyn Lloyd, now Chancellor of the Exchequer, had introduced corrective measures in July, which included an unpopular pay pause and a ten per cent rise in purchase tax. Bank rate was raised from five per cent to seven per cent. By December industrial production was falling and wage restraint for the nurses, teachers, postmen and railwaymen was being enforced in the public sector. The momentum of rising prosperity had checked at the very time when a more affluent society was becoming increasingly conscious of material benefits and more expectant of improved living standards.

A long series of by-election reverses reflected these adverse factors. The Conservative poll dropped consistently, often by twenty per cent or more, and at Blackpool North the Government majority fell from nearly 16,000 to 973. Even this was eclipsed by a disastrous result at Orpington in March 1962, where a Tory majority of over 14,000 in 1959 was transformed into a Liberal majority of 7800.

Many Conservative Members of Parliament were now demanding economic expansion as the only way of restoring the Government's popularity and the Prime Minister was thinking along the same lines. Selwyn Lloyd was in a dilemma. He was trying to lay the foundations for sustained growth, but the deterioration in the balance of payments prejudiced his policies and delayed the reflation he was anxious to initiate. His National Economic Development Council was an important contribution in focussing attention on the problems of the economy; but Macmillan was becoming impatient with the Chancellor's cautious reluctance to reflate, which he regarded as politically unacceptable, and he decided that a more positive direction could only be achieved if the Treasury was placed in different hands. On 12 July 1962 he summoned Selwyn Lloyd to Admiralty House and invited his resignation as Chancellor of the Exchequer. The new look Macmillan wished to infuse into his administration did not stop there. The following day six more senior Ministers were requested to resign. A third of the Cabinet had been summarily dismissed at a few hours' notice. This display of ruthlessness, or panic, which quickly became known as the 'July massacre', disturbed rather than reassured the public and was followed early the next week by an almost equally draconian purge of junior ministers. Nigel Birch (now Lord Rhyl), never the best disposed of Macmillan's Parliamentary colleagues, wrote to *The Times*:

Sir,

For the second time, the Prime Minister has got rid of a Chancellor of the Exchequer who tried to get expenditure under control. Once is more than enough.

It was rumoured that Macmillan had sacrificed his colleagues to save himself and Jeremy Thorpe commented wittily, if somewhat unkindly, 'Greater love hath no man than this – that he lay down his friends for his life.' The episode did nothing to appease the Parliamentary Party or to enhance Macmillan's reputation.

In *The Art of the Possible* Butler records that, as part of the Cabinet changes, he was given the title of First Secretary of State and 'invited to act as deputy Prime Minister, a title which can constitutionally imply no right to the succession and should (I would advise with the benefit of hindsight) be neither conferred nor accepted'.

The annual Conservative Conference at Llandudno provided a temporary improvement in the Party's prospects. The Prime Minister made Britain's entry into the EEC the centrepiece of his speech on the final day. It was an outstanding performance and ensured an overwhelming vote in favour of our application. But it heralded a false dawn. The unemployment figures were rising and the by-election reverses continued. The Cuban missile crisis, which shook the world, was skilfully and courageously handled by President Kennedy, with the full support of Harold Macmillan, and the danger of nuclear war was averted. But the worst was yet to come.

On 14 January 1963, General de Gaulle vetoed Britain's attempt to join the Common Market. Macmillan had counted upon our admission to revive the country's economy and the political fortunes of the Conservative Party. It was to be his last and most important contribution to public life and our rejection was a bitter end to all his hopes.

The Vassall tribunal, soon followed by the Profumo scandal, neither of which were well handled by the Prime Minister, were further blows to his administration, only partly offset by the negotiation of the Test Ban Treaty and Butler's success at Victoria Falls in winding up the Central African Federation.

Macmillan's health, as well as his morale, had deteriorated during the summer and he thought seriously of resigning as Prime Minister; but he was reluctant to go in the aftermath of the Profumo affair. As he wrote in *At the End of the Day*, 'I was determined not to take any step which would bring my long premiership to an ignoble end or look as if I was afraid of facing any difficulties which might still confront us.' The choice lay between resigning just before Parliament re-assembled in October 'or going right through to and including the election', which was due to take place not later than the autumn of 1964.

The rival claims of possible successors were already being discussed and as early as June Butler noted 'a very strong tide flowing in favour of a young man of the new generation'. His own prospects were uncertain and he had been told very bluntly by John Morrison, the chairman of the 1922 Committee, that 'the chaps won't have you'.

At that time Reggie Maudling, Chancellor of the Exchequer, seemed marginally the most likely choice in the event of Macmillan's retirement; but I sensed that support for him, never very firm, was beginning to ebb by the end of July when Parliament rose for the summer recess. Macmillan did not think him ready for the top job, particularly because of his lack of experience in handling foreign affairs. Certainly there was no clear consensus for Maudling, or indeed for anyone else. Butler took the traditional view that a leader should 'emerge'. The difficulty was that no one had emerged or seemed likely to do so in the near future.

The Prime Minister gave no indication as to his own preference either then or during a talk with Butler at Chequers in early September. Indeed Rab noticed the same inclination as Churchill had shown 'to stay in office and achieve something lasting' in the international sphere. After this conversation Harold Macmillan recorded in his diary his assessment of Butler's position as being ready to accept the premiership 'if there was a general consensus of opinion for him. But he doesn't want another unsuccessful bid.'

Following discussions with a number of colleagues in August and early September, Lord Home had come round to the view that Macmillan 'had lost too much ground to recover his winning form' and ought to resign. He informed the Prime Minister accordingly, but gained the firm impression that he would stay on provided his health was maintained. Two days later, at an audience with the Queen, Macmillan said he would not have an election that year and would not lead the Party at the election when it took place. In his autobiography he stressed his determination to preserve the royal prerogative and the need for his successor to be capable of dealing with foreign affairs.

Although his spirits had improved during the summer recess, the Prime Minister still could not make up his mind whether to go or to stay. He was, however, already suffering from the prostate trouble which was soon to become acute and he thought it wise to discuss with the Chief Whip the procedure for selecting a successor should ill-health force him to resign.

Interest in this subject was already being shown in some constituencies and two resolutions had appeared on the agenda for the Party Conference. The Barry Conservatives expressed 'concern regarding the existing procedure for electing the leader of the Party' and urged that a committee be established 'to consider ways whereby more effective consultation between the interested bodies' could be achieved. And the Chester-le-Street association urged the National Executive to re-examine the method of selection.

Although Macmillan had himself been chosen, in effect, by his Cabinet colleagues, he thought the field of consultation should in future be extended and formalized. He arranged, therefore, that the Lord Chancellor should sound the Cabinet, the Chief Whip the junior Ministers, and he and his assistant whips the Conservative Members of the House of Commons. At the same time the Chief Whip in the House of Lords would consult the Unionist peers, and constituency chairmen, agents and candidates would have an opportunity of expressing their opinions through the Conservative Central Office and the National Union.

In a diary entry dated 6 October, Macmillan was still weighing the arguments for and against resignation. He feared that, if he stayed and then failed to win the election, people would attribute this as 'due to the old limpet'. On the other hand, there was 'no clear successor' and he recorded that he was 'beginning to move towards staying on – for another two or three years'.

On 7 October he saw Butler and thought that he would 'prefer me to go on, for – in his heart – he does not expect the succession and fears it'.

It was ironical that on the very day when he finally decided to remain in office, he was struck down by the illness which terminated his premiership.

The Cabinet met on 8 October. Macmillan did not mention his health, but he was clearly in pain and left the meeting before it broke up. His appearance alarmed his colleagues and after his departure they discussed the possibility of his resignation. Butler, supported by

Home and Maudling, thought the Prime Minister could temporize in his Conference speech later in the week, but Iain Macleod and most of the other Ministers were in favour of a definite decision and wanted Macmillan to stay as leader.

The Lord Chancellor, Lord Dilhorne, informed his colleagues of the new arrangements for choosing a successor if this became necessary and said he would be available to hear their views. Lord Home observed that as he, too, was not a candidate, he would be ready to help Dilhorne in this task. He clearly considered himself ineligible, although the Peerage Act passed in July allowed hereditary peers to renounce their titles and stand for election to the House of Commons.

Meanwhile, Macmillan had seen his doctors, who told him he must enter the King Edward VII hospital for an immediate and serious operation. He therefore sent for the Chief Whip, Martin Redmayne, and asked him to prepare the machinery for selecting a new leader.

A message was sent to Iain Macleod, as chairman of the Party, at Blackpool, to warn him that Macmillan would be unable to address the Conference on Saturday. It was decided that this task should fall to Butler as deputy Prime Minister. The next evening another telephone call brought the news of Macmillan's decision to relinquish the premiership. The leadership crisis had begun.

Looking back over the years, in reply to a question by Sir Harry Boyne, the lobby correspondent of the *Daily Telegraph*, as to which Government post he had found most difficult, Macmillan recalled that the Foreign Secretaryship was the most onerous because one was never off duty:

All through the night something may be happening in some part of the world which requires immediate attention. You may be roused from sleep at 2 a.m. (9 p.m. in New York) by our ambassador at the United Nations requiring guidance on how to vote on some issue which is to be decided within the next few minutes.

He thought the position of Chancellor of the Exchequer was equally difficult because the economy was so unpredictable and because of the need to deny to colleagues the money they required for worthwhile projects on which they had set their hearts. 'The job of Prime Minister is far the best,' he told Boyne, 'because you are the boss, responsible only to the Queen. You can arrange your time as you like and go down to Birch Grove for a look at the daffodils if you feel so inclined.'

Macmillan was never a slave to routine, and it was not unusual to find him leaning against a book shelf in a corridor, absorbed in a volume which had caught his eye as he passed. His breadth of mind gave him many interests outside politics, but he was certainly the most successful Conservative Prime Minister of modern times and the Party owes more to him than to any of its other leaders since the Second World War.

It is impossible to assess whether, had his health remained un-impaired, Macmillan could have led his Party to victory in the general election a year later. The overall Labour majority of four was so minimal that his political skill and great experience might well have tipped the scale in favour of the Government.

His contribution to the Conservative Party and to the country had been distinguished. He had style and his dexterity in guiding and controlling the Cabinet was remarkable. His authority in Parliament was unquestioned and few cared to confront him in debate. He has been criticized as a poseur and an actor, but no one can be an effective public speaker without the ability to act and in his own patrician, almost Edwardian vein, Macmillan was a fine speaker. He understood how to delegate and left his Ministers to handle their departmental work in their own way. He was not only the shrewdest political brain in the Party since Baldwin, but is also a philosophic statesman of impressive range, well read and with a wide knowledge and understanding of history; a fascinating, sometimes brilliant conversationalist, and a man of outstanding intellect. He contrived to combine attractively an inherent and genuine idealism with a good-humoured, worldly cynicism. He is a sophisticated and a very civilized man. I believe he will be remembered in history as one of the great peace-time Prime Ministers of Britain.

6

ALEC DOUGLAS-HOME

Historically, few Prime Ministers have been able, or even anxious, to choose their successors, but Macmillan had strong views and considerable influence on who should and who should not follow him at Downing Street.

During the course of his premiership he had brought forward three younger men who were, by 1963, of sufficient experience to be considered. Reggie Maudling had been Chancellor of the Exchequer for over a year, Iain Macleod was leader of the House of Commons and chairman of the Party organization and Edward Heath had been responsible for the Common Market negotiations. All three were men of ability who had entered Parliament thirteen years earlier in the famous 1950 vintage and had rapidly drawn ahead of their contemporaries. Each had been given opportunities; none had yet emerged as a generally acceptable leader of the Party.

In the last volume of his autobiography, Harold Macmillan wrote revealingly:

I personally favoured either Hailsham or Macleod, preferably the former, for I felt that these two were the men of real genius in the Party, who were the true inheritors of the Disraeli tradition of Tory radicalism, which I had preached all my life. I regretfully had to admit that I did not feel that Butler could win an election or could receive the loyal support of the Party as a whole. I told Hailsham of my views and hoped that he would become a candidate.

In this significant passage, Macmillan publicly acknowledged his opposition to Butler, although he certainly understated it. As Kenneth Young wrote in his biography of Lord Home, it was appropriate that the Prime Minister's postal address at Chequers was Butler's Cross. Indeed, the course of the leadership crisis can only be explained by Macmillan's determination that Butler should not succeed him as Prime Minister. This attitude towards his deputy, well known in the House of Commons, was no doubt based on the view that Butler lacked the steel necessary for strong leadership and the inspiration needed to pull the Party through a toughly fought election. Many members of the Parliamentary Party shared this opinion. Others took the opposite view. They believed, in the words of Iain Macleod, that Butler had one important asset, apart from his great experience of government – that he could attract 'wide, understanding support from many people outside the Tory Party. And without such an appeal, no general election can be won.'

There is no doubt that Butler was the best qualified of the contenders and none of the younger members of the Cabinet in the House of Commons commanded sufficient support to defeat him. In order to ensure his rejection, the Prime Minister was therefore obliged to consider a candidate from the House of Lords, now made possible by the passage of the Peerage Act in July 1963. But for this change in the law, neither Hailsham nor Home would have been eligible for the leadership when Macmillan resigned. On all the evidence the succession would then have gone to Butler. The effect of the Act was to give the Prime Minister a better chance of preventing this. His first choice fell on Lord Hailsham.

Quintin Hailsham had been a splendid chairman of the Party. He was uniquely capable of rousing the enthusiasm of the constituency workers and had made a significant contribution to the Conservative victory in 1959. He has a brilliant mind and, at his best, his speeches can be moving and eloquent. But his advice is erratic and many of his colleagues would have been reluctant to serve under him. They acknowledged that he would make an inspiring leader of the Party at a general election, but they questioned his judgement, should the Conservatives win it, as the leader of the nation.

Nevertheless, the bandwagon was set in motion and the Prime Minister's son, Maurice, and his son-in-law, Julian Amery, arrived in Blackpool to canvass support for Hailsham in the presidential type of campaign which the timing of Macmillan's resignation had made inevitable. Their efforts were assisted (or prejudiced) by the extraordinary performance of Randolph Churchill, hot-foot from the United States, who did little to improve Hailsham's prospects by peddling 'Q' lapel badges and buttons round Blackpool, some of which (quickly consigned to the waste-paper basket) he even presented to Butler.

On the Thursday evening Hailsham was to address a large meeting organized by the Conservative Political Centre. It seemed the obvious opportunity to declare his candidature and my wife and I went along to hear him do it. He had already issued his speech to the press and was obliged to adhere to the text of it. It was rather dull. But, in response to the somewhat perfunctory applause, he added an emotional postscript announcing his decision to give up his peerage and to stand for election to the House of Commons. The demonstration which followed was described to Rab Butler as being 'reminiscent of a Nuremberg Rally'. Hailsham left the hall to a great burst of cheering from his excited supporters and hurried to a Young Conservative dance, where he was greeted, writes Kenneth Young in *Sir Alec Douglas-Home*, 'with the sort of rapture more often accorded by teenage girls to pop singers than to potential Prime Ministers'.

In the result, the uninhibited canvassing for Hailsham reacted against him and alienated more support than it attracted. His lack of judgement seemed confirmed and his too-evident eagerness for the premiership ensured that he would not achieve it. His bandwagon came to a halt almost as soon as it had started to roll.

In the meantime, none of the younger and more peripheral candidates had gained any ground. Despite his able and painstaking conduct of the Common Market negotiations, Edward Heath's departmental experience was limited and he was not yet a serious contender. Iain Macleod, though far better known, was a controversial figure. His Colonial Secretaryship had evoked the enthusiasm and idealism of the left wing of the Party and most of the Young Conservatives, but had antagonized its conservative element. To lead a Party, a man must be acceptable to every section of it and Macleod had forfeited the confidence of the more traditional Conservative supporters. Moreover, the Government's waning popularity and the by-election reverses had inevitably produced an adverse effect upon the reputation of the chairman of the Party. As always, he received a standing ovation for his brilliant Conference contribution, but the applause was for the speech, not the man, and his chance of breaking the deadlock between Butler and Hailsham was negligible.

Initially, Maudling's prospects looked more hopeful and in other circumstances he would have commanded considerable support, but on this occasion the Conference had an unusual influence upon the

Members of Parliament and Maudling is not the sort of speaker to arouse the enthusiasm of a large audience. He and Macleod had a private pact that whichever's star was in the ascendant at the critical moment would not be opposed by the other. Knowing that Maudling's chances were better than his own, Iain tried with selfless generosity to help Reggie with his speech. He coached him tactfully with the timing, the pauses, the turn of phrase and the peroration. But to no purpose. Maudling's performance was pedestrian and his hopes slipped away as the speech sagged heavily to its conclusion. No one felt that he could convert the uncommitted or inspire the faithful to an electoral victory. A better candidate must be found and to the uninformed Butler looked the obvious choice. But Macmillan still had another card to play.

On Wednesday evening, 9 October, the Prime Minister summoned Lord Home to the King Edward VII Hospital and informed him that he should regard himself as a potential leader of the Party. This suggestion astonished Alec Home, who had never even considered such a possibility. He had no intention of resigning his peerage and dismissed the idea as out of the question. He still regarded Hailsham as Macmillan's designated successor and was prepared to support him.

The following afternoon, as that year's president of the National Union of Conservative and Unionist Associations, Home was entrusted with the task of announcing to the Conference the news of Harold Macmillan's resignation and on the Friday morning he began a very good speech in the debate on foreign affairs by saying, 'I am offering a prize to any newspaper man who can find a clue in my speech that this is Lord Home's bid for the leadership.' This disarming remark delighted the delegates. He has always been immensely popular in the constituency associations and when he sat down the prolonged applause was, in contrast to Macleod's, as much for the man as for the performance.

Rumours were already circulating in the Imperial Hotel that Home might be 'drafted' as the compromise candidate and on the Thursday evening Reggie Bennett, MP for Gosport and Fareham, reported to Macleod that there was strong support for the Foreign Secretary to break the deadlock between Butler and Hailsham. 'Don't be so bloody ridiculous,' Iain replied, 'Alec told us in Cabinet that he wasn't a runner.' When Bennett pointed out that, while Home no doubt meant this at the time, he might have come under considerable pressure since then to allow his name to go forward, Macleod still rejected the idea out of hand. In fact, Bennett was right.

Although Alec Home told Butler on more than one occasion that he could not contemplate leaving the House of Lords, he was already being pressed privately by some of his Cabinet colleagues to accept nomination. A stream of visitors to his hotel bedroom included the Lord Chancellor, Duncan Sandys and John Hare. Several senior back benchers, among whom were Selwyn Lloyd on three occasions, Sir William Anstruther-Gray (now Lord Kilmany), Sir Charles Mott-Radclyffe and Colonel 'Juby' Lancaster also called to see him. None of these felt able to support either Butler or Hailsham and they begged Home to enter the contest. He gave no commitment to do so but agreed to consult his doctor as to whether he would be fit enough to assume the leadership. This indicated a considerable change in his previous attitude; but, as late as Saturday, 12 October, when Hailsham asked his opinion, he replied, 'I think you've got a pretty good chance.' Nevertheless, a ground-swell was gradually developing in his favour. A third of the Members were against Butler and a third were against Hailsham. Home was the man to whom there were the fewest objections. He was the compromise candidate and the Party unifier, as Bonar Law had been fifty years earlier.

Meanwhile Macmillan, who was too skilled a tactician to run two candidates at the same time, had received reports from Blackpool that Hailsham's exuberance had lost him the race. The Prime Minister decided to switch his bet to another horse from the same stable. His choice was the Earl of Home.

By now, the Imperial Hotel was a hot-house of gossip and intrigue. Little groups gathered in corners or in hotel bedrooms, discussing the prospects of their respective nominees and criticizing the other contenders. I found this atmosphere distasteful, though to some it seemed a stimulating and exciting drama.

Just before the last Conference session on Saturday, Alec Home, who is a most straightforward man, went to see Rab Butler to inform him that he was going to consult his doctor early the following week. It was a polite way of saying that he was now a rival candidate. That afternoon Butler made the leader's speech. It was a competent, though not particularly impressive performance and did not enhance his claims. In the course of a short introduction, Home made a curious observation. 'We choose our leader,' he said, 'not for what he does or does not do at the Party Conference, but because the leader we choose is in every respect a whole man who in all circumstances is fit to lead the nation.' This was in no way derogatory of Butler, but it was a strange and somewhat unlikely remark if, at that moment, he regarded himself as a candidate.

That evening the Conference broke up and we all returned to London. My wife and I travelled back with Iain Macleod, the Maudlings and Hugh and Antonia Fraser. In the course of the journey I prepared a list of my preferences for the leadership, to be handed in to the Chief Whip on Monday. Iain Macleod was my first choice, although I recognized that he had virtually no chance of being selected, and Reggie Maudling my second. They were not very helpful (or hopeful) suggestions. Maudling's prospects had fallen after his poor Conference speech; Macleod's had not risen despite his brilliant one. It was clear to me by this time that the contest was effectively between Butler and Home. I admired and respected them both and was happy, in my junior post at the Colonial Office, to serve under either. I said so in my letter to the Chief Whip.

On Monday Home's doctor declared him fit to undertake the leadership. During the early part of that week, the whips took their detailed soundings among the junior Ministers and back bench Members of the Parliamentary Party. The Prime Minister sent for St Aldwyn, Redmayne and Oliver Poole to enquire what the reactions were. Redmayne had not underlined the fact that Home was now a certain runner and St Aldwyn suggested that his name should be mentioned to MPs as the candidate most likely to unite the Party. This was not at the Prime Minister's instigation, indeed Macmillan did little to influence the choice at this stage. But Redmayne adopted Michael St Aldwyn's proposal and many Members who had put Home on their lists, but not at the top of them, were asked if their order of preference would be different if they knew for certain that he was prepared to renounce his peerage and was a firm candidate who alone could unite the Party. I am sure Alec knew nothing of this 'second round', but as a result of it several Members revised their lists, raising his name from third to second or from second to first. Iain Macleod was right when he wrote later in the *Spectator* that the whips were working for several days to influence the votes in favour of Home. Many senior back benchers were doing the same. This is not a criticism. They were perfectly entitled to ensure, if they could, the election of the man whom they thought best able to unite the Party and best fitted to lead the country.

In making his report to the Prime Minister, the Chief Whip acknowledged later that he gave weight 'to people on whose opinion one would more strongly rely than on others'. It is at least questionable whether he should have made so personal a judgement about his colleagues in the Party, but on that basis he was able to report that, on first choices, Home was 'marginally' ahead and became 'outstandingly so as you took it further through the field'. Lord St Aldwyn was no doubt on stronger ground when he said that 'the peers were overwhelmingly for Home'. It would have been surprising if they were not.

In contrast to opinion in Parliament, a *Daily Express* poll on 16 October showed Butler in the lead with thirty-nine and a half points to twenty-one and a half for Hailsham, eleven for Maudling and nine and a half for Home. In an effort to keep the door open, Butler pointed out to the Prime Minister the difficulty of bringing in a peer, not only because of the delay this would involve, but also because of the psychological impact such a step would be bound to have in the country.

The Cabinet soundings were far the most important. No one unacceptable to his colleagues could have become their leader and when Dilhorne reported an overwhelming Cabinet consensus for Home, it was decisive. But it is not easy to understand how so large a majority could have been composed. Apart from Macmillan, the Cabinet consisted of twenty members. By this time at least nine (Boyd-Carpenter, Boyle, Brooke, Butler, Erroll, Hailsham, Macleod, Maudling and Powell) were for Butler. At least four (Dilhorne, Hare, Home and Sandys) were for Home and it is almost certain that Heath and Soames were also Home supporters. The views of the remaining five were not known, but even if all were for Home, it is difficult to reconcile the figures with 'an overwhelming consensus'.

On 15 October, the Prime Minister saw Butler, Hailsham, Heath, Home, Macleod and Maudling and, on the 16th Boyle, Brooke, Hare, Joseph, Sandys and Soames. He implied to many of them, where he did not actually state it, that Home was his own choice. In a diary entry on the 16th, he wrote that 'practically all these Ministers, whether Hoggites or Butlerites or Maudlingites, agreed that if Lord Home would undertake the task . . . the whole Cabinet and the whole Party would cheerfully unite under him'. With the exceptions of Macleod and Powell, this assessment proved, in the end, correct. The Prime Minister also saw Selwyn Lloyd, not at that time a member of the Cabinet, who agreed that Home must be Macmillan's successor.

On 17 October it became generally known through reliable press sources that the decision was for Home. When this was confirmed, Maudling and Powell met at Macleod's flat, where Toby Aldington joined them. Later that evening Macleod and Powell spoke to Home on the telephone and told him they could not serve under him. Macleod, Maudling, Erroll and Aldington gathered at Powell's house in South Eaton Place after their dinner engagements for what became known as 'the midnight meeting'. Hailsham kept in touch with them by telephone and was by this time in agreement with the others that Butler should be the new Prime Minister. Maudling, Macleod and Powell then told Butler what had been agreed and assured him of their support. This understanding between Butler, Hailsham and Maudling, three out of the four principal candidates, seemed of importance and they invited the Chief Whip to call round to discuss the matter. He undertook to inform the Prime Minister of their views. In *The Art of the Possible* Butler wrote later:

> One presumes and hopes that the Chief Whip informed the Prime Minister, as he was requested to do, that seven or eight members of the Cabinet were opposed to the choice of Home. What is certain is that Macmillan decided to ignore this powerful objection and acted . . . with utter determination and despatch, making a definite recommendation of Home.

Redmayne had spent the earlier part of the evening, in company with Dilhorne and Selwyn Lloyd, at the Foreign Secretary's home in Carlton Gardens. The opposing camps were aligning their forces for the final decision, but although the Butler faction seemed formidable, Home's supporters had the Prime Minister's ear. When Hailsham telephoned to say he would not serve under Home, Selwyn Lloyd warned him that this would look like sour grapes. At the same time he advised Alec not to lose his nerve. Home was not unnaturally aggrieved by the turn events were taking and telephoned the Prime Minister. He reminded Macmillan that he had been asked to come forward in the interests of Party unity and said that he now felt like withdrawing from the contest. Macmillan urged him not to do so and added, 'If we give in to this intrigue, there will be chaos. . . . Go ahead and get on with it.' From his hospital bed, ill as he was, the Prime Minister was still in control of the situation.

Next day Edward Boyle told Macleod and Powell that he too would decline to join a Home administration, but by Saturday he had changed his mind, partly as the result of a talk with Butler, partly because there were important decisions pending at the Ministry of Education which he was anxious to take.

On the morning of Friday, 18 October, Butler telephoned the Lord Chancellor to invite him to convene a meeting of the rival candidates. Dilhorne tried both the hospital and 10 Downing Street to obtain Macmillan's approval, but received no reply. In the meantime Macleod had arranged and was present at a meeting between Butler, Maudling and Hailsham; but, forewarned by Redmayne, the Prime Minister was too quick for them. He sent his letter of resignation by hand to the Palace and the Queen visited him in hospital later in the morning.

Macmillan received his sovereign in a wheel chair and, as he was too ill to carry on a conversation of any length, he handed her a memorandum incorporating the reports submitted to him by Dilhorne, Redmayne and St Aldwyn. These recommended Home not merely as Macmillan's personal preference, but as the collective choice of the Cabinet and the Conservative Party in both Houses. Given such a document, there could be no question of seeking further advice and the Queen had no option but to send for Lord Home. She did so at once and Home drove to the Palace before lunch. He felt unable to forecast the attitude of some of his Cabinet colleagues and therefore asked for time in which to ascertain whether or not he could form a government. An announcement was made that the Queen had invited him to do so. In this she followed Macmillan's written advice not to appoint Home as Prime Minister but simply to entrust him with the initial task of taking soundings and then reporting the outcome to her.

Alec Home began his interviews immediately. At first Butler, Hailsham, Macleod, Maudling and Powell all declined to serve. In the face of a defection of senior Ministers on this scale, Home would have had to abandon the attempt. Butler was the key. He had only to persist in his refusal to make Home's position impossible. Home told him frankly that the outcome depended on his decision and on Maudling's. He offered the Foreign Office to Butler, who undertook to consider this proposal. At a meeting that evening between Home, Hailsham, Butler and Maudling, Hailsham said that, although he would prefer Butler, he would be willing to serve under Home. He felt that, as a candidate himself, he would have been criticized for not doing so on grounds of personal pique.

Everything still depended on Butler. Mollie Butler, the warmest and most charming of women, who is devoted to her husband and was much more ambitious for him than he was for himself, urged him to stand firm. But Butler considered that Quintin Hailsham's defection amounted to an erosion of support and next morning he agreed to come in. He was genuinely concerned not to split the Party, but there was another reason for his capitulation. In the final analysis he lacked the ruthlessness to fight his own corner. This is an endearing characteristic in the man; it was a fatal flaw in the politician. Quite apart from their personal antipathy, Macmillan had no doubt sensed this and it may, at least partially, explain his determination that Butler should not succeed him. Lord Dilhorne wrote to Butler:

> By your action you have held the Party together at a critical time. I do not doubt that, if you had refused to serve, Alec would have failed to form a Government.... Many would have thought that you had refused ... only to secure your personal advantage.

When Maudling heard that Butler had agreed to join the new Government, he himself followed on the not unreasonable grounds that it was pointless to be more royal than the king. Only Macleod and Powell remained. Alec Home saw each of them again in an attempt to persuade them to change their minds, but they felt unable to do so.

Five resignations, and especially Butler's, would have made it impossible for Home to form an administration. Two were a pity but could be accepted. By lunch-time on Saturday, 19 October, Home was able to drive to the Palace and kiss hands on his appointment as First Lord of the Treasury. The leadership crisis was over.

Enoch Powell is, *sui generis*, a brilliant, unpredictable 'loner' and an almost professional resigner. Macleod was a far greater loss to the Government. His decision not to serve was gravely damaging to his reputation in the Conservative Party and to his prospects of ever becoming its leader. His loyalty and his motives were questioned, especially after his article in the *Spectator* three months later. He was more experienced in government and a far better speaker and television performer than Heath and, had he remained in the Cabinet in 1963, it is virtually certain that he would have become Shadow Chancellor when the Conservative Party went into opposition in

1964, instead of a year later. With his great debating skill he would have fought the 1965 socialist Finance Bill with at least as much success as Heath did. It was from this base that Heath was able to take the leadership when Home retired in the summer of 1965 and from this base Macleod might well have captured the prize.

Home was the first hereditary peer to become Prime Minister since the end of Lord Salisbury's long reign over sixty years earlier. For the three weeks between his appointment on 19 October, and his victory in the Kinross and West Perthshire by-election on 8 November, the Prime Minister of Britain had no seat in either House of Parliament, a situation without precedent in the political history of this country.

By Sunday, 20 October, Home had completed his Cabinet list, which was announced that evening. It was not a difficult task, because the new Prime Minister could scarcely have asked his colleagues to serve under him on Friday and then dropped some of them two days later. The only changes, therefore, were consequential on the resignations of Iain Macleod and Enoch Powell. Home brought in Selwyn Lloyd in succession to Macleod as leader of the House of Commons and appointed John Hare to Macleod's other responsibility as chairman of the Party. Hare was given a peerage as Lord Blakenham and became deputy leader in the House of Lords with a seat in the Cabinet. Peter Carrington took over the leadership in the Lords from Hailsham, who had renounced his peerage but remained Lord President of the Council and Minister for Science. Butler succeeded Home at the Foreign Office. Tony Barber, who had been Financial Secretary to the Treasury, was promoted to Cabinet rank to replace Powell as Minister of Health and Edward Heath moved from his position at the Foreign Office to the Board of Trade, exchanging the ancient title of Lord Privy Seal for the new one of Secretary of State for Industry, Trade and Regional Development, which incorporated and added to the role of President of the Board of Trade.

The outcome of the Kinross by-election was never in doubt and Alec Home's conduct of the campaign was confident and relaxed. He held his informal press conferences in the morning room of his host's house, clad in slacks, a pullover and his habitual red leather slippers. He was accessible to everyone, always in good humour and never in a hurry.

On 11 November he was adopted as leader of the Conservative Party at the traditional meeting at Church House, Westminster.

Lord Carrington proposed him and Rab Butler seconded the motion in a graceful and generous speech. 'Sir Alec stands on the side of progress,' he said, 'I knew this before I consented to serve with him.'

The following day Sir Alec Douglas-Home, as he had now become, entered the House of Commons for the first time for twelve years. Almost at once he came under attack from Harold Wilson. A flippant remark made over lunch nine months before was resurrected and publicized. Sir Alec, laughing at himself, had said, 'When I have to read economic documents, I have to have a box of matches and start moving them into position to illustrate and simplify the points to myself.' This 'match-box economics' was fair game for Wilson's ridicule; but Douglas-Home redressed the balance in a television interview the same evening. Wilson had spoken scornfully of his aristocratic background. 'After half a century of democratic advance,' he declared, 'the whole process has ground to a halt with a fourteenth Earl.' 'When you come to think of it,' Home retorted, 'I suppose Mr Wilson is the fourteenth Mr Wilson.'

Socialist sneers at the aristocracy are no doubt designed to stimulate class hatred as a political weapon, but this can be double-edged. Many people feel that someone of assured position and independent means is less likely to be self-seeking and less liable to have any personal axe to grind than the clever, ambitious man of a different background who has to make his own way in the world. Moreover, the English – even in the second half of the twentieth century – are a race of snobs, many of whom still respect the old aristocracy. The 'grouse moor image' is therefore less of a political disadvantage than some of its critics imagine. Alec Home's lineage is undeniably long, but there should be no shame in the accident of birth.

The recorded history of the Border family of Home goes back to the twelfth century. The third Lord Home fought against the English at the battle of Flodden in 1513 and the sixth was created an Earl by King James I. Another ancestor, the Black Douglas, was a noted warrior in the armies of Robert the Bruce. On his mother's side Home is descended, like Anthony Eden, from Lord Grey of the Reform Bill and from 'Radical Jack', Earl of Durham, through whom Canada achieved Dominion status. As a boy, he was heir to 134,000 acres with an annual rent roll of almost £100,000 and, in addition, substantial royalties from the family coal pits in Lanarkshire.

If Anthony Eden was born with a silver spoon, Home's could be described as gold. He was educated at Eton, where he became captain of his house, president of 'Pop' and played cricket for the school. He spent three years at Christ Church, Oxford, where (partly due to ill-health) he only achieved a third class honours degree. As an undergraduate he took little or no interest in politics, but after leaving the university he became concerned about the problems of poverty and unemployment in Lanarkshire and decided to try and make his own political contribution to their solution. He was actuated more by the family sense of service to the community than by any personal ambition.

Lord Dunglass, as he then was, was elected as MP for Lanark in 1931 and in 1935 he became Parliamentary Private Secretary to Neville Chamberlain, then Chancellor of the Exchequer. In the following year he married Elizabeth Alington, a daughter of his former headmaster at Eton. Their exceptionally happy marriage was of political as well as personal importance because his wife has been a driving force and a spur. She is a warm and human personality whom everyone loves.

As Parliamentary Private Secretary to the Prime Minister, as he had then become, Dunglass was associated with the Munich policy, but, when Chamberlain fell, his career was interrupted not only for political reasons, but by ill-health. He was rejected as unfit for war service, endured a serious spinal operation and was on his back in a plaster case for the next two years. In the 1945 election, he was defeated at Lanark, but won it back by a narrow majority in 1950. A year later his father died and he went to the House of Lords.

When Churchill formed his second administration in 1951, James Stuart became Secretary for Scotland and asked for Home as his Minister of State. ' "Home sweet Home," it shall be,' agreed Churchill; and when Eden became Prime Minister four years later he promoted Home to the Cabinet as Secretary of State for the Commonwealth. In an office which was primarily diplomatic, Home was so successful that in 1960 Macmillan made him Foreign Secretary, despite socialist criticism that he could not answer for his department in the House of Commons. This difficulty was overcome by appointing Edward Heath as his number two at the Foreign Office with a seat in the Cabinet and the sinecure post of Lord Privy Seal.

Some Conservatives had been sceptical of the evidence in support of Home's candidature for the leadership and public expression was given to this view in a brilliantly scathing article by Iain Macleod in the *Spectator*, of which he had become editor after leaving the

Government. The 'magic circle' method by which a leader had hitherto evolved was thought to be undemocratic and on 1 January 1964 Humphry Berkeley, at that time Conservative MP for Lancaster, wrote to Alec Douglas-Home to suggest that the Party should adopt a new procedure for electing its leader. He thought this could take the form of a vote by Members of Parliament in a secret ballot, or perhaps of an extension of the franchise to include representatives of the National Union, the adopted candidates and the Conservative peers. He asked the Prime Minister to arrange for a small committee to consider the matter and to make recommendations. Douglas-Home thought it best to leave the idea in abeyance till after the general election.

One of the most important and controversial Bills of the new session of Parliament was brought in at Heath's insistence and with Home's support against the judgement of some of their Cabinet colleagues. Its purpose was to abolish resale price maintenance, with the object of increasing competition and bringing down prices. Heath fought it through the House of Commons with courage and tenacity and it passed into law in April 1964.

Earlier in that year Winston Field, the Prime Minister of Southern Rhodesia, visited Britain to begin negotiations for the independence of his country on the basis of the 1961 constitution. He was a reasonable man and Home and Duncan Sandys thought they could reach agreement with him; but in April he was replaced as premier by Ian Smith, an inexperienced and unsophisticated politician, who was much more awkward to deal with, and the first opportunity of resolving the Rhodesian issue was lost.

The principal political problem for the new Prime Minister was the timing of the General Election, which had to be held at the latest by early November. Douglas-Home was naturally anxious to select the most favourable date for his Party. Some Ministers, including Maudling, would have preferred to go in May or June, but Sir Michael Fraser and the Party chairman, Lord Blakenham, advised that the Government would lose by between thirty and sixty seats in the summer, but might win in the autumn by the narrowest of margins. In fact the Labour Party achieved an overall majority of four.

On 15 September 1964 the Prime Minister announced the dissolution of Parliament. The general election took place on Thursday, 15 October, and at 3.30 p.m. the following day Douglas-Home went to the Palace to resign as First Lord of the Treasury. He had held the highest office for exactly one year. He left Downing Street that afternoon and, with Harold Wilson's permission, spent the night at Chequers. From there he wrote to a friend, 'I think that the thirteen years was just too much and the public were a bit bored with both Parties . . . being the Government, we got the worst of it.'

It was estimated that if 900 people in eight marginal constituencies had voted Conservative instead of Labour, or had even abstained, the Government would have survived. But the narrow defeat was the beginning of the end for Douglas-Home's leadership of the Party. He had fought a gallant campaign, in which his own speeches were mercilessly heckled and, although he was often denied a hearing, he behaved throughout with dignity and courage.

Some people blamed him, I think unfairly, for the defeat. A former Cabinet Minister of great experience believes that, had Butler been Prime Minister, the Conservatives might have won. In his view Alec Douglas-Home could make no effective appeal in the Midlands and lacked both leadership quality and intellectual distinction. Others attributed the result to the defection the previous year of Macleod and Powell. But I am sure Douglas-Home was right in thinking that the real reason, after thirteen years of Tory Government, was that the electorate wanted a change. This enabled Wilson to capture at least part of the vital middle ground which always decides elections.

After so long in office a Party does not take readily to opposition. Shadow Ministers missed the day-to-day information and the machine which provided it. We were accustomed to being serviced by large departmental staffs and the abrupt transition to one private secretary (or the share of one), supplemented by the help of a small team at the Conservative Research Department, was not an easy one. Ex-Ministers were full of confidence for the first month or two because we knew more about the problems than our successors, but this changed rapidly as the new men became more experienced and the Conservative front bench less well-informed. Although Labour is at heart a Party of protest and many of its leaders were happier criticizing than governing, the Conservatives dislike opposition and are not therefore very good at it.

Alec Douglas-Home's personal position was not an easy one. He could have continued as Prime Minister for another Parliament if he had won the election, but he was less successful in opposition. The state of the economy was the dominant issue of the day and he was no economist. His experience lay mainly in foreign and Common-wealth affairs and he was not sufficiently combative in the House of Commons to restore the morale and arouse the enthusiasm of the Parliamentary Party.

The Tory pack wanted blood. They wanted their leader to show them game and they hoped he would take on Wilson and beat him at the Despatch Box. This was not Home's strong suit. He was a competent speaker, widely liked and respected on both sides of the Chamber, but he has never been outstanding in debate and Wilson was often too quick for him. Realizing his own limitations, he seldom went into bat and, when he did, made few runs. Critical murmurs gradually gathered strength in the corridors of the Palace of Westminster and the press publicized the growing discontent and fanned the flames.

Alec Douglas-Home was sensitive to the suggestion that his election as leader of the Party had been undemocratic. He responded to this criticism by setting up an enquiry to recommend a new procedure for electing the leader. In his biography of Home, Kenneth Young quoted him as saying:

> I didn't think that any election held after my election by the same methods would every carry any public confidence again. . . . People outside . . . thought the matter had been jobbed. I was perfectly happy with the old method, but I wasn't from a future leader's point of view.

On 5 November 1964 Douglas-Home announced to the 1922 Committee that he proposed to review the procedure for choosing the leader. Humphry Berkeley then submitted a memorandum to him, advocating election by Members of Parliament only. This was the conclusion towards which Alec Douglas-Home was himself moving. After Blackpool, a change had become inevitable and would in fact have been made without Humphry Berkeley's intervention. A *Times* editorial on 11 January 1965 reflected public opinion following the circumstances of Home's own election and the interest aroused by Macleod's pungent article in the *Spectator* a year earlier:

> One requirement, perhaps the most important, of any elective or selective procedure . . . is that it should be capable of conferring legitimacy. If enough people come seriously to impugn the procedure, its fairness, its appropriateness, or its freedom from abuse . . . it can no longer provide a sure basis of authority . . . that point appears to have been reached, or approached, in the case of the Conservative Party. . . . The customary

processes of consultation are widely thought to be unrepeatable after the events of October 1963.

The new arrangements, in line with Berkeley's memorandum, were set out in a short paper in February 1965. They are reproduced as an appendix to this book. There were suggestions that Douglas-Home should clarify his own position by himself submitting to a ballot, but he made it clear that the new system would only take effect for any future contest.

After the election defeat in October 1964, Douglas-Home had told the Shadow Cabinet that he would stay on as leader of the Party; but by the beginning of the next year there were already signs of an 'Alec must go' movement. Michael Spicer, the chairman of PEST, a new left-of-centre group in the Party, was quoted as saying, 'We have made our position pretty clear. We say that he symbolizes the wrong forces and his election was a mistake.'

Maudling counter-attacked on Home's behalf on 19 January:

I have grown sick and tired of the constant harping on personalities, the repeated speculation on the so-called 'leadership issue'. . . . I would like to make it clear that, from my point of view, I do not consider there is any such issue. . . . Sir Alec Douglas-Home is, and will remain, at the head of our Party. He is a leader of outstanding qualities and strength of character.

On 4 February Home himself expressed publicly his determination to continue as leader and the next day a statement was issued by the Executive Committee of the National Union re-affirming its 'full confidence and unstinted support'. Nevertheless, criticism continued and the adherents of potential candidates, in the event of Douglas-Home's resignation, began to meet privately to discuss the claims to the succession of their respective nominees.

It was becoming plain that the most probable contenders would be Edward Heath and Reginald Maudling and their prospects were significantly affected during February when Douglas-Home made some interesting changes in the Shadow Cabinet. Maudling was moved from his post of Shadow Chancellor to Foreign Affairs and was replaced by Heath, who had impressed Alec by his hard-working professionalism. As Andrew Roth put it in *Heath and the Heathmen*, 'Unlike Maudling, he was more willing to forgo a good meal or a good wine to attend a meeting on taxation policy.'

Heath's new appointment soon gave him an opportunity, which he was quick to seize, of shining during the debates on the budget and the Finance Bill at a time when the Labour Government's taxation proposals were unpopular.

In March the opposition to Alec Douglas-Home was given new impetus by the Conservative defeat in the Roxburgh, Selkirk and Peebles by-election, won by a young man called David Steel, now leader of the Liberal Party. This was an event of great significance. The seat had been held by Lord William Scott from 1935 until 1950, when it fell to the Liberals. It was won back the following year by Commander Donaldson, whose death in March 1965 caused the by-election. The new Conservative candidate was Robin McEwen, like Alec an Old Etonian Berwickshire laird. Not surprisingly the leader of the Party, who was in any case a personal friend, gave McEwen his full endorsement. But many Conservatives, including the Chief Whip, Willie Whitelaw, saw the danger. One of the criticisms of Douglas-Home was his aristocratic image, which some considered out of date and damaging to the Party. Yet here was a Tory candidate in the same area of Scotland and with the same background, whose defeat would inevitably lend support to the anti-Home campaign. The result was declared on 25 March and next day the *Daily Telegraph* published an article on the front page headed 'Leadership of Home in question', which warned that the by-election reverse 'could lead to the election of a new leader before Easter'.

On the same day a strong article by Alan Watkins appeared in the *Spectator*. 'How much longer can Sir Alec Douglas-Home continue as leader of the Conservative Party?', it began:

One MP compares the situation today to that prevailing immediately before the abdication crisis. Everybody knew that something was wrong, but no one was prepared to say so. No one, that is, until the Bishop of Bradford innocently set things moving. Who will be the Conservative equivalent of the Bishop of Bradford?... It only needs one speech attacking the leadership for the misgivings about Sir Alec to become semi-public property. And sooner or later this is going to happen.

Watkins forecast that if a general election seemed likely in May or June, Home would be safe, because there would be no time for the Party to change its leader, but 'as soon as it becomes evident that Mr Harold Wilson has no desire to go to the country in either late spring or early summer, then we may expect the grumbles about the Tory leadership to take on a new vigour'.

Paradoxically, it was the Conservative success in the local govern-

Benjamin Disraeli, Earl of Beaconsfield, at Osborne towards the end of his life.

LEFT Robert Cecil, Marquess of Salisbury, was leader for nearly eighteen years.

BELOW Lord Balfour and David Lloyd George (*right*) at a garden party in 1922.

RIGHT A. Bonar Law, who became leader in 1911.

BELOW (*From left to right*) J. H. Thomas, Stanley Baldwin and Neville Chamberlain on board the *Empress of Britain* sailing to Canada before the Ottawa Conference, July 1932.

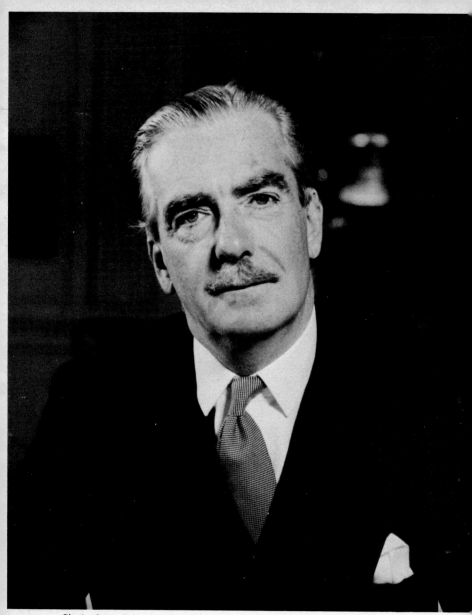

Sir Anthony Eden led the party from April 1955 until January 1957.

Sir Winston Churchill with Harold Macmillan, who was then Prime Minister, in July 1957.

Iain Macleod (*left*) talking to Duncan Sandys outside 10 Downing Street, July 1960.

(*From left to right*) Reginald Maudling, Lord Hailsham and R. A. Butler were contenders for the leadership, won by Lord Home, in 1963.

A Man For All Seasons: how one cartoonist saw Heath during 1974.

Sir Alec Douglas-Home, Margaret Thatcher, Harold Macmillan and Edward Heath at a meeting of the Bow Group, March 1976.

Edward Heath in 1976.

Margaret Thatcher in 1976.

ment elections in May, when the Party gained 562 seats, which made it apparent that the Prime Minister would not risk an election before the autumn at the earliest. This was one of the factors which precipitated Douglas-Home's departure. He knew he must resign, if that was to be his decision, before the House rose for the summer recess, in order to give a new leader the chance to establish himself.

Speaking at Taunton on 28 March, Edward du Cann, the new chairman of the Party, made a vigorous defence of his leader, referring to his high qualities of integrity, honesty and strength of character. The only real complaint against Sir Alec, he declared, was that 'he is not the best actor in the world'. Du Cann denied that any survey of the Party's views on the matter was in progress. 'I have authorized no such survey. I know of no such survey,' he stated. And, on 17 May, in a speech at Glasgow, Iain Macleod also paid tribute to Douglas-Home and gave an assurance that he would serve under him if the Party won the next election. Publicly (and typically) the Conservative hierarchy were closing their ranks and swearing allegiance.

On 26 June Alec Douglas-Home announced that there would be no leadership election in 1965. But at the same time the Prime Minister declared that there would be no general election in that year either. This statement caused renewed press speculation about Douglas-Home's future – a small bonus which Harold Wilson may not have overlooked.

The *Sunday Express* of 27 June headlined a 'Bid to oust Sir Alec by 100 MPs', inspired, it was widely rumoured, by one of Heath's supporters. On the 28th the *Daily Telegraph* published a front-page article headed 'Issue of Tory leadership revived', but on the following day the same newspaper reported that assiduous enquiries had failed to uncover any move to supplant Douglas-Home by Heath. The seesaw of newspaper comment tilted up and down.

One factor was, however, certain. Edward Heath was enhancing his reputation by his brilliant and effective leadership of the Opposition team against the Finance Bill. In the early hours of the morning on 7 July, the Government was defeated in two divisions by fourteen and thirteen votes. To Conservative cheers, Heath rounded upon the Treasury Ministers. 'They have lost control of the House of Commons,' he declared, 'they have lost their majority and can no longer continue their business.'

To many of Edward Heath's supporters, who had been meeting

quietly to prepare the ground, this seemed the time to exert some more overt pressure for a change. Heath's standing in the Party was rising rapidly, Douglas-Home's was clearly in decline. The matter had already been raised in the Executive of the 1922 Committee at a routine meeting on 1 July. Several of its younger members were strongly critical of Douglas-Home, including Neil Marten, a supporter of Reggie Maudling, and even some of the 'Knights of the Shires', who had been entirely loyal to the leader a few weeks before, now agreed that he ought to resign. But the chairman of the 1922 Committee, Sir William Anstruther-Gray, was an ardent supporter of Douglas-Home's and did not report the strength of feeling against him. This invidious task fell, therefore, to Willie Whitelaw, the Chief Whip.

Edward Heath in no sense actuated the campaign against Alec Douglas-Home, but he must have known of it. Indeed, some of the preliminary meetings, designed to put him in an advantageous position should Douglas-Home decide to go, were held at his flat in Albany. He did not encourage the activities of his supporters, but he did not discourage them. He had become attached to Douglas-Home and shrank from any suspicion of disloyalty, but he was personally ambitious and was determined to lead the Party if the occasion arose.

At first Douglas-Home maintained his position. On 9 July he told a press conference at Hull that he would lead the Party until the general election. 'I have made my intentions quite clear,' he said, 'and I mean it.' He repeated this at the weekend and on 13 July *The Times* carried a headline. 'Sir A. Home to remain at the helm. Bid for overthrow fails.' It had been decided that Douglas-Home should soldier on.

The meeting of the 1922 Committee on Thursday, 22 July, was generally acknowledged to be the last opportunity for many months for a final decision and Douglas-Home was expected to declare his resolve to continue as leader and to rally the Parliamentary Party to battle against the common enemy. But, unknown to his followers, Douglas-Home had become increasingly depressed about his own position and much disillusioned by the adverse press publicity. He consulted Harold Macmillan, who urged him to 'stick it out', but he did not accept the advice of his former leader. Macmillan commented later to George Hutchinson, 'He's so generous – a lovely man.'

Douglas-Home spent the weekend of 17–18 July at the Hirsel, trying to reach a decision. An influential article by William Rees-

Mogg, published in the *Sunday Times* of 18 July, may well have tipped the scale. Under the heading 'The right moment to change', Rees-Mogg wrote, 'It is hard to resist the very widespread view that the Conservatives . . . will not win a general election while Sir Alec remains their leader.' As a result of this article, messages began to pour into the Chief Whip's office and Party headquarters the following day, and Willie Whitelaw and Edward du Cann went to see Sir Alec. Du Cann reported that the Party in the country was, on balance, against Douglas-Home staying. Whitelaw warned that, despite majority support, there was a sizeable element in the Parliamentary Party in favour of a change. They advised that, in the prevailing atmosphere, the Party Conference in the autumn could prove awkward to handle. They concluded that he should resign. There were, however, those close to Douglas-Home who took the opposite view. Elizabeth Home, always more ambitious for her husband than he was for himself, urged him to ride the storm. Selwyn Lloyd and Charles Mott-Radclyffe, a vice-chairman of the 1922 Committee, also begged him to stay. Sir Alec said he would sleep on it.

That evening my wife and I attended a party given by Norman St John Stevas at his house in Hampstead and drove Willie Whitelaw back to Westminster after it. We discussed the matter in the car. I was in favour of Sir Alec staying and said so, but I had not realized the extent and gravity of the problem until I saw how distracted and worried Whitelaw was. This normally calm and level-headed man can become emotional in a crisis, as was the case a few months later when the Party split three ways in the vote on the Rhodesian oil sanctions. His position was unenviable. He was personally devoted to Douglas-Home, but his ultimate loyalty was to the Party.

Next day Sir Alec told Whitelaw and du Cann that he had decided to resign. I was shocked when I heard this later, but in retrospect I think he was wise. His selfless loyalty to the Party and to his successor, in marked contrast to the attitude of Edward Heath ten years later, served only to enhance his already great (and grateful) popularity in the Parliamentary Party and in the constituencies. Alec Douglas-Home's standards are high and he could always be relied upon to behave perfectly and to put the country and the Party before his own self-interest. There were also more personal reasons for his decision. His biographer, Kenneth Young, has quoted him as saying:

I didn't see why, after doing Commonwealth and Foreign Secretary and Prime Minister, I should, so to speak, have to fight for position as leader of the Opposition. It didn't attract me. . . . If I'd been ten years younger, I'd have seen it through.

Above all he was a countryman and after a life-time in the public service, it was understandable that the peace and quiet of the Hirsel seemed preferable to the intrigues and drudgery of the Palace of Westminster. He was over-sensitive to the press criticism and there is little doubt that he need not have gone if he had really wanted to stay.

On the Thursday morning before the meeting of the 1922 Committee, Alec Douglas-Home informed his colleagues in the Shadow Cabinet of his decision. Many of them were much distressed by the news, especially Selwyn Lloyd, who tried to persuade him to change his mind, but his resolve was firm and irrevocable.

The main committee met, as usual, at 6 p.m. in room 14. Douglas-Home wasted no time. In a short, simple statement, directly and with great dignity, he said he was going. It was very moving and the Party was stunned into astonished silence. 'No one suggested to me that I should go,' he said, 'but there are those who, perfectly properly, felt that a change of leadership might be for the best.' No doubt there were, but most Members were appalled that a small minority of our colleagues, much assisted by prolonged press speculation, should have brought about the downfall of such a man. We felt a collective sense of guilt that it had been allowed to happen.

I wrote to him within the hour to express my deep regret and characteristically he replied almost as quickly in his own hand. Of the six leaders of the Party under whom I have served in Parliament only two, Alec Douglas-Home and Margaret Thatcher, have habitually written to me in longhand when the occasion arose. It is questionable whether they should have taken the time to do so, but it is this sort of gesture which creates affection and personal loyalty. It may surprise some readers that Harold Wilson often adopted the same practice, even to a political opponent of no importance. As Harold Macmillan once said to me, 'Whatever people may say of Wilson, he has always been most courteous and agreeable to me and of course he has very good manners.'

Elizabeth Home remarked recently, 'I have changed my name five times in my life, but have only been married to one man.' Lord Home of the Hirsel, as he has become in his retirement, is a very modest man: kind, considerate and always ready to help others. In politics, though not an innovator, he was a good chairman – business-like, cool, calm, rational and unruffled. His judgement is good and his sense of humour and of proportion never desert him. More of a diplomat than a politician, he is rightly respected for his loyalty, his integrity and his patriotism. It is difficult to get to the top in politics without a driving, almost ruthless ambition. Alec Home is the exception. He has never been self-seeking. He has never had to be. His own position was assured. His attitude is dispassionate and detached; his manner natural, almost casual. He is, in the terms of the cricket of my youth, a Gentleman rather than a Player and, although he became a professional in the sense that he spent his life in politics, his approach was always that of an amateur. The British people rather like that.

EDWARD HEATH

On the evening of Douglas-Home's resignation, Edward Heath went to Glyndebourne. The opera being performed was *Macbeth*. At the same time Reggie Maudling was meeting his supporters at William Clark's house in Barton Street to plan his campaign. The poll was to take place on 28 July, so there was little time to lose. Although Maudling had discussed future tactics with his friends in the event of Douglas-Home's resignation, they did not start work on his behalf until after the 1922 Committee on 22 July. The same could not be said of Heath's supporters, some of whom had been intriguing against Douglas-Home for several weeks. There is no evidence that Heath himself took any part in these activities and I am sure he did not.

Maudling's team consisted of William Clark, Neil Marten and Sir Frederick Bennett, with some help from Sir John Hall, Patrick Wall, Bryant Godman-Irvine, Eric Bullus, Tony Lambton, Richard Stanley and Philip Goodhart. Clark's adherence was interesting. He had been one of Reggie Maudling's leading front bench aides in 1964 and continued to help Heath in that capacity in 1965. He decided to support and work for Maudling in the leadership election. At the meeting on 22 July the guidelines for the campaign were agreed: there was to be no pressure or pestering of any kind and Maudling directed that no deals were to be done and no promises of future preferment given in return for support during the contest. There was simply to be a canvass to identify the doubtfuls, who then underwent some mild persuasion.

It was a quiet, almost lethargic, but very civilized campaign in which the candidate himself played little part. He did not even canvass his colleagues in the Shadow Cabinet. The tactics were to rely on a reaction against the Heath men for having contributed to

Douglas-Home's downfall and to portray Maudling as the family man, Heath as the bachelor. Photographs appeared in all the newspapers of Reggie and Beryl Maudling with their younger children. Despite this, most press coverage favoured Heath, including *The Times*, *Sunday Times*, *Daily Mail*, *Evening News* and the *Economist*. Anthony Howard described him as 'a tactician rather than a thinker' and there was much comment on his tough, thrusting approach. An unfair and damaging anti-Heath 'Insight' article had appeared in the *Sunday Times* a fortnight before, but this was effectively answered by Tony Barber a week later. The opinion polls showed a public preference for Maudling of forty-four per cent to twenty-eight per cent for Heath and three per cent for Powell, but these were not the voters. Most newspapers forecast a close result

Jo Grimond, then the Liberal leader, said that 'the man who made strenuous efforts to get into the Common Market and abolished resale price maintenance must awake some appreciation in Liberals, if only for his decision and courage'.

In an article entitled 'Grasping for the greasy pole' in the *Guardian*, Mark Arnold-Forster alleged that the Party had chosen Douglas-Home in 1963 'because they were afraid to change the pattern of leadership, to disturb a chain of command which, over the centuries, had almost always found favour with the Cecils. Perhaps this time the Conservatives will feel free to displease Lord Salisbury'. *The Times* was more relevant when it declared that 'whichever succeeds, the Conservative Party will have as its leader a man of quite different background from any of his predecessors'.

Heath's campaign was efficient, well organized and much brisker and more aggressive than Maudling's. It was well run by Peter Walker with the active assistance of Robin Chichester-Clark, Tony Kershaw, Peter Emery and Peter Kirk. Geoffrey Lloyd, Keith Joseph, Jim Prior, John Eden, Ian Gilmour, Dick Nugent, Edward Boyle and Tony Barber also helped in various ways. Walker had been a leading member of a small group who had been meeting from time to time to further the claims of Iain Macleod, but Alec Douglas-Home's retirement came much too soon for Macleod, who knew he had no chance of being chosen and issued an immediate statement saying he was not a candidate. Walker went to see him just before this announcement and told him in the most straightforward way that he was transferring his support to Heath. Macleod endorsed this decision and there was no hard feeling between them. Ian

Gilmour was another friend of Macleod's who joined the Heath camp.

Despite their old friendship, Macleod did not himself vote for Reggie Maudling. He thought Heath would make a stronger, tougher leader and no doubt he was right. Duncan Sandys, who did not usually agree with Macleod, took the same view and tried hard to persuade me to vote for Heath. Heath's biographer, George Hutchinson, believed that Macleod's decision, not to stand for the leadership, presented it to Heath, 'for almost to a man', Hutchinson wrote in the *Spectator*, 'his followers switched to Heath . . . the best estimate is that Macleod would have received forty-five votes. But he would have deprived Heath of such vital support that victory would in all probability have gone to Maudling.' This was no doubt an accurate appreciation, although I cast my own vote for Maudling – and told Heath that I had done so.

I remember Norman St John Stevas, at that time a new Member, seeking my advice as to which of the two was the more progressive. I told him that, although both could be supported by those on the left of the Party, I thought Maudling was, on balance, the more liberal-minded of the two. In fact, it was a difficult choice. Maudling was a more identifiable product of the One Nation school of modern Conservatism. Heath was more dedicated to competition in industry; he was also more positively pro-European. As so often happens on such occasions, the differences between the two were less in their policies and political philosophies than in their personalities. Many people believed that Heath would *do* something, not merely talk, and that he would not dodge or compromise on the big issues.

Peter Walker's team met four or five times during the short campaign at his house in Gayfere Street, Westminster. They split up the Parliamentary Party between them, identified the supporters and the doubtfuls and marked the card. Ted Heath usually looked in at these meetings, but did not personally take an active part in the work. Walker was very efficient and the canvass was a most accurate one, within a few votes of the actual figures.

Heath's 1975 campaign against Margaret Thatcher might well have been more successful if Walker had again been in charge; but by then the two men had drifted apart, perhaps because Peter Walker resented the removal of his departmental responsibility for energy.

Throughout the leadership election, the whips were scrupulously neutral. Willie Whitelaw instructed them not to discuss the succession and he himself did not know what the outcome would be. The Executive of the 1922 Committee also played a much smaller part in 1965 than it did in 1975; and the views of the Unionist peers were unknown to MPs because, although Michael St Aldwyn reported the result of his soundings to the chairman of the Executive, Bill Anstruther-Gray did not pass them on to the Parliamentary Party.

Nominations had to be in by 26 July and it was a surprise to some when Enoch Powell put his name forward, presumably as a 'marker' for the future, since his immediate prospects were negligible. Two other possible runners, Peter Thorneycroft and Christopher Soames, did not enter the lists. Reggie Maudling was proposed by William Clark and seconded by Michael Clark-Hutchinson. More than three quarters of the Shadow Cabinet opted for Heath and, when this became known, it may have influenced some of the younger MPs whose minds were not already made up. Peter Walker's estimate of the outcome was far more accurate than that of Maudling's supporters, whose over-optimistic final forecast was 154 for Maudling and 100 for Heath.

The result was declared at 2.15 p.m. on 28 July. Heath had secured 150 votes, Maudling 133 and Powell fifteen. The margin was below the extra fifteen per cent required for outright victory and could have necessitated a second ballot, but as Heath had obtained more than fifty per cent of the total poll, Maudling wisely conceded. He was lunching in the City at the time and telephoned this decision through to the House of Commons. It was well received in the Parliamentary Party, which always likes a generous loser.

There were no recriminations and no trace of bitterness in the Maudling camp. The new elective procedure had worked well and produced a quick and clear verdict. As James Margach wrote in the *Sunday Times*, 'The magic circle could never have done it. They might have come up with the same result, but inevitably the back-stage jockeying and horse-trading would have left a nasty smell.' The *Daily Telegraph* quoted the view of a senior back bencher, 'We have elected a rough rider and it is time to fasten our seat belts.' Harold Wilson, who disliked Heath, said, 'He's a splitter. If you're not on his side, you're against him. He will split his Party, as Gaitskell split the Labour Party.'

The usual formal meeting to confirm the new leader was held at Church House. A motion of thanks to Sir Alec Douglas-Home was followed by a proposal moved by Peter Carrington for Heath's election. This was seconded by Reggie Maudling who said, 'Ted Heath possesses in full measure all the necessary qualifications for his new position – intellectual brilliance, personal determination, a sense of purpose, a wide experience inside and outside politics, and great physical stamina. . . . He will be a leader of outstanding force.' In retrospect, few would deny that, although not perhaps the only qualities required, the attributes which Maudling ascribed to him were fulfilled in his subsequent leadership of the Party.

Before the war Edward Heath would have been an unlikely Conservative Member of Parliament and a still less likely leader of the Party. His mother was a housemaid before her marriage and his father had started life as a carpenter working for a local builder at Broadstairs in Kent. His aunt is quoted as saying that his grandfather could neither read nor write.

It has always been one of the best features of English life that a man of ability and determination can rise in his own lifetime from the most humble origins to the highest positions in the land. Edward Heath is an outstanding example.

With the help of a loan of £90 a year from the Kent County Council, some sacrifice by his parents and an organ scholarship at Balliol worth £100 a year, he was able to go up to Oxford in 1935, where he became president of the University Conservative Association and later of the Oxford Union. He gained a second class honours degree in Modern Greats, which indicated above-average intelligence but not exceptional brilliance. He was happy and successful at the university, where he earned nothing but good opinions, and in this environment, which he enjoyed, he was relaxed and friendly and seemed almost an extrovert, although in fact he is the opposite. Everyone was nice to him at Oxford and he responded to this atmosphere. He was earnest, efficient, always hard-working, but prematurely serious and even at that age showed no interest in girls, whom he perhaps regarded as a time-consuming diversion, even an obstacle to the fulfilment of his ambitions. His instinct was to draw back if any girl seemed to like him and this inevitably limited his social life. It may have been an especial mortification to be defeated by a woman for the leadership of the Party in 1975.

Heath's commitment to Conservatism was already complete during his time at Oxford and led Anthony Howard to comment many years later that 'nothing makes more effectively for ardent and self-publicizing loyalty to the Conservative Party than a basic feeling of social insecurity'. In fact there is no evidence that Heath felt insecure at Oxford, although I believe he was conscious, when he became leader of the Party, that many of his Parliamentary colleagues came from a different background. They did not care in the least about his relatively obscure beginnings, which made his subsequent achievements all the more to his credit; but if *he* did, it may have contributed to his lack of social self-confidence.

Edward Heath volunteered for the Army on the outbreak of war, but was not called up until August 1940, when he joined the Royal Artillery. His war service brought a mention in despatches and an MBE. By 1942 he had become regimental Adjutant and in 1944 was given command of a battery and promoted to the rank of major. After the war he took command of a territorial regiment and from 1951 to 1954 acted as Master Gunner within the Tower of London.

In 1947 Heath was adopted as Conservative candidate for Bexley, where he won his first election in February 1950 by the narrow majority of 133 votes. In the House of Commons he became a founder member of the One Nation group, formed to evolve and project a modern approach to the social services, which had hitherto been somewhat neglected in post-war Conservative policy. The name of the group was derived from Disraeli's concept that the Tory Party should defend the working class against the rapacious nineteenth-century industrialists who had been supported by *laissez-faire* Liberalism. It consisted initially of nine newly-elected MPs – Cuthbert (now Lord) Alport, Robert Carr (now Lord Carr of Hadley), Richard Fort, Edward Heath, Gilbert Longden, Iain Macleod, Angus Maude, Enoch Powell and John Rodgers.

Heath soon caught the eye of Patrick Buchan-Hepburn (later Lord Hailes), the Opposition Chief Whip, who invited him to join the whips' office within a year of entering Parliament. After the Conservative election victory in the autumn of 1951, he became a Government whip and in the following year was promoted to the post of deputy Chief Whip. When Eden re-shuffled his administration in December 1955, he appointed Heath to succeed Buchan-Hepburn as Chief Whip. It had been a rapid rise to the top organizational position in the Parliamentary Party after less than six years in the House of Commons. He proved his efficiency as an admirable chief-of-staff and gave invaluable service to the Party in keeping it together after the Suez débâcle. Newspaper comment was universally complimentary and Eden went so far as to describe him as 'the best

Chief Whip the Party has ever had'. In argument with a recalcitrant back bencher over the Suez policy, Heath is reputed to have said, 'You were a Communist before the war. Now you are nothing but a bloody Fascist.' When Kenneth Harris asked him if this was a true story, he replied, 'I didn't use the words "nothing but".'

In 1959 Edward Heath entered the Cabinet as Minister of Labour, but after nine months Macmillan moved him to the Foreign Office as Lord Privy Seal to answer for the department in the House of Commons and to take charge of the British application to join the Common Market. He was an enthusiast for this policy and worked immensely hard, with great skill and infinite patience, to bring it to fruition. His expertise and exposition were formidable. It was no fault of his that de Gaulle vetoed our entry at the very moment (and perhaps because) the negotiations were nearing success.

When Douglas-Home became Prime Minister in October 1963, he made Heath Secretary of State for Industry, Trade and Regional Development. He is a good administrator, more at home with facts and figures than with abstract political philosophy, and his new responsibilities suited his temperament. He showed resolution and courage in abolishing resale price maintenance against the wishes of many of his Cabinet and Parliamentary colleagues, who considered (perhaps rightly) that it was a mistake to offend the small shop-keepers, traditional Conservative supporters, on the eve of a general election.

As Shadow Chancellor after the narrow Conservative defeat in 1964, Heath formed an able and effective team to fight the 1965 Finance Bill. Following his election as leader of the Party that July, he made Maudling deputy leader and entrusted foreign affairs to Alec Home and finance and economics to Iain Macleod. Soon after the House re-assembled for the new session he faced his first Parliamentary problem over Harold Wilson's decision to introduce oil sanctions against Rhodesia. He decreed that the Conservative Opposition should abstain and the solid centre of the Party did so, but fifty right-wing Conservatives voted against the order and thirty-one on the left of the Party, including myself, went in to the Government lobby in support of it. The three-way split was a traumatic experience for Heath and his Chief Whip, Willie Whitelaw; and as a Shadow Commonwealth spokesman (which added to my offence since it was a Commonwealth issue), I was sent for to the leader's rooms. 'You can either sit on the front bench and support

Party policy,' he told me, 'or you can go to the back benches and speak and vote as you like.' It seemed to me a perfectly reasonable proposition and shortly afterwards, I think quite rightly, I was dropped from the Shadow team.

In March 1966 Harold Wilson went to the country and increased his majority from four to 100. There was no question of a change in the Conservative leadership; but perhaps because Heath had been elected as a more combative personality than Home or Maudling, he tended to attack the Prime Minister too often in the House of Commons, usually without much success. There was also a strong personal antipathy between the two men which made the atmosphere awkward. Harold Wilson was at his best during this period and at his best he is a very astute and skilled tactician. Heath was often out-manoeuvred. The Labour Government's financial difficulties in the summer of 1966 were, however, politically helpful to the Tories and, with the devaluation of the pound in the following year, the Government's popularity slumped severely, to the corresponding Conservative benefit.

On 20 April 1968, Enoch Powell's immigration speech at Birmingham brought out the best in the leader of the Party. His response was immediate and decisive; it was also correct. He dismissed Powell forthwith from the Shadow Cabinet. *The Times* commented that 'the risk of having Mr Powell as an enemy . . . is less grave than having Mr Powell as a colleague'. Most other members of the Shadow Cabinet were much relieved by his departure. He had argued interminably against many of their collective decisions and had tediously and unnecessarily prolonged their meetings. Although thousands of dockers marched to Parliament in Powell's support, the Parliamentary Party was solidly behind Heath's decision. Powell's enmity soon became personal as well as ideological and a year later this brilliant but bitter man foreswore all his previous pro-European policies and publicly proclaimed his new-found opposition to joining the EEC. In the end he left the Party and advised anti-Common Market Conservatives to vote Labour at the cost, it is thought, of some Conservative seats in the West Midlands. His subsequent speeches on immigration have fomented fear, encouraged prejudice and damaged race relations in Britain.

On 18 May 1970, encouraged by an improvement in the opinion polls, Harold Wilson asked the Queen to dissolve Parliament. Heath fought a good campaign and a month later was able to move into

No 10 Downing Street as Prime Minister of Britain. It was a long road from the Broadstairs boarding house of his childhood, but he was still only fifty-four years old and had climbed to the top rung of the political ladder without any advantages of birth, money or influential friends, at a younger age than any Conservative Prime Minister since Peel.

Heath's personality is contradictory, combining intellectual arrogance with a defensive social diffidence. He is self-contained and self-sufficient. He has a few close friends, notably Madron Seligman and Toby Aldington, but not many people know him really well. Those who do have told me that he is a much more agreeable and a far warmer person than appears on the surface. To acquaintances he is impenetrable and most of us who have served in Parliament with him for more than a quarter of a century feel we know him no better today than when we first met.

As I have never had the opportunity to work closely with him, I am not qualified to make a personal assessment of his faults and virtues. The views expressed here are not, therefore, my own. They are an amalgam of opinions I have collected from his former colleagues in Cabinet and from others whom he would regard as his political friends.

Ted Heath is socially shy and *gauche*. His failure to communicate at a personal level, or even to try to do so, may be partly a deliberate defence designed to avoid the 'small talk' he dislikes. He can seem pompous and priggish, but can be charming and very good company when he is feeling relaxed and is with people he likes. He has a teasing sense of humour, which sounds sardonic but is not meant to be, and some good anecdotes which he recounts rather badly. He can be brusque and rude, often unintentionally, and his prolonged silences are disconcerting. He may feel that silence is sometimes safer than speech. Any subject of casual conversation has to be initiated by those he is with, otherwise no word would be spoken. He is fond of children and good with them and was himself a loyal and devoted son.

Politically, Heath is a man of immense will-power. He has courage, drive and self-confidence, with a forceful determination to overcome any obstacle. He is a decisive and single-minded professional, more a 'do-er' than a thinker, who prefers action to words. Although not an intellectual, he has a clear and powerful mind which enables him to read and absorb a complicated brief with remarkable rapidity.

Almost everyone to whom I have talked has stressed that he is and always has been intensely ambitious. Some have described him as stubborn, but perhaps resolute is a fairer description, because he can be persuaded to change his mind against his initial judgement provided the case for doing so is put well enough and strongly enough. He is more malleable than many people imagine.

As Prime Minister, his style of leadership was military. He knew his own job and expected others to know and do theirs. He was loyal to his colleagues and to those who were loyal to him, but he did not understand the need to be nice to people and seldom bothered to explain the reasons for his decisions in order to carry others with him. Before becoming Prime Minister he was a sunnier and easier person to deal with; later he suffered a little from *folie de grandeur* and became more rigid and authoritarian and less inclined to listen to views which conflicted with his own.

As a speaker he is always competent and fluent, seldom brilliant. He can argue a complicated case convincingly, often without notes and always in perfect sequence. He has no turn of phrase and does not find it easy to move an audience, but exceptionally he can do so when his own emotions are involved, as when he gave the memorial addresses to his friends Sir Timothy Bligh in 1969 and Michael Wolff in June 1976.

Both Heath and Macleod had been confident of victory in the 1970 election, but to many people it came as a surprise and on 19 June the *Daily Telegraph* carried the front-page comments, 'Not since Harry Truman confounded the opinion polls and practically every political prophet in the United States by defeating Mr Dewey in the Presidential election of 1948 has there been such an electoral shock.'

If the election result was a surprise, Heath's Cabinet appointments were not. Predictably, Home returned to the Foreign Office, Maudling became Home Secretary, Hailsham Lord Chancellor, Whitelaw leader of the House of Commons and Carrington Defence Secretary and leader of the House of Lords. Keith Joseph took over the Department of Health and Social Security and Margaret Thatcher the Department of Education and Science. Robert Carr was the new Secretary for Employment and Peter Walker Secretary of State for the Environment. The key appointment as Chancellor of the Exchequer went to Iain Macleod, who died tragically a month later. This was a bitter blow to the new administration and a serious loss to the Party and the nation. Especially after his death, the

Government's approach appeared to many of us to be more right wing than that of any Conservative Cabinet since before the war.

We appreciated that Heath wanted to fashion a tougher, more competitive society, but some of the side-effects were awkward and not always well handled. The ill-considered proposal to sell arms to South Africa was opposed by the Commonwealth, the United States Government, the Foreign Office (though not the Foreign Secretary), the left wing of the Conservative Party in Parliament and of course by the Labour and Liberal Parties. Because of it, the Commonwealth Conference in Singapore was a near-disaster. Heath believed he had made the new Commonwealth countries grow up. He did not understand them and had no appreciation of the love-hate emotions, with a large love element, they felt for their former masters. They expected British Ministers to understand, as Macmillan and Macleod had always understood, the special relationship between us; and Heath's rough tactics were resented, especially by the African leaders, who much preferred Alec Home's tact and good humour. An abrasive attitude is always counter-productive with newly independent nations, particularly when adopted by the ex-Colonial power.

The Conservative manifesto for the 1970 election had included as one of its most important policies the reform of trade union law. Legislation was undeniably overdue and much preparatory work had been done when the Party was in opposition. Barbara Castle's abortive attempt in 1969 to enact a Bill with the same general objectives had been a warning of the difficulties and it was decided to deal with this controversial matter as early as possible in the life of the new Parliament.

The Industrial Relations Bill was published in December 1970 and welcomed by the Confederation of British Industry as 'a considerable landmark in our industrial history', but opposed by the TUC, which decided to conduct a national campaign against it. The second reading was carried on 15 December and the committee stage was debated on the floor of the House for more than 100 hours. The Bill received the Royal Assent on 5 August 1971, but the unions were strongly advised by the TUC not to register under the Act. In April of the following year the Transport and General Workers' Union boycotted the Industrial Relations Court and was fined a total of £55,000 for contempt, but in June the Court of Appeal reversed the IRC rulings and set aside the fines. This spelt the effective end of the

Act. It had contained many useful provisions, but had alienated organized labour and proved unworkable in practice.

In the meantime the deteriorating situation in Northern Ireland had culminated in the introduction of direct rule from Westminster in March 1972. The Stormont Parliament was prorogued for one year and William Whitelaw was appointed Secretary of State for Northern Ireland, with full responsibility for law and order and the invidious, well-nigh impossible task of bringing about a political settlement between the Protestant majority and the Catholic minority in the Province.

In July 1973 a Bill was enacted to provide for a new Northern Ireland Assembly elected by proportional representation. This gave power to an Executive under Brian Faulkner, based on a coalition of moderate Unionists, the Catholic Social and Democratic Party and the Alliance Party, but opposed by the majority of Unionists and two other groups led by the Rev. Ian Paisley and Mr Craig, who all joined together to form the United Ulster Unionists.

In December 1973 a conference was held at Sunningdale between the British Government, the Government of Eire and the new Northern Ireland Executive, at which it was agreed that there would be no change in the status of Ulster against the wishes of the majority of its people. Under pressure from the SDLP, and against the advice of Brian Faulkner, it was also decided to set up a Council of Ireland with equal representation from north and south. This never materialized and was an unwise proposal because it aroused Protestant fears of a 'sell-out' to the south and laid the foundations for the workers' strike which broke the Executive in May 1974 and brought about the return to direct rule.

If the political and security situation in Northern Ireland was worsening, the economy of the United Kingdom as a whole was becoming equally precarious. In July 1971 the National Union of Mineworkers demanded a pay rise of up to forty-seven per cent and, when this was refused, reinforced it with an overtime ban in November and a total strike in January 1972. Attempts by Robert Carr, the Secretary of State for Employment, to negotiate a settlement broke down and a state of emergency to protect vital services and supplies was declared on 9 February. Next day a committee of inquiry was appointed under the chairmanship of Lord Wilberforce. Its recommendations constituted a damaging defeat for the Government by awarding almost the whole of the miners' claim at a cost of £85 million a year. The voluntary incomes policy was in ruins and the floodgates were open to pay claims by any powerful union in the wake of the miners' victory.

Prolonged tripartite talks between the Government, the CBI and the TUC finally collapsed on 2 November, and four days later Heath announced a ninety-day freeze for all pay, prices, dividends and rents. This was followed by stage two of the incomes and prices policy which allowed pay increases of four per cent plus £1 per week in a period of twelve months. Discussions continued between May and September 1973 and on 30 October a new counter-inflation order was published incorporating stage three of the policy. This was a little more flexible and rectified some obvious anomalies. It permitted extra payments for unsocial hours and provided for increases of seven per cent with a maximum of £350 p.a. But the statutory policy was unpopular both in the country and with many members of the Parliamentary Party, who regarded it as the negation of true Conservative principles.

Throughout his premiership Edward Heath's strategy for a modernized, more efficient Britain, ready to take her place as a leader of Europe, was unshakeable, but he was always prepared to change his tactics to achieve his objectives. This gave rise to the U-turns which succeeded the tough approach of the early days of his administration. Rolls Royce was rescued and partly nationalized; the fixed parity of the pound was abandoned and strenuous efforts were made to reduce the unemployment figures now moving menacingly towards the dreaded one million. The rising number of unemployed was causing strong pressure at Westminster and genuine anxiety in Whitehall and the Government decided to reflate the economy in order to alleviate this problem. But income restraint to curb inflation did not combine easily with the increase in the money supply which was bound to worsen it. Nearly £2000 million was injected into the economy, with special help for areas of heavy unemployment.

In an editorial in October the *Guardian* asserted, 'Mr Heath has staked everything – including his chances of winning the general election – on being able to sustain growth through the next twelve or eighteen months ... [he] has already gambled so heavily, with the balance of payments damaged, a pound floating downwards and a Party in near revolt, that his only course is to gamble further.' *The Times* remarked that 'Mr Heath is extraordinary because he is so willing to take up positions of total risk'. And in November the *Daily Telegraph* commented that the Government had nailed its flag to the mast and assumed full responsibility, but that meant that it must 'take the blame for whatever goes ill, as well as the credit for whatever goes well'.

Tony (now Lord) Barber has been criticized somewhat unfairly for the growth of the money supply. It was a Cabinet decision, endorsing the Prime Minister's policy, not the Chancellor's. Under these circumstances, what is a Chancellor to do? If he resigns in protest, the reasons are known and are damaging not only to the Party but to the nation. If he continues in office, he has to accept the responsibility for the policy if it fails.

Although Heath underestimated the degree of reflation required to reduce unemployment to any substantial extent, the gamble on growth, fully endorsed by the TUC, might have succeeded but for bad luck. Unfortunately it coincided with a rise in commodity prices. The cost of the primary products we were obliged to import rose steeply and added to the inflationary spiral. The Middle East oil crisis was the final misfortune which gave the miners the extra industrial power they needed to blackmail the Government. Even so, the confrontation between the Ministers and the National Union of Mineworkers might have been averted but for ill-luck and unskilful tactics.

As far back as July, Heath had made a secret deal with Joe Gormley, the president of the Union: in return for a special concession to the miners based on their unsocial hours of work, the Union would accept stage three of the incomes policy and a winter of industrial peace would be ensured.

On 10 October the Coal Board made an offer to the miners equivalent to a thirteen per cent rise in pay. Having regard to the stage three limit of seven per cent this was generous, but it had been written into a Green Paper as being available to any union which could satisfy the Pay Board that its hours of work were unsocial, so – for the miners – it was not special enough.

It was also virtually the Board's final offer, announced at the outset of the negotiations, and left nothing for the union moderates to be seen fighting for. With all the goods in the shop window, their negotiating position was undermined and it became a field-day for the militants. Gormley was unable to deliver the deal he had agreed with the Prime Minister and the initiative passed to men like Mick

McGahey, the Marxist vice-president. An attempt by the TUC to mediate was treated by Ministers with suspicion and the drama moved like a Greek tragedy to its fatal climax.

The first murmurings of discontent with Edward Heath's leadership could occasionally be heard in private conversations at Westminster in the autumn of 1973, but a general election is a great unifier and the Party entered the February contest united behind its leader. There had, however, been much doubt and indecision about the timing of the election. Some members of the Cabinet and of the Parliamentary Party thought it should have been held earlier, others that the Government should have soldiered on until circumstances looked more propitious. On 7 February 1974 Heath announced that polling day would be on 28 February. In the event, public opinion was not ready for a confrontation with the National Union of Mineworkers. The electorate preferred Labour's policy of appeasement and the hope of industrial peace. In fact, the Conservatives secured a majority of the votes, but Labour returned to Westminster with 301 seats to the Tory total of 296. The Liberals trailed behind with a meagre fourteen seats, although they had achieved nearly twenty per cent of the poll.

There was some criticism of the abortive private negotiations for a Conservative-Liberal coalition during the weekend after the election, but this was unfair both to Edward Heath and Jeremy Thorpe. The Liberals, rightly from their point of view, insisted on electoral reform. They knew that if they entered a coalition without some system of proportional representation, they would be quietly absorbed by the Conservative Party, as the Liberal Nationals had been in the pre-war years after joining the National Government in 1931. But Heath is an honest man and he could not give an undertaking that Parliament would pass the legislation. He offered to refer the matter to a Speaker's conference and to recommend to the House of Commons whatever electoral system the conference proposed. He could not guarantee that up to sixty Conservative Members of Parliament would commit political suicide by voting for it. Without such an assurance, Jeremy Thorpe could not persuade his Liberal colleagues to join a coalition. It was a pity, but it was no one's fault.

The issue is still a subject of interest and of debate, especially since the report of Lord Blake's enquiry into electoral reform. The present voting system is manifestly unfair and a reform which resulted in a succession of Conservative/Liberal or Labour/Liberal governments

for the foreseeable future would have many attractions for the basically moderate, middle-of-the-road British electorate. Industry would
be able to plan ahead without the risk of wasting its investments due
to further nationalization or other extreme left-wing measures. The
Marxist aim of the total socialization of Britain would be averted.

When the negotiations with Jeremy Thorpe proved abortive, Heath
went to Buckingham Palace to resign as Prime Minister. He had held
office for three years and eight months. Many of the policies on which
his government were elected had been abandoned under pressure of
events. He had been dogged by ill-luck, beginning with the loss of his
most brilliant lieutenant, Iain Macleod. His style of government had
become authoritarian and he had often imposed his views on his
colleagues. His team of Ministers was not a strong one and he has
been criticized for not bringing forward enough of the young talent
in the Parliamentary Party. But he had one great and lasting achievement to his credit: he had taken Britain into the European Economic
Community.

In his own country Heath was underrated. His impact on international politics was far greater than most people realized and he was
certainly more honoured abroad than at home. During a visit to the
Bonn concert hall, half the German Government turned out to
receive him, as though he was still Prime Minister, and one of the
Ministers asked, 'Are the British Conservatives mad, that they have
got rid of this man?'

When he became Prime Minister he had not travelled extensively
in the Commonwealth and had far less knowledge, particularly of
Africa and its leaders, than his two Conservative predecessors. His
handling of his first Commonwealth Prime Ministers' Conference
was brusque and unsympathetic, but he learned from it and the
second Conference in Canada was a success. Chou En-Lai, the Shah
of Iran, President Pompidou and Pierre Trudeau were among the
then world leaders who much admired him.

Heath is a very patriotic man and his main objective as Prime
Minister was to restore the economic strength and influence of
Britain at home and overseas. Above all, perhaps, he is a man of
determination and courage. James Barrie once said, 'Courage is the
thing. If that goes, all goes.' It is a quality Heath has never lacked.

Despite the Conservative defeat in the February election, there was
no move overt or, as far as I know, covert to change the leadership

139

of the Party. Harold Wilson was in office with a minority Government and would obviously go to the country at the earliest opportunity in an attempt to secure an overall majority. Under these circumstances it would have been suicidal for the Tories to appear publicly disunited.

Within the Shadow Cabinet there was less harmony. Sir Keith Joseph and Margaret Thatcher were deeply disturbed by the rising tide of inflation and by the lack of any Conservative policy adequate, in their view, to cure or even contain it. As Ministers they had had a heavy work-load in their own departments and had been excluded from the central planning of economic policy. They began, now, to challenge the pragmatism which had hitherto prevailed and to advocate the monetarist system. They received some, at first tentative, support from Sir Geoffrey Howe.

Edward Heath resented the arguments which developed, but had to keep his team together for the election. The majority in his Shadow Cabinet were prepared to concede to Keith Joseph that cuts in public expenditure and a stricter control of the money supply could contribute to a solution, but did not agree that a monetarist policy should be applied too strongly or could provide more than part of the answer to the overriding problem of inflation.

The Conservative Party is more discreet and conceals its differences more skilfully than the Labour Party. Public disagreement was avoided, but it soon became clear that the views long advocated from the back benches by Nicholas Ridley and John Biffen were receiving powerful endorsement from within the Shadow Cabinet itself; and when Keith Joseph began a series of speeches in the country, he was, in effect, laying the ground, not only for changes in economic policy but for a change in the leadership of the Party.

The establishment of his Centre for Policy Studies was almost an announcement of the growing differences of approach. He ceased to defend Conservative policies and argued that past mistakes must be admitted before the Party could expect to return to power. But it was neither practical on the eve of an election, nor in Edward Heath's character, to acknowledge errors in policies of which he had been the author.

As Prime Minister of Britain and as the leader of the Conservative Party, Heath had to be successful to be supported. His strength of character and honesty of purpose were respected and his firmness and resolution admired, but he was not loved. His colleagues in Parliament accorded him the loyalty due to the leader of their Party; but few felt any great personal loyalty to him as a friend.

There is very little gratitude in public life and when men are unlucky or mistakes are made and policies prove unpopular, leaders need the understanding and support of their colleagues, preferably in all Parties but essentially in their own.

I remember, many years ago, James Stuart (later Lord Findhorn), then Secretary of State for Scotland, making an appallingly bad speech when he was winding up an important debate for the Government. The House was crowded and the issue controversial, but no one on the Opposition benches made the least attempt to interrupt or shout him down. When I asked a Labour friend why they had let Stuart get away with it so easily, he replied, 'Because we like him so much.' The House of Commons can be rough, but it can also be generous. Unfortunately Ted Heath did not enjoy this sort of personal affection and had done little to earn it. He finds it difficult to communicate at a public or private level and has only a handful of close friends in Parliament. Nor does he take kindly to criticism.

On one occasion when the poor public relations of the Government were the subject of much adverse comment in the Party and in the press, the Executive of the 1922 Committee, of which I am a member, was having one of its periodic meetings with him. I therefore raised the matter, only to be brushed aside with the remark that he understood the press officers in some Government departments were inadequate. I suggested that good public relations come from the top and that the criticism was not of the public relations officers but of senior ministers in Whitehall and of No 10 Downing Street itself. He looked askance, grunted crossly, 'That is a point of view' and turned abruptly in his chair to begin a discussion on a different subject.

This was not an isolated example. He treated most of his Parliamentary colleagues with ill-concealed contempt, especially the Executive, whose meetings with him appeared to us to be no more than a necessary nuisance so far as he was concerned.

Throughout his premiership, Heath totally dominated his Cabinet colleagues. This was bad for him and bad for them. Some of them resented it and would have preferred a more collective, less individual style of leadership. Many Ministers found him intimidating and did not stand up to him. This was a mistake. As one of his colleagues said to me, 'He is not a bully by nature, though he may seem to

be,' and it was better to fight your own corner and argue your case
if you disagreed with him. He might not accept it at the time,
but he absorbed and often acted upon it later. Nor was he as
impervious to advice as most people imagined; he sometimes even
took it!

In his business dealings, Heath had only one level of communication. It consisted of combative, apparently hostile questioning and of
strong, provocative, even discourteous argument. He used this technique deliberately, in order to elicit information or bring out a point
of view, but it made him sound obstinate and opinionated and gained
him more critics than admirers.

The story is told of a prominent and influential farmer with whom
he had such a fierce argument about agricultural policy that the man
told his MP afterwards that he never wished to speak to Ted Heath
again. When agriculture was under discussion in the Cabinet a few
days later, Heath propounded precisely the views which the farmer
had expressed. He had listened and absorbed, but he did not appreciate that, from the point of view of personal relations, it was as
bad not to have *seemed* to listen as not to have listened at all. I have
heard the same criticism from important industrialists and leading
figures in the City of London.

Unlike Harold Wilson, Ted Heath never took the trouble to
propitiate his Ministerial and Parliamentary colleagues. He can be
very kind, but he is rude, often quite unintentionally, and he tends to
become tongue-tied with acquaintances or strangers. This may be
due partly to preoccupation with more important matters. He cannot
express personal things easily and finds it difficult to thank even
friends for their loyalty and support.

Heath's categories of acquaintance are different to, and more
restricted than other people's. He has few social friends and dislikes
social occasions. He is a self-contained man, close to his family and
to a few others like Madron Seligman, who shares his enthusiasm for
sailing and music, but he is a somewhat solitary figure. This may have
contributed to his rather remote relationship with the electorate,
but it gave him more time to devote to his responsibilities and to his
outside interests. His concentration and professionalism are almost
as great when he is sailing his boat or listening to or conducting an
orchestra as when he is engaged on a political problem. He finds it
difficult to relax and seldom needs to. He seems able to live on his
nerves, yet – at least outwardly – remain calm and contained.

Physically, he can immerse himself in yacht racing and it takes away the tensions. He never cruises, but enjoys to race and to win. His victory in the Sydney-Hobart race in 1969 and his captaincy of the winning British team in the Admiral's Cup in 1971 were triumphant successes which he richly deserved. As he had not sailed seriously until he was fifty, it is remarkable (though in a way typical) that he became so proficient in so short a time.

Music is an emotional outlet. Visitors to his flat in Albany frequently found him playing the piano, from which he desisted with reluctance to greet them. His knowledge of music is extensive and his observations on the subject can be pungent. Peter Walker tells an amusing story of his reaction to a new work being played for the first time. A music critic asked for his opinion and he replied, 'I was interested in being present for its first, and I trust only, performance.'

Such is the weight of public business in modern times and its impact upon the lives of the people that, in our system of government, Ministers become very departmentalized and most have little influence on important matters of general policy. This is especially true of junior and middle-rank Ministers, who feel isolated and out of touch. Heath tried to overcome this by regular written briefs, but there was no feeling that 'we are all in this together' and when the election for the Party leadership took place, several of those who had been junior Ministers in his government did not vote for him.

The inability of the leader of the Party to communicate at a public level was as marked as that of the man at a personal level. His immense application and capacity to read and absorb quickly have contributed to a remarkable grasp of public affairs. He is very effective in question and answer sessions on television, but his personality does not come through as well if he is talking straight to camera; and, with a few notable exceptions, his speeches in Parliament and in the country, although fluent and often without notes, are uninspired and therefore uninspiring. They are usually delivered in a flat monotone. He has no gift of phrase and his knowledge and appreciation of music do not extend to the spoken word.

In one of the best speeches he has ever made in the House of Commons, he was criticizing the Labour Government's failure to explain its policies when, in an aside of endearing and unusual humility, he interpolated, 'But who am I to talk about communicating?' It was his main weakness as a leader and it is a near-fatal weakness in a democracy. There can be no doubt that this flaw in his political make-up contributed more than any other single factor to his defeat in the leadership election. It is a tragic defect because his ability is outstanding and most people would agree that he is nearly a very great man.

8

MARGARET THATCHER

At 2.30 p.m. on 12 September 1974, on the eve of the second general election in the year, the 1922 Committee of Conservative back bench MPs, supplemented by any peers and adopted Conservative candidates able to attend, met at the Europa Hotel in Grosvenor Square under the chairmanship of Edward du Cann. Edward Heath addressed the meeting and outlined the Party's policy and strategy for the forthcoming contest. It was a competent but uninspiring speech. After he had spoken, the 1922 Executive assembled in the Duchess suite for the first time since the adjournment of the House of Commons at the end of July. It was decided to hold a normal routine meeting on Monday, 14 October, the earliest convenient date after the declaration of the poll on 10 October.

There were two reasons for this: the Executive had to make the usual arrangements, at the beginning of a new session of Parliament, for the election of officers for over twenty Party committees and of a new Executive for the 1922 Committee. We also wished to be available in case our views were sought, following what might be a close election result. In the previous February, when the possibility of a coalition with the Liberals was under discussion, the members of the Executive had been scattered and it was not easy (in response to an urgent request from the leader of the Party) to obtain a collective view. We were anxious to avoid this or a similar situation in October. Our purpose was not to discuss the leadership of the Party, which was not then in our minds and was never even mentioned at the September meeting.

Edward Heath's election objective was to avoid another 1966 result and in this he succeeded. There could have been a landslide against the Party. He fought a good campaign and the manifesto was

145

the best written since the Second World War. Its theme was well received in outer London suburbs like my own and in southern England generally, but apparently made a less favourable impact in other parts of the country.

Margaret Thatcher's promise to peg the mortgage rate at nine and a half per cent was helpful to the Party and to her own standing in the country. Paradoxically, it was not her own idea. She had been reluctant to give a commitment to extra Government expenditure but, once persuaded to do so, she publicized the policy with skill and effect.

There had been no argument in the Shadow Cabinet over the national unity approach which Heath developed as the election progressed. It might have been better if he had launched this idea sooner and with greater emphasis, in order to achieve a wider acceptability. It is always wise to give the electorate time to get used to a new concept and to reinforce its message by constant repetition. If he had gone further and come out unequivocally for a coalition, it might have tipped the scale in our favour; still more so had he offered to stand down if other Parties made this a condition for entering a coalition. He would not have risked much by such an offer. If the Conservatives had won, his position would have been a very strong one; if they lost his leadership would in any event be challenged. The arguments against the offer were that it would have demoralized the Party activists, who were already lukewarm about national unity and would have preferred a more full-blooded Conservative campaign, and that it would have been pilloried by Harold Wilson. Even the talk of coalition evoked a typical rejoinder. At his press conference on 5 October, the Prime Minister described it as

a desperate attempt by desperate men to get back into power by any means. . . . Beneath the soft, the pleasant and the adjustable face of today's coalition lies the old and, if I may borrow a phrase from the Conservative leader, 'unpleasant and unacceptable face of capitalism'. Coalition would mean Con policies, Con leadership by a Con Party for a Con trick.

I believe that we should have taken the risk and staked everything on the coalition concept and I wrote to Willie Whitelaw, the Party chairman, to urge a far more direct and forthright appeal on these lines, including an offer by Heath to sacrifice himself if necessary. Quite apart from the electoral response from the floating vote, already alienated by abusive and abrasive Party politics, I believed that in order to resolve the coming economic crisis, the Government would in any case need the support of a large majority of the electorate and this could only be achieved through a coalition. One of the problems was that the ground had been ill prepared and many people did not appreciate how grave the economic position was, yet this was a pre-condition for the credibility of a coalition campaign. As I saw it, we had an election winner, which we only half-exploited and which failed through mismanagement and lack of resolution.

The election resulted in 319 seats for Labour, 276 for the Conservatives and thirteen for the Liberals. The Nationalists took twelve seats in Scotland and two in Wales and the United Ulster Unionists won ten out of the twelve seats in Northern Ireland. Although the Government's overall majority was only three, in practice it was between twenty and forty on most issues, owing to support from one or other of the minority parties.

Heath had averted an innings defeat, in itself quite an achievement, but it was disturbing that 164 of the 276 Conservative seats were con-concentrated south of a line drawn between the Severn and the Wash. We held only one third of the constituencies in the Midlands and the industrial north, a mere sixteen in the whole of Scotland, eight in Wales and none in Northern Ireland. We had become, for the time being, a Party based mainly on the rural areas, the suburbs and the seaside resorts.

There was one disquieting experience shared by almost every Conservative candidate in the country. It was quickly apparent from the personal canvassing we all undertook that the leader of the Party had become an electoral liability. Unlike Churchill, Eden and Macmillan, Heath's personality had never been a positive asset; but in previous elections, although not as popular with Conservative voters as Alec Douglas-Home, he had not been seriously criticized by members of his own Party. In October 1974 it was different. On nearly every doorstep, if a conversation developed, one's constituent – whether man or woman, Conservative, Liberal or Labour – would say, 'I'd vote for you except for Heath,' or 'You'll never win with Heath,' or, quite simply, 'I don't like Heath.'

It was this reaction in the constituencies, following two election defeats in quick succession, which touched off the leadership crisis in the Party. During the three days which followed the poll on 10 October, I and almost every other member of the Executive of the 1922 Committee received messages, telephone calls and letters from our Parliamentary colleagues urging us to take immediate steps to ensure early consideration of the leader's position.

As arranged a month earlier, the Executive met at Edward du Cann's house in Lord North Street at 11.45 a.m. on 14 October. Although no announcement of the meeting had been made, the house was besieged by reporters, photographers and television cameras when we arrived. None of us made any public comment as we entered or left an hour later. It is a happy characteristic of the Executive, rare in any political group meeting regularly, that it is and always has been remarkably secure.

The routine business, though important, was dealt with as quickly as possible. Everyone knew that we must grasp the nettle of the leadership issue. This had not been mentioned at any previous meeting of the Executive and was not debated even on 14 October. We had all had the same experience in our constituencies and the same messages from our colleagues. There was very little discussion and no argument.

We were seated in a semi-circle in the drawing room and Edward du Cann adopted the procedure of inviting each of us, from right to left as we faced him, to express our opinion. We did so very briefly. No one spoke for longer than half a minute, most confined themselves to two or three sentences. We were unanimous that an election for the leadership must be held, not necessarily at once but in the foreseeable future.

The fact that there was not a single dissentient was significant. The Executive consists of the chairman of the 1922 Committee, the two vice-chairmen, the treasurer, two secretaries and twelve members, who are all elected at the beginning of each new session of Parliament, to serve for one year until the following October. It has not always been so, but in the previous few years the Executive had covered the entire spectrum of political opinion in the Parliamentary Party from John Biffen and Angus Maude, who would be regarded as on the right, to Charles Morrison, one of our vice-chairmen, and myself, who may be thought to reflect the views of the left wing of the Party. Most of the other members were broadly representative of the centre. We were also a cross-section in terms of age and geography. Thus, there was no political motive underlying our belief that it was time for a change. Indeed, we had all fought the election on the same manifesto, to which, with varying degrees of enthusiasm, each had subscribed.

The chief function of the Executive is to represent the opinions and wishes of the Parliamentary Party and to act in a consultative and liaison capacity between it and the leader of the Party, so that 'executive' is, in a sense, a misnomer. But on this occasion it was in fact executive – and powerful – because it was the only vehicle through which Parliamentary opinion could not only be expressed but implemented. Although the main Committee had not met and could not do so until the new Parliament assembled, we believed we knew the views of the majority of our colleagues and we were to be proved right in this supposition.

Edward Heath had been our leader for nearly ten years. Under modern conditions the strain and responsibility and the sheer volume of work make this a long time at the top. It was not Heath's fault that he had led us to three defeats out of four, but it seemed time – and the reactions on the hustings and the doorsteps underlined it – to try and give the Party a new and more attractive look. Indeed it is probable that, had the Labour Party lost the election, there would have been the same pressures to replace Harold Wilson; so the October election, which was really an extension of the February election, had put the existing leadership at risk in both Parties.

As soon as our unanimity became clear, it seemed right to convey the views of the Executive to Edward Heath. It was not our intention to rush him into a decision either to resign at once or to hold an immediate election; but with press interest at fever-pitch, it would not have been possible to conceal for long the advice we had decided to offer him and speculation and uncertainty would have been damaging to the Party. We invited Edward du Cann to seek an interview with him that day.

It is right to place on record that, throughout the whole leadership crisis, du Cann himself advocated restraint and time for reflection. He, more than anyone on the Executive, was reluctant to force Heath's hand; but he could not decline to convey our message and he agreed to do so that afternoon. He also arranged to see William Whitelaw, as chairman of the Party, and Humphrey Atkins, the Chief Whip, to inform them of the action we had taken.

I suggested that members of the Executive might wish to hear the leader's reaction to our advice. It would have been difficult to give this news to each member by telephone and in any case there might be need for further discussion in the light of Heath's response to our message. We therefore agreed to meet again next morning; but it was not so easy to decide where. No doubt Lord North Street would again be picketed by the press and the House of Commons was not available for meetings until Parliament assembled on 22 October. It was decided to foregather at 10.30 a.m. at the offices of Keyser Ullmann, the merchant bank of which du Cann was then chairman, in Milk Street in the City.

We realized that a second meeting of the Executive in two days would be headline news for the popular press and that this sort of publicity would be harmful to the Party. There was need for prudence. We therefore arranged – somewhat light-heartedly, as we did not really expect to be followed – to arrive separately and at short intervals, some by car or taxi, others by bus or underground. We entered the building unobserved and congratulated ourselves upon our discretion.

Our self-satisfaction was short-lived. When the meeting ended soon after noon, the first members to leave were confronted by reporters and cameramen as on the previous day. The rest of us beat a hasty retreat into the building and bided our time until we were able to leave unnoticed by another route. Betty Harvie-Anderson and I eventually reached Westminster by underground, after successfully avoiding all the photographers. Some of our colleagues were less fortunate and the *Evening Standard* featured many of them in its next edition, with a sensational story that the Executive, now christened 'the Milk Street Mafia', had met again to plan secretly the political assassination of the leader of the Party. This was both untrue and unfair. We resented the 'Mafia' label, which we were advised was libellous, and wrote a letter of protest to the *Evening Standard*. The story did the Party no good and for a few days, until the explanation became known, it made members of the Executive look like fools or knaves or both. My own telephone rang incessantly with furious protests from friends and constituents, who were ardent supporters of Edward Heath and violently critical of the alleged machinations of the 1922 Executive.

We naturally investigated the source of the leak. This had been accidental in the first instance, but the news of our meeting reached the ears of a member of the staff of the leader's private office some-time during the morning of 15 October, after we had assembled at 25 Milk Street. This official apparently regarded the information as an heaven-sent opportunity to discredit du Cann and the Executive and to win sympathy for Heath. He immediately telephoned Robert

Carvel of the *Evening Standard* to suggest that, if reporters and cameramen were despatched to Milk Street, they would glean some valuable material during the course of the morning. The *Daily Express* was also informed of the meeting.

It is not suggested that Edward Heath himself knew anything of this manoeuvre. He is a man of the highest integrity and would, I am sure, have vetoed such tactics had he been aware of them.

In the end, the operation was counter-productive, because the true source of the leak to the press soon became known in the Parliamentary Party and served to enhance rather than detract from the support for the Executive. It was the first of the 'dirty tricks' with which we had to contend during the next few weeks.

During the meeting at Milk Street, Edward du Cann acquainted the Executive with the leader's response to our message: though amicable, the interview had been short. There is an often-expressed assumption in Parliament that personal relations between the two men have never been close or cordial and it is true that du Cann resigned as chairman of the Party because they differed about the way it should be managed. This may have contributed to the communication gap, of which their interview on 14 October is evidence.

The Executive was disturbed to hear that du Cann had not been given an opportunity to discuss the situation in depth and feared that Heath might have gained a mistaken impression. We therefore drafted a letter to him, setting out our advice in the way du Cann would have expressed it had he been given the chance to do so. This letter was read over the telephone to Humphrey Atkins, who suggested a minor amendment which was incorporated. In it, the Executive invited Heath to address the first meeting of the main Committee, should he wish to do so. He published his reply (though not our original letter), declining this suggestion. This seemed a strange way to behave to colleagues.

Heath indicated that he would be prepared to discuss the situation with the Executive but only after its re-election. The inference, underlined in corridor conversations by his supporters, was that the Executive had no authority to speak for the Parliamentary Party until its own elections had been held. This was a disingenuous and historically incorrect interpretation of the constitutional position, as Philip Goodhart, a joint secretary of the Committee, was able to point out in a letter to *The Times* on 22 October.

Some members of the Executive thought that Heath could perhaps have defused the situation by a statement to the main Committee that he understood the views of the Parliamentary Party and, although the European referendum and the grave economic situation might make an early leadership election unsuitable, he would certainly hold one at a convenient time within the next year. This, it was thought, might have satisfied many Members, whose main anxiety was that the Party should not be saddled with Heath as leader for the next general election, but who did not regard his replacement as a matter of urgency.

There were, of course, serious disadvantages in this way of handling the matter: the meetings of the 1922 Committee, although nominally private, are notoriously insecure and the newspapers next day would certainly have carried an account of the leader's speech and the Party's reaction to it. Whatever this might have been, the very announcement of a deferred election would have derogated from Heath's authority in the intervening period, caused endless speculation in the press, given ammunition to Harold Wilson in the House of Commons and would also, no doubt, have led to much intrigue and lobbying within the Parliamentary Party.

There were several other options open to Ted Heath, all of which were considered by his advisers:

1. He could ask the 1922 Committee for an immediate vote of confidence – which he would almost certainly not have obtained.
2. He could resign the leadership as Alec Douglas-Home had done nine years earlier.
3. He could ignore the advice of the Executive and go on as though nothing had happened; this would have destroyed the unity of the Party and provoked a great storm at Westminster.
4. He could temporize and consider what would be best in the light of events as they developed.

It is not in Heath's character to run away from a difficult situation or to take early and dramatic action before he has made up his mind, so he followed the fourth course.

He may, indeed, have felt vindicated by the result of the general election. Against the odds, he had almost denied Labour the victory, when many people had expected a landslide against him. Moreover, he was confident that his warnings of the coming economic crisis – higher inflation, growing unemployment and the need for a prices and incomes policy – would soon prove justified, as in fact they were.

Heath and some of his advisers believed that the Labour Government might break up either over the economy or the EEC issue and that his chance of forming an all-Party coalition might then materialize. This was the logic of his case for delaying a decision on the leadership. His sense of being sniped at may also have hardened his resolve not to be forced into premature resignation. He asked the Chief Whip to collect the views of MPs and the chairman of the Party to seek soundings in the constituency associations.

William Whitelaw's position, as a likely contender for the leadership, was a difficult one. He and Sir Michael Fraser were rightly anxious to keep Central Office out of the controversy and, although they did not fully succeed in this aim because some officials were ardent Heath adherents, Whitelaw himself was scrupulously loyal and objective.

Nevertheless, it is not easy to obtain reliable constituency opinion on anything at short notice. In one association, the chairman of the Women's Advisory Committee was telephoned and asked to report the views of her members. No meeting of her Committee was due before the deadline she had been given. She was herself a keen Heath supporter and telephoned two of her officers who shared her opinion. She then reported to Central Office that the Women's Advisory Committee was overwhelmingly for Heath!

By this time a renewal of support for him was in fact developing in the constituencies, but it was largely confined to the Party workers, traditionally loyal to the leadership, and did not extend to those normally Conservative voters who had become disillusioned with politicians in general and with the Conservative leader in particular. I had many letters from my own area between October and Christmas urging Heath's early replacement.

Of more immediate significance was the advice he was receiving from those in his confidence. Most of his closest Cabinet colleagues and political associates had advised him either to resign immediately after the general election, or to seek an endorsement of his leadership from the 1922 Committee. Alternatively, they thought he should offer his resignation and hold out the prospect of an early election. Many of those who had worked for him including Jim Prior, Sara Morrison and his two Parliamentary Private Secretaries, Kenneth Baker and Sir Timothy Kitson, believed that a gesture of this kind would have been his best chance of survival. This was also the collective opinion of the 1922 Executive.

Although Peter Carrington did not at first share this view, he and

Michael St Aldwyn subsequently advised that Heath should accept it. Carrington is a very intelligent politician, well-liked, objective and experienced, and Heath should have paid more attention to this advice.

Some supporters of his policies thought, no doubt correctly, that if he could be persuaded to withdraw quickly and gracefully, a consensus could be formed for Whitelaw, whereas a more drawn-out process would allow other contenders to emerge, which would prejudice Whitelaw's prospects.

After Macleod's death, Maudling's oblivion and the elimination of Powell, there was a dearth of talent at the top and – following his success in Northern Ireland – Whitelaw had become the apparent beneficiary. The opinion polls reflected his popularity and his accession would not have involved any radical changes in policy.

Whitelaw himself realized that Heath could not survive; but he did not advise him to go. Indeed, as at that time the most likely successor, he could scarcely have done so. He had been a popular and successful Chief Whip and understands the Conservative Party very well. It was unfortunate that he was 'out of play' for advice at the time when it would have been most valuable. Humphrey Atkins, the present Chief Whip, although entirely loyal, did not have a very close relationship with his leader and his predecessor, Francis Pym, thought Heath should play for time.

Others, notably Lord Aldington and Peter Walker, told Heath they hoped he would fight and they thought he would win. Harold Macmillan, by this time less closely in touch with Parliamentary opinion, gave the same advice when Ted Heath consulted him. No doubt Toby Aldington's counsel carried special weight. He is an able, attractive, straightforward man, respected and popular in the Party. Heath has a real affection for him and relies upon his judgement. But he had left the House of Commons thirteen years before and, like Macmillan, no longer knew the majority of the Conservative members; nor had he shared their experience on the doorsteps in October. He was himself well aware of this and qualified his advice accordingly. In the end, as everyone always does, Heath took the advice he wanted to hear.

The new Parliament assembled on 22 October for the election of the Speaker and the swearing in of Members. No other public business was transacted that week, but the Executive met three times in Edward du Cann's room at the House of Commons. The first meeting of the main Committee was due to take place on 31 October.

The leadership issue was certain to be raised and the Executive did what was possible beforehand to ensure that this would be done in a restrained and responsible way. Du Cann told us that he intended, as usual, to call every Member in the exact order in which they caught his eye and that he would prolong the meeting, if necessary, to make sure that no one who wanted to speak was prevented from doing so.

He followed this procedure with meticulous care and we were therefore astonished when nearly all the Sunday newspapers that weekend carried the same story – that the meeting had been deliberately rigged by the chairman who, it was alleged, had only called those members known to be critical of Edward Heath. This was such a travesty that it could only have been inspired by a deliberate press briefing, designed to denigrate the chairman and Executive and win public support for Heath. It was another of the 'dirty tricks' and was again counter-productive, because all those who attended the meeting (virtually every member of the Parliamentary Party) had seen with their own eyes how fairly it had been conducted. One of the most telling contributions came from Kenneth Lewis, the Member for Rutland, who initiated the debate and made the point that the leadership of the Party was a leasehold, not a freehold.

It was at about this time that some members of the Executive were approached with the implied threat that, if we were not careful, we would all be replaced when the elections for the new Executive were held. As most of us are fairly senior in the Party and are there without fear or favour, this amateurish attempt at intimidation was inept and maladroit. Indeed, throughout these early weeks Ted Heath's cause was badly served and mishandled by some of his supporters in Parliament.

As things turned out, the chairman, officers and Executive were in fact re-elected *en bloc* on 7 November. As far as I know, this was unique in the annals of the 1922 Committee and was a clear and unequivocal endorsement by the majority of our colleagues of the course we had followed. The loud and prolonged applause which greeted Edward du Cann's unopposed re-election as chairman was further evidence that he had correctly represented the views of the Parliamentary Party and should have been a warning to Heath that his own position was, to say the least, precarious.

Before his re-election, and presumably in order to prevent it, personal attacks on du Cann began to appear in the press. This was part of the establishment policy to denigrate those who were genuinely trying to discharge a difficult task in a responsible way.

By now it was clear that Heath, unlike Douglas-Home, had no intention of resigning. The Executive had a duty to bring the matter to a head and pressure to revise the rules for a new election was in any case becoming overwhelming. Revision was necessary because the existing rules only provided machinery for an election when the position of leader was vacant. It had not occurred to anyone when the rules were first devised in 1965 that a leader who had lost the confidence of a substantial section of the Party would wish to continue in office.

Edward Heath acceded to the request that a rules committee should be established and asked that its recommendations should be submitted to him before the end of the year. At the suggestion of the Executive he invited Alec Douglas-Home to accept the chairmanship. The members were as follows: Edward du Cann as chairman, and Sir John Hall and Charles Morrison as vice-chairmen, of the 1922 Committee; William Whitelaw, as chairman of the Party organization; Humphrey Atkins, as Chief Whip in the House of Commons; Lord Carrington, as leader of the Party in the House of Lords; Lord St Aldwyn, as Chief Whip in the House of Lords; Sir John Taylor, as chairman of the Executive Committee of the National Union; Sir Alastair Graesser, as chairman of the National Union. Sir Michael (now Lord) Fraser, though not officially a member of the committee, attended all its meetings.

There were thus five elected Members of Parliament on the committee and four others appointed to it because of their positions in the Party. The composition of the committee, recommended to Heath by the Executive, was in fact the same as in 1965 except for two extra representatives of the Parliamentary Party in the House of Commons and one extra representative of the National Union.

The committee held five meetings, the first on 22 November and the last on 10 December. Its report was submitted to the leader just before the House rose and Members of Parliament had plenty of time to consider it during the Christmas recess.

As compared with the 1965 rules, three changes were recommended: the first was the provision for an annual election. The second concerned the requirement that, to be elected on the first ballot, a candidate must obtain not only an overall majority, but also fifteen per cent more of the votes cast than any other candidate.

This was altered to read fifteen per cent of all those eligible to vote. Heath disliked this small change and was hurt by its inclusion. He thought it militated against his chances by making the hurdle higher. The number of votes required for election on the first ballot was 139. The third change was to formalize and extend the process of consultation with the areas and the constituency associations and, through them, with members of the Party in the country.

The 1922 Executive had met on 11 and 12 November to consider the advice our representatives should tender to the rules committee. There was some discussion about the composition of the electoral college. I would not myself have objected to the inclusion in this of a small number of peers to represent the Party in the House of Lords and of an equal number of National Union nominees to represent the Party in the country – perhaps fifteen of each. This would have gone some way to facilitate the transmission of opinion in the constituency associations to the Party in the House; and Edward du Cann represented this view to the rules committee. But the majority of the Executive thought that the 1922 Committee would expect to retain the sole franchise, which they had been accorded in 1965 when the elective system was first introduced. There is much to be said for this because it is certainly true that no leader can survive for long without the support of his Party in the House of Commons.

Consideration was given, both in the Executive beforehand and in the rules committee when it met, to the advisability of annual elections for the leadership or the alternative of an election at the beginning of each new Parliament. Opinion in the Executive was divided, so we could give no clear lead to our representatives on the rules committee. In the result, the Labour Party's system of annual elections was adopted, mainly because this makes an election less of an event than if it is held only once in a Parliament.

The representatives of the National Union would, not unnaturally, have liked a moderate extension of the electoral college, which might have given voting rights to the area chairmen and, through them, to the Party in the country; but the peers did not want any votes and this no doubt inhibited the National Union nominees from pressing their case.

When Parliament re-assembled after the Christmas recess, the Executive Committee of the National Union recorded its preference not only for a wider electoral college and elections once in each Parliament, but also for an additional provision that no new candidate should be allowed to contest a second ballot who had not come forward for the first. None of these changes were included in the report of the rules committee. The peers accepted the report with some relatively minor reservations; and, at the suggestion of the Executive, the 1922 Committee accepted it with the qualification that some of its recommendations should be re-examined at a later date.

The main anxiety of most Members of Parliament was to hold an early election and get the whole distasteful business over as soon as possible. They knew that any further delay would be damaging to the Party and would make the task of any leader more difficult. Edward Heath was by now equally conscious of the need to resolve the matter and, once the 1922 Committee had approved the report, he knew he could not delay an election without prejudice to his own prospects of winning it. He accordingly accepted the report and called an election, to be held as soon as the arrangments for it could be made.

Meanwhile much discussion was taking place in the Party about the contenders who might come forward and their rival qualities and weaknesses as future leaders. Provided the majority of Members still supported Heath's policies, the establishment front-runner was clearly William Whitelaw, if he would agree to stand; but it was soon known that he had decided not to do so, at any rate on the first ballot.

There was considerable feeling in the Parliamentary Party that Heath should go if a viable alternative could be found and Whitelaw was embarrassed by the pressures upon him to declare his candidature. He thought it would be divisive for the chairman of the Party to oppose the leader who had appointed him. He had also been Ted Heath's Chief Whip for many years and owed him some personal loyalty. He is the most honourable of men and these factors weighed heavily with him. Moreover, he knew that he would lose all influence with Heath if he stood against him and lost.

The other obvious potential candidate was Keith Joseph. As a convinced monetarist, he represents what may loosely be described as the right wing of the Conservative Party in economic policy, but his reputation as an enlightened Secretary of State for Health and Social Security propitiates the centre and left. He has the intellectual brilliance and the administrative capacity to lead the Party and his candidature would have offered an interesting challenge to the consensus politics of post-war Britain; but he lacks one essential requisite

– or so it seemed to his admirers – the quality of political judgement.

During the summer and autumn of 1974 Joseph made two important speeches, some points in which were highlighted by the press in a way he had not intended. The first was concerned mainly with the problem of unemployment, the importance of which he seemed to minimize. This presented the Labour Party with useful ammunition for the October election.

The second speech was even more controversial. It contained much that was of value, which needed to be said, and any Conservative would have agreed with ninety per cent of it; but there were two or three sentences, unnecessary to the main theme, which took every headline. They appeared to advocate contraception on a class differential basis. Of course he meant no such thing, but his failure to appreciate that the newspaper reporters would pick out this passage to publicize at the expense of the rest of the speech was disturbing. Such unawareness of inevitable press reaction was bad enough in a Shadow Cabinet minister; it would have been fatal in a Party leader. We could scarcely elect someone to the top position who, after each of two major speeches, had been obliged to explain and excuse his own statements the next day.

Following the second speech, Joseph made an objective assessment of his own suitability and, after an accurate and exceptionally clear-sighted process of self-analysis, decided against himself. He told Edward Heath and the Chief Whip that he did not intend to contest the leadership and then informed Margaret Thatcher and Geoffrey Howe, who were friends and political allies.

I know from personal experience that Joseph is a very kind man who will take infinite trouble to right a wrong, but he has one personal defect of which he is probably unaware. He is intellectually almost in a class of his own in the Tory Party, and this sometimes makes him seem brusque in his dealings with ordinary mortals. When I asked a friend in the Shadow Cabinet what he thought of Keith Joseph as a possible leader of the Party, he made the witty, if rather unkind rejoinder, 'My dear Nigel, if you chose Keith instead of Heath, it would be like going straight from the fridge into the freezer.'

As it became known that both Willie Whitelaw and Keith Joseph had decided not to run for the leadership, the Party began to realize its dilemma. We had created a considerable agitation to be rid of the very able leader we already had without, so far, any credible candidate to put in his place. Margaret Thatcher had not at that time thrown her hat in the ring and was not yet seriously considered as a contender.

In early November I met an old friend, now a member of the Upper House, who strongly advocated the qualities of Richard Wood as a solution to the problem, and indeed Wood's character and high reputation in the Party would have been a considerable asset. The idea never got off the ground and I only mention it in order to record Wood's own endearing and typically modest reply when the suggestion was made to him. 'Some of my friends,' he said, 'have ideas above my station.'

There was, however, one other possibility whose name had at once occurred to those of us who had worked closely with him – Edward du Cann, the best chairman the 1922 Committee had had in living memory, untarred by the failures of the Heath administration, of which he had not been a member, and a man of great charm and ability, universally popular in the Parliamentary Party. We had to find a candidate who could command wide support and he seemed a likely choice if he would consent to stand.

The idea had occurred to me immediately after the October poll, when I realized that Heath's downfall was inevitable. I discussed it with Peter Tapsell, whom I met by chance on 15 October, a week before the re-assembly of Parliament. Between us we knew of six or seven colleagues who were also interested in du Cann as a candidate. I invited them to come and have a drink at my flat on 22 October and we agreed that I should approach him, which I did the following day, to find out if he would stand. He did not reject the idea out of hand, but said he would only consider it if there was evidence of wider support.

Further private meetings of what became known as the du Cann group were held during November, with a gradually increasing membership, which eventually reached over twenty-five in number. I took the chair on these occasions and reported progress to du Cann afterwards. He attended none of the meetings himself and always made it clear that he was a most reluctant runner and would only become a candidate if no electable alternative to Heath came forward for the first ballot.

The existence of the group and its purpose quickly became known at Westminster, where no secrets can be kept for long, and, perhaps to disarm a potential opponent, Heath soon offered Edward du Cann a place in his Shadow Cabinet. After being ignored for eight years, it was not surprising that Du Cann declined this overdue and oddly timed promotion.

There was one obvious disadvantage, which I did not disguise from du Cann and of which he was himself very conscious. We recognized that his City image might be a liability in the country and the group decided that enquiries should be made. We felt that if du Cann became leader of the Party and if anything came to light later to his or his firm's discredit, it would be a grave embarrassment not only to him personally but to the Party as a whole. We did not for a moment question his own business integrity, but in public life guilt by association can be almost as damaging as a personal involvement.

When I mentioned these doubts to du Cann, he immediately urged me to make the most searching enquiries. I therefore called to see an old friend, the chairman of one of the leading and most reputable merchant banks in Britain. He was unenthusiastic about some of his business connections, but confirmed that nothing was known in the City against Edward du Cann himself. In the meantime two other members of our group were making enquiries of their own. Neither discovered anything to du Cann's discredit.

At about this time it was being said in Parliament that Transport House had a dossier on du Cann's business activities which would be used to damage the Conservative Party if he became its leader. No one ever produced any hard facts, or evidence of any kind, to substantiate these rumours, but it seems likely that this campaign of quiet but persistent denigration was part of the strategy adopted by some of Heath's adherents to prejudice the prospects of any potential candidate. Margaret Thatcher was also attacked as soon as she announced her candidature.

It was impossible to launch any campaign in support of du Cann as long as he declined to declare himself a runner. The group tried to bring matters to a head by sending him a formal letter, drafted at a meeting held at the House of Commons on 19 December, which read as follows:

Now that the procedure for electing a new leader has been devised, we feel that it is not only important that there should be an election fairly soon, but that the Party should have the opportunity of choosing from those best able to shoulder this burden.

For some time it has been increasingly obvious to a number of us that you have the qualities which are required in a new leader: your warmth, your ability to present our case forcefully and sympathetically, your skill as chairman and, above all, the affection in which you are held by your colleagues, make it essential, as we see it, that you should offer yourself for the leadership of our Party. Indeed, we consider it is your duty to do so.

We know that it has not been your wish to stand for election, but during the space for reflection that the Christmas recess will bring, we ask you to consider your position and what we have said, and we earnestly hope that you will feel able to allow your name to go forward on the first ballot when nominations are made.

This was signed by fifteen colleagues, the only members of the group able to attend this hastily convened meeting on the eve of the recess. I delivered it by hand that evening to du Cann's house in Lord North Street and received a reply the next day, promising to consider the matter carefully over the Christmas holiday. He added, however, that Margaret Thatcher's decision to stand had made him even more reluctant to do so.

At du Cann's suggestion, he and Mrs Thatcher had talked the matter over and agreed that neither would oppose the other. They both realized that a credible candidate who could command support must come forward on the first ballot. Margaret Thatcher had had the courage to do so and du Cann was content to give her his backing, but at that time he still looked the more electable of the two and she would have stood down if he had agreed to run. It was for this reason that we still persisted in our attempts to persuade him to accept nomination.

Following a visit to the du Cann's home in Somerset at the end of December I formed the clear impression that he had decided not to stand and this was confirmed when I went for a ride next morning with his wife, Sallie. She was against him running for family reasons: she has no political ambitions and prefers country to London life; she had not been happy when he was a Minister and later chairman of the Party; and she dreaded the security precautions which would have surrounded her three young children had du Cann become leader of the Opposition and subsequently Prime Minister, although she would of course have supported him whatever he decided.

A talk with du Cann as soon as Parliament re-assembled on 13 January convinced me that his decision was final and irrevocable. Apart from family considerations, there were strong business reasons against any closer involvement in politics at that moment. The property market was falling catastrophically at the time and Keyser

Ullman was experiencing difficulties as a result of its past lending policies. In these circumstances du Cann felt he should continue as its chairman rather than disengage immediately, as he would have been obliged to do if elected as leader of the Party.

I convened a meeting on the evening of 15 January 1975, attended by about twenty-five of the group, to tell them of his decision. At our previous meeting just before Christmas, when du Cann's candidature had begun to look increasingly doubtful, Airey Neave, who had long been a friend of Margaret Thatcher's and greatly admired her qualities, had put forward the suggestion that, if du Cann decided not to stand, the group should transfer its support to her. He now reverted to this proposal and asked me to continue as its chairman and run her campaign.

If one thought, as I did, that Ted Heath was almost certain to be defeated by any other strong candidate, it was clearly in my own interest to accept Neave's invitation. I was not so sure that it would be in Margaret Thatcher's. I did not at that time know her at all well and although I had every intention of voting for her on the first ballot, but I was still uncertain whether to support her on the second ballot, if it came to that, I wanted to see what other candidates might enter the lists at that stage before committing myself. To do justice to the person one is working for, I believe one's commitment must be total and unqualified in a matter of this kind. I was not sure that mine would be and I therefore declined Airey Neave's suggestion and instead proposed that he should take the chair himself for the rest of the meeting and persuade as many of our group as possible to transfer their allegiance to Mrs Thatcher. There was some discussion and in the end about fifteen out of the twenty-five members present agreed to give active help to Neave in his campaign. They proved an invaluable, indeed essential, nucleus of support for Margaret Thatcher.

Edward du Cann had earlier informed me, to my amazement, that although she had been a potential candidate since the end of November, Margaret Thatcher had not even thought of recruiting any organization and her only declared supporters were Fergus Montgomery and William Shelton. Shelton was relatively junior in the Parliamentary Party and Montgomery was departing next day on a pre-arranged visit to South Africa from which he was not due to return until after the first ballot had been decided. This was to take place in less than three weeks, on Tuesday, 4 February. There was no time to be lost and Airey Neave did not lose any. He made immediate contact with Bill Shelton and together they assembled one of the most efficient and best organized teams ever recruited for an operation of this kind. In the end it comprised as many as fifty Members, but the effective nerve centre was small and close-knit and was run throughout by Neave and Shelton. They worked hard and in complete harmony.

For some time after the October election, Margaret Thatcher had been diffident about her own qualifications for the leadership of the Party. She knew her experience in high office was limited and that she had very little knowledge of foreign and Commonwealth affairs. Her ambition was to be the first woman Chancellor of the Exchequer, not to be leader of the Opposition or Prime Minister. But she was aware that the Parliamentary Party wanted a change and that there had to be an acceptable alternative. She would not have stood if either Keith Joseph or Edward du Cann had come forward, but when they both declined, she realized that someone must oppose Heath on the first ballot. As soon as she had decided to do so, she went to see Ted Heath to tell him. This required some moral courage, a quality she does not lack. She knew she was putting her head on the political chopper, but she did not hesitate. Understandably, her reception by the leader was cold, abrupt and very short. The interview lasted exactly one and a half minutes.

Soon afterwards stories began to circulate to her detriment: 'Thatcher the snatcher' (the withdrawal of free school milk when she was Minister of Education) was revived in the press and an interview allegedly advising pensioners to hoard household goods against rising prices was given wide publicity. But these were pin-pricks, not deterrents. In any event, she was far too busy to worry about her public image. She had work to do in Parliament, with which her candidature for the leadership could not interfere.

To many of us who remembered Ted Heath's own leadership election in 1965, one of his most surprising actions was his appointment of Margaret Thatcher to lead the Opposition team for the committee stage of the Finance Bill upstairs. It was from this base that he had himself gained the Parliamentary *réclame* which was a significant factor in his defeat of Reggie Maudling after Alec Douglas-Home's resignation. It seemed a hostage to fortune to give an opponent the same opportunity.

Perhaps this aberration can be explained by the intellectual self-confidence in his make-up. He had a high (and justified) opinion of his own abilities and thought his rivals for the leadership were, by comparison, inadequate. It is an error into which others have fallen in the past. Lord Randolph Churchill forgot Goschen. To be fair to Edward Heath, he did not try to cling to the leadership for purely personal reasons. He genuinely believed he was the best Conservative leader available to serve the interests of the Party and the country.

Many Members of Parliament shared this view, but not the majority. There were two distinct strands of opposition – the political and the personal. Some, mainly on the right wing of the Party, were critical of his policies. They included both the monetarist followers of Sir Keith Joseph and others who had been enthusiastic supporters of the so-called 'Selsdon' style of Conservatism. This, they complained, had been eroded or abandoned by the U-turns and policy changes which events had forced or influenced Heath to make.

His personal critics were more numerous. They consisted of the disappointed and of those who disliked him. In any Party there are people whose ambitions exceed their abilities and who have not therefore been given the preferment to which they consider themselves entitled. As the number of aspirants is always greater than the number of posts available, there is not much a leader can do about them except, in suitable cases, to make judicious use of the honours system. Perhaps in reaction to its arguable over-use by Harold Macmillan, Ted Heath scarcely bothered with this form of political patronage.

Most of the more junior Conservative Members did not, however, expect honours or employment. They would simply like to have been recognized by sight, known by name and occasionally spoken to. The truth is that Ted Heath was not friendly enough, or even polite enough, to nearly enough of his followers in the Parliamentary Party. The different categories of critics combined in their resolve to teach him a lesson and at least force a second ballot.

Nominations for the election had to be in by 30 January. They consisted of Edward Heath, Margaret Thatcher and Hugh Fraser. Fraser's candidature was a surprise to some Members. This scion of a noble Scottish house is a charming, politically impetuous, slightly eccentric Highland aristocrat, who sits for a constituency in the English Midlands. Although he is a Privy Councillor and had been a middle-rank Minister in Macmillan's government, he had never sat in Cabinet or Shadow Cabinet and cannot have expected to become leader of the Party. His purpose in standing was to refocus Conservative thinking along more traditional Tory lines. What has failed, he contended, is not capitalism but 'the multi-welfare interventionist State, which has created the weakest economy in Western Europe', and he blamed Heath's government as much as Wilson's for Britain's economic ills. His unexceptionable platform was the defence of the unity of the kingdom, the preservation of the constitution and the supremacy of Parliament which 'has been overwhelmed by a mass of unnecessary legislation and by the centralization of executive power'. He called for a return to more identifiable Tory leadership and to Tory policies based on Tory principles. He had no campaign organization, did no canvassing for votes and had received sixteen when the result of the first ballot was declared.

The real struggle was between Edward Heath and Margaret Thatcher. Their backgrounds, totally different to Fraser's, are not dissimilar. Ted Heath's father was a master builder in Broadstairs, Margaret Thatcher's a respected grocer in Grantham. The democratization of the Tory Party in Parliament, which began in the early 1950s, has only reached the leadership level in the last decade.

Edward Heath and Margaret Thatcher both owe much to their parents and to their hard-working, Christian upbringing. They reflect in their own century the precepts laid down by Samuel Smiles in his Victorian classic, *Self-help*. Each achieved a scholarship or bursary to Oxford, where Heath became president of the Union and Mrs Thatcher president of the University Conservative Association. Both are self-made, although, of the two Margaret Thatcher seems to have achieved this rather more easily and naturally. The Conservative Party has always been evolutionary in men as well as measures and has had the good sense to accept and use ability whatever its origins. Disraeli is an obvious earlier example.

The leadership campaign was run in both camps, especially Mrs Thatcher's, in low-key. It was impossible for Ted Heath, as leader of the Party, to do much personal electioneering. His main involvement was to give a series of small lunch, drink and dinner parties, which looked a little too obvious and were probably counter-productive. His rather rare visits to the Members' smoking room were unrewarding because, as a friend of his put it to me, he could not talk about unimportant things to unimportant people. It bored and embarrassed him.

One young Member, whom he had never addressed before, was startled when he felt a hand on his shoulder and turned to find the leader of the Party offering him a drink at the bar. Heath's somewhat forced bonhomie did nothing to improve this unlikely gesture. Yet he is not normally an insincere man.

He is often more at ease with groups of people outside the House of Commons than with individual members of it. When Tim Kitson took him to meet some small farmers in his Yorkshire constituency, they loved him. He enjoys talking about music or sailing, but only about politics at his own intellectual level and to people who understand and can contribute to the subject under discussion.

Peter Walker would have been prepared to act as campaign manager, as he had done so successfully in 1965. In fact, it was run on this occasion by Tim Kitson and Kenneth Baker and Walker's principal part in it was to produce an over-optimistic list of adherents. He was not alone in this. Almost all the reports reaching Heath were too hopeful.

Kitson recruited a small group of six colleagues to help identify support. There was no overt canvassing for votes. The method employed was simply to 'collect the voices', but it may have been a mistake to leave the conduct of this operation mainly to those known by everyone to be most closely associated with Heath. When one of his Parliamentary Private Secretaries approached an ambitious young MP on behalf of the leader of the Party, the temptation to say 'Yes, of course I shall support Ted' must have been considerable. I know of several younger Members who had no intention of voting for him, but who preferred not to say so and replied instead that they had not yet made up their minds. As a result the supporters and doubtfuls were certainly overestimated. The canvass showed 129 'certainties' and seventeen 'hopefuls'. Tim Kitson thought Heath's vote would probably be between 125 and 130 and that 133 was the maximum he could expect on the first ballot. Even if this had been achieved, it would have meant that the leader had lost the confidence of more than half the Parliamentary Party.

The misleading impression created by the canvass was enhanced by many of Heath's friends, who thought and said that his ability and experience were so outstanding that Margaret Thatcher could not conceivably be a danger. Some of them proclaimed openly that he was winning easily. This was an error because most Members did not want him to win and it reinforced their resolve to make sure he would not.

Airey Neave's campaign was more sophisticated. He is an interesting politician, ideally qualified to manage an enterprise of this kind. He is a quiet man, calm, cool and unruffled, who speaks in a soft voice and seldom wastes words.

He had been to see Ted Heath in the middle of December with the suggestion that he should stand down to avoid the humiliation of defeat. Heath declined sharply. He did not believe Margaret Thatcher could constitute a serious threat. This may explain the ill-judged opportunity he gave her to shine in the committee on the Finance Bill. He then gave Neave a lecture on the impropriety of the 1922 Executive, of which Neave was a member, trying to 'take over' the Party. He had not apparently realized that we accurately reflected the views of our Parliamentary colleagues, upon whose support his leadership depended.

In truth, throughout the whole leadership crisis, the Executive – largely due to the statesmanlike chairmanship of Edward du Cann – maintained a remarkable degree of stability in the Party. We all trusted each other and there was never a serious disagreement or a self-seeking thought in our discussions. At no time in its history had the Executive been so important or so united.

It was a loss when Airey Neave retired from the Committee, but du Cann was concerned to preserve our collective neutrality and thought it better for a campaign manager, so closely associated with one of the candidates, not to remain a member.

Before Neave assumed control, there was very little declared or positive support for Margaret Thatcher. Most members were reluctant to commit themselves, many thought she was unelectable and a few were openly anti-feminist. Neave built rapidly on the support he had inherited from the du Cann group. Those whose political sympathies lay with Keith Joseph now realized that Margaret Thatcher was their best available alternative and volunteered their help. But this was not confined to the right wing. Neave's own position is a little to the left of centre and he was careful to recruit assistance from a broad cross-section of the Party.

Bill Shelton was an invaluable lieutenant. His voting assessments, compiled every few days from 21 January until the poll, were increasingly encouraging. It became clear that Margaret Thatcher was gaining ground at every count and, by the time the first ballot was held, Shelton judged her pledged votes to be 122 and estimated Ted Heath's at the same figure. There were still some, though far fewer, doubtfuls and it was difficult to assess the number of deliberate abstentions, absentees and Fraser supporters. Even Shelton did not forecast Mrs Thatcher's final total.

Airey Neave was very cautious. When I asked him how the campaign was going, he replied, 'Margaret is doing very well, but not quite well enough.' It was the perfect answer, no doubt repeated to all enquirers. The impression created was that she was well worth support, but needed more. The effect upon the doubtfuls was exactly as Neave intended – it was no use abstaining or voting for Hugh Fraser: anyone who wanted to stop Heath must vote for Mrs Thatcher.

Neave's tactics were shrewd and quite simple. There was no canvassing. He did not attack her opponents, either in the first or second ballot, and instructed his assistants not to do so. Their job was to ascertain support and above all to identify the doubtfuls. This was done by giving each member of the team three or four of their own personal friends to approach in apparently casual conversation. Unlike Heath, Margaret Thatcher wisely did no entertaining. Her role was to see small groups of selected doubtfuls and answer their questions on policy. This was effective and won over many who had been hesitant.

No professional public relations experts were employed, but, as Mrs Thatcher's prospects improved, press interest became more intense and Neave realized he needed some outside help, especially to deal with the mass of newspaper enquiries. On Sunday morning, 26 January, he telephoned Joan Hall at her home in Yorkshire and asked if she was free to come to London. She at once got in touch with Mrs Thatcher, who also urged her to come if she could and added, 'But what about your finances?' It was a considerate, human thought. She arrived in London on Tuesday, 28 January, and went straight to work in Airey Neave's room at the House of Commons.

Joan Hall had been MP for Keighley from 1970 until her defeat in the February 1974 election. During this period, she had come to know Margaret Thatcher well and was one of her admirers. She had been much impressed by a visit Mrs Thatcher paid to Keighley, as Secretary of State for Education in the summer of 1972, when she took the trouble to talk to everyone, including the least important, in the most friendly and informal way. She has a genuine charm and warmth, important in any voluntary organization.

For the last week before the first ballot, Joan Hall dealt with all the press and other telephone calls, acted as chauffeur for Margaret and helped her at home. The telephone and front door bells never stopped ringing. Most women cannot compartmentalize their minds as easily as men, but Margaret Thatcher has this facility. At one moment she may be a housewife rushed off her feet with domestic chores; at the next she can take a large press conference with total calm and self-control.

As 4 February, the date of the first ballot, drew nearer, the atmosphere in the Parliamentary Party became more tense and the election inevitably and increasingly became the main subject of conversation between colleagues.

Most Members of Parliament had organized meetings of their constituency executive councils during the month of January, in order to obtain the views of their leading supporters; but the majority of these were held before the list of nominations was known, so they were of rather limited value and many, as in my own association, were indecisive. A more up-to-date assessment of constituency opinion was soon to be available.

At 2.30 p.m. on Monday, 3 February, the representatives of the peers and the National Union came to room 14 in the House of commons to report the results of their soundings to the Executive of the 1922 Committee. Peter Carrington was abroad, so Michael St Aldwyn spoke for the peers. He told us that they had not wished to take a formal vote, so he had inserted a notice on the whip, inviting his colleagues to send their views in writing. This was issued to every member of the House of Lords in receipt of the Conservative whip. There was a fifty per cent response for the first ballot, which in fact represented seventy-five per cent of those who were at all regular in their attendance. The outcome was not given to the Executive in precise figures, but St Aldwyn informed us that there had been a large majority for Ted Heath.

A more detailed report was made by Sir John Taylor on behalf of the National Union. He had asked the area chairmen to telephone each of their constituency chairmen, who in turn made immediate contact with their branch chairmen and with the officers and members of the executive councils in the local associations. These enquiries only began on the previous Thursday and the answers were required by Sunday, so the work had to be done quickly, but it was well organized and was all completed in forty-eight hours.

In most areas it was very thorough. Some constituencies checked as many as 1000 opinions and many obtained the views of 400 or 500 of their members. No doubt most chairmen were content, as in my own division, to talk to the members of their executive councils, but even these would have numbered fifty or sixty in each constituency; so the poll of Party workers was a reasonably large one and we were informed that the voting was much the same in proportion, whatever the extent of the canvass. Nearly every constituency took part and, as with the peers, the result was a large majority for Heath. There had been reservations and criticisms of his leadership in several of the divisions which, by a majority, had returned a pro-Heath vote; but the overall result was clearly in his favour. The franchise however, lay not with the constituency associations but with the Parliamentary Party. A separate assessment was given for Scotland, but it did not differ substantially from that for England and Wales.

Before these reports were made, Edward du Cann had discussed with the Executive and with Michael St Aldwyn and the representatives of the National Union the procedure for making known the results of the soundings to the Parliamentary Party, so that Members of Parliament could take them into account before deciding how to cast their votes in the actual election next day. It had been agreed that, for the remainder of Monday afternoon and evening, every member of the Executive should be available in the House and readily accessible to any colleague who asked for the information. We could also volunteer it to any Member we met. Several did in fact consult me that day. In addition, the area chairmen had notified MPs of the results in their own areas. In these ways there is no doubt at all that Members knew, or could have known, the outcome of the soundings before they themselves voted. There was also an establishment attempt, through the newspapers, to pressurize the Party in the House of Commons by stressing the strength of support for Heath in the constituencies.

Any Members absent abroad had been notified that their votes would be counted if they were received, by letter or telegram, by the chairman of the 1922 Committee not later than the morning of 4 February.

Members of Parliament are not delegates and although some may have been influenced by the views of their leading constituency supporters, I suspect that most had by this time made up their own minds and did not change them. I had no inhibitions myself because I had, in effect, been given a free hand by my constituency executive

171

to vote as I thought best. My supporters took the view, I believe rightly, that I knew the qualities and personalities of the rival candidates better than they did and should therefore form my own judgement. I voted without any hesitation for Margaret Thatcher. No doubt out of loyalty to Ted Heath, the large majority of the Shadow Cabinet did not. Indeed, it is probable that only Keith Joseph supported her on the first ballot, though Norman St John Stevas voted for her in the second ballot after Heath had withdrawn from the contest. She would certainly not have achieved the leadership under the old consultative system because there would have been no consensus for her in the then Shadow Cabinet.

The election was held between 12 noon and 3.30 p.m. in room 14 and was supervised by the chairman and officers of the 1922 Committee. Each member received a ballot paper as he entered the room, on which the names of the three candidates were printed. Having marked his X against the name of his choice, he put the ballot paper in a black box at the end of the room. This culmination of so much argument and activity, spread over a period of four months, took less than half a minute of each Member's time.

The result was announced by Edward du Cann at 4 p.m. The voting was as follows:

Margaret Thatcher	130
Edward Heath	119
Hugh Fraser	16
Abstentions or absent	11

No one had achieved the magic number of 139 votes, so a second ballot now became necessary.

There was a milling throng of Members and lobby journalists outside room 14 just before du Cann came to the door to announce the figures. Each candidate had sent a 'runner' to obtain these in advance of the declaration and to convey them privately to his principal. When Tim Kitson hurried out looking grim and distressed, it was an indication that Heath had not polled as well as he expected and presumably had not secured the 139 votes required for an outright victory; but not even the most optimistic of Margaret Thatcher's supporters can have expected that she would actually achieve a convincing lead on the first ballot. There was a moment of almost awed silence as we absorbed the figures and realized the implications of what we had done; then a buzz of excited comment and speculation.

Heath's ten-year reign was over. It was the end of an era in Conservative politics and no one could tell what the next decade would bring – certainly a new style of leadership; hopefully a more successful one. The Conservative Party does not like defeat and ruthlessly devours its leaders when they fail.

If the result was a triumph for Margaret Thatcher, it was a tragedy for Ted Heath. No one could have worked with greater dedication for his Party and for the country; yet it had all ended in the personal humiliation of rejection by those he had sought so steadfastly to serve. This was the fate which the 1922 Executive and so many of his friends had feared in the immediate aftermath of the October election.

Willie Whitelaw, Jim Prior, John Peyton and Kenneth Baker were with him in his room when Tim Kitson brought the news. It was a great shock to him, but initially he took it very well. Without a wife or children to turn to in time of trouble, Ted Heath must sometimes be a lonely man, and even those of us who, like myself, had contributed to his downfall, could scarcely bear to think of his bitter disappointment. Like most of my colleagues, I wrote him a letter of genuine sympathy and soon received a magnanimous and generous reply in his own hand.

Heath had suffered a year of almost unrelieved disaster: he had lost the premiership of Britain and two general elections; his yacht, *Morning Cloud*, had foundered in a storm and his godson, one of the crew, had been drowned; a bomb had damaged his house and destroyed the chair he usually sat in, so that he had nowhere to live for the next two months. Tim Kitson came to his aid with the offer of his own flat until the house could be repaired.

Soon after the result of the first ballot was announced, I went along to Airey Neave's room, only a few doors from my own, to congratulate him on the brilliant campaign he had conducted for Margaret. By chance she was there too, with Neave, Joan Hall and Bill Shelton. As soon as I entered the room, she jumped to her feet, kissed me on both cheeks and said, 'Isn't it exciting, Nigel, isn't it exciting?' It was a spontaneous reaction, typical of her whole attitude to people. Little gestures like these, which create affection and personal as opposed to political loyalty, stand leaders in good stead in times of adversity. She owes much to Airey Neave, but he had very good material to work on.

173

Edward Heath wisely withdrew from the contest after his defeat and appointed Robert Carr as temporary leader of the Opposition for one week until the second ballot could be held. The field was now open for those who had felt unable to stand against him. A colleague commented a little unkindly that the other candidates were Margaret Thatcher's greatest asset. All are able and well-liked, but each appeared to lack one of more of the qualities required for the highest position.

The best known to the public was William Whitelaw. He is the most friendly and approachable of men and had been a successful Chief Whip, an agreeable leader of the House of Commons and a good Secretary of State for Northern Ireland at an exceptionally difficult time. Indeed, he must have been almost the first English politician to have come out of Ireland with an enhanced reputation.

Whitelaw's personal popularity in Parliament was an asset, but in the mood of the moment the fact that, after Heath's fall, he was the establishment candidate may not have been to his advantage. He was too closely identified with the old regime and with the old policies to be acceptable to those who wanted the leadership to have a new look. Nevertheless, had Heath retired in October, Whitelaw was at that time his most likely successor. The long delay, during which as a non-runner he could not campaign, was detrimental to his chances and allowed Margaret Thatcher to emerge and take the stage as the only serious contender. This was not of course Ted Heath's intention. He would have preferred Whitelaw to succeed him. Although the style of leadership would have been quite different (and more acceptable to most) the policies would have remained the same.

The trade union leaders respect Heath, but they like and trust Whitelaw, hold him in the highest regard, and speak of him with personal affection. This is not surprising. He is an honest and very likeable personality, completely frank, open and uncontrived. Characteristics of this kind tend to make a man vulnerable, but they bring out the best in others and no one would willingly let Willie Whitelaw down. It was significant that, with only one exception, everyone who had ever worked for him, either as a junior minister or Parliamentary Private Secretary, came forward to help in his campaign. They included Sir Paul Bryan, Christopher Tugendhat and David Howell. Tim Raison and Nicholas Scott were also supporters, but when they were made members of the Shadow Cabinet in October, they felt inhibited in the amount of assistance they could give him.

Despite his many qualities of character, Whitelaw would have had weaknesses as a Party leader. He knows nothing about economics. Some economists do not consider this a disadvantage, but it cannot be an asset in these days. He is not an inspiring speaker and his performances in the House of Commons or on a public platform, although adequate, are seldom eloquent. He cannot arouse the faithful or fire the imagination of the public; and his television appearances, though friendly and avuncular, are pedestrian. He has no cutting edge. He is a shrewd politician and understands how to handle the House of Commons, but he would not claim to be of the same intellectual calibre as Edward Heath or Margaret Thatcher. He could have supplied the warmth and compassion, but not the firm, thrustful leadership the Party also needs and demands. Some of his advisers thought he should try and create a more dynamic and purposeful impression; but he took the view, I am sure correctly, that he could not change his personality overnight and that it would be unwise to attempt such a metamorphosis.

Paul Bryan called a meeting of twelve known supporters on the evening of 4 February to plan the brief campaign. Thereafter they met at 6 p.m. every day until the second ballot a week later. There was very little time to organize anything and most of the arrangements were improvised at short notice. The new Members did not know Whitelaw, so he made himself available in Nick Scott's room during part of each afternoon to meet them and any others who wished to put questions to him.

By ill luck his secretary was away and he rightly refused to use any Central Office assistance. Michael Mates, who had only entered the House in October, volunteered to act as his ADC. Mates had recently retired from the regular Army as a young colonel and was a fortunate and extremely efficient addition to the team. His task was to organize the week and fit in press and television interviews with other prearranged commitments. The televised spectacle of William Whitelaw washing dishes, probably for the first time in his life, looked out of character and was. He agreed to do it without thinking, to please a persistent programme producer, but later television interviews with Michael Charlton and David Dimbleby were more serious and more effective.

On Friday, 7 February, Michael Mates, at no notice at all, contrived to produce a constituency audience for him of 300 people. He made a very good speech, in the preparation of which David Howell

175

gave him valuable help. Howell also organized much of his press publicity.

The following day he and Margaret Thatcher were due to speak at a Young Conservative conference at Eastbourne. Margaret took the opportunity to make a key-note leadership speech, which she had not been billed to do. Willie, perhaps more scrupulously, thought it his duty to the YCs to talk about devolution, the subject he had been asked to deal with, but which had little relevance to the leadership contest. Not unnaturally, this cost Whitelaw the limelight and gave his opponent the newspaper headlines. But by this time the tide was flowing for Margaret Thatcher and Whitelaw knew it.

One allegation made against him was quite unjustified. I remember a meeting of the Party's National Executive, on which I serve, when several members of it were strongly critical of candidates who, they suggested, were afraid to run against Heath on the first ballot and instead 'hid behind the lady's skirts' to see what would happen before they ventured to enter the contest. This oblique attack, made in his presence, was hurtful and very unfair to Whitelaw. No one who knows him could ever accuse him of cowardice or opportunism.

Paul Bryan's tally of potential support was unreliable because of defections in the last few days. The tallest oak in the forest had fallen and after her unexpected lead on the first ballot, Margaret Thatcher was virtually unstoppable. The only doubt was whether the anti-Heath, but not necessarily pro-Thatcher, votes would remain firm. In fact, they never wavered and more were added. Bryan's final count for Whitelaw was depressing but realistic. He estimated a total of eighty-one votes, only two more than the actual poll. The last-minute multiplicity of peripheral candidates lowered morale in the Whitelaw camp and cost him more votes than it cost Margaret Thatcher, but in the end made no difference as she achieved an overall majority.

Willie Whitelaw never expected to win on the second ballot, but he thought he might have succeeded on a third. This worried him because he knew that such a result would have divided the Party, not only in the House but in the country. People would have thought it incredible if, having led in two ballots, Margaret Thatcher had been defeated by second preference votes in the third. The same thought had occurred to others and influenced some who were still hesitant to vote for Mrs Thatcher on 11 February.

The two leading candidates had a good personal relationship and Whitelaw was anxious that there should be no bitterness after the election. He instructed his supporters to say nothing detrimental about Margaret and he accepted his defeat gracefully and without any trace of rancour or resentment. He knew the Party wanted a change, and that he could not give it as new a look as his rival. In retrospect he acknowledged that the outcome was in the best interests of the Party and is content with it. You cannot become the leader of a great political Party unless you very much want to lead it. Perhaps Willie Whitelaw, like Rab Butler, did not want it enough. He is a very generous and magnanimous man and his loyalty to the new leadership is a guarantee of cohesion and stability in the Conservative ranks.

The next candidate to enter the field was James Prior. For reasons of personal loyalty and obligation, he could not possibly have opposed Heath, but he was now free to accept nomination and several of his friends urged him to do so, in order to give the Party a wider choice. They also argued that, if he did not stand and instead supported Whitelaw, it might look as though the establishment was deliberately combining against Margaret Thatcher.

Jim Prior is florid, almost bucolic, in appearance, but this belies a shrewd political brain. He had been a loyal and efficient Parliamentary Private Secretary to Ted Heath before becoming a Minister and is well liked in the Parliamentary Party. His candidature was conducted in deliberately low profile at his own insistence. It so happened that his leading supporter, Michael Jopling, had influenza throughout the short second ballot period, so little, if anything, was done to promote his claims. Jopling thinks Prior would have secured twice as many votes if the poll had been held earlier and confirms that opinion veered strongly towards Margaret Thatcher in the last few days.

One of the reasons for this may have been a feeling of resentment that the proliferation of new candidates was an unnecessary distraction, which could lead to fragmentation and to the danger of the final outcome depending on second preference votes. This view was so strongly held that Edward du Cann was asked to discuss with the candidates, other than Whitelaw, whether they thought it necessary and appropriate to stand. He did so, but without effect.

There could in fact have been even more entrants, but Maurice Macmillan and Julian Amery, each of whom had some support, decided not to allow their names to go forward. Amery told a political correspondent of *The Times* that he thought 'the scramble for the

leadership . . . is damaging to the dignity and to the unity of the Party'
and that he did not feel justified in adding to it.

John Peyton looked at the matter differently. He has a great
admiration for Heath and would never have opposed him. Indeed,
he nominated Heath for re-election in the first ballot; but after his
withdrawal Peyton thought there would be no harm in seeking a
platform for the views he wished to express. He is a combative,
caustic and often witty Parliamentarian of great experience; no
respecter of persons, least of all of Labour Ministers, and not at all
the sort of man who would have stood for reasons of personal
aggrandizement. He did not canvass or campaign in any way and
his candidature left no scars.

Sir Geoffrey Howe was the last to enter the lists. He had been on
a lecture tour in Canada and did not return to England until 3
February, the day before the first ballot. He voted for Heath and,
after the former leader's withdrawal, was undecided whether to run
himself or not. He is a distinguished QC, with enlightened views on
social policy, but he had not been in Parliament for very long and
was not well known to the general public. His friends urged him to
stand in order to obtain greater exposure to the world outside
Westminster and to put down a 'marker' for the future.

Howe had the support of the Bow group and of nine or ten
Members of Parliament, including Anthony Buck, David Walder,
Kenneth Clarke and Ian Gow. They thought he could bridge the gap
between the progressive element in the Party and the monetarists, on
the basis that, while sympathetic with Margaret Thatcher's views, he
had a more open economic approach and a more liberal philosophy.
Just as Jim Prior was an alternative to Willie Whitelaw, Howe was
the left-of-centre alternative to Margaret Thatcher. There was, however, no concerted plan to split her vote. His adherents hoped he
would get enough support to be the third runner and gain a respect-
able position in a third ballot if that became necessary.

Howe did not campaign himself, but was available to anyone who
wished to see him to discuss his political outlook. He would not have
stood if Whitelaw had been Margaret Thatcher's only opponent, but
when the others entered the ring he thought he should do so too. In
the result, he made a somewhat disappointing showing, but his
candidature did him no harm, as became evident when he was
appointed Shadow Chancellor soon afterwards.

Meanwhile the lady herself was going from strength to strength.

Airey Neave had gallantly described her as 'the promise of Spring' and her unaffected friendliness and charm were making new converts every day. The male prejudice against a woman as leader of the Party may still have been felt by a few, but was no longer openly admitted. Her advisers had made only one error, which was to admit a television camera to the private champagne celebration party in Neave's flat at Westminster Gardens after the result of the first ballot was announced. This struck a discordant note at a moment when there was a natural wave of sympathy for Heath in the chagrin of his rejection. It was an insensitive mistake, due to lack of thought.

Bill Shelton was a little shaken by the lack of first ballot support in the constituency associations, revealed by Sir John Taylor's report to the 1922 Executive; but his House of Commons figures were clear, accurate and encouraging and they were the ones that mattered.

On Monday, 10 February, the eve of the second ballot, the BBC invited all the candidates to appear on *Panorama*. Wisely, Margaret Thatcher enquired what form the programme was to take. As by now the front-runner, she was to appear first, followed by short interviews with people in the street, picked at random, and then by each of the other candidates in turn. She was to have no right of reply. As she hesitated, the BBC producer made the mistake of becoming somewhat peremptory. That decided her. 'I will not be bullied,' she said, and she won't be, ever. To those who were watching the programme, her non-appearance was a disappointment; but she had a pre-arranged commitment to see a group of still hesitant Members at the House of Commons that evening and they were the electorate, not the television viewers.

Nominations for the second ballot had to be in by Thursday, 6 February. Michael St Aldwyn for the peers and Sir John Taylor for the National Union were obliged to go through the same hurried procedure as they had undertaken for the first ballot a week earlier. This time the response in the Lords was a little over the fifty per cent and in the areas and constituencies, though not quite as extensively canvassed as before, the poll was still very high. The reports were again made to the Executive on the following Monday afternoon, 10 February.

After the first ballot, there had been some resentment in the local associations that their support for Edward Heath had not been reflected in the votes of the Parliamentary party, but on this occasion there was adverse comment about the number of late entrants and

it is interesting to note that the general preference in the constituencies was for Margaret Thatcher in almost exactly the same proportion as the actual vote in the 1922 Committee next day.

The voting procedure on 11 February followed precisely the pattern
of the previous week. I was embarrassed to find myself entering
room 14 to cast my vote at the same moment as Willie Whitelaw. He
is an old and valued friend and it distressed me, and may have hurt
him, that I could not wish him the best of luck, as I normally would
have done, because it would have been too hypocritical just after
marking my ballot paper for Margaret Thatcher. Politics, when
personalized, can be a distasteful business.

I was present in room 14 when Edward du Cann announced the
final figures that afternoon. They were:

Margaret Thatcher	146
William Whitelaw	79
James Prior	19
Geoffrey Howe	19
John Peyton	11

There was no need for a third ballot. Margaret Thatcher had
secured an overall majority. She was now leader of the Opposition,
though not formally the leader of the Conservative Party until
confirmed by the Party meeting at the Europa Hotel a few days
later.

The public and much publicized election for the leadership was
over – to the infinite relief of the Party as a whole and especially of
the members of the 1922 Executive who had, in a sense, initiated and
perforce conducted this invidious, sometimes traumatic, operation.

If the general Conservative reaction to Margaret Thatcher's election was one of relief and, for the majority, of new hope, the attitude
of Labour Members was a mixture of irritation – that, by the choice
of a woman, we might have stolen a march on our opponents – and
speculation as to whether the apparent move to the right, which
Mrs Thatcher's leadership portended, might be electorally advantageous to the Labour Party.

Margaret Thatcher's public life has not left her family unaffected.
Politics are a divisive factor in any marriage, particularly where the
wife is the politician, and for the family a high price is exacted in
human terms. It is no doubt willingly paid, but must still entail an
invasion of privacy for her husband and children. Denis Thatcher is

devoted to his wife and very proud of her, but their home life is inevitably affected by the calls made on her time.

Margaret Thatcher remembers everyone she meets by name and sight, is good with people and cares about them. She is also articulate and can communicate easily and naturally at any level. She understands that in a democracy the ability to persuade other people that your policy is the right one is as important as the policy itself. She has a touch of steel in her character, but her clear, analytical mind is allied to a warm heart. She is a very human person, genuinely interested in others and in the problems which affect and beset their lives. Many leaders have felt the same concern; not all have been able to show it.

Margaret Thatcher's election represented a break with the past and gave the Party the new and more interesting look it needed. Many of her votes came from the younger Members and she drew support not only from the right wing, as I have seen suggested, but from across the political board. I and others who share my views might not have voted for her political approach; we voted with enthusiasm for her personal qualities.

With the exception of Lord Hailsham, Harold Macmillan and Iain Macleod were the last of the Tory romantics and since their day the Conservative leadership, although well-intentioned, has seemed dull and managerial, without style or inspiration. Margaret Thatcher has had the imagination to change this. She understands that the heart is as important in politics as the head, and she speaks clearly, concisely and compassionately to ordinary people in a language they can understand.

No one is perfect and Margaret Thatcher has a problem in overcoming the suburban image she has acquired in some people's eyes. She soon discarded the hats for which Tory ladies were once mockingly derided. It has been more difficult for her to shed the carefully modulated tone of voice which irritates some listeners because they think it sounds simulated and unnatural. In fact, one is not conscious of it in private conversation and, as her confidence increases, her television performance is becoming more relaxed.

In an article in the *Sunday Times* Rebecca West wrote:

Margaret Thatcher's great strength seems to be the better people know her, the better they like her. But of course she has one great disadvantage – she is a daughter of the people and looks trim, as the daughters of the people desire to be. Shirley Williams has such an advantage over her because she's a member of the upper-middle class and can achieve that distraught kitchen-sink-revolutionary look that one cannot get unless one's been to a really good school.

Soon after her election, the new leader made her first appearance at a crowded meeting of the 1922 Committee. She had an almost ecstatic reception when she entered the room and, significantly, even louder and more prolonged applause after she had spoken. This was not so much due to what she said as to the way in which she said it. Her grace and a modest, almost diffident, manner literally charmed hardened old cynics like me, who had seen this sort of thing done before, but seldom so well done. She does not scorn to use her femininity as an asset; and she has style. The Tory Party likes this and had seen very little of it since the days of Harold Macmillan. She had made a good start.

We waited with interest and a slight sense of apprehension for her debut at the Despatch Box for Prime Minister's questions. Harold Wilson was an agile and experienced tactician and a formidable opponent across the floor of the House, who scarcely ever missed an opportunity to score. We need not have worried. Instinctively, Margaret Thatcher has the wisdom to watch and to wait for the right moment. Her interventions are relatively rare, but always crisp, clear and to the point – one point. Most Members try to cover too much ground, so their questions are diffuse and lose impact. Lloyd George used to say that, even in a speech, no back bencher should make more than one point, no Minister more than two and that even Prime Ministers should restrict themselves to a maximum of three points – and preferably to only two!

Immediately after her election, Margaret Thatcher embarked on an exhausting schedule of speeches and public appearances in the country. She was sensitive to the suggestion that her appeal would be confined to the suburbs and quickly disproved this. Great crowds gathered to greet her and her early visits to the north of England and Scotland were like a triumphal progress. Everyone wanted to see and hear her and every minute of every day was committed for weeks ahead. When, in May 1975, the American Ambassador invited her to dinner, she was forced to reply that she had no free evening until the second half of July. She was seriously overworked.

Fortunately, she has the power of total concentration, an immense capacity for work and great physical stamina. This is unusual in a woman and essential in a Party leader under modern conditions.

Margaret Thatcher needs and possesses this asset. She makes very little use of speech-writers and prefers to prepare her own material in whatever time is available. This is often limited to the hours between midnight and three or four in the morning. Even so, she is up again at 7 a.m., ready to start another full day. She can manage for days on end with four hours sleep a night.

This facility stood her in good stead during the committee stage of the 1975 Finance Bill, much of which coincided with her leadership campaign. To those who worked with her on the Bill, her resilience was remarkable. Night after night, and often very late at night, she led the debates with complete clarity of thought and expression; and the following day, apparently untired and always attractive and well dressed, she would embark on an endless round of press conferences, television interviews, public speeches, discussions with colleagues and the dictation of her constituency correspondence. In addition, she received 18,000 letters during the campaign, many of which she dealt with personally. My wife wrote to congratulate her on her victory and received a charming reply in her own hand within three days.

There was one controversial incident after her election which received so much press publicity at the time that the facts should be recorded. On 12 February, the morning after the final result was declared, she went to see Edward Heath at his home in Wilton Street. The visit had only one purpose – to ascertain whether Heath would be willing to join her Shadow Cabinet and if so in what capacity. Until she knew his answer, she could not begin to fill the other positions. She came quickly to the point. 'I have said publicly that I would ask you to join the Shadow Cabinet. Will you do so?' Heath at once declined and added that he intended to spend a period on the back benches. Margaret Thatcher then suggested that he might be willing to take charge of the Conservative Party's European referendum campaign from an official position. Again he refused, but said he would take an active part in the referendum with a private programme of speeches all over the country.

Subsequently Heath denied publicly that he had been offered the Shadow Foreign Secretaryship or any other specific post. This was no doubt technically true, although Margaret Thatcher thought she had offered him anything he wanted and, by implication, the position of Shadow Foreign Secretary, if he would accept it. Given the rather tense atmosphere of the interview, it is arguable that there was a genuine misunderstanding, but, to a senior colleague who was not present, it seemed as though Heath's version of what transpired was 'a quibble and unworthy of someone in his position'.

Even before the leadership contest, relations between the two, although courteous and correct, had never been cordial. One member of the Conservative Cabinet told me that Margaret Thatcher was inclined to be argumentative, over-emphatic and 'rather tiresome' in discussion. A different version was given to me by another senior ex-Minister, who said that she was 'very clear and articulate in Cabinet', and then, as an afterthought, 'Ted didn't always like that.'

The truth is that Edward Heath had run his government in a somewhat authoritarian way, so it would not have been easy for him to serve under anyone, still less under a woman, least of all under Margaret. His experience and stature, even his force of character, would have been an embarrassment to them both and to their colleagues at the meetings of the Shadow Cabinet. There was another personal factor: as long as Keith Joseph was at her right hand as chief policy-maker, it would in any event have been out of the question. Heath and Joseph had disagreed too strongly and too often to work happily together. Under all the circumstances Edward Heath was right to refuse to serve.

Since then, his attitude towards Margaret Thatcher has been less easy to justify. After his notable contribution in the referendum campaign, when he toured the country with a series of powerful and successful speeches, she paid him a most generous public tribute in the House of Commons. I was only a few places from him and was able to watch his response. He sat, granite-faced, staring straight in front, with never a smile or an inclination of the head and without even glancing in her direction or acknowledging her compliments in any way. It seemed an ungracious reaction, which was noticed by everyone and caused much unfavourable comment.

With the passage of time Heath's attitude has not changed. This is both unhelpful to the Party and unfair to Margaret Thatcher, its democratically elected leader. As George Hutchinson wrote in an open letter to Ted Heath in *The Times*, she did not cause the leadership election and did nothing to bring it about; she did not seek to undermine Heath's position beforehand; she simply stood as a candidate when the Parliamentary Party had already and clearly indicated that a majority of its members wanted a change of leader. It is true that Heath did mention her approvingly in his speech at the

1976 Party Conference at Brighton and was much applauded by the delegates for doing so, but it was a tepid reference which disappointed those who had hoped for something warmer and more forthcoming.

Heath himself relied upon the loyal allegiance of Alec Home during the long years of opposition from 1965 to 1970, yet felt unable to grant the same generosity to his own successor. When he was asked in a television interview in July 1976 whether he would for once say something agreeable about Mrs Thatcher, he replied coldly, 'When she became leader of the Party I wished her well and I wished her every success. I don't think anyone can do more than that.' When invited to express an opinion as to whether she would make a good Prime Minister, he merely said it was difficult to know until she actually became Prime Minister. The British people do not like a bad loser and Heath's attitude has done more to damage his own reputation than to harm hers.

Margaret Thatcher came to the leadership without any close knowledge of how the Party machine functions and the initial absence, through ill-health, of Peter Thorneycroft, the new chairman of the Party, made her work-load in this, as in other ways, unusually heavy. She has, however, made a great effort to hold her Shadow Cabinet together. She listens to her colleagues and enjoys the intellectual stimulus of discussion with them. She is not too proud to learn and she learns very quickly.

One early success did much to restore Conservative morale after the two general election defeats and the long-drawn-out battle for the leadership: the Tory victory in the West Woolwich by-election was a tonic for the Party and for Margaret Thatcher, who courageously defied the long-established convention that Party leaders take no part in by-elections. She is not afraid to break with tradition and has more than her share of tenacity and nerve. She inherited the leadership when Party morale was at a low ebb, but in her first six months she showed the quality described by Rab Butler as 'the patience of politics' and nursed the Party back to health and self-confidence.

There followed in September 1975 her successful visit to the USA and then her remarkable speech at the Party Conference that October, which every newspaper and televison commentator described as a triumph – and for once the word was not misused. This one speech justified to the country her choice as leader by the Parliamentary Party and established her authority beyond challenge. There is still a need for her Shadow Cabinet and Parliamentary colleagues to 'sell'

Margaret Thatcher in the constituencies as we successfully sold Harold Macmillan in his early days as leader of the Party.

The Conservative Party, often so much less conservative than the Labour Party, had had the imagination – in International Women's Year – to elect a woman as its leader; but she was chosen despite, not because of, her sex. She was chosen on her merits as the best candidate in the field.

At least seven qualities are required in a national leader: courage, a first-class mind, application, the ability to communicate and persuade, an understanding of people, the power of decision, and good political judgement. I believe Margaret Thatcher has all these and that, by choosing her, the Conservative Party has given the people the chance of electing the first woman Prime Minister of Britain.

APPENDIX I

In 1975 the new consultative arrangements for the constituency associations left many Conservative activists with a sense of grievance. Their main criticism was that Margaret Thatcher's success in the first ballot revealed that Members of Parliament had attached little importance to the strength of support for Edward Heath outside the Palace of Westminster. This complaint cannot be conceded because an expression of opinion is not the same as an instruction; if it was, the MPs would be delegates. At least the constituency associations were able to express their views, which was an advance on the previous arrangements.

A major impetus for giving more power at grass-root level has since occurred with the election by the constituences of David Steel as leader of the Liberal Party. This is an innovation in British politics which could be followed by the two main Parties, though I hope it will not be.

The new rules adopted by the Liberals require candidates for the leadership to be Members of Parliament and to be nominated by one-fifth of all Liberal MPs, or five of them, whichever is less. All paid-up members of a constituency Party are entitled to vote and each constituency gains extra votes where the local Party polled strongly in the last general election and also if it was affiliated to the Party headquarters the previous year. The votes of the constituency are cast in the national poll in the same proportion as the preferences expressed at the local meeting. By keeping the nominations in the hands of Members of Parliament the Parliamentary Party retains an important control. This rule prevents a candidate being imposed on the MPs from outside; indeed it is theoretically possible for the Members to nominate only one candidate, which would effectively debar the constituencies from participating in the election process at all.

It is a matter of opinion whether the new method of choosing their leader has improved the Liberals' image. There was more emphasis on the personalities of the two candidates than on any differences of policy and this is no doubt an inevitable consequence of the system. Although hastily devised, the complicated procedure worked smoothly and efficiently, but the simpler Conservative and Labour leadership elections in 1975 and 1976 were conducted with greater dignity and despatch.

It would be a sharp breach with Conservative tradition to give the Party outside the House a decisive vote in the election of the leader. The National Union, though autonomous and entitled to express views at variance with those of MPs, has never been able to give directions to Members and the Parliamentary Party has always been careful to exclude 'outsiders' from involvement in the election of the leader. When Balfour resigned in 1911, MPs hurried the election of his successor because of their fear that the National Union – due to meet in a few days' time – might intervene. In support of an early decision, Austen Chamberlain, who was one of the contenders, observed:

If the MPs didn't decide on Monday, the Leeds Conference [of the National Union] would take it out of their hands; there would be resolutions, speeches, every kind of lobbying and intrigue. The Party must be summoned to decide at once.

These fears were confirmed half a century later when the announcement of Harold Macmillan's resignation at the Blackpool Conference in 1963 did indeed give rise to considerable confusion, lobbying and intrigue, which was fully publicized by the newspapers and the television. Lord Butler commented in his book, *The Art of the Possible*:

I cannot imagine an atmosphere less suited to such a declaration with scores of journalists, television interviewers, *et hoc genus omne*. It turned Blackpool into a sort of convention *à l'Américaine*.

Two recent attempts to widen decision-making have been prevented. In 1969, the Greater London Young Conservatives in their pamphlet, *Set the Party Free*, complained of the lack of democracy in the Party. They instanced the method of electing the leader, and the leader's sole right to appoint the Cabinet or Shadow Cabinet, the whips and the Party's principal officers. A Review committee was set up under Lord Chelmer to examine ways of making the Party more democratic. Its report recommended greater power for the National Union, though it did not suggest an end to the autonomy of the Party in Parliament. Its most controversial proposal was for the establishment of constituency selection committees, which would be allowed to consider alternative candidates at the time of re-adopting their Member. Not surprisingly, the 1922 Committee opposed this recommendation and it was not implemented, although it has in fact been the practice for many years of the Unionist Party in Northern Ireland.

There was also an attempt by the Executive Committee of the National Union to involve its members directly in the election of the Party leader. In its submission to Sir Alec Douglas-Home's committee in 1974, the

Executive recommended that the eleven area chairmen in England and Wales should form part of the electoral college. This was rejected by the Douglas-Home committee, which, instead, proposed the consultative process whereby local associations would consider the claims of the respective candidates and send their conclusions via the area chairmen to the chairman of the National Executive, who would then pass them on to the Executive of the 1922 Committee.

The Conservative Party's procedures were adopted before the days of a mass electorate and grew gradually outwards as the franchise was extended. In contrast, the Labour Party, based on the trade unions, had at first very few Members in the House of Commons, so there is no tradition of deference to a superior political leadership. Consequently, power is more diffused between the leader, the Parliamentary Labour Party, the National Executive and the annual Conference. But, as the Labour Party attained the status of the official Opposition and its leader became the potential Prime Minister, he assumed a more dominant role and, until recently, there has been no support for the view that his election should be taken away from the Parliamentary Party.

Following the Liberal innovation, it is not surprising that there have been demands for the involvement of the mass membership or the Conference in the selection of the Labour leader. But the Party would be faced with special difficulties if it adopted such a course. In contrast to the Conservative and Liberal Parties, whose membership is of individuals in the constituency associations, the Labour Party also has an affiliated membership through socialist societies, the co-operatives and the trade unions. The unions provide nearly six millions or seven eighths of the membership and would effectively control a leadership election. Indeed, the six largest unions command more than half the total Conference vote; if the block vote system (allowing each union to cast its total vote according to the majority view of the union delegates) was retained, it would be possible for a series of narrow majorities in these six unions to outvote the rest of the Conference. There are also doubts about the representative status of trade union leaders. They are elected on very low polls and trade unionists do not necessarily speak for the Labour voters. Many of these indirect members of the Party have only a tenuous connection with it and may not even sympathize with its policies, but they are enrolled by their affiliated union unless they specifically object and contract out. About a quarter of trade unionists usually vote Conservative.

An alternative would be to confine the election to the 300,000 or so individual members. These are, however, often quite unrepresentative of the views of Labour voters as a whole. This was clearly demonstrated in the 1975 referendum on the European Common Market. The Conference, the National Executive committee and the Trade Union Congress were against British membership of the EEC, but most Labour supporters voted

189

for staying in the Community. Surveys on attitudes to nationalization also show how out of touch Labour activists are with Labour voters. The election of Labour MPs after being rejected by their local associations – S. O. Davies at Merthyr in 1970, Dick Taverne at Lincoln and Eddie Milne at Blyth in February 1974 – again illustrate how Party workers can misjudge the views of the voters they claim to speak for, They are usually more extreme (more to the right if Conservative and more to the left if Labour) than ordinary voters, who are much less interested in ideology; and they are also more extreme than most MPs, who have to take into account the practical difficulties of implementing apparently attractive policies. It is often a commitment to political principles that disposes the voluntary workers to carry out the thankless routine chores of canvassing and addressing leaflets, but, if the Party activists chose more extreme leaders, it might sharpen the divisions between the main Parties, increasing the likelihood of damaging reversals of policy whenever there was a change of Government.

There are other cogent reasons for rejecting the Liberal innovation and leaving the choice of leader to the Members of Parliament:

1   At a time when the influence and status of Parliament is in decline, such a change in the system would be a further blow.

2   What the Liberals do is irrelevant to the two major Parties because there are very few Liberal MPs in proportion to Liberal support in the country and so small a group has correspondingly less authority to speak for the Party as a whole. Moreover, Liberals are engaged in choosing a Party leader, not an actual or potential Prime Minister. Their prospects of forming a government are negligible, none of the Liberal MPs have ever had any Ministerial experience and their policies have no chance of being implemented unless they are adopted by one of the major Parties. With these differences in experience, responsibility and Parliamentary strength, the Liberal experiment is not relevant to the Conservative or Labour Parties and should not be adopted by them.

3   Leadership of the two major Parties involves the exercise of special talents – skill in debate, the ability to master a brief quickly, to rally one's own supporters and point out the weakness of the Opposition's case, to weld the front bench into a coherent, competent team, and to gain the confidence and respect of one's colleagues. In addition, the leader must have a broad electoral appeal in order to win or retain office. It is a reasonable assumption that the best judges of a person's ability to cope with the pressures of leadership are those who work with the leader day in and day out in the House of Commons.

Walter Bagehot wrote in 1867 in *The English Constitution*:

Constituency government is the precise opposite of Parliamentary government. It is the government of immoderate persons far from the scene of action, instead of the government of moderate persons close to the source of action.

Bagehot also noted that the opinions of the leaders were subject to discussion with both supporters and opponents and had to be formed with the responsibility of acting on them in mind.

4 Both the Conservative and Labour Parties have lost members in recent years. Between 1953 and 1975 Conservative membership dropped from about 3 million to 1.5 million and Labour's from approximately 1 million to 300,000. This fall in membership almost certainly means that the Party workers are more extreme and less representative of the ordinary voters than before. It poses a problem, particularly for the Labour Party, because the decline in active members has made local associations vulnerable to takeovers by small left-wing groups. Reg Prentice, then a member of the Cabinet, was not re-adopted as Labour candidate for Newham because of the opposition of a small number of new members in his local party. An extension of the electoral college would not necessarily, therefore, make the system more democratic or representative of the Party as a whole.

5 Leadership elections are inevitably divisive. But most Members of Parliament are more concerned than the constituency associations to maintain Party unity, and it was this factor which brought about the emergence of compromise Conservative leaders in 1911 and 1963. It is interesting that the 'first-past-the-post' system for Parliamentary elections is not used by either the Conservative or Labour Parties for the election of a new leader. Both Parties require further ballots if no contender receives an absolute majority on the first ballot. The elimination of lower-placed candidates ensures that the Party leader is endorsed by more than half the MPs, even if he or she is not their first choice at the outset. In their successful elections Harold Wilson, Edward Heath, Margaret Thatcher and Jim Callaghan all led, but did not win outright, on the first ballot. By confining the election to MPs, together with the provision for new and compromise candidates to enter the contest if the first ballot fails to produce a result, it is more likely that a unifying figure, acceptable to most sections of the Party, will be chosen.

6 The new Liberal system would increase the probability of conflict between rival groups. Historically, the Labour Party has been dogged by the competing claims of the Parliamentary Labour Party and the annual Conference. The Parliamentary Party has persistently asserted its autonomy, while the Conference has insisted that MPs should respond to its policy decisions. In recent years there have been cases of Labour Cabinet Ministers speaking and voting in the National Executive Committee against Cabinet policy. This is a situation which the Conservatives have managed to avoid since Lord Randolph Churchill's attempt to use the National Union as a lever for his own ambitions.

7 There is the related consideration that the claims made for control of a Party by the mass membership are scarcely compatible with a *Parliamentary* democracy, in which an MP's primary responsibility must be to the voters

who elect him and indeed to the whole of the constituency which he represents.

Examination of the methods adopted in other countries can be used to support arguments for and against a change in the system. In most European Parties, the leader is elected by fellow members of the legislature. The main exceptions are communist Parties, whose leaders are elected by the national executive committee outside Parliament, and the socialist Parties in Sweden and Switzerland, where the leaders are elected by the Party Congress. In these cases, the method of election is a reflection of the greater influence of the Party organizations outside Parliament.

In the United States and Canada the Parties have developed convention systems for electing their leaders. Canadian conventions represent all sections of the Party, with votes allocated to MPs, local constituency associations, members of provincial legislatures, Party officials and women's and student organizations. The Canadian method merits study if British Parties wish to move further in the direction of widening the electoral college.

The American system for electing delegates to the nominating conventions permits a larger number of Party members to participate, but it carries certain drawbacks. The voters do not themselves elect a candidate. They choose delegates who do so. Not all American states hold primaries and, as each state decides how and when its delegates are selected for the convention, there is a bewildering diversity of arrangements. Although the Presidential candidate becomes its standard bearer for one election, he is not the formal leader of his Party. Indeed, the United States system of government is so different from our own that it does not provide any useful guidance.

There are, of course, valid arguments in favour of extending the suffrage for leadership elections. To do so would no doubt increase interest in the Parties and boost their membership at a time when there is some pressure for greater internal democratization, and such a system would make the Parliamentary leadership more attentive and accountable to the views of the constituency membership; but it is fair to conclude that the new system adopted by the Liberals is less suitable for the larger Parties.

Whether one supports the election of the Party leader by the MPs only, the mass membership only or by some combination of each depends on which criteria one applies and which type of leadership one prefers. Elections by MPs, on the one hand, and Party members on the other are likely to emphasize different qualities and promote different leaders. MPs are more influenced by a candidate's Parliamentary skills, his ability to unite the Party and his appeal to the electorate, including the uncommitted floating vote. The constituency members are more concerned with the candidate's adherence to 'true' Party principles. The difference between the two sets of electors is between a Parliamentary and a partisan approach, appealing to a national or to a Party constituency.

Some idea of the different types of leaders who would emerge under the two systems is suggested by the campaign for the Labour leadership in March 1976. Many Labour MPs found a larger body of support for Wedgwood Benn and Michael Foot in the constituencies than at Westminster and appreciably less support for Roy Jenkins. In 1963 it is probable that Lord Hailsham would have been the choice of the Conservative rank and file whereas he had much less support among MPs. Rab Butler had a higher public poll rating than any of the other candidates and might have won the 1964 election for the Conservatives since, unlike Hailsham and Home, he appealed to the middle vote, without which elections cannot be won.

In the United States in recent years there have been two examples of Party activists dominating the selection of Presidential candidates and imposing their choice on the Party's establishment. These were Barry Goldwater for the Republicans in 1964 and George McGovern for the Democrats in 1972. The narrow electoral appeal of both men and the divisive impact which they had on their respective Parties resulted in the disasters that overtook their campaigns for the Presidency. The very reasons which make a candidate popular with the Party membership may reduce his appeal to the wider electorate. The paradox is that, as the Parties embrace internal democracy and respond to their grass-roots supporters, they become less representative of the ordinary voter.

At present the Labour and Conservative Parties elect their leaders according to clear and well-understood rules. Both Parties now provide for re-election contests which allow for change without risk of a revolt or crisis in the Party. The low-key campaigns which result leave little bad blood among the candidates, who in any event will have to work together as colleagues. Members of Parliament constitute a knowledgeable electorate who know the contenders personally and are the best judges of their qualities. They should not be unaware of the views and feelings of their constituency supporters and if their judgement is acceptable on other issues, there is much to be said for also trusting them to elect their own leader.

APPENDIX 2

PROCEDURE FOR THE SELECTION OF THE LEADER OF THE
CONSERVATIVE PARTY

Timing of Elections and General Responsibilities

1   If the position of leader of the Party is vacant, an election shall be held as early as possible.

2   Otherwise there shall be an election in the House of Commons beginning within twenty-eight days of the opening of each new session of Parliament, except that in the case of a new Parliament the election shall be held not earlier than three months nor later than six months from the date of assembly of that Parliament. The actual date will be determined by the leader of the Party in consultation with the chairman of the 1922 Committee.

3   The chairman of the 1922 Committee will be responsible for the conduct of all ballots and will settle all matters in relation thereto.

Nominations and List of Candidates

4   Candidates will be proposed and seconded in writing by Members of the House of Commons in receipt of the Conservative whip. The chairman of the 1922 Committee and scrutineers designated by him will be available to receive nominations. Each candidate will indicate on the nomination paper that he is prepared to accept nomination, and no candidate will accept more than one nomination. The names of the proposer and seconder will not be published and will remain confidential to the scrutineers. Nominations will close by noon on a Thursday five days before the date of the first ballot.

5   If only one valid nomination is received, the chairman of the 1922 Committee shall declare this person elected. If more than one valid nomination is received, the chairman of the 1922 Committee and his

scrutineers will publish a list of the valid nominations and immediately transmit a copy to the two vice-chairmen of the 1922 Committee, the Chief Whip in the House of Commons, the chairman of the National Union, the chairman of the Executive of the National Union, the president of the Scottish Conservative and Unionist Association, the chairman and deputy chairman of the Party, the chairman of the Party in Scotland, the leader of the Party in the House of Lords and the Chief Whip in the House of Lords.

Procedure for Consultation with Members of the Party Outside the House of Commons

6 During the period between the close of nominations and the date of the first ballot, it shall be the responsibility of the constituency associations, represented by Conservative Members of Parliament, to inform the Member of their views regarding the candidates.

7 Similarly, the leader of the Party in the House of Lords and the Chief Whip in the House of Lords will make such arrangments as appropriate to obtain the views of peers in receipt of the Conservative whip.

8 In order that all sections of the Party shall be consulted, area chairmen of the National Union will obtain the opinions of constituency associations, through their chairmen, and report their findings to the chairman of the National Union and the chairman of the Executive of the National Union. In Scotland the area chairmen will similarly consult and report to the president of the Scottish Conservative and Unionist Association. They will also report to Conservative Members of Parliament within the area of their responsibility the views of constituencies not represented by a Conservative Member of Parliament.

9 The leader of the Party in the House of Lords, the Chief Whip in the House of Lords, the chairman of the National Union and the chairman of the Executive of the National Union, together with the president of the Scottish Conservative and Unionist Association, will on the Monday attend a meeting of the Executive of the 1922 Committee for the purpose of conveying to them the collective views of the peers in receipt of the Conservative whip, the National Union and the Scottish Conservative and Unionist Association respectively.

First Ballot

10 The first ballot will be held on the Tuesday immediately following. For this ballot the scrutineers will prepare a ballot paper listing the names of the candidates and give a copy for the purpose of balloting to each Member of the House of Commons in receipt of the Conservative whip.

11 For the first ballot each voter will indicate one choice from the candidates listed.

12 Where any Member is unavoidably absent from the House on that

day, through sickness or by being abroad, the scrutineers will make arrangements to receive their votes.

13 The ballot will be secret and neither the names of those who have voted for a particular candidate nor the names of those who have abstained from voting shall be disclosed by the scrutineers.

14 If, as a result of this ballot, one candidate *both* (i) receives an overall majority of the votes of those entitled to vote *and* (ii) receives fifteen per cent more of the votes of those entitled to vote than any other candidate, he will be elected.

15 The scrutineers will announce the number of votes received by each candidate, and if no candidate satisfies these conditions a second ballot will be held.

Second Ballot

16 The second ballot will be held on the following Tuesday. Nominations made for the first ballot will be void. New nominations will be submitted by the Thursday, under the same procedure and with the same arrangements for consultation as described in paragraphs 4–9 for the first ballot, both for the original candidates if required and for any other candidates.

17 The voting procedure for the second ballot will be the same as for the first save that paragraph 14 shall not apply. If, as a result of this second ballot, one candidate receives an overall majority of the votes of those entitled to vote, that candidate will be elected.

Third Ballot

18 If no candidate receives an overall majority, the three candidates receiving the highest number of votes at the second ballot will be placed on a ballot paper for a third and final ballot on the Thursday following.

19 For the final ballot each voter must indicate two preferences amongst the three candidates by placing the figure 1 opposite the name of his preferred candidate and the figure 2 opposite the name of his second choice.

20 The scrutineers will proceed to add the number of first preference votes received by each candidate, eliminate the candidate with the lowest number of first preference votes and redistribute the votes of those giving him as their first preference amongst the two remaining candidates in accordance with their second preference. The result of this final count will be an overall majority of the votes cast for one candidate, and he will be elected.

Party Meeting

21 The candidate thus elected by the Party in the House of Commons will be presented for confirmation as Party leader to a Party meeting

constituted as follows: Members of the House of Commons in receipt of the Conservative whip; Members of the House of Lords in receipt of the Conservative whip; Adopted Parliamentary candidates; Members of the Executive Committee of the National Union not already included in the above categories.

APPENDIX 3

Section 2.

LEADERS OF THE CONSERVATIVE PARTY 1885–1975

Name	Length of Parliamentary Service before Elected to Leadership (c)	Age at election (c)	Date	Rivals	Length of Service as Leader
Marquis of Salisbury (1830–1903)	28 years (15 Commons 13 Lords)	55	1885	—	16 years, 9 months (Nov. '85–July '02)
A. J. Balfour (1848–1930)	26 years	54	1902	—	9 years, 4 months (July '02–Nov. '11)
A. Bonar Law (b) (1858–1923)	11 years	53	1911	1. Walter Long 2. Austen Chamberlain (both stood down)	9 years, 4 months (Nov.11–Mar.21) +7 months (Oct. '22–May '23)
Austen Chamberlain (1863–1937)	29 years	57	1921	—	1 year, 7 months (Mar. '21–Oct. '22)
Stanley Baldwin (1867–1947)	15 years	55	1923	Lord Curzon	14 years (May '23–May '37)
Neville Chamberlain (1869–1940	18 years	68	1937	—	3 years, 5 months (May '37–Oct. '40)
Winston Churchill (1874–1965)	38 years	65	1940	Lord Halifax	14 years, 6 months (Oct. '40–Apr. '55)
Sir Anthony Eden (1897–1977)	31 years	57	1955	—	1 year, 9 months (Apr. '55–Jan. '57)
Harold Macmillan (1894–)	30 years	62	1957	R. A. Butler	6 years, 10 months (Jan. '57–Nov. '63)
Sir Alec Douglas Home (1903–)	27 years (15 Commons 12 Lords)	60	1963	1. R. A. Butler 2. Q. Hogg 3. R. Maudling	1 year, 9 months (Nov.'63–Aug.'65)
Edward Heath (a) (1916–)	15 years	49	1965	1. R. Maudling 2. E. Powell	9 years, 6 months (Aug.'65–Feb.'75)

| Margaret Thatcher (1925–) | 15 years | 49 | 1975 | 1st ballot 1. E. Heath 2. H. Fraser 2nd ballot 1. W. Whitelaw 2. J. Prior 3. G. Howe 4. J. Peyton | (Feb. 75–) |

Notes:

a. Edward Heath was the first Conservative Leader to be elected by a ballot of MPs.

b. Bonar Law, 1911–21, and Chamberlain, 1921–2, were leaders of the Conservative Party in the House of Commons. Formerly, when the party was in opposition, there were separate leaders in the Commons and Lords. The title 'Leader of the Conservative and Unionist Party' did not exist until it was conferred on Bonar Law in October 1922.

c. Length of Parliamentary Service: the column contains completed years from election to Parliament to selection for leadership. Age at election is given as the age at the last birthday on the date of selection or election.

INDEX

Acheson, Dean, 80
Aden, 76
Africa, 93–4
Aldington, Lord, 61, 108, 132, 154
Alexander, A. V., (Earl), 51
Alliance Party, 135
Alport, Lord, 129
Amery, Julian, 102, 177
Amery, Leo, 32, 37, 38, 41–2, 43, 45, 49
Anstruther-Gray, Sir William (Lord Kilmany), 45, 105, 120, 127
Arnold-Forster, Mark, 125
Asquith, Herbert (Earl of Oxford and Asquith), 21–2, 24, 34, 42
Assheton, Ralph (Lord Clitheroe), 63
Astor, Viscountess, 45
Astor, Viscount, 38
Atkins, Humphrey, 149, 151, 154, 156
Atlantic alliance, 60, 68
Attlee, Clement, (Earl), Norway debate, 41; suggests Halifax as Prime Minister, 42–3; and Chamberlain's resignation, 47, 48–9; supports choice of Churchill as Prime Minister, 49–50; relationship with Churchill, 23, 51; forms government, 60; loses 1951 general election, 65

Baker, Kenneth, 153, 167, 173
Bagehot, Walter, 190
Balcarres, Lord, 22–3
Baldwin, Mrs, 26
Baldwin, Stanley, (Earl), 10, 24, 25, 26–30, 58, 70; background and early career, 8–9, 27; becomes Prime Minister, 28, 88–9; becomes leader of the Conservatives, 5, 6, 28, 198;

government, 58; retires, 3, 28, 30; suggests Chamberlain should form National Government, 42; character, 5, 23, 29; Eden's admiration for, 64; on Eden, 81
Balfour, Arthur, (Earl of), 1; background and early career, 20; becomes leader, 5, 6, 20, 31, 198; as Prime Minister, 20–1; in opposition, 21–2; electoral record, 4; critics of, 4; resignation from leadership, 3, 22; estrangement from Conservative Party, 28; 1922 election, 25; character, 23
Barber, Anthony, (Lord), 111, 125 137
Barrie, Sir James, 139
Beaverbrook, Lord, 23, 26, 49, 53, 85
Belgium, 48, 76
Benn, Wedgwood, 193
Bennett, Sir Frederic, 124
Bennett, Reginald, 104–5
Berkeley, Humphry, 114, 116, 117
Bevan, Aneurin, 12, 35
Bevin, Ernest, 60, 61
Biffen, John, 140, 148
Birch, Nigel (Lord Rhyl), 92, 95–6
Birkenhead, Earl of, 25, 28, 46
Blake, Lord, 23, 138
Blakenham, Viscount, see Hare, John
Bligh, Sir Timothy, 133
Boothby, Lord, 32, 37, 38, 43, 49
Bow group, 178
Bower, Robert, 37
Boyd-Carpenter, John, (Lord), 107
Boyle, Sir Edward, (Lord), 78, 107, 109, 125
Boyne, Sir Harry, 99

Bracken, Brendan, (Viscount), 2, 37, 42, 47, 49

Branston, Ursula, 60, 61

British Broadcasting Corporation (BBC), 179

Brooke, (Lord Brooke of Cumnor), 107

Bryan, Sir Paul, 174, 175, 176

Buchan-Hepburn, Patrick (Lord Hailes), 129

Buck, Anthony, 178

Bullus, Sir Eric, 124

Butler, Mollie, (Lady), 87, 110

Butler, R. A., (Lord), 12, 103, 177, 185; and possibility of Halifax as Prime Minister, 46, 49; in Chamberlain's government, 36; on Eden, 56, 68, 82; and Conservative Research Department, 63, 88; in opposition, 1945–51, 64; in Churchill's government, 1951–55, 65, 67; acts as head of government for Churchill, 66; in Eden's government, 70; acts as deputy to Eden, 69, 80, 88; as possible successor to Eden, 5, 72, 73, 77, 83–7, 89, 198; and Suez crisis, 73, 76–7, 85–6; and Eden's resignation, 81; in Macmillan's government, 89, 96; acts as deputy to Macmillan, 93; and Macmillan's resignation, 99, 188; as possible successor to Macmillan, 5, 97, 98, 101–9, 115, 193, 198; refuses to serve under Douglas-Home, 109; agrees to join Douglas-Home's Cabinet, 110, 111; seconds Douglas-Home as leader of Conservatives, 112; character, 87–8

Butler, Sydney, 87

Callaghan, James, 3, 8

Campbell-Bannerman, Sir Henry, 21, 33

Carlton Club, 22–3, 25–6, 27, 28

Carr, Robert, (Lord), 129, 133, 135, 174

Carrington, Peter, (Lord), 10, 111, 112, 127–8, 133, 154, 156, 170

Cartland, Ronald, 37

Carvel, Robert, 151

Castle, Barbara, 134

Cato, 28

Cattell, Dr, 65–6

Cavendish-Bentinck, Lord George, 16

Cavendish-Bentinck, Lord Henry, 16

Cecil family, 9, 20, 125

Cecil, Viscount, of Chelwood, 38

Central African Federation, 96

Centre for Policy Studies, 140

Chamberlain, Sir Austen, 30, 58, 188; seeks leadership of Conservatives, 22–3; becomes leader, 6, 24, 198, 199; loses leadership, 3, 4, 5, 25–6; Law wishes to be succeeded by, 27–8

Chamberlain, Joseph, 19, 20, 22, 30

Chamberlain, Neville, 113; becomes leader, 5, 9, 198; unpopularity with Labour Party, 29, 30–1; World War II, 32, 34; relationship with Churchill, 35; Eden's opposition to, 36–8, 58; and Churchill's Norwegian plan, 39, 40; Norway debate, 41–3, 43–5; resignation, 3, 6, 46–9, 50, 67; remains in Churchill's government, 50–1; retains leadership of Conservative Party, 52–3; ill-health and death, 53, 54; character, 34, 54–5

Channon, Sir Henry, 36–7

Charlton, Michael, 175

Chelmer, Lord, 188

Chichester-Clark, Sir Robin, 125

Chou En-Lai, 139

Churchill family, 9

Churchill, Lady, 66

Churchill, Randolph, 56, 76–7, 85, 102

Churchill, Lord Randolph, 6, 18–19, 32, 165, 191

Churchill, Sir Winston, 4, 20, 88, 90, 147; background and early career, 28, 32–3; in Chamberlain's War Cabinet, 33, 34–5; 'Churchill group', 37; Norwegian plan, 38–40; as possible Prime Minister, 42, 45–8; Norway debate, 44–5; and leadership of Conservatives, 6, 9, 53–4, 198; becomes Prime Minister, 5, 30; forms government, 49–52; relationship with Conservative Party, 51; chooses Eden as heir-apparent, 58–9, 62, 69; Eden's relationship with, 61; relationship with the press, 61–2; loses 1945 general election, 2–3, 55, 60; and Attlee, 23; post-war political career, 64; 1951 general election, 65; 1951–55 government, 10, 65–9, 113; delays resignation, 66–7, 97; ill-health, 66; retirement, 3, 68–9; and Eden's successor, 85;

character, 68–9; oratory, 29, 34–5, 52; on leadership of Conservative Party, 3; on Baldwin, 26–7; on Austen Chamberlain, 25
Clark, William, 124, 127
Clark-Hutchinson, Michael, 127
Clarke, Kenneth, 178
Coal Board, 137
Colville, Sir John, 68–9
Commonwealth, 93–4, 134, 139
Confederation of British Industry (CBI), 134, 136; see also Federation of British Industries
Confederation of Ship-Building and Engineering Unions, 91–2
Conservative Central Office, 2–3, 18, 98, 153
Conservative Party, origins of, 15; functions of leader, 1; qualities needed for leadership of, 4–5; age of leaders, 9; security of leadership, 3–4; leadership elections, 7–8; Members of Parliament, 8–14; modernization of, 62–3
Conservative Party Conferences, 1946, 63; 1962, 96; 1963, 7, 103–4, 105–6; 1975, 185–6; 1976, 185
Conservative Political Centre, 103
Conservative Research Department, 12, 63, 88, 115
Cooper, Duff (Viscount Norwich), 37, 38, 44
Council of Ireland (proposed), 135
Courtauld, Mollie, 87
Courthorpe, Sir George, 54
Cousins, Frank, 92
Craig, William, 135
Cranborne, Viscount (5th Marquess of Salisbury), 36, 38, 61, 66, 69, 73, 81, 83–5, 90, 125
Cromwell, Oliver, 41–2
Crookshank, Harry, (Viscount), 64
Crossley, Anthony, 37
Cuban missile crisis, 96
Curzon, Marquess, 5, 6, 26, 27, 28, 30, 198
Cyprus, 76

Daily Express, 85, 107, 151
Daily Herald, 85
Daily Mail, 85, 125
Daily Mirror, 85
Daily Telegraph, 54, 84, 86, 89, 99, 118,
119, 127, 133, 137
Dalton, Hugh, 36, 46, 49, 60
Davidson, J. C. C. (Viscount), 28, 29
Davidson, Joan (Viscountess Davidson and Baroness Northchurch), 26
Davies, Clement, 38, 42–3, 44, 45, 49
Davies, S. O., 190
Dayan, Moshe, 79–80
De Gaulle, General, 93, 96, 130
Derby, Earl of, 16, 53
Devonshire, 9th Duke of, 90
Dewey, Thomas Edmund, 133
Dilhorne, Viscount, 99, 107, 108, 109
Dimbleby, David, 175
Disraeli, Benjamin (Earl of Beaconsfield), 6, 9, 16–18, 19, 129, 166
Donaldson, Commander, 118
Douglas-Home, Sir Alec, 22, 147; background and early career, 9, 10, 112–13; and Norway debate, 44; and Suez crisis, 73; and Macmillan's resignation, 97, 99; as possible successor to Macmillan, 102, 104–9 113–14, 125, 193; becomes leader of Conservatives, 7, 9, 111–12, 198; relinquishes peerage, 6, 99, 102; forms government, 10, 109–11, 130; as Prime Minister, 5; ill-health, 113; loses 1964 general election, 4, 114–15; in opposition, 1964–70, 115–17, 130; reviews procedure for choosing leader, 8, 116–17; possible successors to, 117–20, 124–7; considers resignation, 119, 120–1; resignation, 3, 121–2, 152, 165; in Heath government, 133, 134; chairman of rules committee, 156, 188, 189; loyalty to Heath, 185; character, 122–3; public image, 2
Douglas-Home, Lady, 113, 121, 122
Du Cann, Edward, 145; defends Douglas-Home, 119, 121; and opposition to Heath's leadership, 148, 149–51, 155–6, 157; as possible successor to Heath, 160–3, 164; and 1975 leadership election, 168, 171, 172, 177–8, 180
Du Cann, Sallie, 162–3
Duggan, Hubert, 37
Dulles, Foster, 72, 73–4, 76, 78
Dunglass, Lord, see Douglas-Home, Sir Alec
Durham, Earl of, 112

Economist, 125
Eden, Sir Anthony (Earl of Avon), 12, 147; background and early career, 9, 56–8, 112; in Government, 33, 58; opposition to Chamberlain, 36–8, 58; and Chamberlain's resignation, 47, 48; in Churchill's government, 51, 59; as heir apparent, 56, 58–9, 62, 69; relationship with Bevin, 60; becomes leader, 5, 31; in opposition, 1945–51, 60–4; knowledge of foreign affairs, 62; political philosophy, 63–4; establishes Parliamentary Secretariat, 63; in Churchill's government, 1951–55, 65–6, 67–8; takes Britain into European military alliance, 67–8; succeeds Churchill, 68–9, 198; forms government, 10, 70–1, 113; problems of inflation, 70, 71; Suez crisis, 72–81; ill-health, 59–60, 65–6, 78–9, 80–1; resignation, 3, 81–2, 84–5, 90; on Heath, 129–30; character, 61–2, 70, 82
Eden, Clarissa (Countess of Avon), 78–9, 80, 89
Eden, Sir John, 125
Eden, Marjorie, 56
Eden, Sir Timothy, 57
Eden, Sir William, 56–7
Edward VII, King of England, 20, 56
Edward VIII, King of England, 37
Egypt, Suez crisis, 72–80
Eire, 135
Eisenhower, Dwight D., 74, 91
Elizabeth II, Queen of England, royal prerogative, 8; and Churchill's retirement, 66, 69; knights Eden, 68; and Eden's retirement, 81; and Eden's successor, 83, 84–5, 88; and Macmillan's resignation, 97, 109
Elliot, Walter, 64, 90
Emery, Peter, 125
Emrys-Evans, Paul, 37, 38, 44
Errington, Sir Eric, 90
Erroll, Lord, 107, 108
Eton, 10–11
European Economic Community (EEC), Britain's first application to join, 94, 96, 103, 130; Britain enters, 139; referendum, 152, 153, 183, 184
Evans, Sir Harold, 91
Evans, Sir Horace, 84

Evening News, 125
Evening Standard, 85, 150, 151

Faisal II, King of Iraq, 79
Faulkner, Brian, (Lord), 135
Federation of British Industries (FBI), 71; *see also* Confederation of British Industry
Field, Winston, 114
Finance Bill, 1975, 183
Finland, 39
Fisher, Lord, 40
Fleming, Ian, 80
Foot, Michael, 193
Fort, Richard, 129
'Fourth Party', 19, 20
France, and Suez crisis, 73, 74–6, 79–80, 91
Fraser, Lady Antonia, 106
Fraser, Hugh, 106, 165, 169, 172, 199
Fraser, Sir Michael (Lord Kilmorack), 87, 114, 153, 156

Gaitskell, Hugh, 8, 75, 127
Gandhi, Mahatma, 46
general elections, April 1880, 18; January 1906, 21; January 1910, 21; December 1910, 21; November 1922, 26; July 1945, 2, 60, 113; February 1950, 12, 64; October 1951, 65; May 1955, 70; October 1959, 2, 91, 93; October 1964, 2, 4, 100, 114–15, 130; March 1966, 2, 118–19, 131; May 1970, 131–2, 134; February 1974, 2, 138–9, 145, 149; October 1974, 145–8, 149, 159
Geoffrey-Lloyd, Lord, 10, 125
George V, King of England, 26, 28, 42
George VI, King of England, 30, 42, 49, 50, 58–9
Germany, World War II, 32, 33–6, 38–40, 48, 59; joins NATO, 68
Ghana, 93
Gilmour, Sir Ian, 125, 126
Gladstone, W. E., 16, 18, 19
Goldwater, Barry, 193
Godman-Irvine, Bryant, 124
Goodhart, Philip, 124, 151
Gore-Booth, Lord, 75
Gormley, Joseph, 137
Goschen, Viscount, 165
Gow, Ian, 178
Graesser, Sir Alastair, 156

Granby, Marquess of, 6
Greenwood, Arthur, 32, 43, 47, 48, 49, 51
Grey, Earl, 57, 112
Griffiths, James, 43
Grimond, Joseph, 125
Guardian, 41, 85, 125, 136
Gunston, Sir Derrick, 37
Guttsman, W. L., 9

Hailsham, 1st Viscount, 38
Hailsham, 2nd Viscount (Quintin Hogg), 45, 181; background, 10; as possible successor to Macmillan, 7, 101–7, 193, 198; supports Butler for premiership, 108, 109; refuses to serve under Douglas-Home, 108, 109; agrees to join Douglas-Home's government, 109–10, 111; in Heath government, 133
Halifax, Earl of, 6, 38; in War Cabinet, 36; Watching Committee, 38; and Churchill's Norwegian plan, 39, 40, 41; as possible Prime Minister, 6, 42, 43, 45–50; in Churchill's government, 51; proposes Churchill for leadership of Conservatives, 53–4; becomes ambassador to United States, 58
Hall, Joan, 169–70, 173
Hall, Sir John, 124, 156
Hare, John (Lord Blakenham), 105, 107, 111, 114
Harris, Kenneth, 130
Harris, Ralph, 87
Harvie-Anderson, Betty, 150
Heath, Edward, 1, 4, 11; background and early career, 9, 128–30, 166; in Eden's government, 71, 129; and Suez crisis, 81; and Macmillan's succession to premiership, 84, 89; in Macmillan's government, 113, 130; and Britain's first application to join EEC, 94, 130; as possible successor to Macmillan, 101, 103; abolishes resale price maintenance, 114, 130; and Douglas-Home's succession, 107; in Douglas-Home's government, 111, 130; as possible successor to Douglas-Home, 117–18, 119–20, 124–7; becomes leader, 8, 111, 127–8, 164–5, 198, 199; in opposition, 1965–70, 21, 130–1; relationship with Wilson, 131; wins 1970 general election, 131–2; forms government, 10, 133–4; as Prime Minister, 133–9, 140–1; problems of inflation, 71–2, 136; takes Britain into EEC, 139; loses 1974 general election, 138–9, 145–8, 149; in opposition, 1974–75, 139–40, 145; opposition to leadership of, 3, 4, 121, 147–58, 165; possible successors to, 158–65; 1975 leadership election, 126, 166–74, 176, 178, 180, 184–5; declines to join Margaret Thatcher's Shadow Cabinet, 183–4; attitude towards Margaret Thatcher, 184–5; character, 34, 127, 132–3, 141–4; public image, 2, 147–8
Henry, Anthony, 15
Herbert, Sydney, 37
Hicks-Beach, Sir Michael, 6
Hitler, Adolf, 4, 28, 35, 39, 40, 48, 67, 72
Hoare, Sir Samuel, 52
Hogg, Quintin, *see* Hailsham, Viscount
Home, Earl of, *see* Douglas-Home, Sir Alec
Hopkinson, Henry (Lord Colyton), 63
Hore-Belisha, Leslie, 45
Howard, Anthony, 125, 128–9
Howe, Sir Geoffrey, 140, 159, 178–9, 180, 199
Howell, David, 174, 176
Hutchinson, George, 120, 126, 184

India, 4, 93
Industrial Relations Act, 1971, 134–5
Industrial Relations Court, 134
Iran, Shah of, 139
Iraq, 79
Ireland, 4, 135
Iremonger, Tom, 84
Israel, 73, 74–5, 76, 79–80

Jenkins, Roy, 193
Joint Planning Committee, 39
Jopling, Michael, 177
Jordan, 73, 74, 79
Joseph, Sir Keith, 107; supports Heath in 1965 leadership election, 125; in Heath government, 133; advocates monetarism, 140; as possible successor to Heath, 158–60, 164; opposition to Heath, 165; and 1975

leadership election, 168, 172; chief policy-maker to Margaret Thatcher, 184

Kennedy, John F., 96
Kershaw, Anthony, 125
Keyes, Sir Roger, 40, 41
Keyser Ullman, 150, 162–3
Kilmuir, Earl of (Sir David Maxwell-Fyfe), 11, 64, 70, 81, 83, 86–7
Kindersley, Guy, 12
Kirk, Sir Peter, 125
Kitson, Sir Timothy, 153, 167, 172–3

Labour Party, election procedures, 8; functions of leader, 1; leader's length of stay, 3; Members of Parliament, 14; becomes official Opposition, 24; and Baldwin, 29; supports choice of Churchill for Prime Minister, 49–50; and Suez crisis, 75; 1964 general election, 114; 1974 general election, 138, 146, 147, 159
Lambton, Viscount, 124
Lancaster, Colonel 'Juby', 105
Lansdowne, Marquess of, 23
Law, Andrew Bonar, background and early career, 8–9; as deputy to Lloyd George, 23, 24, 51; becomes leader, 5, 23–4, 25–6, 105, 198, 199; as Prime Minister, 26; resignation, 3, 26, 27–8; character, 4, 5, 23
Law, Richard (Lord Coleraine), 2, 37, 38
League of Nations, 33, 58
Lebanon, 79
Lewis, Kenneth, 155
Liberal Party, origins, 16; in nineteenth century, 18–19; influence on Conservatives, 12–13; October 1974 general election, 138, 147; and electoral reform, 138–9
Liberal–Unionists, 19, 20
Lindsay, Sir Martin, 84
Liverpool, Lord, 19
Lloyd, 1st Lord, of Dolobran, 38
Lloyd, Selwyn (Lord Selwyn-Lloyd), in Eden's government, 70–1; Suez crisis, 72, 74, 75, 80; and choice of Eden's successor, 84; in Macmillan's government, 89, 95; supports Douglas-Home, 105, 107–8,

121, 122; in Douglas-Home's government, 111
Lloyd George, David, (Earl), 25, 27, 29, 30, 182; coalition, 4, 5, 24; Bonar Law deputy to, 23, 24, 51; 1909 budget, 21; on Bonar Law's election, 23; resignation, 26; in Norway debate, 43–4; oratory, 34–5
Lloyd George, Gwilym (Viscount Tenby), 65, 77
Lloyd George, Lady Megan, 43
Locker Lampson, Oliver, 58
Londonderry, Marquess of, 38
Long, Walter, 22–3, 198
Longden, Sir Gilbert, 129
Lothian, Marquess of, 58
Luxembourg, 48
Lyttelton, Oliver (Viscount Chandos), 60, 61, 64, 65

MacDonald, Ramsay, 30, 58
McEwen, Robin, 118
McGahey, Michael, 137–8
McGovern, George, 193
Macleod, Iain, 12, 34, 77, 119, 134; in Conservative Research Department, 63; in Eden's government, 71; in Macmillan's government, 94; and 1958 busmen's strike, 92; and Macmillan's resignation, 99; as possible successor to Macmillan, 101, 103, 106, 110–11; on Butler, 102; pact with Maudling, 104; opposition to Douglas-Home's leadership, 106, 110, 113–14, 116; supports Butler for premiership, 109; refuses to serve under Douglas-Home, 108–11, 115; as possible successor to Douglas-Home, 125; supports Heath for leadership, 126; in OneNation group, 129; in opposition, 1964–70, 130; 1970 general election, 133; death, 133, 139, 154; character 181
Macmillan, Alexander, 90
Macmillan, Lady Dorothy, 88, 90
Macmillan, Harold, 11, 12, 13, 134, 147, 186; background and early career, 90–1; on Baldwin, 29; in Eden group, 37; on Watching Committee, 38; foresees Labour victory after war, 60; 1945 general election, 2; in opposition, 1945–51, 64; on Churchill's delayed resignation, 67;

in Eden's government, 70–1; and Suez crisis, 73, 76–7, 78; as possible successor to Eden, 72, 73, 77, 83–7; succeeds Eden, 9, 81, 198; becomes Prime Minister, 88–90; government, 1957–63, 91–100, 113, 130; political patronage, 165; foreign policy, 93–4; 'July massacre', 95–6; ill-health, 96, 98–9; considers resignation, 96–9; resignation, 3, 7, 89; possible successors to, 101–9; opposition to Butler, 101–2, 110; urges Douglas-Home to remain as leader, 120; on Wilson, 122; advises Heath to enter leadership election, 154; character, 100, 181, 182; public image, 2; on royal prerogative, 8

Macmillan, Maurice (father of Harold Macmillan), 90

Macmillan, Maurice (son of Harold Macmillan), 102, 177

Malta, 76

Margach, James, 62, 127

Margesson, David, (Viscount), 47, 49, 52

Marlborough, 7th Duke of, 32

Marten, Neil, 120, 124

Masaryk, Jan, 60

Mates, Michael, 175, 176

Maude, Angus, 129, 148

Maudling, Beryl, 125

Maudling, Reginald, 154; in Conservative Research Department, 63; and Macmillan's resignation, 99; as possible successor to Macmillan, 97, 101, 103–4, 106, 107, 198; pact with Macleod, 104; supports Butler for premiership, 108, 109; agrees to join Douglas-Home's government, 110; 1964 general election, 114; supports Douglas-Home as leader, 117; as possible successor to Douglas-Home, 117, 120, 124–5, 126, 127, 164; on Heath, 128; in opposition, 1964–70, 130; in Heath's government, 133

Maxwell-Fyfe, Sir David, see Kilmuir, Earl of

Menzies, Sir Robert, 74

Military Co-ordination Committee, 35, 39

Milne, Edward, 190

Monckton, Sir Walter, (Viscount), 3, 73

Montgomery, Fergus, 163

Moore, Jaspar, 10

Moran, Lord, 66, 67

Morrison, Charles, 148, 156

Morrison, Herbert, 43, 46, 49, 61

Morrison, John (Lord Margadale), 84, 97

Morrison, Sara, 153

Morrison, W. S. (Viscount Dunrossil), 64

Mott-Radclyffe, Sir Charles, 105, 121

Musketeer, operation, 75–6

Mussolini, Benito, 72

Nasser, Colonel, 72–5, 79

National Economic Development Council, 95

National Executive Council (NEC), 2

National Union of Conservative and Unionist Associations, 1; established, 18; Randolph Churchill and, 19; and Neville Chamberlain's election as leader, 31; and Churchill's election, 53, 54; Eden's election, 69; Macmillan's election, 90; and Douglas-Home's election, 7, 98, 114; supports Douglas-Home as leader, 117; 1975 leadership election, 157–8, 170–1

National Union of Mineworkers, 135, 137–8

NATO, 68

Neave, Airey, 163–4, 168, 169, 173–4, 179

Netherlands, 48, 76

News Chronicle, 85

Nicolson, Harold, 32, 37, 38

Nicolson, Nigel, 77–8

Nigeria, 93

1922 Committee, Churchill rarely speaks to, 64; and Suez crisis, 77; and review of election procedure, 116; and opposition to Douglas-Home's leadership, 120, 122, 124; and 1965 leadership election, 127; relations with Heath, 141, 168; 1975 leadership election, 145, 148–58, 160, 170, 173, 180; support for Margaret Thatcher, 182

Northcote, Sir Stafford (Earl of Iddesleigh), 6, 18–19

Northern Ireland, 135

Norway, 38–40, 44

Nugent, Lord, 125

Nutting, Sir Anthony, 78

One Nation Group, 129

Pahlavi, Mohammed Reza, Shah of Persia, 139
Paisley, Rev. Ian, 135
Panorama, 179
Parliament Act, 1911, 28
Patrick, Mark, 37
Pearson, Lester, 76
Peel, Sir Robert, 15, 16, 18, 132
Peerage Act, 1963, 99, 102
PEST, 117
Peyton, John, 173, 178, 180, 199
Pineau, Christian, 73, 74
Pitt, William the younger, 9
Poland, 35–6
Pompidou, Georges, 139
Ponsonby, Lord, 35
Poole, Oliver, (Lord), 84, 106
Port Said, 76
Portland, Dukes of, 16
Powell, Enoch, 63, 154; resigns from Macmillan's government, 92; supports Butler for premiership, 107; refuses to serve under Douglas-Home, 108, 109–11, 115; as possible successor to Douglas-Home, 125, 127, 198; in One Nation group, 129; immigration speeches, 131
Prentice, Reginald, 191
Pretyman, Captain, 6
Primrose League, 18
Prior, James, 125, 153–4, 173, 177, 178, 180, 199
Profumo, John, 45, 96
Pym, Francis, 154

Quarterly Review Journal, 15

Raison, Timothy, 174
Ramsden, Sir Eugene, 54
Redmayne, Martin, (Lord), 99, 106, 108, 109
Rees-Mogg, William, 120–1
Reform Act, 1832, 15
Reform Bill, 1867, 19
Rhodesia, 114, 121, 130–1
Ridley, Nicholas, 140
Rodgers, Sir John, 129
Rolls-Royce, 136
Roosevelt, Franklin D., 36, 59

Roth, Andrew, 117
Rothermere, Viscount, 49
Rothschild, Lord, 17
rules committee, 156–8
Russia, World War II, 39; and Suez crisis, 74, 76, 78; Macmillan visits, 93

es-Said, Nuri, 79
St Aldwyn, Earl, 106–7, 109, 127, 154, 156, 170, 171, 179
St John Stevas, Norman, 121, 126, 172
Salisbury, Marchioness of, 20
Salisbury, 3rd Marquess of, 3, 4, 18, 19–20, 32, 111, 198
Salisbury, 4th Marquess of, 38, 45
Sandys, Duncan (Lord Duncan-Sandys), 37, 61, 81, 105, 107, 114, 126
Sassoon, Sir Philip, 26
Scott, Nicholas, 174
Scott, Lord William, 118
Scottish Nationalist Party, 147
Seligman, Madron, 132, 142
Shakespeare, Sir Geoffrey, 13
Shelton, William, 163, 168, 173, 179
Simon, Sir John, (Viscount), 52
Sinclair, Sir Archibald, (Viscount Thurso), 41, 51
Smiles, Samuel, 166
Smith, Ian, 114
Smith, W. H., 6, 20
Smuts, General, 28, 29
Soames, Sir Christopher, 66, 107, 127
Social, Democratic and Labour Party (SDLP), 135
South Africa, 76, 134
Spaak, Paul-Henri, 68
Spears, Sir Edward (Louis), 37, 38
Spectator, 106, 110, 113–14, 116, 118, 126
Spens, Sir Patrick, (Lord), 38
Spicer, Michael, 117
Stamfordham, Lord, 28
Stanley family, 9
Stanley, Oliver, 60, 61, 64
Stanley, Richard, 124
Steel, David, 118, 187
Stuart, James (Viscount Findhorn), 113, 141
Suez Canal, 4, 17, 72–81, 85–6, 87, 91
Suez Canal Users' Association, 74
Sunday Express, 119

Sunday Times, 50, 121, 125, 127, 181
Sunningdale Conference, 1971, 135
Swinton, Earl of, 38

Tapsell, Peter, 160
Taverne, Richard, 190
Taylor, Sir John, 156, 170–1, 179
Thatcher, Denis, 181
Thatcher, Margaret, 159; background and early career, 9, 166; in Heath government, 133; advocates monetarism, 140; October 1974 general election, 146; as possible successor to Heath, 160, 161, 162, 163–5; 1975 leadership election, 126, 166, 168–80, 183, 184–5; as leader of the opposition, 8, 182–6, 199; Heath's attitude towards, 184–5; character, 122, 170, 181–2
Thomas, J. P. L. (Lord Cilcennin), 11, 37
Thorneycroft, Peter, (Lord), 2, 92, 127, 185
Thorpe, Jeremy, 96, 138, 139
The Times, 54, 73, 85, 88, 95–6, 116, 120, 125, 131, 136–7, 151, 178, 184
Trade Union Congress (TUC), 71, 134, 136, 137, 138
Transport and General Workers' Union, 92, 134
Tree, Ronald, 37
Trenchard, Lord, 38
Trudeau, Pierre, 139
Truman, Harry, 133
Tugendhat, Christopher, 174

Ulster, 135
United Nations, 59, 74, 75, 76, 78
United States of America, Vice Presidents, 5; and Suez crisis, 73–4, 75, 76, 78–9; relations with Britain after Suez, 91; opposes arms sales to South Africa, 134
United Ulster Unionists, 135, 147

Vassal, 96
Vicky, 93
Victoria, Queen of England, 17, 19

Walder, David, 178
Walker, Peter, 125, 126, 127, 133, 143, 154, 167

Wall, Patrick, 124
Waller, Ian, 72
Walpole, Sir Robert, 29
Ward, Dame Irene, (Baroness), 84
Watching Committee, 38, 45
Watkins, Alan, 118
Wellington, Duke of, 15
Wells, Sumner, 36
Welsh Nationalist Party, 147
West, Rebecca, 181
Whitelaw, William, 146, 149; background, 10; and advice on Douglas-Home's leadership, 118, 120, 121; 1964 leadership election, 126–7; and Rhodesian sanctions, 130; in Heath's government, 133, 135; as possible successor to Heath, 153, 154, 158, 159, 199; and 1975 leadership election, 156, 173, 174–7, 178, 179, 180; as a politician, 175
Wilberforce, Lord, 135–6
Williams, Shirley, 182
Williamson, Sir Thomas, 71
Wilson, Harold, 2, 142, 149, 152, 166; becomes leader of Labour Party, 8; attacks Douglas-Home, 112; 1964 general election, 118–19; becomes Prime Minister, 115, 116; and Heath, 127, 131; introduces oil sanctions against Rhodesia, 130; 1970 general election, 131–2; October 1974 general election, 146; 1974–76 government, 140; Prime Minister's questions, 182; resignation, 8, 22; public image, 2
Winterton, Earl, 45
Wolff, Michael, 133
Wolmer, Viscount, 37, 38
Women's Advisory Committee, 153
Wood, Sir Kingsley, 46–7, 48, 49, 52
Wood, Richard, 160
Woolton, Earl of, 63, 67
World War I, 23
World War II, 32, 33–52, 59

Yorkshire Post, 69
Young, Kenneth, 101, 116, 121–2
Young Conservatives, 7, 11, 62, 103, 176
Younger, Sir George, 25

The Murder
Before Christmas

A Charlie Kingsley Mystery

Other books by Michele Pariza Wacek

The Secret Diary of Helen Blackstone
(free novella available at MPWNovels.com)

It Began With a Lie (Book 1 in the "Secrets of Redemption" series)
This Happened to Jessica (Book 2 in the series)
The Evil That Was Done (Book 3 in the series)
The Summoning (Book 4 in the series)
The Reckoning (Book 5 in the series)

The Third Nanny

The Stolen Twin

Mirror Image

The Murder Before Christmas

A Charlie Kingsley Mystery

by Michele Pariza Wacek

ISBN 978-1-945363-32-0

Library of Congress Control Number: 2021949748

For my family, for always believing in me.

Chapter 1

"So, Courtney, is it?" I asked with what I hoped was a comforting and nonthreatening smile. I set the mug holding my newest tea blend I'd created for the Christmas season—a variety of fresh mint and a couple of other secret ingredients—down on the kitchen table. I called it "Candy Cane Concoctions", and hoped others would find it as soothing as it was refreshing. "What can I do for you?"

Courtney didn't look at me as she reached for her tea. She was young, younger than me, and extremely pretty, despite looking like something the cat dragged in. (And believe me, I know all about what cats can drag in. Midnight, my black cat, had presented me with more than my share of gifts over the years.) Courtney's long, wavy blonde hair was pulled back in a haphazard ponytail, and there were puffy, black circles under her china-blue eyes. She was also visibly pregnant.

"Well, Mrs. Kingsley," she began, but I quickly interrupted her.

"It's Miss, but please, call me Charlie." Yes, she was younger than me, but for goodness sake, not THAT much younger. Maybe it was time to start getting more serious about my morning makeup routine.

Her lips quirked up in a tiny smile that didn't quite reach her eyes. "Charlie, then. I was hoping you could make me a love potion."

I quickly dropped my gaze, busying myself by pushing the plate of frosted Christmas sugar cookies I had made earlier toward her, not wanting her to see my shock and sorrow. She was pregnant and wanted a love potion. This just couldn't be good.

"I don't actually do love potions," I said. "I make custom-blended teas and tinctures."

1

Her eyebrows knit together in confusion. "But people have been raving about how much you've helped them. Mrs. Witmore swears you cured her thyroid problems."

I tried not to sigh. "My teas and tinctures do have health benefits, that's true. Certain herbs and flowers can help with common ailments. In fact, for much of human civilization, there were no prescription drugs, so all they had to use were herbs and flowers. But I can't promise any cures."

"What about Ruthie?" Courtney asked. "She claims those heart tinctures you made are the reason Bob finally noticed her."

I gritted my teeth. When Ruthie's dad was recovering from a heart attack, I made a couple of teas and tinctures for him. Ruthie, who had a crush on her coworker Bob for years, was apparently so desperate for him to notice her that one day, she decided to bring one of my tinctures to work (I'm unclear which) and slip it into his drink. And apparently, shortly after that, Bob started up a conversation with her, and eventually asked her out on a date.

It didn't help matters that Jean, Ruthie's mother, had claimed my tinctures had reignited her and her husband's love life, which is probably how Ruthie got the idea to try them with Bob in the first place.

Needless to say, that was an unintended benefit.

"I didn't give Ruthie a love potion," I said. "I gave her dad some tinctures and teas to help his heart."

Courtney gazed at me with those clear-blue eyes, reminding me of a broken-down, worn-out doll. "Well, isn't that where love starts?"

"Maybe," I said. "But my intention was to heal her father's heart, not to make anyone fall in love with anyone else."

"But it worked," she said. "Can you just sell me whatever you gave her? I have money. I'll pay."

"It's not that simple," I said. "I really need to ask you some questions. It's always good to talk to your doctor, as well."

She bit her lip and dropped her gaze to the tea in her hands. She looked so lost and alone, I felt sorry for her.

"Why don't you tell me a little bit about who you want this love potion for?" I asked. "That would help me figure out how best to help you."

She didn't immediately answer, instead keeping her eyes down. Just as I was starting to think she wasn't going to say anything at all, she spoke. "It's for my husband," she said, her voice so low, it was nearly a whisper.

I could feel my heart sink to the floor. This was even more heartbreaking than I had imagined. "You think your husband fell out of love with you?"

"I know he has," she said. "He's having an affair."

"Oh Courtney," I sighed. "I'm so sorry to hear that."

She managed a tiny nod and picked up her tea to take a sip.

"Have you two talked about it?"

She shook her head quickly.

"Does he know you know?"

She shrugged.

"Maybe that's the place to start," I said, keeping my voice gentle. "Having a conversation."

"It won't help," she said, her voice still quiet.

"How do you know if you haven't tried?"

She didn't answer … just stared into her tea.

"Have you thought about marriage counseling?"

"He won't go." Her voice was firm.

"Have you asked?"

"I know. He's said before he thinks therapy is a waste of money."

"Okay. But you have a baby on the way," I said. "You need to be able to talk through things. I understand it might be difficult to talk about something like *this*, but ..."

"He's in love with her." The words burst out of her as she raised her head. The expression on her face was so anguished that for a moment, it took my breath away.

"But how do you know if you haven't talked to him about it?"

"I just do," she said. "When you're married, you know these things. You can sense when your husband has fallen out of love with you. Hence, my need for a love potion. I need him to fall back in love with me. You can see how urgent this is." She gestured to her stomach. "In a few months, we're going to have a baby. I just *have* to get him to fall back in love with me."

Oh man, this was not going well. "I see why you would think that would be easier, but the problem is, there's no such thing as a love potion."

"Can you please just sell me what you made for Ruthie's dad? So I can at least try?"

"Whatever happened between Ruthie and Bob had nothing to do with one of my tinctures," I said flatly. "I don't want to give you false hope. I really think your best course of action is to have an open and honest conversation with him about the affair."

She was noticeably disappointed. It seemed to radiate out of every pore. I hated being the one to cause that, but I also wasn't going to sell her anything that could be misconstrued as a "love potion." Not only for her sake, but my own. The last thing I needed was lovesick women showing up at my door to buy something that didn't exist.

"Okay," she said quietly as she ducked her head so I couldn't quite see her face. "No love potion. How about the opposite?"

I looked at her in confusion. "The opposite?"

"Yes. Something that would kill him."

My mouth fell open. "Wha ... I'm sorry, could you repeat that?" I must have heard her wrong. She was still talking so quietly, not to mention hiding her face.

Courtney blinked and looked up at me. "I'm sorry?"

"I didn't hear what you said. Could you repeat it?"

"Oh. It was nothing." She offered an apologetic smile.

"No, really," I said. "I thought ..." I laughed a little self-consciously. "I thought you said you wanted something to kill your husband."

She blinked again. "Oh. Yeah. It was just a joke."

"A joke?"

"Yeah. I mean, you know. Sometimes married people want to kill each other. No big deal." Now it was her turn to let out a little twitter of laughter. "Have you ever been married?"

I shivered and put my hands around my mug to absorb the warmth. "No." Which was true. I had never been officially married, but that didn't mean my love life wasn't ... complicated.

Nor did it mean I didn't know exactly what she was talking about.

"Well, you know, sometimes married people can just get really angry with each other, and in the heat of the moment, even want to kill each other," she explained. "But they don't mean it. It's just because they love each other so much that sometimes that passion looks like something else. In the heat of the moment, in the middle of a fight, you can say all sorts of things you don't mean. But of course, they wouldn't *do* anything about it."

"Of course," I said. I decided not to mention that when she said it, she wasn't actually arguing with her husband. Nor did I bring up how perhaps she was protesting a bit too much.

I gave her a hard look as I sipped my tea.

She kept her gaze firmly on the table, refusing to meet my eyes. "Did I tell you how wonderful this blend is?" she asked. "It's so refreshing. Reminds me of a candy cane."

"Thanks. It's called 'Candy Cane Concoctions,' actually. I created it for the holidays," I said.

"It's wonderful." She took another hurried drink and put her mug down, tea sloshing over the side. "Are you selling it? Could I buy some?"

"Sure," I said, getting up from my chair. "Hang on a minute. I'll get you a bag."

She nodded as I left the kitchen to head upstairs to my office/work room. Although, to be fair, it was so small, it wasn't uncommon to find drying herbs or plants throughout the house.

I collected a bag and headed back to the kitchen. When I walked in, Courtney was standing up, fiddling with her purse. I instantly felt like something was off. Maybe it was the way she was standing or the bend of her neck, but she oozed guilt.

"Oh, there you are," she said, fishing out her wallet. "How much do I owe you?'

I told her, and she pulled out a wad of cash, handing me a twenty.

"I'll have to get you some change," I said.

"That's not necessary," she said, taking the bag. "You were so helpful to me, and besides, I need to get going."

"But this is way too much," I protested. "Just let me find my purse."

She waved me off as she left the kitchen and headed for the front door. "Nonsense. Truly, you were very helpful. No change is necessary." She jammed her arms into her coat, and without bothering to zip it up, opened the front door and headed out into the cold.

I closed the door after her, watching her through the window as she made her way down the driveway and into her car. She didn't seem very steady on her feet, and I wanted to make sure she got into her vehicle safely. After she drove off, I went back to the kitchen to look around.

Nothing appeared to be out of order. If she had been digging around looking for something (like something to kill her husband with), it wasn't obvious.

Still, I couldn't shake that uneasy feeling.

I went to the table to collect the dishes. Midnight strolled in as I was giving myself a pep talk.

"I'm sure she didn't mean it," I said to him. "She was probably just upset. I mean, she wasn't getting her love potion, and clearly, she was uncomfortable having a conversation with her husband. Although you'd think that would be a red flag."

Midnight sat down, his dark-green eyes studying me.

"Of course, that's hardly my business," I continued. "She's upset with him, and rightfully so. Who wouldn't be? Even if she wasn't actually joking in the moment, she was surely just letting off steam."

Midnight's tail twitched.

"Maybe this was even the first time she said it out loud," I said as I moved to the sink. "And now that she said it, she realized how awful it was. Of course she would never do anything like that." I turned to the cat. "Right?"

Midnight started cleaning himself.

"You're a lot of help," I muttered, turning back to the sink to finish the washing up.

As strange as that encounter was, it was likely the end of it. I hoped.

Chapter 2

"Did you see the paper yet?"

"Good morning, Pat," I said into the phone. "So nice to hear from you. Oh, why yes, I did have a Merry Christmas. How was yours?"

"Go get your newspaper, and I'll be right over." There was a click, and the line went dead.

I replaced the receiver but didn't immediately move. There was a prickle of unease near the base of my skull. I had a sneaking suspicion I wasn't going to like what I saw in the newspaper.

Therefore, I took my time getting to it. I heated up water for a fresh pot of tea and put out some muffins I had baked the day before along with my new Christmas plates and napkins. Even though it was only me and Midnight, I still decorated the house—especially the kitchen. Normally full of sunflower decor, I had switched everything out for Christmas-themed items, complete with a small tree in the corner.

The whole Christmas season was bittersweet for me, but Christmas day was especially so. Christmas had always been my favorite holiday, but I missed seeing my niece Becca and my nephews, especially CB. My relationship with my sister Annabelle was still a little frosty. So, talking on the phone with them was easier.

After our call the day before, I'd spent a good chunk of the day baking before heading over to Nancy's house for Christmas dinner. Nancy, who owned the Redemption Inn, didn't have local family either, so we typically spent the holidays together at her place, where she could keep an eye on the inn.

The kitchen ready for Pat, I was about to fetch the paper when I decided I should maybe dress in something other than the old pair of grey sweatpants and sweatshirt I was wearing. I threw on a pair of jeans with one of my Christmas sweaters, red with a green tree in the center of it and ran a comb through my unruly brownish-blonde hair. It was somewhere between curly and frizzy, depending on the humidity, and today was definitely one of its wild days, so rather than deal with it, I pulled it back into a ponytail. I took a quick glance in the mirror, studying my eyes, which were an interesting mix of green, brown and gold, along with my full lips and narrow face, and wondered if I should dash on a bit of make up as well. I decided I didn't have enough time to mess around with it, and headed for the front door instead.

It was a cold, grey day outside. No snow yet, which was disappointing, as it would have been nice to have had a white Christmas. Still, it looked like it might start snowing any minute.

The paper was in the middle of the driveway, which meant I needed shoes. By the time I located my tennis shoes and laced them up, Pat had arrived and was heading up the driveway.

"Want to grab my newspaper while you're there?" I called out.

Her mouth dropped open. "You mean, you don't know yet?"

"It's Boxing Day, Pat," I said. "I didn't want to ruin Boxing Day."

"I don't even know what 'Boxing Day' means," Pat said as she detoured to scoop up my paper.

I shut the front door, knowing she would let herself in, and headed back to the kitchen to finish making the tea. I heard the front door open and close, and Pat appeared in the kitchen, her nose and cheeks bright red from the cold.

"I can't believe you didn't drop everything to get the paper," she grumbled, tossing it onto the table and snatching a muffin. Pat was a good decade or so older than me, and the best way to describe her was "round." She was plump, with a round face, round black-rimmed glasses, and short, no-nonsense brown hair that was turning grey. She had been one of my first customers, referred by Nancy, and had also become a good friend.

"Do you want to read it for yourself, or should I tell you?" she asked, taking a bite of the muffin. Like me, she also had on a Christmas sweater, except hers sported a family of snowmen holding song books and presumably caroling.

I brought the tea pot to the table and picked up the paper. "Neither," I said. "I told you, it's a holiday. Well, at least in Canada and the UK. We should be planning a shopping trip, not reading unpleasant happenings in the newspaper."

Pat rolled her eyes. "Trust me, you're going to want to see this," she said with her mouth full. "And, in case you didn't notice, we don't live in either Canada or the UK."

With a sigh, I slid the rubber band off and unrolled the paper.

A Murder Before Christmas, blared the newspaper. *Man Found Dead. Poisoned Present Suspected.*

"Poisoned *what*?" I muttered, reading the headline again. "Are they for real?"

"Don't worry about the headline," Pat said. "Just read the article."

I started to skim it.

Dennis Fallon, aged thirty-nine, was found dead in his home on Christmas Eve.

His wife, Courtney Fallon, aged twenty-five and six months pregnant, found him and called 9-1-1 ...

The words began to swim before my eyes. *Courtney Fallon ... six months pregnant.*

Had she told me her last name? I couldn't remember. But surely, this couldn't be the same woman.

An image of the haunted young woman who had sat in my kitchen a few weeks ago drinking my Candy Cane tea and asking for a potion to kill her husband appeared in my mind's eye.

It had to be someone else.

I quickly skimmed the article, searching for a photo of Dennis and his bride, when suddenly, my stomach twisted into a giant knot.

There, near the bottom. On their wedding day.

No question it was the same Courtney.

I looked up to see Pat pouring the tea. She handed me a mug. "You're going to need this. In fact, do you have anything stronger?"

I grasped the tea with limp fingers and collapsed into one of the chairs. "Pat, could I be responsible?"

Pat pulled out a chair and sat down across from me. "I don't know. Were you the one who sent him the poisoned brandy?"

"Poisoned bra ... *he was really poisoned*?"

"You didn't finish reading the article, did you?"

"No, I was just looking for a picture."

Pat shot me a look. "How many Courtneys do you think live in Redemption? Especially six-month pregnant ones?"

I picked up my tea to take a drink. It was hot and burned my tongue, but I drank it anyway. "I can't believe this is happening."

Pat reached for another muffin. "Oh, believe it. Do you want a muffin? Or should I find some Christmas cookies? I know you have some stashed in here somewhere ..."

Even though I had lost my appetite, I reached for a muffin. Maybe Pat had the right idea, and the sugar would help.

After Courtney left that day, I couldn't stop thinking about her. As much as I tried to write off what happened as frustration on her part—she didn't *really* want to kill her husband—I couldn't shake the feeling that something else was going on.

"Do you think I should tell someone?" I had asked Pat over tea and cookies.

Her expression was puzzled. "Who are you going to tell?"

"I don't know. The police?"

She blinked at me. "The police?"

"I mean, isn't that who you're supposed to tell if you have information about a crime?"

"Charlie, what exactly do you think you know? Someone came in here asking for a love potion because she's pregnant and her husband is cheating on her, and when it was clear she wasn't getting one, she asked for something else. You're talking about a pregnant woman who's upset because her husband is having an affair. There are probably a lot of women in that situation who have fantasized about killing their husband. Wouldn't YOU?"

I chewed on my lip. "I suppose."

What Pat had said made sense. The chances of her actually meaning it were pretty low.

And yet ...

Staring at Courtney's shy smile on the front page of the newspaper brought all my doubts back.

"So, do you want to tell me what happened, or do I need to read the article?"

Pat broke off a piece of muffin. "A package arrived for the mister on Christmas Eve. It appeared to be a present from one of his cousins, who just happened to be spending the holidays overseas. The note said something like 'Open me first for a little Christmas Eve cheer.' Inside was a bottle of his favorite brandy, so of course he had a little drink. Apparently, that's all it took."

"Where was Courtney when all this happened?"

"In the kitchen. She claimed they had decided to spend a quiet Christmas Eve at home, just the two of them, and she had spent the afternoon making a nice dinner. When he didn't show up, she went looking for him and found him lying on the floor of his study, dead."

My eyes widened. "Seriously?"

Pat nodded. "Yeah. Kind of weird, isn't it?"

"I'll say. Why would he be in his study drinking by himself when they were going to spend Christmas Eve together?"

"Good question."

"And she didn't hear him fall?" I continued. "You would think if a grown man collapsed, she would have heard it."

"Maybe she had Christmas music playing."

"Maybe." I frowned. "It still seems odd. So, after she found him, then what? Was she the one who called the cops?"

"Yep. And they pronounced him dead on the scene."

"This really does sound like she did it," I mused.

"Yeah, it does."

"Has she been arrested or charged or anything?"

"The paper didn't say," Pat said. "I would imagine they're keeping a close eye on her, though, at least."

"Maybe I should go talk to her," I said as I went back to studying Courtney's wedding photo. She looked impossibly young in a gorgeous wedding gown, her thick blonde hair piled on the top of her head. Her new husband was beaming at her.

"And say what? 'Hey, did you decide to poison your husband after all?'"

"Something like that, but maybe not quite as blunt." I couldn't tear my eyes away from her husband. Even if the news story hadn't mentioned his age, it was clear just in looking at him that he was much older than her, with his thinning hair and slight paunch.

But it was the look of love and adoration in his eyes that kept me glued to the page.

"I don't get it," I said.

"Get what?"

"Why he would cheat." I flipped the paper around to show Pat what I meant. "First of all, look at the age difference. She's young and pretty, and he's nearly middle age."

"So because he's middle aged, he wouldn't cheat?"

"No, but why *would* he? She appears to be a perfect trophy wife, if that's what he was looking for. But even more than that, look at how he's looking at her." I tapped the newspaper. "That doesn't look like a guy who doesn't love his wife."

Pat peered at the picture. "Maybe he fell out of love with her. We don't know when they got married."

"She's still pretty young. It couldn't have been that long ago."

"Maybe he's one of those guys who never wanted kids. And now that his wife is pregnant, he's lost interest."

"Possibly."

Pat glanced up at me, her eyes narrowing. "What are you saying? You don't think he was cheating on her?"

I thought about the visit with Courtney—how exhausted and depressed she had looked, and how sad she had been about her marriage. It sure didn't seem like she was acting; I had really felt her sincerity in thinking her husband was cheating on her.

"I'm not sure," I said. "I mean, Courtney sure seemed like she believed he was. But maybe she was wrong. Maybe he wasn't."

"How could she be wrong about something like that? How did she find out?"

"I don't know," I said. "I didn't ask. It didn't seem important at the time. But I do know they had never talked about it. So, it's possible she thought he was cheating for some reason, but he actually wasn't."

"Man, wouldn't it suck if she poisoned him over a misunderstanding?"

"What a nightmare." I sat back in my chair and stated twisting my ponytail around my hand. "I have to go see her. I mean, either he *was* cheating on her, which is unfortunate and kind of weird as she does seem to be a trophy wife, or he wasn't, but for some reason, she thought he was. Which is also weird."

"Or ..." Pat said, glancing at me out of the corner of her eye as she broke off another piece of muffin. "She made the whole cheating thing up."

I hadn't considered that theory. Was it possible she had invented the whole thing? I pictured her sitting at my kitchen table again, her beautiful blue eyes filled with sadness and grief. The idea she could have been faking caused a shiver to run up my spine.

I had to know the truth. Or at least, make an effort to find out what was going on. I ignored the little voice inside me that reminded me that this likely wasn't any of my business, and I had better things to do. I pushed myself out of my chair. "Want to come with me to visit the grieving widow?"

Pat tossed the last bite of muffin into her mouth. "Are you kidding? I wouldn't miss it for the world."

Chapter 3

Courtney's house was located on quiet cul-de-sac on the other side of town near the lake. It was a large, two-story colonial home with red and white bricks, white trim, and a huge yard filled with trees and a massive garden. During the summer, it would probably be a real showstopper, but with dead grass, naked trees, and the garden a huge, dark gash in the middle of the yard, it looked barren and depressing.

Pat and I made our way up the driveway. The house was decorated with Christmas lights along with a plastic Santa in a sleigh and a family of snowmen, which was probably festive and fun at night, but in the middle of an overcast, grey day, it just added to the gloom.

I rang the doorbell and waited. The old wooden door was decorated with a cheery red and green wreath. I found myself wondering if all the holiday touches were Courtney's idea, and if so, if she would continue to do them next year. I hoped so, for the sake of her unborn child. He or she would probably have enough issues growing up without a father without losing Christmas, as well.

"Think she's not home?" Pat asked, stamping her feet and shoving her hands in her coat pockets.

"I guess we should have called first," I said, reaching over to ring the doorbell again.

The door burst open, causing me to jump. "Mrs. Kingsley! I mean Charlie. What are you doing here?"

Courtney looked awful. Her nose was bright red, and her face was puffy, like I had just interrupted her in the middle of a crying binge. Only part of her blonde hair was in a ponytail—the rest of it hung in a greasy, tangled mat around her shoulders. She wore a stained grey sweatshirt and sweatpants.

"I ... I'm so sorry for your loss," I said, feeling awkward and clumsy. I was ashamed that it hadn't occurred to me that I might be interrupting Courtney's grieving. I kept picturing her asking me for something to kill her husband with over and over, and I wondered if I had really seen the coldness in her eyes when she'd asked. "I wanted to come by and see if you needed anything, but I probably should have called first rather than barge in like this."

She sniffed loudly, rubbing her cheeks with a wet, crumpled tissue. "Do you want to come in?"

I glanced at Pat. "Well ... sure. If it's not too much trouble."

She shook her head. "The place is a bit of a mess, but if that doesn't bother you, come on in."

I stepped over the threshold, introducing her to Pat and handing her a basket filled with muffins. She sniffed again as she took it. "You didn't have to."

"It was no trouble," I said, wishing I had taken the time to make a casserole or something heartier than my leftover muffins.

She went to the kitchen while Pat and I moved toward the pristine living room. I wasn't entirely sure what she was talking about when she said the place was a mess. The only thing that seemed even a bit messy was the coffee table, which was covered with stacks of paperwork. The room was decorated in soft, pastel colors—yellows, pinks, and baby blues. The sofa and matching chairs were cream-colored with pillows and afghans matching the accent colors, and the hardwood floor was covered by a complementary braided rug. In the corner next to the fireplace was a huge Christmas tree with gaily wrapped presents beneath it.

"She's going to have to do a lot of baby proofing," Pat said, shaking her head as she sat down gingerly on the sofa.

Courtney came in at that point, saving me from answering. "Oh, where are my manners? Did you want anything? I could make a pot of coffee or tea. I still have some of that wonderful mixture I bought from you, or ..."

"We're fine, Courtney," I said gently. "Why don't you sit down?"

She looked a little lost, like she had her mind set on complet- ing the task of making us something to drink, and now that she didn't have to, she wasn't sure what to do. But after a moment, she lowered herself into the chair.

"Are you doing okay?" I asked, feeling my face turn red in reaction to how stupid it sounded. "I mean," I started again. "The baby, and all."

"The baby is fine," she said, blowing her nose. "I'm doing about as well as can be expected, I guess. There's just so much to do, and I don't know where everything is. Dennis took care of all of that, but he's not here, so ..." Her face crumpled, and she scrubbed at it again with the tissue. "I'm so sorry. I'm emotional at the best of times, which these aren't. Thank you again for coming. That was so nice of you. Other than the cops and my mother, no one has stopped by."

I glanced at Pat, who raised her eyebrows at me. "No one has come by to offer their condolences?"

She shook her head. "It's probably because it's Christmas, you know. People are busy with their families and have oth- er commitments. I'm sure they'll come once everything calms down in a few days."

"I'm sure that's all it is," I agreed, hoping she was right, and that it wasn't because everyone thought she had poisoned her husband. "Do you want to talk at all? About what happened?"

She blew her nose. "We were supposed to go to a party on Christmas Eve, but I wasn't feeling up to it. This whole month of December, it seemed all we did was go to one party after anoth- er. Not to mention all the gift-buying and decorating ... it was exhausting. Dennis had said we should take advantage of the fact that the baby wasn't here yet and do as much entertaining as possible, as next December, we would probably be homebod- ies. Initially, I agreed. It made a lot of sense. But, as December wore on, it just got more and more tiring. Christmas day was going to be a packed; we were seeing my mom for lunch and his family for dinner, and I just didn't think I could handle one more party. So, I asked if we could stay home and celebrate Christmas Eve with just the two of us. I would cook us a nice dinner, and we could light a fire in the fireplace and turn on the Christmas tree lights and have a nice, quiet evening.

"He agreed, so that afternoon I was busy in the kitchen cooking. I heard the doorbell ring, but I was in the middle of prepping the beef wellington, so I called out to Dennis to answer it. He came in to show me what Arthur had sent. It was beautifully wrapped … gold paper with a red box. He said it was too pretty to unwrap, and maybe we should leave it, but he also couldn't resist seeing what it was, especially after he read the card. 'Open me first for some Christmas Eve cheer.' I think those words are burned in my brain." She sucked in a shaky breath. "Anyway, after Dennis read the card, he said something like, 'Leave it to Arthur to always know when to send a party in a box.'"

"Arthur is Dennis's cousin?" I asked.

She nodded. "He often sends things out of the blue, especially when he's traveling. He travels a lot."

"For work or …?"

"Yes, for work, but for fun, too. I think he's in France now … or maybe the Swiss Alps. It's hard to keep track of where he is most of the time." She paused, as if thinking about having a cousin who sent out-of-the-blue gifts and was difficult to get ahold of would be the perfect way to unsuspectedly slip someone some poison.

"What do you mean about the 'party in the box'?" Pat asked.

Courtney bit her lip. "Dennis wasn't happy about missing the Christmas Eve party," she said quietly. "He didn't say much about it, but I know he was disappointed. He was really looking forward to that one in particular. His client, Harry, was known for hosting really lavish parties. And, with the baby coming, this might be the last year in a long time we would be able to attend, at least the Christmas one. And …" her voice trailed off before she gave herself a quick shake. "It doesn't matter now."

"What?"

She shook her head firmly. "No. It doesn't matter anymore. He was disappointed that we weren't going to the party. Period."

I glanced at Pat, seeing the same question in her eyes. What wasn't she telling us? "Was he upset with you about it?" I asked.

Her expression was puzzled. "Upset? No, not at all. He said he understood. He knew this holiday season was hard on me. It was just ... unfortunate. Bad timing. I should have mentioned something earlier, and we could have skipped some of the other parties instead of that one, and he was right ... I should have said something sooner."

"It's not your fault, you know," I said. I didn't particularly like how her wanting to stay home on Christmas Eve turned into her being at fault, but I also wasn't sure if I was simply reading too much into it. Her husband was dead, and maybe if they had gone to the party, he wouldn't be. It was natural for her to blame herself, even if it made no sense.

She gave me a watery smile that didn't quite reach her eyes. "I still should have said something sooner. Dennis was right. I should have trusted him to help me."

I thought about my initial conversation with Courtney, when she had first revealed that Dennis was cheating on her. She hadn't wanted to bring it up to him. Maybe this was more of a recurring theme. "Did you often not tell him things?"

She shrugged, staring down into her lap. "Sometimes. I don't know. His job was really stressful, and I didn't like adding to that."

"What did Dennis do for a living?"

"He's a financial advisor. He had his own business ... well, him and Glenn. That's his business partner."

Apparently, they were pretty successful at it, if the size of the house was any indication.

"What's going to happen to the business now?" Pat asked.

Courtney squeezed her tissue into a tighter ball. "I'm not sure. I guess Glenn takes it over completely."

Pat and I glanced at each other. I could see the same question mirrored in her eyes again. Is taking over a business a motive for murder?

"That does sound stressful," I said. "Managing other people's money."

"You have no idea," she said. "He had so much trouble leaving work at the office. Even though he has a home office, I felt like my role was to create a sanctuary for him here … a place for him to rest and recharge. He often told me how much he loved coming home, because it was just so soothing and peaceful after all the stress of the day. So, you can imagine how I didn't like to … disturb the peace, so to speak."

There was something there. I could feel it in the tension of the room. I wanted to keep asking questions to try and get to the bottom of whatever it was, but I didn't feel like it was the time or place. I wasn't sure if any of it was relevant to who killed Dennis, either.

I studied Courtney, who still had her head bowed. Every part of her screamed misery, from her collapsed shoulders to how her body seemed to want to curl into a tiny ball. Was asking her questions about her marriage really what I should be doing right now?

Probably not, I decided.

"So, back to the gift," I began. Courtney raised her head but didn't meet my eyes. I was feeling guilty pushing her with all my questions. No matter what happened in her marriage, she was way too young to be a widow. Especially since, in just a few months, she would also be a single mother. I needed to be more sensitive. "Dennis called it a 'party in a box' because he had to miss the Christmas Eve party?"

She nodded. "Yes, I think getting his favorite brandy … well, it felt like a sort of consolation prize or something. It really brightened his mood." She was silent for a moment, lost in the memories. I was expecting another bout of tears, but she remained dry-eyed.

"So, then what happened?" I prodded. "Did Dennis pour himself a drink?"

She shook her head. "No. Or at least, not in the kitchen. He told me he'd get out of my hair while I finished cooking. It was clear I wasn't really paying attention." She sucked in a shuddering breath. "Maybe I should have been more attentive. Then he might have stayed in the kitchen to have a drink with me instead of going off to his study. I could have seen when he collapsed and called the paramedics sooner. Maybe I could have saved his life."

"It's more likely that it wouldn't have mattered," I said. "Once we know what the poison was, we'll know more, but there's a number of them out there that either have no antidote, or they're so fast-acting, they might as well have no antidote."

Courtney didn't respond, instead reaching for a new tissue.

"So," I continued. "You don't know exactly when he had the brandy."

She shook her head. "I was so focused on making dinner, I wasn't really paying attention to the time. It wasn't until I had the stuffed mushrooms arranged on a plate that I realized I hadn't seen him for a while. That's when I found him in his study."

She pressed the clean tissue against her eyes for a moment. "He was slumped over, half on the sofa and half on the floor."

"Sofa?" I asked.

She nodded. "Along with his desk, he's got a black leather sofa in there. He likes, err *liked*, to sit and read on his sofa rather than at his desk. Especially right before dinner. That's how he unwound at the end of the day. He'd sit on the couch with a drink and a magazine or newspaper. He was forever reading financial publications." She paused again, took another shuddering sigh.

"As soon as I saw him, I ran over and touched him. I thought maybe he was having a heart attack or something. I shook him, and he collapsed the rest of the way onto the floor. It was at that point I knew he was dead."

That explained why Courtney didn't hear him fall. He must have been sitting on his sofa with his brandy when it happened.

"I called the paramedics," Courtney said. "At least, that's what I thought I was doing when I called 9-1-1. I was hoping they could revive him, but deep down, I knew it was too late. I still thought it was a heart attack or a stroke, even though he didn't have any medical issues ... other than stress, of course. It didn't even occur to me he was poisoned. It was only when the cops arrived with the paramedics that I started to realize they thought something else was going on."

I glanced over to the hearth where the wedding photo that was in the newspaper was displayed. While it was clear Dennis was older than Courtney and that he had a few extra pounds on him, he didn't look like a candidate for a heart attack or a stroke.

Could she really be innocent? Despite asking about something to kill him with just a few weeks before?

"What did the cops say?" Pat asked.

Courtney balled her hands into fists. "They haven't said much yet, but it's clear they suspect me. They already came back to interview me again, although they pretended it was just to give me an 'update,'" she answered, adding air quotes around the word "update."

"What was the update? Do they know what killed Dennis?"

"Not yet. They're still waiting for the toxicology report. They're also testing the brandy and trying to get in touch with Arthur." She rolled her eyes. "Basically, they had absolutely nothing to report, but they certainly had a whole lot more questions for me. Why don't they do their job and investigate first, instead of harassing me?"

I forced myself to avoid looking at Pat. "Well, you do have to admit it looks suspicious," I said, trying to be gentle. "Your husband was poisoned at home, and you're the only witness."

"But it wasn't me!" she cried out. "I told them the brandy was a gift. I showed them the card. How could they think it was me?"

"Well," I said cautiously. "I'm guessing they might think you faked it."

Courtney's eyes went wide. "Faked it? How could I fake it? The gift arrived when I was in the kitchen."

I reminded myself that Courtney was grieving and not thinking straight. "The cops only have your word that the gift was delivered on Christmas Eve," I said. "Were you able to tell them who delivered it?"

"No, I told you. I was in the kitchen when the doorbell rang."

I nodded. "So what about Arthur? What kind of relationship did he have with Dennis?"

She gave me a perplexed look. "Arthur wouldn't have poisoned Dennis. That's ridiculous."

"But the gift came from Arthur ..."

"No, someone must have pretended," she said, like I was a particularly slow child. "If it did come from Arthur, it was clearly an accident. Arthur and Dennis got along great. Arthur would never have hurt Dennis on purpose."

"So you're saying someone sent the gift pretending to be Arthur, so Dennis wouldn't be suspicious about drinking it?"

"Yes. What else would it be?"

She still didn't seem to be grasping the situation she was in. "Okay, so let's look at this from the cops' point of view," I said. "You claim that this gift arrived on Christmas Eve for Dennis. You don't know how it arrived—you only heard the doorbell. Dennis tells you the brandy is from Arthur, who you're saying would never poison him. You're saying that there is someone out there who wanted to kill Dennis, and also knew him well enough to know he had a cousin named Arthur who is overseas right now. This person also knew you both would be home on Christmas Eve and not at this big party. And, you are the only witness to what happened that night."

Her face grew paler as I talked. "I'm in trouble, aren't I?" she asked faintly.

"It doesn't look good," I said. "You may want to call a lawyer."

She slumped over. "But it wasn't me. I swear. I'm telling the truth."

She was so distraught, I almost believed her. More than that, I *wanted* to believe her, but there were too many things that didn't add up. "Do they know about the affair?"

Courtney looked away. "I didn't tell them."

"Why not?"

"Because it doesn't matter anymore," she said. "Dennis is dead."

"Yes, but you must know they'll find out. If you don't say anything, it'll look even more suspicious."

Courtney chewed on her lip. "Well, they don't know I know."

She couldn't be this naive. It had to be an act. "What if they ask someone who knows you know?" I asked. "Like someone like me, who you told you wanted to kill Dennis ..."

Courtney jerked her head around, horror in her eyes. "I didn't mean it! I told you I didn't mean it!"

"I know," I said, trying to calm her down. "But what if you said something to someone else? Like Ruthie, when she told you about the love potion?"

Courtney was violently shaking her head. "I didn't tell anyone else. I swear. It just ... slipped out with you."

I found that difficult to believe. "Okay, okay. But how did the subject come up with Ruthie?"

Courtney rolled her eyes. "It was all her. She was telling everyone. I didn't have to ask."

If that was the case, I wondered how Bob would feel when he found out that Ruthie gave him a love potion. Although it was possible that he already knew and found it flattering she would go through such lengths for him.

"But," Courtney continued, her face brightening, "you could tell them."

I looked at her in confusion. "I could tell who, what?"

"The cops," she said, clapping her hands together. "You could tell the cops what I said."

My mouth dropped open. "You want me to tell the cops that you talked about killing your husband?" I couldn't be hearing her right.

"Yes," she said. "Charlie, don't you see? If I was really going to murder my husband, I wouldn't have told anyone about it. But the fact I talked about it with you proves I wasn't serious."

I eyed Pat, who looked as dumbstruck as I felt. "I don't think it works that way," I said cautiously. "I think the cops might consider that motive. Plus, I'll have to tell them that you knew about the affair, and then they'll think you definitely had motive."

Courtney's face crumpled. "I really messed things up, didn't I?" she asked softly.

"Maybe not," I said, even though I didn't believe it. "I'm not an attorney. I think you might want to call one."

She was shaking her head, her face anguished. "You gotta help me."

"I'm not really sure how I could," I said.

"Can you go talk to the cops?" she asked. "Maybe see if you can find out what they're thinking?"

"I don't think they're going to tell me that."

"But they have before," she said. "You've helped them with other cases. I remember hearing something about it. Maybe you could help them find who really killed Dennis."

Briefly, I closed my eyes. While it was true that I had worked with a couple cops previously—okay, one cop, Officer Brandon Wyle—it wasn't like we were friends or anything. More like they tolerated me.

Barely.

"I'm not sure my talking to the cops on your behalf would actually help you," I said. "I think a lawyer would be your best bet."

"But I don't have a lawyer right now," she said. "I have you. Will you please help?"

Those clear, china-blue eyes pleaded with me. Her chin quivered.

It was a bad idea. I knew it was. I should have listened to the little voice earlier, when I was home in my kitchen, that told me I should leave well enough alone. I really needed to just say, "No, I'm so sorry. This was a mistake." Then, if I still felt guilty, I could bring her a pan of my world-famous lasagna, so she at least wouldn't have to cook.

"Okay," I said instead. "I'll see what I can find out. But I don't want to have to lie about you knowing about the affair."

"You don't have to," she said quickly. "It's not like I lied to them. They asked if we had any problems in our marriage, and I said not any more than other couples. I mean, all couples have problems, right?"

"Yes, but ..." I started, but Courtney kept going.

"It's not like we fight or anything. We really don't. We've always gotten along so well." Her eyes filled with tears, and she blinked them back. "That's why I don't understand why he would do such a thing."

"Men are pigs," Pat said. "That's why."

I glanced back at the wedding photo again, at the look of love in Dennis's eyes. It didn't make sense to me either, but alas, it was too late to ask him now.

"The cops are still going to wonder why you didn't bring it up," I said.

"I'll just tell them I wasn't thinking straight. That I thought it was an accident, or the doctors made a mistake, and he had really died from a heart attack. I'll say I didn't think our private life was relevant."

I wasn't sure the cops would buy such a story, but if Courtney was as distraught with them as she had been with us, it was possible. Grief did make people do strange things.

"I'd feel better if you got yourself an attorney," I said. "An attorney might have a much better explanation."

"Okay, fine. I'll call and see if I can find one," she said. "But you're still going to go talk to the cops, right?"

"Yes," I sighed. "I'll see what I can find out. But no promises. Chances are, I will learn nothing helpful."

Courtney nodded her head vigorously. "Of course. And you'll tell them I didn't do it?"

"I'll do my best," I said.

Which I would, although I wasn't completely convinced of her innocence.

On one hand, it seemed like she had been completely blindsided by her husband's murder. And it also seemed like she truly loved him.

But, on the other, there was something off about her ... the way she was careful to avoid my gaze and hide her expression.

She was hiding something. I was sure of it.

The problem was, I had no idea what.

Chapter 4

"Tell me again—why are you here?" Officer Brandon Wyle shifted his lean, lanky figure into a more comfortable position as his chair squeaked in protest. His dark hair was longer than he normally wore it, curling around his collar and into curtain bangs that he absentmindedly brushed off his forehead. I found myself wondering if it was a new hairstyle, or if he kept forgetting to make an appointment with a stylist. His expression was carefully blank, but his dark eyes didn't miss a thing.

I was doing my best to sound more confident than I felt. The longer I sat there, the more convinced I was that it was a huge mistake. But at that point, it would have been even worse if I'd left, so I had to brazen my way through it. "She's my client," I said, which was true. She had bought some tea from me. Once. "And you've seen her condition."

Wyle's eyebrows went up. "'Condition'? You mean her pregnancy?"

"Exactly. Stress isn't good for mothers-to-be. Well, stress isn't good for any of us, but it's especially not good when you're pregnant. And she's already dealing with the stress of losing her husband ..."

"Who she likely poisoned," Wyle said.

Now it was my turn to raise eyebrows. "Are you saying she's a suspect?"

More squeaking as he moved again. We were sitting by his desk, which was tucked away in the corner of the police station. The room was too hot—Wyle had mentioned there was something wrong with the heater—but the combination of the heat, cigarette smoke, and the burnt-coffee-old-sweat odor made my stomach turn. Even though we weren't alone, no one appeared to be paying any attention to us. The constant collective noise of the phone ringing, typewriters clacking, and people talking filled the space. "Oh come on, Charlie. You're smarter than this. Everyone is a suspect in the beginning. Heck, you even made the list."

I was aghast. "Me?"

"Yes, you. Don't you think it's pretty suspicious you're even here?"

"I never even met Dennis," I said.

"You don't need to meet the guy to sell his wife some poison."

"I don't sell poison," I said firmly, deciding I would definitely not be mentioning Courtney's request for something to kill her husband to Wyle. "I sell teas and tinctures."

"Uh huh." Wyle tapped his pen on his notebook, which was balanced precariously on top of a stack of paperwork. His eyes continued to study me.

Wyle was not my first choice. I'd have preferred a cop who didn't know me from Adam. Preferably someone who would be open to my flirtations and maybe let slip a tidbit or two, so I would have something to tell Courtney. And Pat.

Even better, one who wouldn't think to tell anyone I had come by asking questions.

Instead, I got my last choice. Well, maybe my second-to-last. Officer Murphy might be a better last choice. He was sure I had something to do with a couple of disappearances a few years before, but could never prove anything, which meant he continued to regard me with great suspicion … even when it was clear I had nothing to do with the case at hand.

Tough call.

But, seeing as I was stuck with Wyle for the moment, I was going to have to make do. "Look," I said. "Don't you think it's too obvious to be Courtney? I mean, if you were going to kill your husband, why on Earth would you do it when it was just the two of you alone in the house? You're just asking for 'number one suspect' status."

"You're assuming criminals are smarter than they are," Wyle said.

"Have you spoken to her? She's grieving pretty heavily."

"Could also be a guilty conscience."

"Wyle, come on," I said. "Would it be possible to investigate a few other people before throwing the book at her?"

Wyle started jotting down a note. "Who would you like to start with? You, perhaps?"

I ignored that. "Have you talked to Arthur?"

"It's not him."

"How can you be so sure?"

Wyle sighed. "Well, first of all, the package wasn't mailed. It was delivered by courier. And, before you ask, yes, we were able to track down Arthur, and it seemed pretty clear he didn't know anything about it."

While I figured Arthur was a long shot based on Courtney's reaction, it was still a little deflating to hear he had been ruled out. "Did you ask the courier who sent it?"

Wyle's eyes went wide. "Oh, what a good idea. You should be a detective."

I gave him a look. "I guess that means the courier was a dead end."

"You guessed right. The package was mailed to the courier with instructions to deliver it on Christmas Eve."

"Who mailed it?"

"It arrived a few days ago, so all the mailing material had been thrown away. And before you ask, the person paid with cash and left delivery instructions. I guess this isn't that strange—people mail or drop packages off with special delivery instructions."

Wyle was right; that wasn't very helpful. "What about his business partner?"

Wyle shrugged. "What about him?"

The fluorescent lights flickered. I wasn't sure what was worse: the lights, the heat, or the smell. Regardless, it—or maybe the combination—was starting to give me a headache. "Well, don't you think it's at least worth having a conversation with him?"

"Why? Is there something suspicious about him or the business?"

"No, not that I know of," I said. "But that doesn't mean there isn't something TO know."

Wyle gave me a look and wrote something down with an exaggerated flourish. "Talk to business partner, check. Anyone else?"

My headache was getting worse. I started rubbing my temple, trying to ease the pain. I really ought to bring up the affair. The sooner I did that, the sooner I could get out of the whole ordeal. But they were already so suspicious of Courtney … wouldn't that make it worse?

Wyle's eyes narrowed. "Charlie? What is it?"

I sighed. If they didn't know about it now, they were going to find out at some point, and maybe I could try and mitigate some of the damage. "Dennis was having an affair."

Wyle's expression didn't change, but something seemed to shift in it—like he was suddenly hyper-focused. "Do you know with who?"

I shook my head.

"Does Courtney know?"

I looked away. I didn't want to answer as I felt like all I was doing was driving more nails in Courtney's coffin. "She thought Dennis was having a heart attack," I said.

"He's thirty-nine. Pretty young for a heart attack."

"Yes, but he's quite a bit older than she is," I said. "And remember, she's pregnant and not thinking straight."

Wyle gave me a look.

"For the record, I told her she should have told you," I said. "She said she didn't because she didn't think it mattered anymore. He's dead."

"But we told her we thought he was poisoned," Wyle said.

"She didn't believe you," I said. "She thought there had been some sort of mistake, or that it was an accident."

Wyle didn't look convinced.

"Everyone grieves differently," I said. "And yes, I get that it sounds suspicious, but she's really not thinking straight."

"I'll make a note," he said drily. "How long has the affair been going on?"

"I don't know the details, but it's been a while," I said.

He nodded and wrote a few things down. "Is that it?"

I paused, trying to figure out if I'd made things worse for Courtney. I had an unpleasant feeling the answer was "yes." Was there anything I could do to make it better?

No. I'd better stop while I was ahead.

"Yes, that's it." I stood up. Wyle stood as well.

"Thanks for coming in," he said. "I'll definitely look into all this."

"Of course," I said, picking up my purse.

Wyle didn't move. "Which means you don't need to do anything more."

"What more do you think I would do?"

Wyle huffed a sigh. "No investigating. We'll take it from here."

I gave him a thin smile. "I don't know what you're talking about. I don't investigate anything. I make teas." I turned and headed toward the door.

"I'm serious, Charlie," Wyle called out.

I waved at him without turning around. I couldn't get out of there fast enough.

***

"Well, that was pretty unproductive," Pat said, picking up a fry. "Unless you count getting yourself added to the suspect list. Then, it was definitely a win."

I made a face at her.

We were sitting in Aunt May's Diner. After leaving Courtney's house, Pat assumed she would be accompanying me to the police station. I assumed I was dropping her off at her house. While in the car, we'd had a brief (but heated) discussion about it. I argued that me showing up at the station was odd enough as it was, let alone arriving with a second person, which would surely raise even more red flags. In the end, we came to a compromise. Pat agreed, a little less graciously than I thought warranted, to not try and weasel her way into the station with me. I agreed to meet her at Aunt May's afterward to give her the lowdown.

"And you better not leave anything out," she warned as she slammed the car door. I gave her a cheery smile as I pulled away from the curb. She stood in front of Aunt May's, watching me drive away and shaking her head.

"We for sure now know Courtney is a suspect," I said, playing with the straw in my ginger ale. My stomach was still queasy, although as soon as I got out of the station, I started feeling much better. I decided on the grilled cheese with tomato soup, which was also helping. "And the cops don't seem to be looking at anyone else."

"Wyle did say lots of people were on the suspect list," Pat said, wiping her hands with a napkin. She had ordered a club sandwich and eaten most of it while waiting for me. "It's possible they haven't settled on Courtney yet."

"True," I said, frowning darkly at my own sandwich as I pictured Wyle's smug smile while making a point of taking notes. Oof, that man drove me crazy. "But it feels like they've decided it's Courtney, and all that's left is for them to cross all their T's and dot their I's."

"It's hard to blame them," Pat said. "It does look suspicious."

I eyed her. "You think she's guilty, too?"

Pat shrugged. "You were there with me. She's hiding something."

"Yeah," I said glumly, going back to staring at my sandwich. "I wish I knew what that was."

Pat regarded me thoughtfully. "Why does it bother you so much to think she might have killed her husband? I mean, you barely know her. She wasn't a client. Buying one bag of tea doesn't count, so it's not like you're going to lose business."

"It doesn't bother you?"

Pat shrugged. "Sure, it's a little creepy to think we were sitting in a murderer's living room, but he *was* cheating on her. It's not like we were in danger."

"But was he?" In my mind's eye, I saw the wedding photo again.

Pat pursued her lips. "People fall out of love, Charlie," she said, as though reading my mind.

"I know."

"And just because someone is unfaithful, it doesn't mean he doesn't love his spouse."

"I get it," I said impatiently. "But that doesn't change the fact that there's just something about this that doesn't add up." I paused and started playing with my straw again. "I can't put my finger on it."

"Maybe it's because you've never chit chatted with a murderess before."

I jerked the straw so hard, ginger ale sloshed out of the glass.

"Or," Pat continued, not noticing the mess I'd made, "maybe Courtney is being set up."

I gave Pat a hard look. "Weren't you just trying to convince me that Courtney is guilty?"

Pat grinned at me. "I didn't say I believed it. I was just throwing it out there as a reason for your uncomfortable feeling." Her smile disappeared. "But seriously. I agree with you. There's something not quite right about all of this. But what?"

But what, indeed. Was it because Courtney was being set up for her husband's murder? Or was she responsible?

Or was something else going on completely?

I picked up my sandwich. "I suspect we'll never know the truth."

Pat huffed a dramatic sigh. "And that's probably the truest statement we've heard today."

Chapter 5

I was in the middle of creating a customized tea blend for one of my clients when the doorbell rang. Hoping it wasn't her yet, as I was running behind, I hurried to the door.

However, the woman standing on the other side of the door was a stranger.

"Can I help you?"

She was older, her face soft with wrinkles. Her blonde hair streaked with silver was pulled back in a stylish bun, and her clear, blue eyes studied me from behind silver, cat-eyed frames. She wore a long, cream-colored wool coat and a bright-red scarf around her neck. She seemed familiar, but I couldn't place her.

"Are you Charlie Kingsley?" she asked.

"I am. And you are ..."

"Violet. Violet Simson." She held out her hand. "I'm Courtney's mother."

Of course. The resemblance was striking; I couldn't believe I hadn't seen it sooner. I reached out my hand to shake hers, but then I realized I was letting all the heat out of the house, so I stepped back to invite her in. She took a moment to stomp her feet on the doormat before coming inside.

"Do you want some tea?" I asked, shutting the door behind her.

Her face brightened. "Do you still have some of the candy cane kind?"

"Sure do." I headed to the kitchen to get a pot started. "Just hang your coat on the rack and come join me."

She appeared in the kitchen a few moments later, wearing a bright-blue sweater that matched her eyes and black slacks. "Your kitchen is so big," she exclaimed.

I glanced around, taking in the white cabinets, grey counter-tops, and huge island in the center. I still had my Christmas decorations up, including the tree in the corner and a Santa cookie jar. "Yes, it certainly is."

"I miss my big kitchen," she said with a sigh. "My apartment is nice, but I sure miss my kitchen. And wow! Your garden!" Violet had moved to the large window and was longingly staring out.

"Not much to look at now, I'm afraid," I said as I carried the tea and a couple of mugs to the table.

She waved a hand dismissively. "I can get a good idea of what you're doing. My garden is something else I miss." She sighed again.

"I'd miss my garden and kitchen too," I said as I deposited the last of my leftover Christmas cookies in the center of the table next to the pot. They were nearly a week old, but they still tasted fine. Hopefully, Violet would finish them, or maybe I could persuade her to take the rest with her, as I was Christmas-cookied out. I poured the tea as she took a seat. Immediately, she cupped the mug with her hands, but she didn't drink.

"How is Courtney?" I asked, figuring the question would eventually lead to why she had turned up on my doorstep.

She let out a deep, painful sigh. "That's why I'm here today."

I pushed the Christmas cookies a little closer to her. A little sugar and fat certainly couldn't hurt. "I thought that might be the case."

She smiled, but it appeared strained, and her eyes remained worried. "I knew you'd understand. I had a feeling you were the right person to talk to."

I could feel prickles of unease start to rise on the back of my neck, but I kept my expression neutral. "Oh?"

She nodded. "Courtney needs help."

I had no doubt Courtney needed help. Probably a lot of it. "Has she hired a lawyer yet?"

Violet sighed again and looked up at the ceiling. "She's called a few people, but everyone thinks she's guilty."

I restrained from saying the obvious—that a lot of people thought Courtney was guilty because she looked pretty guilty—hence, her need for an attorney. The sooner the better. "Is that what they said?"

"Not in so many words."

"Are they refusing to work with her?"

"No, they're all willing to represent her."

"Then what's the problem?" I didn't understand what Violet was upset about, nor what she thought I could do to help. Was she looking for suggestions?

"She has no one on her side," Violet burst out, sloshing her tea over the side of her mug and onto her hand. She quickly jerked her hand away and thrust one of her fingers into her mouth.

"Did you burn yourself?" I asked, getting out of my seat. "Let me get you a washcloth."

"It's nothing," she mumbled around her fingers, but I was already at the sink, wringing out a washcloth for the table and a clean one for her hand. I handed her one and wiped up the table with the other.

"Okay," I said, sitting back down. "Let's back up here. First off, how can you be so sure no one is on her side?"

"Isn't it obvious?" Violet asked, finally succumbing to the lure of the sugar and reaching for a cookie. "No one is coming by. No one. Not to bring food, not to see how she's doing. They're not even sending flowers."

"Well, it's tough to know what to say or do in these situations," I said. "Her husband has been murdered. It's not like he died of cancer or a car accident."

"And they think she did it."

"Well, some probably do," I agreed. "But some probably don't know what to think."

Violet took a bite of the cookie, spilling crumbs over the table. I made a mental note to bring small plates to the table with snacks. Seeing Violet at the door had thrown me off my game. "If they were real friends, they would come by," Violet said darkly, brushing a few crumbs off her chin. "These cookies are very good, by the way," she added. Before I could respond, she kept talking. "But it's more than just her so-called 'friends,'" she said around another bite of cookie. "The cops think she's guilty, too."

"The cops think everyone is guilty," I said. "It's their job."

"Yes, but if they're already convinced Courtney is guilty, they're not going to look at anyone else."

This was true, and it was something that had bothered me, as well. But, somehow, coming from Courtney's mother, it simply ratcheted up my uneasy feeling.

"That's why I thought Courtney should get herself a good attorney," I said.

Violet pressed her lips together into a straight line. A couple of crumbs were stuck to the corner of her pink-lipsticked mouth. "If the attorney thinks she's guilty, too, he isn't going to try and find the real killer, either," she said. "Courtney needs someone in her corner. Someone who will fight for her."

Oh no. I had a terrible feeling where she was going. "Have you thought about hiring a private investigator?" I asked. "I mean, if you think the cops aren't going to look hard enough, a PI could help."

She waved her hand in a dismissive way. "A PI is going to be just like an attorney. He'd take her money, sure, but he'll assume she's guilty and not try all that hard."

"I don't think it works that way ..." I started to say, but Violet interrupted me.

"That's why she needs you." She looked me directly in the eyes. "She needs you to help investigate and find the real killer."

My stomach twisted in a knot. I thought about Wyle a few days before, his dark eyes boring into mine as he told me to leave the investigation alone. What would he do if he knew the mother of his number one suspect was in my house trying to get me to do exactly what he warned me against doing? "You do know I'm not a detective or anything," I said. "I make teas and tinctures."

"But you have done some investigating before," she said. "Right?"

"Yes, but ..."

"And you believe she's innocent, right?"

I wouldn't say that, exactly. But her eyes, so like her daughter's, were so hopeful, I couldn't bear to crush her spirits. "Believing in her guilt or innocence doesn't have anything to do with finding the person who is responsible."

"But you'll try harder if you believe in her innocence," Violet insisted. "We can pay you, if that's what you're worried about."

"No, that's not it." My tea business did pretty well, better than I ever thought it would, and my trust fund covered the mortgage payment, so money wasn't an issue. I took a deep breath. "I'm just a regular person," I said. "I don't have any special skills or a license or anything. I don't know if my poking around is going to help Courtney or make things worse." Thinking about my previous conversation with Wyle, I was leaning toward it making things worse.

"But that's not true," Violet said. "Courtney told me you already talked to the cops on her behalf."

"Yes, but I don't know how helpful I was." I had called Courtney to give her an update, which I didn't think was terribly optimistic. I told her the cops now knew about the affair, but that I had also pushed them to question other people, including Dennis's business partner. I didn't mention that I didn't think I was terribly successful at the latter, although in retrospect, I probably should have. Both mother and daughter now appeared to think I had made a difference in the case, hence their desire for me to keep investigating for them.

"The point is, you're trying to be helpful," Violet said firmly. "And that's what we need. Will you help us?"

I looked into Violet's clear, china-blue eyes, so like her daughter's, and inwardly sighed. How did I get myself into these messes?

"I'll see what I can do," I said, and Violet clapped her hands.

"I knew you were the perfect person! I just knew it."

I smiled back, but it felt forced and uncomfortable. Hopefully, I would accomplish more than just turning myself into more of a suspect.

***

"Do you even know the first thing about investigating a crime?" Pat asked.

We were sitting in the living room with the lights off and Christmas tree on. I figured since it wasn't yet New Year's, we could still enjoy the Christmas tree without guilt. I had also poured us both a healthy glass of red wine. I wasn't much of a drinker, maybe one or two glasses a month, but it felt warranted.

"I've done it before," I said.

Pat raised her eyebrows over the rim of her wine glass. "You got lucky before," she corrected. "This is a little different."

"How so?"

"Well, to start, do you know where to begin?"

"Violet gave me the names of Dennis's business partner and, uh, mistress."

Pat's eyes went wide. "Mistress? So Courtney knows who she is?"

I took a sip. "Apparently so."

"Did Violet tell you how Courtney found out?"

"I didn't ask. Trust me, it was weird enough getting that information from Courtney's mom." I could still remember the face Violet made as she wrote down the woman's name, address, and phone number.

"I'm just ... I can't believe Courtney didn't say something to Dennis about it before. If I had found out the name of some floozy Richard was cheating on me with, you can bet your bottom dollar we would have had a chat about it."

"I don't understand it either," I said.

"So, is that it?"

"For now," I said. "I also got some background information on Dennis. As it turns out, he was married before, to a woman named Nina."

Pat rolled her eyes. "Let me guess. Divorced."

"You win the prize."

Pat shook her head. "So, Courtney really was a trophy wife. Did he leave Nina for her?"

"That I don't know, and I could hardly ask her mother."

Pat inclined her head. "Fair enough. Are you going to have a chat with Nina?"

"I'm strongly considering it. An ex-wife would certainly have motive to not just murder her 'husband,' but set his new wife up for the crime. The timing doesn't make a lot of sense, though. Courtney and Dennis have been married a couple of years now. I would have thought if Nina was inclined to do such a thing, she would have done it before now. Especially as Courtney has a baby coming."

"Maybe the baby is what pushed her over the edge," Pat said. "Maybe Nina wanted a baby, and Dennis kept refusing, and then she found out the new wife is pregnant."

"Hmm, good point," I said, drumming my fingers on my wine glass. "I think I definitely need to pay her a visit."

"Anyone else on your list?"

"Not yet. I asked Violet to think about any other people who would have known about Arthur and would want to hurt Dennis."

"What about Dennis's family?"

"I asked, but Violet doesn't really know them very well. She was going to get a list together for me with some notes. But clearly, she wanted me to start with Glenn and, uh, Tiffany."

Pat's jaw dropped. "Tiffany? Really? That's his mistress's name?"

"It gets worse."

"Worse?"

"She's an aerobics instructor."

Pat choked on her wine. "Wow. I feel like I'm living in a bad soap opera. Tiffany the aerobics instructor! I can practically picture what she looks like." She wagged her eyebrows at me, and I snorted.

"But seriously," Pat continued. "I'm glad you got the names, but how on Earth are you going to approach either of them?

You're not the cops. You can't just sashay in and start asking questions about Dennis."

"Let's just say I have a few tricks up my sleeve," I answered mysteriously.

Chapter 6

"Get those knees up," Tiffany shouted from the front of the room. "You don't want those Christmas cookies stuck on your thighs."

I groaned. At this point, I didn't care if every Christmas cookie I had ever eaten decided to move into my thighs. They could even bring their friends.

"And smile!" Tiffany demonstrated by pointing at her own wide grin.

I groaned again.

Back when I lived in New York, I regularly attended aerobics classes. Moving to Redemption, I had been so busy with gardening and tea-making, not to mention cleaning my huge old house, that I never seemed to have the time to go to aerobics. But when I called the Fit for Life health and fitness club for Tiffany's teaching schedule, I figured it wouldn't be a big deal. I mean, I was a little out of shape, but I was sure the class was nothing I couldn't handle.

I thought I was going to die.

Tiffany, in contrast, didn't even look like she had broken a sweat. Her platinum-blonde hair was pulled back in a high ponytail that bounced merrily along with the music, and her hot-pink and green leggings with matching pink leotard seemed to glow under the fluorescent lights. Her body was tight and firm, including her derrière, which I caught frequent glimpses of in the wall-to-wall mirror. My own reflection wasn't nearly as flattering.

All in all, Tiffany looked exactly like one would imagine an aerobics instructor named "Tiffany" who was having an affair with a married man would. I knew without any doubt that Pat would be rolling her eyes if she were there. Of course, she would never be in such a class with me, because Pat was also much smarter than me.

This was definitely not one of my best ideas.

It got even worse. Tiffany put us through a torturous routine of leg lifts and sit-ups before guiding us through a few stretches to end class.

I mopped off my face with a towel and uncapped my water bottle for a drink, trying to pull myself together enough to have a conversation with Tiffany. Although I was wondering if I should figure out another way to run into her going forward— something that didn't involve me doing aerobics.

"Nice to see a new face in class."

Startled, I nearly choked on my water. There she was, standing right next to me. Now that I was closer, I could see she was both older and sweatier than I had thought. Tiny lines fanned out from a pair of intense green eyes, and beads of sweat dotted her forehead and cheeks, almost puddling on top of her heavy makeup.

"Thanks," I said. "It's been a little while since I've been to a class. I'll definitely be feeling it tomorrow."

She grinned. "I'll take that as a compliment. I don't remember seeing you around. Are you new?"

"Sort of. I moved to Redemption from New York a few years ago. When I lived in New York, I was pretty religious about attending aerobics class, so I thought maybe it was time to get back into the groove."

"Well, you're starting at the right time," she said. "We have a special going on, a New Year, New You type of thing. Half off monthly membership dues for six months."

"That's a great deal and probably exactly what I need," I said as I fell into step next to her.

"I can get you signed up if you want," she said and laughed. "Sorry, not trying to be pushy. But I also know human nature. If you don't plunk down a payment, you're far less likely to come back."

"Ain't that the truth?" I said. "I'm just not used to an aerobics teacher selling me memberships."

"Oh, I'm more than an instructor," she said. "I own the place."

My eyes widened. Violet hadn't mentioned that. "Oh, wow. I didn't realize."

"Yeah, it's all mine." She waved her arm in a big flourish, the gesture encompassing the locker rooms, weight room, cardio room, and aerobics studio. "It's probably not as impressive as what you're used to in New York, but it does the job."

"I think it's lovely." Which was true. While it wasn't as shiny and polished as the clubs in New York, it was clean and bright, with pale-yellow walls, hardwood floors, and colorful inspirational posters all around. The one in the hallway had a kitten dangling from a rope, with the words "Hang In There" printed across the bottom. The location wasn't bad, either. It was a couple of blocks away from downtown, and it had a nice, big parking lot in front.

Her face flushed with pleasure. "Thanks. You should have seen it before the remodel. It was a wreck." Her hands fluttered around, as if giving me a tour of what it once looked like. "I'm Tiffany, by the way. Tiffany Gold."

"Charlie Kingsley." We shook hands. Her nails were long and polished in a bright, cheery red, probably in celebration of Christmas.

"So, Charlie, think I'll be seeing you again?"

I smiled. "Probably." *Most definitely.* I suspected I would need at least one or two more visits before I was able to start asking her about Dennis and Courtney.

Her smile was wide. "Great. Let me get you the paperwork. You can take it home, of course, or we can fill it out here."

"That works," I said as I followed her to the cozy lobby filled with comfortable chairs and small tables. The color scheme was muted and soothing—browns, beiges, and blues, and there were more framed inspirational posters featuring cats, like the one with a cat balancing on a branch and the words "Believe in yourself, and you can do anything." The Christmas decorations were still up, including a tree covered with red and gold tinsel. On the opposite wall from it was a bar with a couple of poinsettias on it. Three high chairs stood in front of what looked like a place for meal preparation, but other than a tall fridge filled with water and energy drinks, it was bare.

"What do you do, Charlie?" Tiffany asked as she headed for the desk that stood next to the front door. There had been someone manning it when I walked in—a tiny, perky thing who didn't look old enough to drive—but the room was empty now. I saw Tiffany shake her head slightly as she walked over to the desk.

"I sell teas and tinctures," I said.

She paused and glanced over her shoulder to look at me. "What kind of teas?"

"My own custom blends mostly. The tinctures are custom, too."

She turned all the way around. "Really? Where do you get the ingredients?"

"Grow them. Mostly. Not all, of course. It's a little too cold for a lemon tree, for instance. But I grow many of the flowers and herbs myself."

"Are they organic?"

"Yep."

She clapped her hands together. "This is amazing! I've been looking for someone like you!"

"Really?" I hadn't expected that. "Do you have something going on that you think an herbal tea would help with?"

"Maybe. I've been using herbs and teas for years. But the distributors are all out of town, so they have to mail me products and mixtures. Which is fine, but it won't work with the idea I had."

"Which is ..."

"Doing something here."

"Here?"

She nodded toward the long counter. "I've been wanting to offer some healthy beverages, and maybe some snacks, so people can sit after their workout and have something. I could offer coffee, but ..." she made a face. "I don't know. Coffee doesn't feel like it belongs. It's got all that caffeine, and I don't know if people should be drinking caffeine after a workout when they should be rehydrating. But herbal tea, that's perfect."

"Maybe I could come up with a post-workout blend," I said, the wheels already turning.

Her eyes widened. "You could do that?"

"Yeah, something to help relax the body and reduce inflammation. Maybe rose and chamomile. Ginger would be good, as well. I can play around, maybe come up with a couple of versions."

She let out a little squeal. "Oh! I love that idea. Yes, a custom tea blend. Maybe we can make it exclusive to Fit for Life."

"Maybe." I hadn't thought about doing custom tea blends for another business, but the idea intrigued me.

Tiffany was so excited, she looked like she might break out into another aerobics routine. "This is so perfect. It's exactly what I hoped would happen."

Hoped would happen? I shot her a funny look. "What do you mean?"

She gave her head a quick shake. "Nothing. Well, almost nothing. It's just I never wanted this to be solely a health and fitness club. I always wanted it to be more holistic. You know, offer healthy foods, maybe teach classes on nutrition and stress reduction, like meditation and yoga. You know, everything that goes into being fit for life." Her smile was a little self-conscious. "But it's been a more difficult road than I thought to add those other pieces. Just running the fitness part has taken up most of my time."

"Is there anyone who can help out? Maybe a family member or husband?" I tamped down my eagerness, not wanting to scare her off. Maybe I would be able to get more out of her today than I had hoped.

She let out a bitter laugh. "No, my family doesn't live that close, not that any of them would be interested. And my husband considers this my hobby." She rolled her eyes.

I tried not to let my shock show.

She had a husband.

I had assumed she was single.

"He thinks this is a hobby?"

She nodded. "He makes enough that I don't need to work, but I was getting so bored with volunteer work, and this was what I always wanted to do. So, he did give me the money to get it going, and I'm grateful, but ..." her voice trailed off, and she looked away. I could see a muscle tightening in her jaw. "Oh my goodness, look at the time! I have another class coming up. Do you want to come back later, maybe in a couple of days, and we can hammer out the details to sell your tea?"

"Sure." I was dying to ask more questions, especially about this non-supportive husband, but the brittle smile she had plastered on her face made it clear she was done talking about it. At least for now.

"Jillian," she called out, and the petite teenager I'd seen earlier appeared from the hallway. "Can you help Charlie here? She's going to be a new member. And schedule a time for us to meet in a couple of days."

"Sure," Jillian answered in a sing-song voice as she headed to the desk.

Tiffany's smile turned frosty. "And please remember what I told you about not leaving the front desk unattended."

Jillian bobbed her head, her ponytail bouncing up and down. "Yes, Ms. G."

"Thanks," Tiffany said shortly before turning to me with a slight nod. "See you soon."

"Can't wait." Which was absolutely true. There was clearly more going on than what "met the eye," and I was impatient to discover what was lying beneath the surface.

Chapter 7

"So, Mrs. Kingsley, why don't you tell me a little bit about yourself?" Glenn smoothed his red tie as he seated himself behind the imposing oak executive desk in front of me. Like Dennis, he appeared to be in his late thirties or early forties, with a receding hairline and the beginnings of a round, soft belly. A mustache covered what appeared to be a pair of thin lips, and his cheeks and nose were ruddy, as if he'd enjoyed a little too much alcohol over the years. He adjusted his well-cut navy suit jacket and selected a pen from a holder.

"It's 'Ms.,'" I said, trying to unobtrusively make myself more comfortable on the hard-backed chair in front of him. "I'm not married."

He made a note on the empty notepad in front of him. "Widowed or divorced?"

"Neither," I said.

The faintest hint of surprise crossed his face, so quickly I thought I might have imagined it. But I was pretty sure I hadn't. He made a second note. "So how can I help?"

There was a fussiness about him that I found off-putting. Something about the meticulously clean desk, save for the notepad, a black and gold blotter, a matching black and gold pen holder, a letter tray (empty, of course), a gold-framed picture angled so I couldn't see who was in it, and a mug with the words "World's Best Boss" printed across it set my teeth on edge. There was no sign of any Christmas decorations, although to be fair, it was after the new year. And last but not least, the uncomfortable chairs. I was starting to wonder if Glenn chose them specifically because of how uncomfortable they were—a subtle hint to not linger or waste any time with friendly banter.

Even though I had never met Dennis and really didn't know anything about him (other than his taste in women), I found myself wondering how he put up with Glenn as a business partner.

"I have a trust fund," I said, immediately recognizing the expression in his eyes—"Oh, so that's where she got her money." I paused to take a breath, even though part of me had to admit he wasn't exactly wrong. Yes, my tea business paid the bills, but it would be far more challenging for me without the trust fund. "While the person who manages it is based in New York, since I'm here to stay, I thought it might make sense to also look for someone local to manage part of it."

He was busy with his notes. "Yes, that is definitely something we can help with. I'll need a few details."

He asked a bunch of questions, which I did my best to answer in a way that sounded more promising than the situation was. Truth be told, there was really no way Mr. Farley would ever give up one iota of control.

When he was satisfied with my answers to his questions, he leaned back in his chair to give me his little sales pitch: how long he's been in business, how many satisfied customers he had, and what I could expect working with him.

I smiled and nodded during his little spiel, and when he was finished, he asked if I had any questions.

"Not really," I said. "You came highly recommended."

He smiled wide, revealing a lot of teeth. "Can I ask who? We love rewarding happy clients."

"Of course. It was my client, Courtney Fallon."

His smile faded a little, and he suddenly became very busy straightening up his desk. "Well, that's sweet, that she did that. I'm sure you must have heard about her husband."

"I did," I said.

"I'm surprised you came in now after what, err, happened."

"Well, to be frank, I meant to come in earlier," I said, flashing him an embarrassed smile as I lied through my teeth. "But, with the new year, I thought it would be smart to make the move. However," I continued, and Glenn's expression, which had started to relax, tensed up again. "I *was* wondering how you were handing things, in light of Dennis's death."

"An excellent question," Glenn said, although the stiffness of his body screamed otherwise. "I can assure you that, as a client, there will be no issues on your end. Of course, we will have a transition here, and I already have feelers out for a new financial advisor to take his place, but I can promise you that we will do everything in our power to make our team transitions as painless and seamless as possible for you."

I smiled. "That's great to hear. I'm glad you're already on top of things. It must have been a huge shock when it happened. No one would blame you if you needed to take some time off to grieve and regroup."

Glenn smoothed his tie again. "Yes, it was a shock," he said. "I suppose that's the case when anyone dies. My father was sick for a long time, and even though we expected his death, when it happened, it was still a shock. Under these circumstances, it's especially so. I thought about shutting the business down for a few days, but quite honestly, working helps me. I know if I were sitting at home, all I would be doing is thinking about the business anyway, and how to move forward with Dennis gone." He gave me a thin smile, but I could see the tension and stress behind it. "Plus, this time of year is always busy, so it's better to keep working."

I nodded, my expression understanding. "I can imagine how difficult all this is for you. I'm having trouble getting my head around what happened, and I never even met Dennis. And while I'm not especially close with Courtney, I personally can't believe she had anything to do with his death."

Glenn's smile froze. He started fiddling with the items on his desk again, shifting them and moving them around. "How well do we know anyone, really?" he asked. "Aren't we all capable of violence under the right circumstances?" He glanced at me then, his expression embarrassed, as if suddenly realizing I was still in the room. "Sorry," he said. "Clearly, I'm not myself. I've known Courtney since the beginning of their relationship. I was even the best man at their wedding. It's been ..." he paused, shaking his head, his fingers continuously rearranging items, as if they had a mind of their own. "Difficult."

I nodded again, making sure I kept my face arranged in a compassionate-yet- interested expression. "Was their marriage troubled?"

"What marriage isn't?" He must have seen something in my face, because he forced a smile. "I just mean, it's difficult to re-ally know what's going on inside a marriage when you're on the outside looking in. On the surface, they seemed happy enough, but ..." he shrugged.

"Do you know any reason Courtney might have had for wanting to hurt Dennis?" I watched him closely. He must know about Dennis's affair. I couldn't believe as his business partner, he wouldn't have noticed something—long lunches, leaving early, working late. Maybe Tiffany even came by the office a few times for a quickie on the desk.

Glenn stopped fiddling and straightened up, smoothing his tie and folding his hands on his desk. "I'm sure the police will sort it out," he said dismissively. "Do you have any other ques-tions for me about our services?" It appeared we were done talking about Dennis and Courtney.

"Mr. Haggard?" The secretary cracked open the door and poked her head in. She was probably around my age with short, dark hair, dark eyes, and a thin mouth that a heavy coat of red lipstick couldn't completely mask. "Mr. Christof is on the phone for you again."

Glenn pressed his lips together. "Not now, June. Can't you see I'm with someone?"

"But he was very insistent ..."

"Not now," Glenn snapped. "Tell him I'll call him back when I'm done with my meeting."

"Of course, Mr. Haggard," June murmured, her expression reminding me of a kicked dog. She slunk out of the office, clos-ing the door behind her.

Glenn straightened up. "I apologize for that," he said. "As you can imagine, it's been an adjustment for everyone, including our clients. While it's normal for people to want to make sure all will be well when it comes to their money, a few of them have been quite concerned. We're doing our best to reassure them as much as possible, but it's going to take some time."

"Of course," I said. "I understand."

He smiled a tiny smile. "So, do you have any other questions?"

I shook my head. "No, you've been very helpful. And you've given me a lot to think about."

"Let me know if you think of any others."

I reached down to collect my purse when my eye caught the framed photograph. During Glenn's fiddling, he had shifted it, so I could now see who it was—a woman with carefully styled blonde hair, perfect makeup, and intense green eyes.

I had to blink a few times, sure I was seeing things. It couldn't be her.

It just couldn't.

"Mrs., err, Ms. Kingsley? Is everything all right?" Glenn was staring at me, his expression concerned.

My mouth had gone dry. "Sorry. I just ... is that your wife?"

Glenn glanced at where I was pointing. "Ah, yes. That's Tiffany."

"She's ... she's lovely," I said faintly, but inside, I was screaming. Dennis was sleeping with his business partner's wife? That couldn't be right. Violet must have gotten the names mixed up. Surely, this information was too important not to share with me, had she known.

Glenn beamed. "She is, isn't she? She owns a health and fitness club here in town. Fit for Life. Have you been there?"

I swallowed. "Yes, actually. I was thinking about getting a membership for the new year. You know, a New Year's resolution."

"Ah, yes. You would definitely be in good company."

I stood up, wanting nothing more than to get out of that stuffy, sparse office. "Thank you for your time. I'll be in touch."

Glenn stood as well, reaching across the desk to shake my hand. "It was nice meeting you, Ms. Kingsley. I trust you won't let our current ... well, 'troubles,' dissuade you from using our services."

His hand was hot and heavy, and his grip was tight. Uncomfortably tight. Like he was purposefully squeezing my hand. His eyes had a strange glint to them, and I was suddenly aware of how alone we were. June's desk was down the hall and near the front door. With the door closed, would she even hear me if I screamed?

I pulled my hand away. "Of course not," I said. "It's not like it was your fault Dennis died. Right?"

I couldn't believe the words had come out of my mouth. *Charlie*, a little voice snapped inside of me. *Are you trying to get yourself in trouble?*

Glenn also seemed in disbelief. His eyes widened, and his jaw dropped open. We started at each other in silence for a moment before I forced myself to laugh.

"Sorry," I said. "Just a bad joke. I shouldn't have said it."

Glenn's mustache twitched as he frowned in disapproval. "No, you shouldn't have."

"I'll ... um ... I'll just go." I turned and hurried down the hallway, forcing myself not to run.

Are you out of your mind? The little voice hissed at me. *If he IS Dennis's murderer, do you really think antagonizing him was a smart move?*

While the little voice had a point, what I saw in Glenn's eyes was worth the risk.

There was something underneath the shock. Something that shouldn't have been there if he were completely innocent.

Fear.

Chapter 8

"Hold on," Pat said, holding her hands out as if she could physically stop the flow of words from my mouth. "Dennis was having an affair with his business partner's wife?"

I yanked the Tupperware container out of the cupboard, spraying flour into the air like a white cloud. When I was upset, I baked. "Don't you think that would have been good information to have shared with me?" I asked, presumably to Pat, but I could have just as well been talking to the stick of butter sitting on the counter waiting to be turned into gingerbread, or Midnight, who had meandered into the kitchen and was sitting by his bowl.

I had called Violet the moment I walked in my house. Violet's response: "You mean you didn't know Tiffany is Glenn's wife?"

"How could I have?" I demanded.

"Well, I just figured you knew."

"They have different last names," I nearly shouted.

"Oh, oh," Violet said, suddenly sounding lost and confused. "I just ... it's such a blur. Was it important to tell you?"

I clamped my jaw together and forced myself to count to ten as I paced around the kitchen as far as the cord would go. *She's an old woman*, I reminded myself, *and her daughter, her pregnant daughter, is suspected of killing her husband. Of course she isn't thinking straight.* "If I'm going to help you, I need to know everything," I said. "Otherwise, I could screw something up and not even know it."

"Oh, of course. That makes sense," Violet said. "I should have thought of that. Forgive me."

"It's fine," I said. "Just please don't hide things from me."

"Did you say anything to Courtney?" There was an edge to her voice that hadn't been there before.

"What does that matter?" I asked.

"Does that mean you didn't?"

"No, I didn't say anything to Courtney. Why?"

Violet let out a sigh of relief. "She doesn't like talking about it, as you can imagine. It really upsets her. And she's upset enough right now. I told her I'd handle it. So, if you wouldn't mind ..." Her voice trailed off.

"I won't say anything," I said. "But that means you need to be honest with me. Is there anything else I should know?"

Her voice was hesitant. "I ... I don't think so. But let me think about it and get back to you."

I hung up, sure she still wasn't telling me everything. But what was she hiding? And why?

"So, why didn't they tell you?"

I grabbed the sugar out of the cupboard and nearly dropped it. I had forgotten I had just filled it, so it was much heavier. "Violet thought I knew."

Pat looked perplexed. "But how would you? Their last names are different."

I pointed my wooden spoon at Pat. "Yes! My point exactly."

Pat shook her head as she picked up her tea. "This is really bizarre. Maybe Courtney is guilty after all."

I plucked the baking soda out of the cupboard with a lot less force than before. "Maybe. But Glenn sure was acting like he had something to hide. And he had motive, as well. Just as much as Courtney."

"You're assuming Glenn knows about Dennis and his wife."

And just like that, all my anger and frustration drained out of me. I slumped against the counter, letting out a deep sigh. "That's true. I just don't know what to do," I said. "Maybe it was an honest mistake. Violet is pretty upset and isn't thinking straight. Or maybe she was embarrassed. I mean, it's embarrassing that her son-in-law was cheating on her daughter with his business partner's wife. Or maybe she really didn't think it was that important. So, it's possible her not telling me really doesn't mean anything. But ..." I chewed on my lip.

Pat raised an eyebrow. "You think it does?"

"It seems suspicious," I said. "Not to mention I think there's more she didn't tell me. She asked me to help her, so why is she keeping secrets? Doesn't that seem suspicious to you?"

Pat shrugged. "I don't know. You could be right about why Violet didn't tell you. Should it be considered 'suspicious?' Maybe, but maybe not. As for other stuff she's hiding, everyone has things they would prefer others don't know. It could be just something embarrassing or dumb they did when they were younger. But again, not necessarily criminal, or even something to be concerned about."

"But you and I both felt like Courtney was hiding something when we talked to her," I said.

"It's like you said before. What would be the point of intentionally not telling you? Especially since you would likely find out."

I went back to my baking. "Maybe to confuse things?" I guessed. "I mean, if Courtney really is guilty, maybe Violet is hoping I do mess things up. That would make it more difficult for the cops to make a case against Courtney."

"I think you're reaching," Pat said.

"You're probably right," I agreed. "Especially since everyone seems to be acting guilty. Glenn sure seemed like he was hiding something. And Tiffany is clearly not happy in her marriage."

"Well, if you want my two cents, at this point, I would probably assume Violet not telling you was an innocent mistake and take a much harder look at Tiffany and Glenn. Especially Glenn."

"Yeah, Glenn has certainly moved to the top of my list of suspects now that I know he had motive," I said. "He had the means, too. He would have known Dennis's favorite brandy. He would have known about Arthur, the cousin. Heck, he probably would have even known that they weren't going to the Christmas Eve party, so he would have had the opportunity to set it up to look like Courtney did it."

"But that brings up another point—why would he do that to Courtney?" Pat asked. "Wasn't she as much a victim as he was? Why would he do that to her?"

"That's true." I hadn't thought about that angle, and I mulled it over as I started my KitchenAid mixer and dug the loaf pan out of the cabinet. "Maybe he didn't mean to set her up. Maybe it was an accident."

Pat raised an eyebrow. "He set her up by accident?"

"Yeah, I mean, it's possible. We still don't know what he was poisoned with," I said. "Maybe Glenn used something that he thought would mimic a natural death. Let's not forget, Courtney did think he had a heart attack."

"You think Glenn would have been stupid enough to believe the cops wouldn't test the brandy?"

I shrugged. "Who knows what he thought? Maybe he didn't think it would happen that quickly. If Dennis had collapsed after he put the bottle away, maybe the cops would have assumed he died from natural causes. Then, they wouldn't test the brandy."

"Sounds a bit like reaching again."

I poured the batter into the loaf pan. "Glenn is a financial advisor, not a doctor. He would have no idea what he was doing, in that respect, and it wasn't like he was in the room with Dennis. It's also possible he thought that because the brandy showed up as a gift, the cops would assume it was someone other than Courtney. Why would Courtney go through all the trouble of packaging up a bottle of brandy and sending it as a gift? She could just quietly poison something in the house."

"Which would lead back to her," Pat pointed out.

"Maybe, maybe not," I countered. "It depends on what she did. Like, for instance, if she poisoned him slowly, over time, it might just look like he got really sick and never recovered."

Pat shivered. "That would take nerves of steel, to watch someone slowly die."

I thought about Courtney, and how she could barely hold it together when we had visited her. "Yeah, I don't think she could do it either," I said. "But there's other ways you can kill someone without poisoning him. Make it look like an accident."

"That's true, but what if Courtney is counting on that?" Pat asked. "That people would assume if it were her, she would have done it differently. And that's exactly why she chose this method."

I popped the gingerbread into the oven. "I suppose that's possible, too." I shook my head and picked up my tea.

Pat gave me a sympathetic look. "How will you figure it out?"

"I guess I keep digging," I said. "I'm working on setting up a meeting with Nina. I left her a voicemail, but she hasn't responded. And I'm seeing Tiffany tomorrow to talk about sup-plying tea to Fit for Life. In fact, this is the tea I created for it. Do you like?" I held up the mug.

She took another swallow. "Ah, I thought it was new. It's good. So, this is the post-workout tea?"

"Yep," I said. "It's designed to help with muscle soreness and inflammation."

Pat took another sip, then leaned over to prop her elbows on the counter. "You know, you're probably going to lose her as a client once she figures out what you're really after."

"Which is why I tested it on you," I said. "I figured if it's any good, I can sell it myself."

Chapter 9

"So sorry to keep you waiting," Tiffany said, peeling off a pair of bright-yellow rubber gloves as she breezed into the closet that doubled as an office. Her hair was slicked back into a ponytail, and she had a smudge of something on her chin. She gave me a quick smile before squeezing behind her overflowing desk. Tiffany definitely used the "pile" method of organization. Mounds of paper were everywhere, including on the chair underneath me. When Jillian showed me to Tiffany's office, she told me to "put the pile anywhere." The only problem was that there wasn't really "anywhere" to put it, as the only empty spaces appeared to be the walkway. But then I realized the space under my chair was empty, so I shoved the pile there.

"No problem," I said. "You have something here," I added, gesturing toward my own chin.

She stared at me, then touched her skin. "Oh, it's a piece of wet paper towel." She brushed it away, smudging her pink lipstick in the process. "I was doing a little cleaning. I hate leaving it all 'til the end of the day, as I'm usually tired then. Trying to get it all done at that point can be overwhelming."

Cleaning? Didn't she have a cleaning service? While I got the fact that you wear a lot of hats as a business owner, being the janitor, too, seemed a little much.

She must have seen something in my face, because she continued talking. "It's only temporary. My last cleaning service wasn't working out, so we parted ways a month ago. You wouldn't believe how difficult it is to find someone new during the holiday season, so I figured it was just easier for me to handle it until I could look for someone when the new year started."

"I guess people want their evenings free for holiday parties," I said.

She flashed me another smile. "Yeah, that's probably it. Anyway, I'm so glad you're here. I've been excited to talk with you."

"Me too. In fact," I pulled out the little bag from my purse. "I brought you some tea to try."

Her face lit up. "Oh! I love that. Let me just heat up some water. I'll be back in a jiff." She meandered her way between the piles, and I had to admire how well she was able to navigate. Maybe all the aerobics classes really do pay off.

She brought back two mugs of sort-of-hot water. I made a mental note to have a conversation with her about an easier way to get hotter water. She was also going to need more tea infusers, as all my tea was loose. I had brought only one with me, so I used it for her cup. "I have another one around here somewhere," she fretted, looking around the office.

"Don't worry about it," I said. "I've already tasted it."

She gave me a sideways smile. "One of these days, I'll clean up in here. I always intend to, but there are just never enough hours in the day."

I smiled reassuringly. "I get it."

While we waited for the tea to steep, she explained her proposal. I would sell on consignment, with a 60/40 split (she would get the 60). I would be in charge of regularly checking in and keeping inventory stocked, whereas she would handle collecting the money.

"So, if people want to make a cup of tea and sit in the lobby, how will that work?" I asked.

She took another sip of hers, which she clearly loved. "What do you mean?"

"Well, I thought that was part of what you wanted—a place for your clients to enjoy a cup of tea after their workout."

"Oh, yes." She frowned. " It would have to be self-service. I guess I could offer some paper cups … "

"So, you'll need a way for people to get hot water," I said. "And you'll probably want to offer other fixings, too, like fresh lemon, honey, and cream. And you'll need tea infusers."

The more I talked, the more her face seemed to close down. "That's a lot of work," she said, her voice hesitant. "Especially when we don't even know if it will sell or not. What if we just sold packages they could take home?"

"We could certainly start with that," I said. "That's probably smart. To test out the concept."

Her smile was relieved.

"Of course," I continued. "Sales would be better if we could have them taste it first. I've found providing a sample sells the tea itself."

Her smile faded. "That makes sense," she said. "I don't know, but I was hoping this would be really simple to start. I'm just so busy with everything."

"We can keep it simple," I said, even though her reluctance puzzled me. Hadn't she realized all that would be involved in selling tea to her customers? Or had she just not given it much thought at all? "If you do ever want to start selling cups, you might want to think about offering coffee, as well. I know you didn't want to, but a coffee maker would also heat the water for you, so it would make sense to have both."

"Yeah, you have a good point. I'll look into it. Anything else?"

I actually did have more questions—the 60-40 split, for one—as it seemed like I would be the one doing all the work and shouldering the expenses. But her whole demeanor was so strange. The conversation was not going at all like I'd expected.

Normally, I would have waited until she was in a better mood before I brought up her husband, but watching her energy level plummet, I wasn't sure if I would get another chance to talk to her privately. "Not about the tea, at least for right now," I said, plastering a smile across my face. "But I *did* want to tell you … I met your husband."

Her eyes grew wide. "You met Glenn?" Her voice was strained, and she seemed shocked.

I bobbed my head up and down. "Yep. I'm looking for a financial advisor. I had a meeting with him yesterday."

"A meeting?" She had gone from shocked to flustered. "How did you know I'm married to him?"

"He has a framed picture of you in his office," I said. "I was surprised, because you two don't have the same last name."

She chuckled, but it sounded a little forced. "When we got married, I was pretty established under my own name. Plus, I never really loved the idea of women having to change their names when they marry."

"Established?"

"I was working as a model," she said.

"Wow. A model. How exciting."

She laughed, and it sounded much more natural. "Not really. A lot of hurry up and wait. Plus, being photographed for hours can get old pretty quickly. But I still enjoyed it." Her face had a faraway look. "I knew it wouldn't be forever, so I thought rather than try and build everything back up with a new last name, I would just keep going with my maiden name. I figured I could change it later, like if we had kids … but unfortunately, that doesn't seem to be in the cards." Her eyes were sad.

"Sorry," I said, feeling a little pang of sadness myself. There was a time when I thought I was going to have it all: the husband, the 2.5 kids, the white picket fence … but it didn't end up working out that way.

She gave her head a quick shake. "Nothing to be sorry about. Clearly, it's not meant to be." She gave me a faint smile.

A part of me wanted to ask her more questions, but it didn't seem like she wanted to talk about it. "Well, Glenn was great," I said. "It must be nice having a financial advisor as a husband. You don't have to worry about any of that. And didn't he lend you the money, as well? That was nice. I mean, not having to go through a bank."

"Yeah, I am grateful for the loan. And he does take care of all the finances. Our personal as well as the business's. So yes, it's nice to have those tasks off my plate."

She shifted in her chair, like she was done with the conversation and ready for me to leave. I quickly plowed on, before she could make an excuse about getting back to work. "I was surprised he was taking appointments, though."

Her lips curled down. "You're talking about what happened to his business partner." Her voice was flat.

"Yes. It was really shocking to read about in the paper. I mean, it was a shock for me, and I've never met Dennis. Just his wife ..."

"You know Courtney?" Tiffany blurted out, interrupting me. Under her makeup, her face had gone pale.

"Yes, she's my client," I said.

"Your *client*?"

"Yes, she buys my teas." I cocked my head and studied her. "Is there a problem? Do you not like her?"

Tiffany had collapsed into her chair. "I just ... I didn't realize you knew her."

"Redemption is a small town," I said. "It might be more un-usual if I didn't know her." I smiled, trying to lighten the mood.

Tiffany didn't smile back, instead picking up her tea and cup-ping her hands around it as if for warmth. "I'm sorry. My reac-tion was probably pretty confusing. It's been tough, as you can imagine. I've ... we've known Dennis for years. It's been such a shock."

"I can imagine," I said. "I'm just amazed at how well the two of you are holding up."

She gave me a twisted smile. "It's not always easy, believe me. I've had my moments. But for the most part, I've discovered that working helps keep my mind off things, which is good, be-cause with the holidays, I'm even more short-staffed than usual. So, I really have to work."

I wondered about her being more short-staffed than usual. There was something there. I could feel it, but I also didn't want to lose the opportunity to ask about her relationship with Court-ney and Dennis, so I mentally filed it away to deal with later.

"So, you knew Courtney as well, right?" I asked.

"Of course. Actually, I was the reason Courtney and Dennis met."

I nearly fell off my chair. It was all I could do to keep a straight face. "Really?" I asked, hoping Tiffany hadn't noticed whatever crazy, shocked expression was surely on my face. Would I ever get to the bottom of the surprises in this case?

"Yeah," Tiffany said. "She was one of my aerobics instructors. One evening, Glenn and I were going to a work dinner with Dennis. Glenn was going to pick me up here, so I didn't have to waste time driving home to change. For some reason, Dennis came with him. Actually, now that I think about it, Dennis was having car trouble, so Glenn was going to give him a ride. Anyway, Courtney had finished her class and was leaving as Dennis and Glenn arrived. I wasn't quite ready yet, so Dennis and Courtney ended up chatting for a few minutes, and that was all it took." She shrugged and smiled, but it wasn't a happy one. "Dennis found out when Courtney was teaching next and showed up to ask her out. It was a whirlwind courtship, and then, they were engaged."

"Wow," I said. "That's kind of romantic."

"I guess it was love at first sight." She started playing with her cardboard cup, swirling the tea around. "As you can imagine, we did a lot of double dating, both before they were married and after. And Glenn was Dennis's best man at his wedding."

"This must be awful for you," I offered. "Especially knowing them the way you did. And, especially with what the cops are saying ..." My voice trailed off.

Tiffany eyed me. "What about the cops?"

I leaned forward slightly and lowered my voice, like we were two old friends about to indulge in a good gossip. "They think Courtney was the one who killed Dennis. Can you imagine? Courtney? I can't picture it, especially in her condition. But I also haven't known her very long. Can I ask what you think? If you don't want to talk about it, I understand, but it's really been bothering me. I mean, a client of mine maybe being a murderer, and I didn't even know it ..."

Tiffany glanced away, seeming to focus instead on another inspirational poster hanging on the wall—yet another cat, and the words "When life leaves you hanging, DON'T QUIT."

"I know how you feel," she said in a low voice. "I'm having trouble believing it, as well. Especially when I think about all the time we spent together, having them over to our house for dinner, eating at their house." She shivered. "Was it the pregnancy hormones? Did she just snap?"

I stared at her, trying to process what it was that I was hearing. "So you think Courtney did it?"

She must have heard something in my voice, because she quickly started backtracking. "Well, I don't actually know," she admitted. "But it just seems really suspicious. Dennis poisoned? By his favorite brandy? How many people even know about his favorite brandy? Or his cousin? It would have to be someone close to him."

"Can you think of anyone else?" I asked. "You knew Dennis a long time. Maybe he had a falling out with a friend or family member? Or maybe a disgruntled client?"

She was shaking her head. "Everyone loved Dennis. He handled most of the networking and meeting and greeting." She smiled as she talked, a different smile than any I'd seen so far. It softened her face and brought out her beauty in a way that all the thick makeup failed to do. "Glenn is ... well, you met him. He's the numbers guy. He's a little more ... buttoned up, than Dennis ever was. Which made them a good team, because Glenn dealt mostly with the numbers, and Dennis dealt mostly with the clients. I don't know what's going to happen with Dennis gone." She bit her lip and turned away, but not before I saw a sheen of tears in her eyes.

Tiffany had real feelings for Dennis. That shocked me a little, even though it shouldn't. If they were having an affair, then it made sense. But still, the idea that she was in love with her husband's married business partner felt messed up ... like witnessing an episode of *Jerry Springer*.

"Is the business doing well?" I asked. I wasn't sure what prompted that question. Based on Courtney's house and that she apparently didn't work, I assumed it was. But, based on Tiffany's reaction, it appeared I hit a nerve. She snapped her head around to stare at me, nearly knocking her piles of paper to the ground.

"Why would you ask such a question?" Her voice was high, too high, and she paused to take a breath.

"I ... I didn't mean anything by it," I said. "I guess I was still thinking about the disgruntled client scenario. Maybe an investment didn't turn out as planned, and some clients got upset or something."

Her eyes grew wide. "You think an investment not going well would lead to murder?" Her voice was still too high, and suddenly, all the strange little things I'd been noticing came together like an image from a kaleidoscope.

Tiffany not having enough staff, even having to do her own cleaning. Her reluctance to buy the supplies needed to sell the tea. Her membership sale, and how quick she was to push me to sign up.

Tiffany was having money problems.

And, just as clearly, Glenn was refusing to give her another loan.

I wondered why. Was it because Tiffany wasn't a good businesswoman, and Glenn didn't want to dump good money after bad? Or because his business wasn't doing well, either, and he didn't have the money to give?

Or was he lying to Tiffany, telling her the business wasn't doing well because he didn't want to tell her the truth about why he didn't want to give her a loan?

"Um ... well, I thought the two biggest motivations for murder were love and money," I said. "Clearly, it's not a healthy reaction, but people aren't always thinking clearly in those moments."

"It still seems extreme," she insisted.

More than a wife murdering a husband? I wanted to ask, but then again, there is a reason cops look at the spouse first when foul play is suspected. And usually, at the end of the day, the spouse IS the guilty one.

"I agree, it does seem extreme," I said. I'm just throwing out people other than Courtney who might have done it. As far as I can tell, Courtney didn't have much of a motive. I thought she and Dennis were happy. She said they never fought. Or is that not true? Was there a problem with their marriage?"

As I spoke, I closely studied Tiffany's face. From the little I knew about her, she was pretty much an open book, her feelings clearly revealed on her face.

She probably knew that, too, because she turned away from me. "If there was a problem, I wasn't aware of it either," she said softly. "They always seemed happy to me. Of course, who knows what goes on inside a marriage ... especially when you're on the outside looking in."

I sucked in a quick breath of air. Glenn had said almost the exact same thing. It made me wonder which marriage they were talking about—Dennis and Courtney's, or their own?

I also couldn't figure out if she was telling the truth or lying. Her eyes were turned away, still staring at the DON'T QUIT message, no doubt. But, if she was telling the truth, why would Dennis cheat?

And what would be the purpose of lying? The whole conversation seemed to be about throwing Courtney under the bus. So why not share the juicy gossip about the marriage being in trouble?

Nothing about this case made sense.

Suddenly, she started. "Oh, look at the time. I have to go." She jumped to her feet and started weaving her way to the door.

I stood, as well. "So, the tea ...."

"Yes, yes, just bring in some bags, and let's see if we can sell it," she said, practically pushing me out the door. There was a flustered, frantic energy about her, and she was careful not to look at me. "Don't bring in a lot, though. Just enough to test the concept. Sound like a plan?"

"Sure," I said, even though I still didn't like the split. Although honestly, did it even matter? Bringing in a few bags of tea would be the perfect opportunity to continue this conversation after doing a little more digging on my end. And chances were, the more questions I kept asking, the less likely Tiffany was to want anything to do with me, so any tea-selling opportunity would disappear anyhow. "I'll be back once I get the bags together."

Her smile was perfunctory. "Great." She turned to walk away, still talking to me over her shoulder. "Just stop by. If I'm not around, Jillian can help you."

I watched her disappear into the aerobics room. I suspected I had one, maybe two more conversations with her before she was done.

I was definitely was going to have to make the next one count.

Chapter 10

I finished parking my car alongside the curb, turned the engine off, and paused for a moment, staring at Courtney's house.

I knew Pat would be furious with me for going without her, but there were answers I needed from Courtney, and I had a feeling I would be more likely to get them alone.

I also had a feeling that I might be more successful with this meeting if I had the element of surprise.

I was tired of finding out vital information about Courtney from other people. Something needed to give. And since I didn't want to go through her mother, I needed to talk to her directly.

But still, I paused. I was used to people dropping by unexpectedly—it kind of came with the territory of operating a business out of a home. But it wasn't the norm for most. I also had to keep reminding myself that Courtney was not only very pregnant, but grieving.

The polite, compassionate move would be to call and see if she was okay with seeing a visitor.

However, after learning that Tiffany was not only Glenn's wife, but also Courtney's former boss, I was feeling less than charitable.

I got out of the car and headed up the driveway. If she wasn't there, or if she wasn't in a good frame of mind to talk, I would leave and make an appointment with her for a different time, I told myself.

But I wanted to try this first.

The house was quiet as I approached, making me question whether she was home. I stepped onto the porch and rang the doorbell. As I stood there waiting for her to answer, I mentally sent Pat an apology and promised to tell her everything.

For a moment, there was silence, making me think again that I would have to call to arrange a time to talk to her, but then, I heard faint footsteps before the door cracked open.

"Charlie?"

My eyes widened in shock as I looked at her, although I tried to cover it up. She looked awful. Her face was way too thin, her cheeks hollowed out and an almost greenish tint to her skin. This couldn't be good for the baby. Looking at her, I started to question the wisdom in asking her a bunch of uncomfortable and likely unwelcome questions.

On the other hand, if she ended up getting charged with murder, her life was going to get about twenty times more stressful than anything I could do to her. If she wanted my help, whatever games she was playing had to stop. Now.

"How are you doing?" Even as I asked, the words sounded ridiculous. Obviously, she wasn't doing well. You only needed eyes to see it. But societal norms are deeply engrained.

She forced a smile. "I've been better. Did you want to come in?" She held the door open a little wider.

"Just as long as I'm not bothering you," I said as I stepped through.

"No bother," she answered, her voice quiet and a little wistful. "I wouldn't mind a little company."

Another pang of guilt shot through me. I should have been more attentive ... should have stopped by sooner and not waited until I had an agenda. But too late now. "How is the baby?"

She smiled, a true smile, and pressed a hand against her belly. "Kicking away. I think he might be a soccer player."

I raised an eyebrow. "He?"

Her smile turned mischievous. "None of the doctors told me, if that's what you're asking. I just have a feeling. Do you want anything to drink? Coffee? Tea? Water?"

"I'm fine ... you don't need to trouble yourself," I said, taking my coat off.

"It's no trouble. I was thinking about making myself a cup of tea." There was something about how she was standing there looking at me, an almost desperate eagerness to please in her energy, that broke my heart.

"Tea would be great," I said. "It's nippy out there. A nice cup would do the trick."

Her smile was relieved. "I have just enough of your Candy Cane Concoctions for one more pot. I save it for special occasions, but even so, I'm almost out. It's so good."

"I can bring you more," I said, kicking myself for not having thought to do so. "I also have some great blends for expectant and new mothers I can bring by."

Her eyes lit up. "That would be great. Do you want to go sit in the living room? I've got a fire going."

"You don't want any help with the tea?"

She waved her hand, brushing me off. "No, no. I've got it. Go sit by the fire and relax."

She moved into the kitchen, a hand on her lower back, and I went to do as she said.

The living room was in much better shape than the last time. The papers on the coffee table had been put away, and the room had signs of recent dusting and vacuuming. I wondered if Courtney was doing it herself, or if she had someone helping her … maybe her mother. Someone had also put all the Christmas decorations away, which made me sad for some reason. I wondered again if her child would grow up never enjoying Christmas because of what happened this season.

"Here we go," Courtney said as she entered the room. She was carrying a tray loaded with the tea pot and mugs, and with every step, the pot rattled. I quickly got up to take the tray from her.

"Thanks. I looked for some cookies, but I guess the baby must have been hungry," she said, trying to joke.

"That's okay," I quickly assured her. "Trust me, I eat enough baked goods on my own. I don't need any more."

I set the tray down on the coffee table as Courtney lowered herself into the chair in front of me. I poured both mugs and handed one to her. She accepted hers, and we both took a sip.

"So, my mother tells me you're helping find out the truth," Courtney said.

I set the mug down on the table. "I'm certainly trying."

She looked up at me, her clear, china-blue eyes reminding me so much of a child. "Thank you," she said. "I really appreciate it. And if you need money ..."

I shook my head. "No, no. I'm fine. It's not like I'm a professional at this or anything."

"Well, if you need anything," she said. "Anything at all, I'm here for you. Have you come to give me an update? Should I call my mother, as well?" She started moving, as if to head toward the phone, but I held my hand out.

"Hold on. Yes, I'm here for an update, but I also have some additional questions, too. Maybe we bring your mother in later. If you want."

Courtney slowly lowered herself back into her chair, her expression wary. "Questions?"

I gave her what I hoped was a reassuring smile. "So, I spoke to both Glenn and Tiffany."

I paused, watching her closely to see if she reacted to Tiffany's name. Even though I had promised Violet I wouldn't bring it up, I was hoping for an opening, so I could talk to her about it.

But Courtney didn't seem to react, other than dropping her gaze to look down at her hands.

"I didn't realize that Tiffany was your former boss, or that you met Dennis through her," I continued, deciding to skip the cheating for now.

Courtney remained silent, still staring at her hands. Her blonde hair had fallen across her face like a curtain at the end of an act, so I couldn't even get a look at her expression.

I stayed quiet as well, waiting her out. The silence stretched longer than I expected, making me wonder if she was ever going to break it.

Finally, she stirred, lifting her head so her hair fell away. "We ... I should have told you," she said softly.

"Why didn't you?"

She looked down again. "I'm not really sure. I guess ... I was ashamed."

I didn't expect that response. Was Dennis still married when he got together with Courtney? "Why would you be ashamed?"

"I guess ..." she bit her lip. "I always felt a little guilty about how Dennis and I met," she said in a rush.

Immediately, I started thinking back to the conversation with Tiffany, trying to remember if she had talked about Dennis's marital status. I didn't recall anything, which of course didn't mean he was single. "Why?"

She let out a heavy sigh, almost as if that statement alone was causing a deeply buried secret to emerge. "It's a long story," she said.

"I have plenty of time," I replied, making a point of sitting back in my chair, as if settling in for the long haul. I was getting the feeling that whatever she was going to confess had been troubling her for a very long time.

She looked down into her tea again, as if searching it for strength, before finally beginning to speak. "When I was thirteen, my father had a midlife crisis and ran off with a younger woman. A MUCH younger woman. My mother was devastated. It completely blindsided her emotionally, of course, but even more than that, it was financially devastating. My mother hadn't had a job in years, since before I was born. She had no real job skills, no prospects, no nothing. It was awful. The only job she could get was low-paying temp work through an agency. We had to move out of our beautiful home and into a dreadful apartment. The walls were so thin, I could hear her crying after I went to bed every night. It was just awful."

"But what about the courts? Didn't your father have to pay alimony and child support?"

"When I say, 'ran off,' I mean literally," she said bitterly. "One day, he drained our bank accounts and vanished with that woman. Cops were no help, because it's not against the law to disappear when you're an adult. And we didn't have the money to hire a private investigator to find him. If you don't know where he is, you can't get money from him."

"What about family? Could they help you financially?"

She sighed. "My mother's parents did what they could, but they were living on a fixed income themselves. On my dad's side, his mother was in a nursing home and had dementia, so she wasn't much help, and his father wasn't in the picture. He never talked much about his father, but I got the sense that his dad had left his mother much like he left us." She paused, as she swirled the tea in her cup. "His mother died a few years ago. I think, of all the things my father did to us, that's the one thing my mother really found unforgivable. That he left his mother like that. We continued to visit her until the day she died, and she never stopped asking about my father. It was ..." she shook her head.

"Anyway, I helped as much as I could, but I was only thirteen when it happened, so I couldn't get a real job. I did other things ... helped around the house, babysat, got a paper route, and did other odd jobs. Whatever I could do to help earn a little money.

"When I turned sixteen, I got my first real job, cleaning offices and commercial buildings at night. My mother didn't want me to do it. She wanted me to focus on school, but she also knew we needed the money. By then, she was working two jobs and still barely able to make ends meet. She wanted to go back to school ... maybe study to become a nurse, so she could get a decent-paying job. She was always interested in health, medicine, and natural remedies and whatnot. But there was no time or money for that, either. Anyway, eventually, we reached an agreement that I could take this job as long as it didn't impact my studies.

"Needless to say, that didn't last long. I took as many shifts as they would give me, which of course cut into school, and after a few weeks, I dropped out. My mother didn't find out for several months, mostly because neither of us were home very much. She was furious." Courtney grimaced at the memory. "I told her it was temporary. I could work multiple jobs for a while, which would free her up to go back to school. Once she had a decent job, I could go back and get my GED and figure out what I wanted to do. She didn't like that plan at all. She thought it made more sense for me to get my schooling and a good job, but I told her that would take longer, since I still had to finish high school. It made more sense for her to go first. Plus, I was younger and didn't mind working multiple jobs. She wasn't happy about it, but at that point, there was nothing she could really do. I had quit several months before, so there was no going back.

"Fast forward a few years later, and Tiffany hires me to man the front desk on weekends. It was a bad time for me. I was exhausted. I had been working 60-70- hour weeks for years by then, in mostly menial jobs like waitressing and cleaning, and it was exhausting. My mother was in nursing school, and it was going a lot slower than either of us had anticipated. It was a huge adjustment for her to become a student again after so many years. Plus, she was still working full-time as a temp on top of her studies, so it was just … well, difficult. *Everything* felt difficult. I was feeling really beat down and discouraged with life. At that moment, I couldn't see a way out of the slog of working all the time I had found myself in. I was feeling very sorry for myself.

"It was during this time that I started to get to know Tiffany. Working at Fit for Life was becoming the bright spot of my week. I got to sit at a desk all weekend, which felt like heaven, and the little bit of cleaning, straightening, and organizing I was supposed to do was so easy compared to my other jobs. I was flying through it and even doing extra tasks, just because it was easy for me. And I didn't mind.

"Well, Tiffany noticed I was going above and beyond and started stopping in on the weekends to talk to me. I guess we became friends, in a way, if you can even be friends with your boss. She knew my history and about all my other jobs. After a few weeks, she asked if I'd like to work full-time with her. It was a pretty decent salary increase, so of course I said 'yes.' At the same time, Glenn, her husband, needed a new secretary at his office, and they offered the job to my mother. Again, it was more money than what she was making as a temp.

"It was great. I could quit my other jobs because I was making more. I was also able to work out and take classes for free, which I really enjoyed. I didn't think I was going to like aerobics, but I discovered the opposite. Because of my interest, Tiffany encouraged me to become an instructor, and I just adored it. I felt like I had figured out what I wanted to do with my life. For the first time since before my father left, I was happy."

She paused, taking a sip of her tea, which had to be cold by now. I waited in silence. While I still didn't understand where the guilt was coming from, it was giving me a glimpse into who Courtney was as a person and what made her tick.

"I knew about Dennis, of course. My mother talked about him, as did Tiffany. I knew he was married, but his marriage was basically over. They weren't divorced, but they were separated. He had moved out of the house, and they were in that space where they were both trying to work out if they wanted to stay together or end it. It was during this time that Tiffany one day asked me if I wouldn't mind teaching her late-afternoon aerobics class, as she was going to a work dinner with Glenn, and there wouldn't be enough time for her to shower and get ready if she taught it. She apologized, saying she had gotten the dates wrong, or she would have planned better.

"Of course I said 'yes.' I would have done nearly anything for Tiffany. I was so grateful for all the help she had given me. She thanked me and then said something about getting Karen, who was one of our personal trainers, to watch the front desk until I could get back after class. Now, Karen was a great personal trainer, but not great at watching the front desk. She loved talking to people and could easily get distracted and not check people in properly, which then created more of a headache for me to fix after the fact. So I said that wouldn't be necessary, as Tiffany wasn't leaving until after class was over. I could just pop out as soon as I was done and cover the desk, so Tiffany could leave.

"I remember how Tiffany got the oddest expression on her face. She said, 'No, Karen can handle it.' I told her it was no trouble, that I didn't mind at all. I'd done it before, and it wasn't a big deal.

"Then she started telling me it would be better if I didn't come out early. In fact, I should stay away until after she left. When I asked her why, she started telling me that Dennis was coming as well, and as this was the first time he was going to one of these dinners single, it would be best to keep things simple for him. Then she went on to talk about how she thought it was a mistake that he'd moved out, and she wished he was bringing Nina, as they really ought to be working on their marriage. She thought it was best that Dennis didn't have any other distractions until he 'got his head on straight and went back to his wife.'

"Well, none of it made any sense to me. I didn't understand how my being at the front desk would have any sort of effect on his relationship with his wife. Then I was hurt, because I thought Tiffany was ashamed of me. I asked Tiffany if that was the case, and she was floored. It was clear she hadn't been thinking that, and she kept assuring me it had nothing to do with me. She just wanted Dennis to do the 'right thing.' Which, again, made no sense to me.

"I couldn't stop thinking about it all day, so of course by the time class was over, I was in the lobby. By that time, I was super curious and wanted to see Dennis for myself.

"I was surprised at how handsome he was. I remember I kind of stood there, uncertain, feeling like I wanted to go back to the ladies' locker room, when he turned. His eyes met mine, and that was it. The attraction was instant, like I had touched a live wire. He came over to introduce himself, and we started talking in the lobby, which is where Tiffany found us after she had finished getting ready.

"I was a little nervous, because it was the first time I didn't do as she asked. My attention was torn between Dennis and watching for her, so I saw her the moment she stepped out of the hallway. Her face went white, and she stopped dead in her tracks. I felt sick. Neither Glenn nor Dennis was paying any attention to her, so they didn't see it, but I knew the truth. It was because I had disobeyed her.

"I rushed up to her, apologizing, telling her I thought she had left. She recovered quickly and gave me this flat smile that didn't reach her eyes before hurrying everyone out of the building. Of course, Dennis wasn't so easily swayed, and a few days later, he showed up at the end of my aerobics class. It was one of Tiffany's days off, so he kept me company for a while as I manned the desk and eventually asked me to dinner. And the rest is history." She hunched over, folding both arms across her belly, as if shielding her baby from the blows of condemnation she was expecting from me.

I, however, was still trying to sort it out in my head. Listening to the story, it seemed to me that Tiffany sensed, correctly, that Dennis would find Courtney attractive and wanted to keep the two from meeting. But Courtney's response still wasn't making sense. I could understand her feeling guilty in the beginning, but once she knew about Dennis's affair with Tiffany, wouldn't she be upset with Tiffany for manipulating her?

"So, I gather Tiffany was pretty upset," I said, when it became clear that Courtney was waiting for me to say something.

Courtney nodded. Her hair had spilled over her face again, so I couldn't read her expression. "Our relationship was never the same after that. I thought it was because she disapproved of my seeing Dennis. He wasn't officially divorced when we started dating, and maybe she thought I was preventing him from getting back together with Nina. But Dennis assured me the marriage was over. It wouldn't have mattered if he had met me or not. And then I thought maybe it was because I disobeyed her ... that she was still angry about that. I apologized, and she said it wasn't a big deal, but I could still tell something was wrong. I asked her a few times to tell me what it was, but she kept insisting that everything was fine ... that it was all in my head. But I knew it wasn't." She paused again. She still hadn't looked up at me, but she was starting to uncurl herself and sit up a little straighter, as if talking about it was finally beginning to free something up inside her.

"So, what happened?" I asked. "Did she fire you, or ...?"

Courtney shook her head. "No, nothing like that. I worked for her until Dennis and I got married, which took a bit as he first needed to finalize the divorce." She smiled at the memory. "Dennis hated waiting. He wanted to marry me right away, but of course, the wheels of justice move at their own pace. Anyway, once we were married, I dropped my schedule back to just teaching classes. We didn't need the money. Dennis made enough for me to stay home, but I liked teaching." She looked away, her eyes full of grief. "Dennis was so good to us. Did you know he even helped out my mother? He found her the cutest little apartment in one of the complexes he owned, so she didn't have to pay rent. Plus, he kept her on his business's health insurance plan, so she was able to drop down to working part-time. He was so caring. He would have made a wonderful father."

"He sounds amazing," I said, but inside, I was struggling to make sense of all the pieces. How could two business partners have completely different financial situations? On one hand, Dennis was supporting both his mother-in-law and his stay-at-home wife, while presumably also paying alimony to the mysterious Nina, whereas Glenn appeared to be unable or unwilling to give his wife a loan for her business.

Perhaps I was being unfair to Glenn, I considered. Perhaps Tiffany was a horrendous business owner, and it made better financial sense to let her sink or swim on her own.

"Anyway," Courtney continued, wiping her eyes with a tissue. "I tried for a long time to fix my relationship with Tiffany. I even asked her to be my maid of honor for my wedding. She declined. Said she was 'too old' for that sort of thing. I tried to talk her into it. I even told her that I owed her for introducing us, but she was pretty adamant. Eventually, I just gave up."

"But you still had to spend time with them, right?" I asked. "I mean, Glenn and Dennis were still business partners. So there were work parties and dinners together?"

"Some," Courtney said. "The work parties weren't really an issue. We could just avoid each other. There were some dinners at each other's houses in the beginning, but they petered out

over time." She stared off into the corner, her expression dejected.

I was completely gobsmacked. Courtney was acting like she
mourned the loss of the relationship with Tiffany—like they had
been best friends until one day they weren't, and Courtney had
no clear reason why. Which made no sense. Tiffany had been
sleeping with Dennis. Why wasn't Courtney furious with her?
For that matter, why hadn't Courtney even brought up the subject? She knew I knew who it was, because her mother had told
me ...

With a sudden, blinding shock, all the pieces swirling around
in my brain clicked into place.

Courtney had no idea who was sleeping with her husband.

Suddenly, it all made sense.

Violet.

She had worked at the firm. Of course she would have seen
Tiffany hanging around. Maybe she even saw Tiffany and Dennis having their affair. And clearly, she never told her daughter
the truth, maybe to save her feelings.

The only thing that didn't make sense was why her mother
hadn't told Courtney before she married Dennis. If Courtney
had known, surely, she would have called off the wedding.

Wouldn't she?

"I don't think you did anything wrong," I said.

Courtney jerked her head up, and for the first time since she
started the story, met my eyes.

"I would have thought it was a strange request, as well,"
I continued. "And if my boss had said that to me, I probably
would have done the same thing ... gone out into the lobby to
take a look at the mystery man myself."

Courtney smiled. "The whole thing was really weird," she
said. "But then, Tiffany hadn't been acting herself for a while.
Honestly, I was wondering if something else was going on,
something with her health. She wasn't focusing the way she
used to. I would catch her sitting at her desk just staring off into
space. And she was more irrational, as well, and making strange

decisions. It was just a weird time. I still wonder if there was something else going on ... something she wasn't telling me."

There absolutely was something else going on that Tiffany wasn't telling her, but it wasn't my place to get into it.

"I did want to ask you, and I get it, if you don't know the answer, but how is Tiffany as a business owner?"

Courtney looked puzzled. "Do you mean was she a good boss? Yes, she was the best."

"No, not just a good boss, although I guess that's part of it. I meant," I hesitated, trying to figure out the right words. "Was she good with numbers? Was Fit for Life profitable? Was she making money?"

Courtney's face cleared. "Oh. I see. Yes, I mean, I think so. I never saw any numbers either way, but the place was always busy, and she was always talking about needing to expand and grow her team. Why do you ask?"

That didn't necessarily mean she was a good businessperson, but it also didn't sound like she was running Fit for Life into the ground. "It's just, when I saw her, I got the distinct impression she was having money issues."

Courtney looked surprised. "This is always the busiest time of year. People come in and buy new memberships for the coming year ... you know, New Year's resolutions and all that. I can't believe she would be having money issues now. There must be some sort of misunderstanding."

"What about Dennis's business?" I pressed. "Do you know if there were any financial issues going on there?"

Her face turned white, which I hadn't expected. I had thought she would deny it like she had about Fit for Life, not stare at me in horror. "Did the police tell you?" she whispered.

I sat up straighter, alarm bells going off in my head. "Tell me what?"

"About the missing money."

"*Missing*?"

Her whole body was trembling. "Yes, and they think Dennis was the one who stole it." She buried her face into her hands, her shoulders heaving.

I sat there, dumbfounded. Dennis stealing money? Was that why he was killed? Because of money?

"*Was* he stealing money?"

She raised her head from her hands, tears streaking down her face. "No!"

"But ..." I gestured around the house. "How was he able to afford all of this plus take care of your mother?"

"The business does well," she insisted. "Dennis would have no need to steal anything! Plus, he told me he had made good investments of his own over the years. That's his job! He's very good at it. Why do you think the business has done so well?"

"So, is Glenn just as successful?" I asked.

"I don't know why he wouldn't be."

I couldn't think of any reason either. I also didn't have any proof he wasn't, except the niggling suspicion that Tiffany's money woes were somehow connected to Glenn—either because she needed an influx of cash and Glenn couldn't or wouldn't give it to her, or because of money problems, she was having to pull more money out of the business than was healthy.

"Did Dennis ever share any worries about the business?"

She rolled her eyes. "He was *always* worried about business. He was always stressed about something. Managing other people's money is stressful. He didn't want to make any mistakes. I didn't ask about particulars. I didn't want him to associate the stress of business with being at home."

If Dennis had been stealing from the business, it seemed pretty clear that Courtney didn't know anything about it. Unless she was a really good actress, which was also possible.

"What about the cops? Are they investigating the missing money?"

Her mouth flattened into a thin line. "I don't know what's going on. I had one cop tell me they only cared about the murder, not the theft. I guess Glenn doesn't want to prosecute since Dennis is dead ... I don't even know if he could."

I looked at her in surprise. "But doesn't Glenn want his money back? How can he do that without there being an investigation?"

"I didn't say there wouldn't be an investigation. I guess Glenn is trying to track it down. He doesn't want any criminal charges. But I don't know, maybe I'm getting it wrong."

I looked at her curiously. "How do you know that?"

"Because Glenn called me," she said.

"He called you?"

She nodded. "After the cops spoke to me. He called me a day later, apologizing for not telling me first. He said he knew I had nothing to do with the theft, and he was trying to work out a way to get it fixed without it hurting me financially, as he knew I had enough to deal with."

"Wow, that was ... pretty generous of him."

Courtney nodded again, her face expressionless. "Glenn was always a little prickly," she said. "A lot of people found him off-putting. But he was always kind to me. I liked him."

I wondered if Glenn's compassion was because he felt a kinship to Courtney because their spouses were having an affair, or if he had a guilty conscience because he was the one who killed her husband. Regardless, if Dennis truly was stealing from the business, that gave both Glenn and Tiffany motive.

"Is there anything else that has come out about Dennis?" I asked.

"What do you mean?"

"Well, any other secrets that might have led to his death."

She gave me a reproachful look. "Isn't that enough?"

Touché, I thought. "What about his affair?" I asked. "Do you know who it was with?"

Her face closed in on itself. "I don't want to talk about it."

Did that mean she knew, or she didn't? "Courtney," I said as quietly and gently as I could. "This is important. If you want me to help, you need to tell me everything you know. Do you know who it is?"

She sat frozen for a moment, and I wondered if she was even going to answer. But finally, she shook her head.

"Then how do you know he was having an affair?"

"Because of the lipstick."

"Lipstick?"

She nodded. "On his shirt collar. It wasn't my shade ... not that I would have gotten any on his shirt collar anyway."

"But that doesn't mean he was necessarily having an affair," I said. "He could have hugged someone, maybe a client, who wasn't as careful as she should have been."

"That's what I told myself, too. But then," she paused and swallowed hard. "One of my friends told me she saw him with another woman. She didn't know who, because she couldn't see the other woman's face. But she said they were ... were ... kissing."

Inwardly, I sighed. I wondered if the friend was actually her mother. I didn't want to push it though, as I had promised Violet that I wouldn't tell Courtney. "I'm sorry, Courtney."

She shrugged—a sad, pathetic movement that didn't do anything to hide the hurt in her eyes. "Doesn't matter now. It's all just water under the bridge."

I couldn't think of anything to say to that.

"I know I keep asking this, but is there anything else I should know about?"

She looked at me, her eyes red-rimmed and hopeless. But there was something else there. Something I couldn't identify.

"I can't think of anything," she said. Her voice matched her eyes. Hopeless and sad.

The more time I spent with her, the more convinced I was that she had nothing to do with her husband's murder.

But that didn't mean I wasn't equally as sure she was still lying to me.

Chapter 11

"I can't believe you went to Courtney's house without me."

I pushed the lemon meringue pie toward Pat. "Have another piece of pie. Did I mention I baked it just for you?" Pat *loved* lemon meringue pie.

She glared at me as she started to cut a second piece. "Don't think I don't know a bribe when I see one," she growled.

"You know I wanted to bring you," I said. "But I also want to get to the bottom of all these secrets."

"And how did that work out for you?" Pat asked, her mouth full of meringue.

I made a face. "Yes, I admit she's still lying. Everyone is still lying. But look at what I *did* discover."

"Dennis is apparently a thief as well as an adulterer," Pat said. "Who could have seen that coming?"

"And the fact that Courtney's mother didn't tell her it was Tiffany," I said. "I'm still struggling to get my head around that."

"I know," Pat said through bites of pie. "I can't imagine not telling Barbara if I knew that the man she was about to marry was also a cheater." Barbara was her daughter.

I picked up my mug. "Was it the money? Was Violet just so exhausted from working so hard all those years, and she thought Dennis would take care of them financially?"

"It's also possible she didn't know," Pat said, licking her fork. "At least, not before the wedding. Maybe Tiffany never came to the office. She did have a business to run, after all. Maybe she and Dennis were more discreet, and Violet only caught them after the wedding."

I took a sip of tea. "That's possible," I said. "That makes more sense, actually, than her knowing and not telling Courtney. She and Courtney seem pretty tight. I don't see a lot of secrets between them."

"You mean besides this one. Violet still isn't telling her about Tiffany."

"Probably because she doesn't want to hurt her," I said.

"So, what's next?" Pat asked.

I sighed. "I'm not sure. I seem to have just as many suspects as when I started, although I will say Glenn has moved closer to the top of the list. He must have been furious at Dennis."

"I'd say it was more likely he hated him," Pat said. "Dennis stole his wife and his money. Wouldn't you hate him?"

I inclined my head. "It might also explain some of Tiffany's reaction," I said. "On one hand, she was quick to accuse Courtney, but the more we talked, the more she seemed to kind of back off from that. Do you think she might suspect her husband?"

Pat pursed her lips. "Maybe. It might not even be conscious. I've found that to be the case more times than not. People know what's going on, but they're too terrified to admit it to themselves."

"Or, what if it was Tiffany, and she's feeling guilty about pinning it on Courtney?" I mused. "What if she did it in a fit of anger? Maybe she and Dennis were having some sort of lover's spat, and then she found out about the money being stolen and just lost it."

"'Poison is a woman's weapon,'" Pat said. "Didn't Agatha Christie say that?"

"Actually, I think that was Sherlock Holmes," I said. "But yes. The choice of sending a poisoned bottle of brandy to the house doesn't fit as well with Glenn. I don't see him wanting to incriminate Courtney, and that scenario definitely makes her the number one suspect. But Tiffany was clearly upset about Courtney marrying Dennis. Maybe she was jealous, because she wanted Dennis, even though she really had no claim on him. Or maybe it was some sort of rivalry. Courtney was younger and prettier, and Tiffany clearly must have known or sensed she was Dennis's type, or she wouldn't have told Courtney not to come out to the lobby in the first place. But whatever it was, she hasn't gotten over Courtney marrying Dennis, so for Tiffany, Courtney being blamed might have been part of the plan."

"You know, if Dennis was stealing from the business, Glenn might not be the only one upset with him," Pat said. "What if he was also stealing from his clients? Maybe one of them found out and got pretty upset."

"That's true." I thought about my meeting with Glenn and how June had interrupted with the announcement of what sounded like an irate client on the phone. Could that client also have been victimized?

"Maybe I need to try harder to get to Nina," I said. "I feel like I still have more questions than answers, and maybe she can help me figure out which direction I should focus on."

"Good idea," Pat said, and pointed a fork at me. "Just make sure you bring me next time. A lemon pie isn't going to save you if you don't."

* * *

I had just finished straightening up the kitchen when the doorbell rang. Assuming it was Pat returning for some reason (perhaps to take home the rest of the pie, which I had urged her to do, but she'd refused, claiming her waistline didn't need the addition of an entire pie in one day). I opened the door expecting to see her standing on the stoop.

Instead, I found Officer Brandon Wyle.

"Well, hello there, officer," I said sweetly. "Is there something I can do for you? Perhaps a custom-blended tea to help with whatever ails you?"

He shot me a look. "I don't think there's a tea out there than can help with what ails me," he said. "May I come in?"

I leaned against the door, even though I knew all my nice, warm air was rushing out. "That depends," I said. "Is this an official or unofficial visit?"

His eyes narrowed. "Unofficial. For now."

"Well, if that's the case, come right in." I held the door open. "I have homemade lemon meringue pie. Would you like a slice?"

"This isn't a social call," he said, stepping inside and removing his jacket.

"Is that a 'yes'?" I asked, heading to the kitchen. Behind me, I heard a sigh.

I had the pie on the table and was making a fresh pot of tea when he appeared in the kitchen. "You don't have to go through any trouble," he said.

"Nonsense," I said, bringing the tea to the table. "I'm happy to provide our law enforcement with refreshment. Now, how can I be of service?"

He sat down but didn't touch the tea or pie. His dark hair was still on the shaggy side—clearly, he hadn't scheduled that haircut yet. His equally dark eyes were hooded as he studied me. "You lied to me."

I widened my eyes. "That's quite an accusation. I hope you have proof to back it up."

"You said you weren't going to investigate Dennis Fallon's murder."

I reached over and started cutting a piece of pie. "Hmmm. I don't recall making that promise."

"We agreed. I said we had it covered, and you didn't need to investigate, and you agreed."

I tilted my head to one side. "Well, that's not how I remember it. I do remember you telling me you had the investigation covered, but as for me agreeing to anything ... I'm pretty certain that didn't happen."

He blew out a frustrated sigh.

I pushed the piece of pie toward him. "Trust me, that pie will make everything better."

He shook his head, but picked up his fork. "Honestly, you're going to be the death of me."

"All I've done is ask a few questions," I said. "No harm in that, and certainly not against the law."

"It is when it's harassment."

My jaw dropped. "Harassment?"

He nodded as he took a bite. "Glenn Haggard wants to file an official complaint. Said you're harassing him and his wife."

I started to laugh. "What? There was no harassment."

"Why don't you tell me what happened and let me be the judge?"

"Well, it's true I spoke to both of them. I made an appointment with Glenn to discuss him becoming my financial advisor. And I met Tiffany because I checked out an aerobics class at Fit for Life. We got to chatting, and she's interested in selling my teas in her business."

There was a pause as Wyle ate and I sipped my tea. Finally, he gestured with his fork. "Continue."

"Well, that's really it."

He raised his eyebrow. "That's it?"

"Well, yeah. Basically. I mean, I'm sure we talked about other things, but that was the gist of the conversation."

"So, you didn't tell either of them that Courtney is your client and then proceed to ask questions about Courtney and Dennis?"

"Oh! Is that what all of this is about?" I shrugged. "Well, I mean, Glenn's business partner just died, so of course it would have been remiss on my part to not ask how his death will impact the business."

Wyle's lips twitched, as if holding back a smile. "And Tiffany? What was the excuse there?"

I took a moment to think about it. "You know, I can't really remember how it came up. I think it was because I was telling her about my appointment with Glenn."

"Why would you tell her that?"

"Well, because they're married." I rolled my eyes. "I thought she might be interested in hearing that I was considering working with her husband."

"How did you know they're married? They don't have the same last name."

"Glenn has a picture of her on his desk," I said. "I noticed it and asked him about it. Anyone having a meeting with him would have done the same."

Wyle shook his head. "I can't believe it."

"What?" My voice was all sweetness and innocence.

He put his fork down and scrubbed his face with his hands. I had the distinct impression he was trying not to laugh. "Okay," he said, removing his hands and sitting back in his chair. "So, officially ..."

"I thought you weren't here officially," I said.

He glared at me. "Officially, you need to leave Glenn alone. Tiffany, too."

"What if I want to hire him to be my financial advisor?"

He gave me another look. I held up my hands in mock surrender. "Okay, okay. I guess he doesn't want my business."

He shook his head again.

"But all kidding aside, is this complaint something I should worry about?"

"Just as long as you leave Glenn and Tiffany alone, there shouldn't be an issue," he said.

"That's it?" I was surprised. "I would have thought there would be more of a ... 'lawyerly' response to such a complaint."

"Well, depending on what was filed, there might have been. But as there is no official complaint, there's nothing to be done."

"But I thought you said Glenn filed a complaint?"

"I said he *wanted* to," Wyle corrected. "Luckily for you, I was the one dealing with him. I was able to talk him out of doing anything official and instead told him I would take care of it."

I wasn't sure if I heard him correctly. "Wait, you were the one who talked him out of filing a complaint against me? Why would you do that?"

He reached for his tea mug. "Honestly? Because I found his complaint ... suspicious."

"Really?" This was getting more and more interesting. "How so?"

"Let me just say that his story and your story were more similar than not," he said drily. "He admitted you had only come to see him once, and that you claimed to be looking for a new financial advisor. It was less clear about why you were seeing his wife, but again, it sounded like you were showing up in her business during business hours. Regardless, I found I was less interested in what you were doing and far more interested that he was upset enough by your questions that he made time in his busy schedule to come down to the station to make a complaint."

"I find that rather interesting myself," I said. I picked up the spatula and gestured to the pie, my actions asking if he wanted another piece. He shook his head.

"So, do you want to tell me what you talked about that got him so hot and bothered?" He flashed a sudden, unexpected grin at me, which caused my stomach to flip inside out. He was really quite good looking when he smiled. Good thing he didn't do it much.

Instead, I dropped my gaze to my tea and thought about what to do. It wasn't like I was under any sort of obligation to not talk to the cops. I wasn't an actual private investigator or anything like that. Nor had I taken any money for what I was doing. But I still felt vaguely uncomfortable, like I might be sharing a confidence that wasn't mine to share.

I decided to start easy, with the things I already knew the cops knew.

"Well, it seems Glenn and Tiffany are having some financial trouble," I said.

"How do you know that?"

"Tiffany made some comments that inferred her business isn't doing well financially," I said. "And Glenn, of course, is saying that Dennis stole money, so my guess is if there are financial issues, he's blaming the theft."

"You don't think that's the case?"

I shrugged. "According to Courtney, he wants to handle the investigation himself. I would think if there was money stolen, he would welcome official help. Wouldn't you?"

Wyle gave me a sideways smile. "We found that interesting, too."

"As for Tiffany, it's clear she's hiding something. I'm not sure what."

"Do you know who Dennis was having the affair with?"

I gave him a look. "I don't know for sure, but it sounds like you've heard the same rumors I have. That it was Tiffany."

He nodded. "It would appear Glenn had motive to kill Dennis. Plus, he would have known about Dennis's cousin."

"I agree. He does look guilty."

Wyle studied me. "But ..."

"I didn't say 'but.'"

He gave me that sideways smile again. "You didn't have to."

"No wonder they pay you the big bucks," I said with my own half-smile before letting it fade. "If Dennis had been killed in some other fashion, maybe a car accident or robbery gone bad, I would absolutely suspect Glenn was behind it somehow. But this? A poisoned bottle of brandy shows up at Dennis's house. Of course Courtney is going to be the prime suspect. Glenn knows this, and if he knows about the affair, he likely sees Courtney as someone who is equally hurt. So why would he want to pin the murder on her?"

"And if he doesn't know about the affair?"

"I still don't see why he would want to hurt Courtney. If he killed Dennis because Dennis was stealing, he knows Courtney would have had nothing to do with it. Again, it makes no sense to pick a murder method that so obviously lays the blame at Courtney's feet."

"On the other hand, he might be thinking if the investigation focuses on Courtney, he'll be less likely to be discovered. Plus, since Courtney didn't do it, maybe he thinks the investigation will clear her."

I snorted. Wyle stared at me.

"Sorry," I said. "I wasn't trying to be skeptical. But the problem with the poison in the bottle as a Christmas gift is that Courtney can't really prove she didn't do it. Glenn seems smarter than that. Unless he thinks it's such a circumstantial case that it will never go to trial. Speaking of circumstantial, have you identified the poison yet?"

I didn't expect Wyle to answer me. But to my surprise, he took out a small notebook and flipped through it. "It's something called 'Aconitum Napellus.'" He pronounced the words slowly.

It took me a few moments to decipher what he said. "Are you talking about Monkshood?"

He stared at me. "Yes. You know what that is?"

"Yes. It's a very dangerous heart and nerve poison. It's an herb that's usually grown only as an ornamental plant because of its dark purple flowers. It's beautiful, but very toxic. In ancient times, they would dip the tips of spears into a poison made of Monkshood before going into battle."

He shut his notebook. "I should have guessed you'd know about it."

"Well, that is what I do," I said modestly. "But now I'm even more convinced it's not Glenn. How would he know about Monkshood?"

"He could research it. You said he was smart."

"Yeah, but he's a numbers guy. I don't see him spending time in the library going through books on herbs. That seems like too much work when there are other ways to kill someone. Although ..." I paused as a thought struck me. "Tiffany is very much into herbs and natural medicine. It's possible she knows about Monkshood."

"So, you think Tiffany did it?"

"Possibly. Or she's got books at home, and Glenn went through them."

Wyle folded his arms across his chest. "So, now you think it's Glenn?"

"He certainly has the motive," I said, although even to myself, I didn't sound convinced.

"So, if you don't think it's Glenn, then who?"

I sighed. "That's the problem. I'm not sure. If not Tiffany or Glenn, then who? Maybe Nina knows."

"The ex?"

I nodded. "I was hoping she would talk to me."

Wyle narrowed his eyes. "Are you going to harass her, too?"

"That wasn't the plan. Of course, it wasn't the plan to harass Tiffany or Glenn, either."

His lips twitched in a faint smile. "If you want to debrief on what you find out, let me know."

I widened my eyes and pressed my hand to my heart. "Does this mean what I think it does? That you're giving me your blessing to investigate?"

Wyle rolled his eyes. "I think 'blessing' is a little strong, but at this point, it seems clear you're going to do what you want, so if you can help solve the case, I'll take it."

"Well, then since you asked so nicely, maybe I will give you a debrief. Although," I frowned, as if mulling it over. "To be honest, I'd rather 'compare notes' than give you a debrief."

His smile widened slightly as he stood up. "Ours wasn't the most helpful of meetings, but maybe you'll have better luck." He waved me back down as I started to stand. "I can see myself out. Thanks for the pie. You're right, it did make everything better." He flashed one last grin as he sauntered out of the kitchen, leaving me to catch my breath.

Brandon Wyle was trouble. No question about that.

I had just finished cleaning up the kitchen a second time when there was another knock at the door. "Grand central station again," I muttered to myself as I went to answer it.

This time, I checked to see who it was before opening the door. There was a man I had never seen before standing on the porch. From what I could tell, he was definitely attractive, with sandy-brown hair and delicate, almost effeminate features, and a bit of a weak chin. I wondered if he was a potential client. I mostly sold to women, but I did have the occasional man stop by.

I opened the door. "Can I help you?"

He raised his head and stared directly into my eyes. His were dark blue and ringed with thick lashes that were wasted on a man. "Are you Charlie Kingsley?"

"I am. And you are ...?"

"Luke." There was something frantic, almost frenzied, about him that made me want to back up a few steps and shut the door. "Luke Zellner. I'm Courtney's lover."

Chapter 12

I watched Luke demolish the rest of the pie. He had been so distraught, I wasn't sure what to do with him other than offer him a cup of tea and dessert, which he accepted. He didn't seem too keen on the tea, but at least I wasn't going to have to worry about any leftover pie.

He was younger than I thought when I saw him standing outside. He was also more muscular—the thin, pale-blue sweater that matched his eyes stretched across his well-developed chest.

"She couldn't have done it," he kept telling me between bites. "Courtney is absolutely the sweetest, most loving person you could ever meet. The fact that anyone thinks she could have done this to anyone, much less her husband, is ludicrous."

I tried not to roll my eyes. Luke had been basically repeating the same thing since he first sat down in my kitchen.

"How long have you two been ... seeing each other?" I winced as the words came out of my mouth. It sounded like I thought there was nothing wrong with what they were doing, when in reality, I was trying to figure out if Courtney's baby was Luke's.

"A few years," Luke said.

I tried to keep the shock from my face, although Luke was looking down at the pie instead of at me anyhow. A few *years*? That would be most of Courtney's marriage. Maybe even before their marriage. Did this mean Dennis had been seeing Tiffany for years, as well? Were Courtney and Dennis even in an actual marriage?

"You've been having an affair for *that* long?" I asked.

Luke stopped chewing and looked at me, his expression slightly sheepish. "Well, no," he admitted. "We've been friends for that long, but it wasn't until this year that things shifted."

"What changed?"

He gave me a surprised look. "What changed? She found out her husband was a lying, cheating bastard, that's what. He doesn't deserve her."

His tone was so angry, I found myself wanting to push my chair back. I wondered if he was angry enough to do something about it.

"So, she started having an affair with you because her husband was having an affair?"

He dropped his fork onto his plate, the contact making a "clinking" noise. "It wasn't like that," he said forcefully, almost as if he were trying to convince himself. "Yes, she was upset, and yes, I was the person she turned to. I was the only one who listened to her. We *were* friends. But sometimes friendships can develop into something more, and that's what happened. That's all it was."

I wondered if Courtney had the same view of their relationship. "How did you two meet?"

His whole body seemed to relax as his lips curled into a smile. "We worked together at Fit for Life," he began.

It was all I could do to keep myself from interrupting with an "Are you kidding me?" How was it that everyone involved in this case seemed to have worked for either Fit for Life or F & H Financial Advisors?

"I'm a personal trainer," he continued, which certainly explained his muscular chest. "And you probably know that Courtney was on staff there, too."

"You weren't?"

He shook his head. "The personal trainers and fitness instructors were all contractors. We just worked when we had clients. Courtney was the exception, although a couple of the personal trainers would also work a few hours a week behind the front desk."

"Does this mean you knew Courtney before she met Dennis?"

He nodded. "We were friends. I was dating someone else before she started going out with Dennis, or I probably would have asked her out sooner. Of course, I thought there was plenty of time. I was such an idiot." He shook his head.

"So, I gather you stayed friends after she got married."

"Yeah. Courtney didn't have a lot of friends to begin with. She had basically worked through her entire teenage years, so she wasn't able to go out and party like other kids her age. But we always got along." He picked up his fork and started playing with what was left of the pie on his plate. "I had to work a lot, too, so I understood."

"And Dennis knew about your relationship?"

He shrugged. "I think so. I was at the wedding. But it wasn't something Courtney and I talked about."

"What did you talk about?"

"Life, I guess." He gave me a lopsided grin. "What do friends talk about?"

"Let me rephrase," I said. "Was she happy? Was she in love with Dennis? Other than the affair, did they seem happy together?"

He took a few moments to answer. "I think, overall, she was content with her life," he said. "Before she got pregnant, she was a little bored, quite honestly. She loved working out—that was another thing we had in common—and she loved teaching aerobics classes, but Tiffany didn't use her as much as she wanted. She told you about the rift between her and Tiffany?"

I nodded.

"Yes, well, because of that, Tiffany didn't schedule her for classes the way she used to, which I know bothered Courtney. Not that she complained. I encouraged her to go to other health and fitness clubs and line up more teaching gigs. It would be easy for her to do, because she's really good. But for a long time, she resisted."

"Do you know why?"

Luke scooped up a bite of pie and popped it into his mouth. "I think because she didn't want to hurt Tiffany," he said. "I think a part of her really thought Tiffany would eventually come around and want to be friends again, but if Courtney was working for the competition, that would be it. Of course, that didn't happen. I think Courtney had just about decided to shop her talents around when she got pregnant, which of course scuttled those plans."

"Speaking of the baby," I said, grateful he'd brought it up, as I had been trying to figure out how to weave it into the conversation. "Do you know if ..." my voice trailed off as I realized just how nosy I sounded.

"If it's mine, you mean?" He shook his head as he went back to staring at his plate. "It's not. But I wish it was," he muttered into the pie.

I had to wonder about his motives. How much did he *really* wish the baby was his? Enough to send Dennis a surprise gift on Christmas Eve?

"This has been really helpful, Luke," I said with a smile. "But I am curious. Why are you here?"

He stopped eating, his fork still in the air, to stare at me. "What do you mean? Aren't you helping Courtney figure out who killed Dennis?"

I nodded. "I'm trying. Did she tell you to come talk to me?"

"No. She doesn't know I'm here."

"Then how did you know I'm helping her?"

He shot me a look. "Are you serious? This is Redemption. Word gets around."

I supposed it would, especially with Glenn trying to lodge a complaint about me. I could still remember how fast word had spread about my tea business. Still, it left me feeling a bit uneasy. I wasn't keen on starting a detective business.

"So, what did you come to tell me? Just that she couldn't have done it?"

Luke scraped off the last piece of pie. "No. Well, yes, it's true that she couldn't have done it, but mostly, I wanted to tell you who did."

I sat up a little straighter. "You know that? Who is it?"

"A client."

It was all I could do not to roll my eyes. "A client? That's really vague. Any idea which one?"

"Probably one involved in Maple Leaf Grove."

"What's that?"

He gave me a surprised look. "You don't know? It was an investment project F & H was a part of that ended up a complete disaster. You didn't hear about it?"

I shook my head.

Luke settled back in his chair, like he was getting ready to share a story. "Well, one of my clients was involved, which was how I found out about it."

"One of your personal-training clients?" I was trying to figure out how investing and working out went together.

"No, one of my handyman jobs." He saw the confusion on my face and clarified. "I do a lot of odd jobs. Handyman, construction, personal training. Altogether, it's a living. Anyway, Mr. Oldman is a long-time client. I've been helping him out for years. I basically have a standing appointment one afternoon a week to do whatever needs to be done around his house or yard. He's a great guy. Pays me for a full day's work even though I'm usually only there half the day, and I rarely work the whole time then. He always wants me to stay and chat for a while. He was the one who told me about Maple Leaf Grove, because he was an investor and thought maybe I could get some steady work there."

"Well, what is it?" I asked again, trying to hide my impatience.

He picked up his tea and took a sip, making a slight face. "It was supposed to be a brand-new, high-end subdivision outside of Riverview. You know how much that city is growing, right? It's just taking off. Anyway, I'm not sure of all the specifics—you could talk to Mr. Oldman about it if you wanted—but F & H was one of the main investors, along with a bunch of their clients, like Mr. Oldman. The land was purchased, and it was gorgeous. Just a perfect site for a beautiful neighborhood. Plans had been drawn up, contractors were hired, work got started, and then the EPA stepped in and designated it a 'superfund site.' The investors lost hundreds of thousands of dollars."

My eyes widened. "A superfund site? You mean, one of those plots of land that was once home to an old gas station, and the gas tank leaked?"

He nodded solemnly. "Yes, except this was an old chemical waste site, so it was even worse. Apparently, it all happened back in the twenties. The company basically just covered everything with dirt, and after a few years, sold it. I think it was sold a couple other times before it was set to become part of the new Maple Leaf Grove subdivision."

I pressed my hand to my mouth. "Oh no."

"Superfund sites" were called that because some sort of environmental damage had been done—like a leaking underground gas tank—and before you could do anything with the property, like build or develop it, you would have to clean it up. It was incredibly expensive, which is why the EPA had set up a superfund account to help pay for it. The problem was that, even with superfund money, it was too cost prohibitive. So, the properties tended to just sit there, abandoned and forlorn, wasting away.

"I don't understand," I said. "How did they not know? Didn't they do their due diligence?"

Luke shrugged. "That's the question of the hour. How did it get so far in the process without someone, somewhere, realizing what was happening? Why weren't the proper tests done before the sale? Everyone is pointing fingers at everyone else, and as there were multiple entities involved in the deal, it's not clear who was actually in charge."

"What about who sold them the land? Couldn't the investors go back to them and at least get their money back?"

"They're in the process of trying," Luke said. "There are attorneys involved, and lawsuits, but apparently, the company that sold it is claiming they didn't know, and I guess it's a pretty convincing case. So, it's not good."

"Wow. So, F & H was a part of the whole thing?"

"The investment part. They were the ones lining up the investors, so as you can imagine, the other investors are pretty upset."

I wondered if this was what the man who had called Glenn's office the day I was there was upset about. I couldn't think of his name … something German, I thought. But if he was one of the investors, it made sense why he would be agitated, and why Glenn clearly didn't want to take the call. "I agree this all sounds pretty bad, and Glenn really has his hands full right now, dealing with it alongside Dennis's death. But, speaking of Dennis, how does this tie into his murder? I get that the investors would be upset with him, but there's probably a lot of people involved in that debacle for them to be upset with. And as far as I know, Dennis is the only one who is dead."

Luke leaned forward slightly, as if we were in the middle of Aunt May's diner rather than my kitchen, and he didn't want anyone overhearing him. "Well, rumor has it that even though Dennis had brought it up with his clients, he hadn't invested all that much of his own money."

"Really?" That was a bit surprising. "Does anyone know why?"

"Dennis claimed it was because he had money invested in other projects and wasn't liquid enough to put all that much into this one."

"That sounds reasonable," I said, thinking about what Courtney had said about her husband's successful investments. "Did the investors not believe him?"

"Not really. Some of them, like Mr. Oldman, didn't think it was intentional, but rather that he handled things wrong."

I frowned. "Intentional? People really thought Dennis was trying to scam the investors on purpose?"

Luke nodded. "A few did. They thought Dennis knew exactly what was going on and still sold them the opportunity. But I think most of them were of the same mind as Mr. Oldman, which was that Dennis had a feeling something was off and therefore was cautious with his own money. But if that's true, he also shouldn't have sold it to everyone else."

"But why would Dennis sell something that he knew was a bad investment?" I asked. "Was he just a bad person?"

"I don't think that was it," Luke said. "I never got that sense of him. But, yeah, the lack of a motive as to why he would be involved on any level, including tainting his business by association, is why I think most people just figured he was guilty of terrible judgement."

I paused, turning over the new pieces of information in my mind. "The ones who thought Dennis knew," I said slowly. "I take it there's been no recourse? They just think Dennis screwed them, and there's no way to get their money back?"

"Yep," Luke said. "Which is why I think one of them killed him. Not because he thought he'd get his money back, but just because he wanted Dennis to pay."

The more I thought about it, the more it made sense. "What about Glenn?"

"Oh, Glenn," Luke let out a sigh. "He definitely invested a lot. Maybe a little too much. No one thinks he had anything to do with it."

Well, that explained Glenn and Tiffany's financial predicament. If Glenn had lost a ton of money in Maple Leaf Grove on top of Dennis stealing from the business, no wonder things were tight. Add to the fact that F & H had probably lost clients due to this whole fiasco, and Tiffany taking on janitorial duties made sense. It was entirely possible that she was supporting them financially, at this point.

It also moved Glenn to the top of the suspect list again. How angry and resentful must he have been at Dennis?

Enough to kill him?

"Whoever killed him also wouldn't care if Courtney was the one who was blamed," Luke interrupted my thoughts. Flattening his mouth, he continued, "No, they wouldn't care at all."

"Did you tell the police about this?"

He looked away. "Not yet. I know they really zeroed in on Courtney, and if they realize we are involved ..." He raised his hands, palms up.

"Yeah, I can see that." Cleary, if the cops knew Courtney was also having an affair, all that would do is strengthen their case against her. "Do you have the names of the investors who were the most upset?"

"Right here," he said, digging into his jeans pocket. He pulled out a crumpled piece of paper and handed it over to me.

I smoothed out the wrinkles and studied the three names on the list. Walt Barr, Jim Hacker, and Ned Ardelt. None of them rang any bells.

"I gave you their phone numbers, too, as well as Mr. Oldman's contact information in case you want to talk to him," Luke said.

"I see that," I said. "So, I take it it's okay if I call all of them?"

Luke nodded, his eyes bright and eager to please. "My phone number is on there, too. If you need any help. Or anything."

I folded the paper up. "I definitely will."

Chapter 13

"I met Luke," I said.

There was silence on the other end of the phone.

"Courtney? Are you still there?"

The sound of throat-clearing. "I'm still here," she said in a small, quiet voice.

"Luke said you two were having an affair. Is that true?"

More silence.

"Courtney?"

I was about to hang up and drive over to her house to confront her in person when she started to talk. "It was a mistake," she said, her voice still low.

I closed my eyes. "Courtney, I thought you said you were going to be honest with me?"

"I am!"

"Not telling me about an affair you're having is not being honest with me."

"Had, not having," she corrected, her voice forceful. There was a muffled dragging sound on her end, like she was pulling out a kitchen chair to sit down. "Look," she said, her voice so quiet, I had to strain to hear her. "It was one time, and it was nearly a year ago. I had just been told about Dennis kissing another woman, and I was a wreck. Luke met up with me after I taught my class. We went out for coffee, I told him everything, and ... well, one thing led to another."

"Is the child you're carrying Luke's?"

"No!" The answer was immediate and firm. "It was that one time, nearly a year ago. I knew right away I had made a huge mistake, and I told him we could never do it again. He agreed, although I could tell he was disappointed. We still hung out, but nothing else happened."

"You're sure?"

"Yes, I'm sure. I'm telling you the truth." She sounded like she was close to tears. "I know you may not believe this, but I love ... loved my husband. I wanted to make my marriage work. I was devastated when I found out about the cheating and, well, I didn't handle it well. But that mistake woke me up. I got my head on straight and started focusing on making my marriage work."

"Then why didn't you ever tell Dennis you knew he was having an affair?" I half expected her not to answer, as it was really none of my business. But I was also sick of having information withheld from me. I was trying to do Courtney a favor, yet obstacles kept getting tossed in my path at every turn.

She hesitated. "It's hard to explain."

"Why don't you try?"

"Because ... I guess I kind of felt like if he said it, that he was having an affair, it would make it real. And if it became real, then there was the possibility he would leave me for her. So, I guess ... I thought if we didn't talk about it, if instead I just focused on being the best wife I could be, he would ... well, forget about her and stay with me."

There was so much I wanted to say. How trying to build a relationship on a lie never works. That hiding from the truth never worked out for anyone, because the truth always comes out in the end. But what was the point? Dennis was gone. And it wasn't like she had asked for my help with her relationships.

Still, my heart hurt for her. She was so young and already had a lot of strikes against her. I wondered if she would ever be able to move past her trauma and wounds and find the relationship she clearly craved.

For not only her sake, but for that of her baby, I truly hoped she would.

"Do you know about Maple Leaf Grove?"

"Oh no," she said.

I took that as a "yes."

"Why 'oh no'?"

"Because it wasn't his fault!" Her voice was a plaintive cry.

"What wasn't his fault?"

"The project! I know what people are saying, but it wasn't his fault. It wasn't even his idea."

"Courtney, slow down," I said. "Start from the beginning. Are you saying that it was Glenn's idea to invest in Maple Leaf Grove?"

"Yes! That's exactly it." Her voice still had an edge of hysteria to it, but I could tell she was trying to calm herself. "Dennis always had a bad feeling about that project. From the very beginning. But Glenn was so excited about it. He thought it was going to be their big break … put their business on the map, maybe even get them bigger clients out of Milwaukee or even Chicago. Dennis wasn't as convinced." She sighed. "He didn't want to put any money into it, but felt like he had to, mostly to support Glenn. So he purposefully only put a small amount in. If we lost it, we lost it—it wasn't going to hurt us one way or another, and if the project was as successful as Glenn kept saying, well, that would be okay, too. He would admit he was wrong and be fine with the small return. He told me over and over he hoped he WAS wrong. He didn't want to see anyone lose their shirt over this, but unfortunately, he was right."

"If he was so hesitant about Maple Leaf Grove, why did he sell it to his clients?"

"He didn't," Courtney said firmly. "Glenn was selling it. Not Dennis."

"Then why is everyone blaming him?"

"That's the problem. I don't know," she wailed. "I don't understand what's going on. Why does everyone think Dennis was the reason they lost their money? Or why do they think he stole money from F & H? He was a good, honest man. I don't know why they're saying things like this about him."

"Do you have any idea who was to blame?" I asked. "Who else would have been stealing from F & H, if not Dennis?"

"I don't know," Courtney said. "They have a secretary; I can't remember her name right now. There's also a bookkeeper and a couple of junior associates … someone named Rick, I think? Or maybe Dick. I can't remember." She sighed. "I'm not that much help, I know. I didn't know any of them very well, but I can't imagine anyone stealing money from anyone. I keep thinking it's some sort of mistake."

"We can only hope," I said, although I was starting to wonder if Courtney was for real. Could she possibly be that innocent, or was it all an act?

And, if it was all an act, did that mean I was on a wild goose chase, and Courtney was guilty after all?

"I have to ask," I continued, even though I knew I was sounding like a broken record. "Why didn't you tell me about Maple Leaf Grove?"

"Why would I tell you?" she asked, sounding genuinely bewildered. "What does Maple Leaf have to do with Dennis's death?"

I closed my eyes, willing myself to be patient. "Luke was the one who told me, because he thought one of the investors in Maple Leaf might be responsible for Dennis's death."

"What?" Courtney sounded shocked. "No. No, that can't be. Dennis's clients are good people. They wouldn't do something like that."

"It *is* possible," I said. "Both you and Luke are telling me that people were pretty angry at Dennis. Rightly or wrongly, it sounds like they were blaming him."

"But, to kill him? That seems extreme."

"I agree. But people kill people over money all the time."

"But it's not like they'd get their money back if Dennis died."

"Courtney," I was trying really hard not to sound as impatient as I felt. "Who do you think killed Dennis?"

"I don't know," she said. "That's why you're helping me look into it."

"Yes, but you do understand it's likely going to be someone you know, right?"

"But ... no. There must be a mistake," she fretted. "An accident."

"And what if there isn't?" I asked. "What if whoever did it truly intended on killing Dennis?" I didn't really like pushing her. I knew she was still grieving and pregnant, but I also felt that, if she continued to close her eyes to reality, things were going to get a lot worse for her.

"Then it must be someone I don't know," she said. "A stranger."

"How would a stranger know Dennis's favorite brandy? Or about his cousin?"

"Well, maybe Dennis told someone, and someone else overheard?" she guessed. "You know, some sociopath."

"Seriously," I said. "You're going with that?"

"There has to be some explanation."

"There *is* an explanation," I said. "And that explanation is simple—someone you know killed your husband."

"But ... but that would mean I know someone who is capable of doing something like that," she burst out. "And that can't be. It just can't."

"Why not?"

"Because I should be able to sense it!" She was completely distraught. "I should have known. Just like I should have known my father was about to leave us. I caught him as he was packing. I asked him why he was packing, and he said he wasn't ... that he was just packing a bag to donate to Goodwill and would be right back. And I *believed* him. I really thought he was coming right home. I didn't sense anything. And now, you're telling me someone I know killed my husband, and I didn't sense that evil, either? How could I be such a lousy judge of character? What is *wrong* with me?"

I stayed silent, listening to Courtney's hitching breath. It sounded like she was crying. "Courtney," I said very quietly. "It's not your fault your father left you."

"But I should have *known*. Other people know when things are off. Why don't I?"

"Sometimes people know, but a lot of times, they don't," I said reassuringly. "People are blindsided all the time by the actions of others. You wanted to believe your dad. There's nothing wrong with that. And it certainly doesn't mean you're a lousy judge of character."

"But my dad wasn't the only one," Courtney said, her breath hitching again as she tried to control her tears. "Dennis cheated on me, and I didn't know it. And what if ... what if he really *did* steal that money? How could I not have known?"

"Half the spouses in this country are cheating, and most of the time, their partners don't know," I said. "It doesn't mean anything. As for what Dennis did or didn't do, let's just wait and see what happens. Maybe it is all a mistake like you said. Okay?"

"Okay," she said, her voice small.

"Is there *anything* else you should tell me? Even if it doesn't seem like it has anything to do with Dennis's death?"

She paused for a moment. "I don't think so," she said, seeming a little uncertain. Then, more firmly. "No, no, I don't think so."

I wasn't sure if I believed her, but that would have to do.

* * *

"*Courtney* is having an affair, too?" Pat's mouth was open, forming a round O, her expression incredulous. "Are you kidding me?"

"I know," I said, depositing a plate of pumpkin bread in the middle of the table. "It's like every time I turn around, I discover yet another pin dropping."

Pat eyed the plate of bread. "Any more pie?" she asked hopefully.

I shook my head regretfully. "'Fraid not. Wyle and Luke finished it off."

"You should have hidden the leftovers," she grumbled.

I nudged the bread closer. "Pumpkin bread is very festive this time of year. Very soon, there will be no more pumpkin bread— or pumpkin anything—until next fall. So enjoy it."

Pat muttered something under her breath but took a slice. "You know, I do remember hearing about that Maple Leaf fiasco. Richard has a coworker who invested. He had tried to talk Richard into it, too, but Richard wasn't interested. He's not a big on risk-taking. He prefers putting money in savings accounts and US bonds. Needless to say, when it fell apart last summer, his coworker didn't say too much about it."

"Can you ask Richard if his coworker thinks Dennis was to blame?"

Pat frowned as she popped a piece of pumpkin bread into her mouth. "I can ask. I don't know if we'll get the answer, though. The guy is pretty touchy on the subject, mostly because for a while, you couldn't shut him up about it. He was trying to get the entire office to join him. I think one or two did, but he was so obnoxious about it, it turned a lot of people off. But let me see what I can find out. What about the names Luke gave you? Were any of them helpful?"

"They were certainly angry," I said as I twirled my mug around. I had spent the evening after Luke left on the phone, mostly getting yelled at. "Walt was especially furious. The moment I brought up Dennis, he ranted and raved. He even said he wasn't sorry he was dead."

Pat's eyebrows went up. "Really?"

"Yeah." I continued to twirl my mug, remembering how I had to hold the phone away from my ear as I listened to Walt. "He's also pretty convinced that Dennis was stealing from F & H. He's sure Dennis was a shyster, and the world is better off without him in it."

"Do you think Walt could have killed Dennis?"

"It's possible," I said. "I was going to ask him if he knew what Monkshood is, but then I thought it might be better coming from the police. If Walt is the killer, I didn't want to tip my hand."

Pat nodded. "That makes sense."

"I took notes," I said, grabbing a notebook from the counter to show her.

"You're going to give that to Wyle?"

"A copy," I corrected. "But yes. If he's not talking to the Maple Leaf investors, he really should."

"Are you going to tell Wyle about Luke?"

I closed the notebook and placed it next to my tea. "I don't know yet," I said. "I mean, I should. Luke definitely has motive, as he's clearly in love with Courtney. Although that gives Courtney even more motive than she had before. I feel like I should share it, but I don't know."

Pat cocked her head as she studied me. "You don't think Luke did it?"

I sighed. "Not particularly. He didn't *feel* like a killer. You know what I mean?"

Pat gave me a look. "Because you know what a killer feels like, right?"

"Ha," I said, smiling like I was in on the joke as I picked up my tea, if only to give myself a reason to look down and hide my eyes. As good a friend as Pat was, she didn't know all my secrets. She especially didn't know that I actually had quite a lot of experience on the subject of killers.

"But seriously, he had this puppy-dog energy about him. So eager to please. I suppose anything is possible, but Walt felt like a much better lead. Although I don't know if Walt would be all that into poisoning. He seems more like a 'shoot 'em in the parking lot' type of fellow."

"Yeah, the method is the stickler," Pat mused. "There certainly seems to be enough people who were angry enough at Dennis to wish him dead. But to be calculated enough to set up sending him a poisoned bottle of brandy as a pretend gift from his cousin seems a little ... cold-blooded."

"That's where I always get stuck," I said. "Figuring out who has the motive and would pick that specific method. Monkshood, of all things."

"Where would you even find Monkshood?" Pat asked. "Especially now. It's not like it's growing in anyone's backyard."

"Some herbalists sell it," I said. "There are those who claim the herb has some therapeutic uses."

"I thought you said it was quite toxic."

"It is," I said. "I wouldn't use it for anything. But some do. Especially in Chinese medicines. Apparently, it's good for relieving pain, and it also may help with some cardiac problems."

"Really? So you can buy it here?"

I nodded. "The problem is that it's very easy to overdose. It doesn't take much for Monkshood to become toxic. There are other, less lethal ways to help with pain than Monkshood. At least, that's my opinion."

Pat shook her head. "Wow. I had no idea."

"That's the thing. It's not like it's that obvious of a poison to use. The obvious choice would be to get some rat poison. It's easy to get your hands on, and everyone knows it's lethal. But Monkshood? Maybe I'm overthinking things, but right now, all the pieces aren't fitting together. I don't know if I'm missing a couple of crucial ones, or if I'm not looking at what I have in the right way yet."

Pat gave me a sympathetic look. "Well, maybe Wyle can shed some light on this when you give him your notes. When are you going to do it?"

"After I talk to Nina." I grinned at her. "I told him I'd share any insights with him."

Pat stared. "You're talking to Nina?"

"I am," I said, as I stood up. "And so are you. Come on, she's expecting us."

"Seriously? And you couldn't have said something sooner?" Pat glared at me as she finished off the last of the pumpkin bread. "It's a good thing you're such a good cook. Otherwise, we would definitely have issues."

Chapter 14

"So, Charlie," Nina said as she handed me a delicate, white porcelain cup rimmed with gold. "You're the one who makes teas, correct?"

"I am indeed," I said, accepting the cup.

"I've been meaning to call you for a while," she said, giving me a faint smile. "I've been hearing rave reviews."

"It's wonderful," Pat chimed in beside me. "Highly recommend. Best tea you'll ever have."

"Well, then, I definitely feel I should apologize in advance for what I'm serving you. It's store-bought."

"I'm sure it will be fine," I lied. Inwardly, I was kicking myself. I should have brought some samples with me.

Nina gave me another thin smile as she handed a cup to Pat. She was about as opposite of Courtney as one could be. Tall and rawboned, while Courtney was petite and curvy, although the pregnancy certainly added to the curves. Courtney's face was heart-shaped, while Nina's was long, thin, and narrow, with high cheekbones and deep-set, dark-brown eyes. Her brown hair was cut short in a no-nonsense style, which her clothes matched—a dark-blue blazer with a white blouse and black trousers. She would never be called "pretty" or "cute," but she was imposing, and at one time, maybe even striking.

Her house was decorated in a similar no-nonsense manner—navy-blue carpet, beige couch and matching chairs, oak coffee table and bookshelf, and red and blue accents. It was all very neat and sterile.

Nina seated herself in one of the beige chairs and crossed her legs. "Before we get started, I feel like I should warn you that if you're here to talk about Dennis's murder, I'm afraid I'm not going to be of much help. I haven't spoken to Dennis in, oh, at least two years. So, I really don't know anything."

"I'm more interested in learning more about Dennis the person," I said.

Nina's eyebrows raised as she took a sip of tea. "Oh?"

"Yes, I'm hearing a lot of contradictory information about him, and I thought maybe you could fill in some details."

Nina pursed her lips. "I can certainly try."

"So, what was Dennis like?"

"Like?"

"Back when you were married to him," I said. "How would you describe him?"

Nina sat back slightly in her chair. "Dennis was one of those men who could walk into a room and own it," she said. "It's what made him such a good salesman. When he was speaking to you, you felt like the only person in the world. It was truly a gift."

"How did you two meet?"

"Back in college." She paused, her face softening and a smile playing on her lips, and suddenly, I could see the echoes of the beauty she once was. Lacking typical generic prettiness, Nina's looks would have once been unique and noteworthy. "I thought he was such an arrogant jerk. I wanted nothing to do with him. In retrospect, I don't think he was used to anyone saying 'no' to him, which probably really piqued his interest. He asked me out sixteen times before I said 'yes.' For two months, he would wait outside my English Lit class to ask me out again. Finally, I asked what it would take to get him to leave me alone. He said I had to agree to go out with him one time. So, against my better judgement, I did." She shook her head. "The rest is all history."

"How long were you two married?"

"Legally, we were married almost twelve years, but the marriage died way before the legal end."

"Why did it end?"

She sighed. "Because I finally realized I was done sharing him. I wanted a real marriage, not one where I was always in second place."

My eyes widened. Was she talking about Tiffany? "Who were you sharing him with?"

"His work," she said, with more vehemence than I would have expected from someone who had been divorced for several years. "I finally woke up one morning and realized the reason why I was so unhappy was because all along, he had been married to his business, not me. I asked him to move out, said I wanted a trial separation. I thought that might wake him up, but instead, it seemed to put us on a path that ultimately ended in divorce."

While this was certainly consistent with what Courtney said about Dennis working all the time, I wondered if it was the full story. "It was only his work that was the problem?"

Nina lifted an eyebrow. "What else? Or are you asking if he was cheating on me?"

"It's come up that Dennis might not have been completely faithful."

Her smile was sad. "If you're implying that Courtney stole him away, as much as I despise her, it isn't true. We were already legally separated and headed for divorce when Dennis met her. Her being in the picture didn't change a thing."

I wondered about the despising comment, but decided to come back to it. "No, actually it's Tiffany I'm wondering about."

Nina's eyes widened. *Tiffany?* " She burst out laughing. "Oh heaven's, no. He wouldn't have an affair with Tiffany."

Pat and I glanced at each other. "How can you be so sure?"

Nina put her tea down on the table and picked up a napkin to dab at the corners of her eyes. "Because I was there at the beginning. Who told you this nonsense? Was it Tiffany?"

I had a feeling that bringing up Courtney's mother wouldn't be the right move. "It was actually someone who saw them together."

Nina made a face. "What did they see? Them kissing?" She rolled her eyes. "Tiffany has been after Dennis since they first met. Dennis was never even remotely interested in her."

"But ..." I hesitated, glancing again at Pat, who looked as surprised as I. "If they were kissing ..."

"It meant nothing," she said firmly. "It was likely instigated by Tiffany, but whatever that person saw, I can assure you, it wasn't what it looked like."

"How can you be so sure?"

Nina sighed and recrossed her legs. "I take it no one told you how it all started. So, Dennis and Glenn met in college. They were roommates. I'm not sure how Glenn met Tiffany ... I think at a party, maybe ... but they were dating off and on when he brought her to this tailgating party. Dennis and I were both there; we were on our third date, and I still wasn't sure about him. Tiffany took one look at him, and that was it. She was hooked. It was written all over her face.

"Needless to say, Dennis didn't feel the same way. He was cordial and friendly toward her, but that was it. Our relationship was one of those on-again, off-again types back then, and unfortunately for Tiffany, I think she read into that the wrong way. I think she thought Dennis and I were going to break up, and once we did, she would swoop in and get him. But for her to know if that happened, she had to stay in the know. So, she kept dating Glenn.

"Anyway, as you've probably guessed, that didn't happen. It took a couple of years, but eventually, our relationship turned serious, and Dennis and I got engaged. Shortly after that, Glenn asked Tiffany, and she agreed." Nina shook her head. "For the life of me, I don't know why. It was clear she didn't love him. Why Glenn asked her and why she accepted is a mystery. My suspicion is that Glenn didn't have much experience with women, and he didn't think he could do much better than Tiffany. As for Tiffany," Nina shrugged. "Maybe she thought it was her way of staying in Dennis's life ... like one day, he would look up and see her and realize what he had been missing. Or maybe because she had already devoted so much time to being in a relationship with Glenn, she didn't want to admit defeat. But, whatever the reason, about three months after we were married, they tied the knot."

"Still," I said. "Something could have changed. Maybe after you two separated, he started to see Tiffany in a different light."

Nina made a face. "I highly doubt it. First off, Dennis had enough trouble balancing his business and a relationship, much less trying to squeeze in an affair. And second, I can't see him doing that to Glenn."

It was clear nothing I could say was going to convince Nina. I studied her as she sat in the chair, cool and unruffled. Was it possible that Courtney and Violet were both wrong? That Dennis wasn't having an affair? I decided to switch gears. "What was his relationship with Glenn like?"

Nina reached for her tea. "It was a case of opposites attract. And I mean *polar* opposites. Dennis had all the charm and charisma, while Glenn was more on the numbers and analytics side. As far as I could tell, they continued to get along well even when they were business partners. I know that friendships can sometimes fall apart in those situations, but that doesn't seem to be the case with Dennis and Glenn. Dennis would never hear or say a word against Glenn."

I cocked my head. Another odd turn of phrase from Nina. "What was your relationship like with Glenn?"

Nina looked faintly surprised. "How is that relevant? I haven't talked to any of them in years."

I smiled. "Simple curiosity. I'm also just wondering how you would know that Dennis would never say a word against Glenn."

Nin's lips curled up. "Well, to be quite frank, I warned Dennis not to start a business with Glenn."

"Why?"

"I never trusted him. There was something about him. Something ... slippery. Dennis told me it was all in my head."

"Have you heard about Maple Leaf Grove?"

Nina pressed her lips together and shook her head. "A terrible investment. I don't know who was in charge over there or how the necessary testing wasn't completed before the sale."

"Did you know people are saying that it was Dennis's fault?"

"Dennis?" Nina laughed again, but it wasn't quite as hard as before. "That's ridiculous. What proof do they have?"

"That he didn't put enough of his own money in," I said. "He barely invested anything."

"Well of course he didn't. Dennis knows a good investment when he sees one, and he also knows a bad investment. It's like he can smell them. It was why he was so good at his business."

"So you don't think it was Dennis's doing?"

"If anyone was to blame, it would be Glenn," Nina said firmly. "Glenn always had a weakness for get-rich-quick investments. I can't tell you how often Dennis talked Glenn out of one hairbrained scheme or another. Maple Leaf Grove has Glenn's fingerprints all over it."

"Glenn is also saying that Dennis was stealing from the business."

"*What*?" In her shock, Nina spilled her tea onto her lap. Pat reached over to hand her a napkin. "That's even more preposterous than Dennis being in charge of Maple Leaf Grove."

"So, you don't think he was stealing money, then."

"If anyone is stealing money from that business, it's Glenn," Nina said as she furiously scrubbed her pants with the napkin.

Pat and I looked at each other. *Glenn?*

"But, if that were the case, why would Glenn even bring it up?" I asked. "Dennis is gone. So why would he even talk about it?"

"Probably because someone figured it out, and now, he's trying to save his bacon. Glenn never did anything unless there was a clear benefit to him." Nina stopped her scrubbing and eyed both of us. "Look, I know I was married to the man, so maybe you think I'm biased, but it's not even possible that Dennis *could* be stealing. He was the salesman, remember? Glenn was the one who was in charge of the bookkeeping and numbers."

"I thought Courtney said they had a bookkeeper."

"So what if they did?" Nina said impatiently. "I said Glenn was in charge, not the one necessarily doing the work. He's the CFO, so if anyone could cook the books, he could."

I was starting to get a very bad feeling about the whole thing. "If what you're saying it true, do you think Glenn is capable of killing Dennis to hide all the lying and stealing he was doing?"

Nina looked me directly in the eye. "Absolutely."

Chapter 15

As we were leaving, I asked Nina about what she'd said about Courtney. "You said you despised her," I said. "I'm just curious as to why. Do you think she might have had anything to do with Dennis's death?"

Nina let out a short bark of laughter. "Oh, heaven's no. It's ... well, it's a little hard to explain."

I was by the front door, about to open it, but I stopped and turned around. The hesitancy in Nina's voice was like nothing I had heard from her throughout the entire interview.

She stood there biting her lip. "She's just so ... submissive. Her entire life revolved around Dennis. I never could stand women like that. All my life, they irritated me. 'Have a life,' I would think to myself. 'A man doesn't define you—only you can do that.'" She paused and gave me a twisted smile. "I knew the moment I met her that Dennis would adore her. A big reason why our relationship wasn't working was because we both had completely different careers and focuses, and he really needed a woman who would be there for him. She was exactly right for that." Her smile turned sad. "Maybe I despise her because she was able to give him what I never could."

"You were married a long time," I said quietly. "It sounds like he really tried to make it work. Clearly, he did love you."

"Unfortunately, despite what they say in romance novels, love isn't always enough."

I had no good answer for that, so instead, I thanked her for her time and squeezed her hand. I could write a book on how love isn't always enough.

"That was something," Pat said after we stepped outside, the door closed firmly behind us. "Are we back on the Glenn-did-it train?"

"Maybe," I said. "Nina was certainly compelling." I glanced over my shoulder at the neat and tidy ranch house and could have sworn I saw a curtain fall, as if Nina had moved to the window to watch us go. "But I think we need more."

Pat turned to me, an eyebrow quirked up. "More? As in more evidence? How are we going to get that?"

We reached the car, and I went over to unlock Pat's door before moving to my side. I waited until we were both settled inside before I answered. "If what Nina said is true, it's possible Dennis suspected something was wrong in the business. According to Courtney, Dennis seemed more upset and preoccupied with work than usual these past six months or so. That could be why."

"It's also when Maple Leaf was falling apart," Pat said. "That would certainly cause a lot of stress."

I frowned. "Possibly. It would cause stress, yes. But I don't know. Courtney made it seem like he was bringing more work home than usual. What work would he have with Maple Leaf? It doesn't sound like he had that much to do with it at all."

"Maybe he was trying to save the business by finding more investments."

'Maybe. Or maybe he was starting to suspect Glenn."

"Okay, so what if you're right?" Pat asked. "Where are we going to look for evidence? It's not like we can search Dennis's office at F & H. Even if Glenn didn't call the cops the moment he saw you, he's not just going to let us stroll in there and start digging around. Especially if he has something to hide."

I started the car. "I seriously doubt Dennis would have kept anything incriminating in his F & H office. My bet is, it's in his home office. Got time for a quick stop at Courtney's?"

"I wouldn't miss it," Pat said, settling back in her seat. "Let's just hope Glenn hasn't already gone by to search it."

* * *

"Why do you want to search Dennis's office?" Courtney asked.

We were standing in the living room, having just removed our coats. Courtney looked better than she had in a while. She had recently showered and dressed in clean clothes—an oversized Green Bay Packers sweatshirt and old, navy blue sweatpants. Despite the fact that both items were clearly too big for her, they still pulled against her swelling belly. Her face still showed the ravages of grief, but there was now a little peace mixed in, as well. Maybe her outburst during our call had helped her release some of her emotions. I hoped that was the case. In the background, I could hear Violet banging around in the kitchen, presumably making tea.

"I'd like to try and clear his name," I said. "That's what you want, right? Evidence he had nothing to do with Maple Leaf Grove or stealing from F & H? It's possible there's something in his office that can help us."

Her eyes widened. "You really think so?" Her voice was eager.

"It's certainly worth a try."

She nodded. "Of course, go ahead and look."

"Was anyone else in there?" I asked.

"The cops," she said, frowning. "They took some things, though I'm not sure what. I had to sign a paper."

My heart sank. Hopefully, they'd just focused on the brandy and packaging and left the files alone.

"I'll stay with you," Pat said, glancing at me.

"Oh." She seemed flustered. "You don't have to. My mom is here."

"That's okay," she said, tucking her arm through Courtney's. "I wanted to find out more about how you're doing. With the baby, and all. My mother died when I was pregnant with Barbara, and dealing with that grief was really rough." She patted Courtney's hand.

Courtney's face squished up. "Oh, I'm so sorry. I don't know what I'd do without my mother. And while you were pregnant … was Barbara your first?"

"She was," Pat said, leading Courtney to the couch and nodding at me over her head. I quickly disappeared down the hall

We had agreed in the car that Pat should stay in the living room with Courtney while I searched Dennis's office. Should we find something that implicated Dennis, we reasoned, neither of us wanted Courtney to wander in and find out. It seemed safer for me to search while Pat kept her busy.

Even though I had forgotten to ask Courtney where Dennis's office was, it was easy to find. As soon as I opened the door, I could tell. Oak wood paneling on the walls, hardwood floors covered with a thick bear rug, and a heavy, oak executive desk against the back wall pretty much screamed "man office." A black leather coach was pushed up against the opposite wall and a small cart for drinks stood nearby. Overstuffed bookcases lined the walls, although I didn't see any filing cabinets. I wondered if the cops took them, or if Dennis just didn't store many files at home. There didn't seem to be any room for filing cabinets anywhere else, so I thought it must be the latter.

I went around to his desk and started searching the drawers. The contents of the top drawer were typical: pens, paperclips, staples and whatnot. The next drawer slid out, displaying a tray of hanging files. I quickly searched through them, but they appeared to be personal. They were labeled "Insurance," "Warranties," "Receipts," and "Medical Bills." I didn't see anything labeled "Income" or "Tax," and wondered if the cops took those.

I closed that drawer and opened the next. This was another with hanging files, but they appeared to be stuffed with research. There were articles torn from magazines and newspapers, neatly labeled with the name of the periodical.

Frustrated, I slammed it shut. Now what?

I looked around the office. Even with the overstuffed bookcases, Dennis was surprisingly neat. Even the top of his desk was organized—there was one empty, stacked letter tray, a cup of pens, a phone, and one of those desk-pad calendars. It was December's, and it was filled with notes written in Dennis's careful hand. There were reminders of appointments outside the office along with what looked like general reminders.

Call Jim tomorrow.

Check out TG.

Ask Hans about records.

Hans. I kept staring at the name. Why was it so familiar?

"Knock, knock." Violet stuck her head inside the door, a smile on her face. "I thought you might like a nice cup of tea while you search."

I sat straight up. "Thank you. That would be lovely." I watched her as she came forward, holding the cup of tea carefully in front of her so she wouldn't spill.

"I wanted to thank you for everything you've been doing," she said. "I appreciate you looking after my daughter."

"Of course," I answered, taking the cup from her. "I'm happy to help."

She nodded her head slightly and turned to go, but I continued to talk, speaking in my normal voice. "Speaking of helping, why didn't you tell your daughter the truth about Tiffany and Dennis?"

She froze for a moment, before throwing a panicked glance over her shoulder. She hurried over to the office door and quietly asked, "Did you tell her?"

I didn't immediately answer. Instead, I simply watched her for a minute. Her face was frantic. "I did not," I finally said.

Relief swept her face. "Thank you," she breathed.

"Don't thank me," I said. "It was sheer luck I didn't mention it. Why didn't you tell me Courtney didn't know?"

Her cheeks flushed pink, and she ducked her head, seemingly unable to meet my gaze. "It was stupid not to tell you," she said. "Because you're right ... you easily could have mentioned something to Courtney. I guess ... I didn't want to get into why I didn't tell her."

"I don't understand," I said. "You wanted me to help, but you didn't want to tell me everything? You trust me to help, but not enough to give me an explanation? How do you expect me to be able to be of any use at all?"

She kept her eyes glued to the floor. "It was stupid," she said again, biting her lip. "I didn't want you to think badly of me. Of us."

I was floored. "Why would I think badly of either of you? Neither of you were doing the cheating."

Finally, Violet raised her head. "Because we were fools," she said, her voice bitter. "We should have known. I should have known. How did I miss the signs?"

"Why do you assume the affair was going on before Courtney was even in the picture?"

Her smile was rueful. "It's easier. Makes it worse to think it didn't start until he and Courtney were married, don't you think?"

I had to admit, she had a point.

"I felt so foolish," Violet continued. "I couldn't bear to tell you, or anyone else. I didn't think I could stand it if I felt like you were judging me. Even silently. I was already judging myself enough. How could I have let my daughter marry someone who was sleeping with his business partner's wife? And I was their secretary. How could I have not known what was going on?"

"Is that why you didn't tell Courtney?"

She bit her lip again and shook her head. "No. I didn't tell her because it would have broken her heart," she said, softly. "Even more than it already was. You have to understand. Courtney adored Tiffany. She would have done anything for her. Anything."

Anything but hide away when Dennis came to the club, like Tiffany told her to, I thought, but I held my tongue and let Violet continue.

"If she had known Tiffany was the one, I don't know what Courtney would have done. She was already in such a state when she found out. I was afraid it might push her over the edge."

Considering the fact that Courtney's reaction after finding out about Dennis's infidelity was to run out and jump in bed with another man, Violet had another point. At the same time, Nina's conviction that Dennis wasn't having an affair, much less with Tiffany, kept circling around in my head.

"How did you find out about the affair?" I asked.

She sighed. "I saw them."

"You saw Dennis and Tiffany?"

She nodded. "It was after my rotary club meeting. I was on the other side of town—normally, we do it at Fran's house, but she was in the middle of redoing her kitchen, so that day, we were at Gladys's—which was near Mario's ... have you been there? Cute little Italian restaurant. They have the best eggplant parmigiana. So, as I was driving by, I thought maybe I should treat myself to a late lunch—maybe even splurge on a glass of wine and skip dinner. I drove around the block, pulled into the parking lot, and got out of the car. I hadn't shut the door yet when I saw the restaurant door open and two people come out. It was Tiffany and Dennis. My first instinct was to start waving and calling out to them, to find out what they were doing at Mario's, but another instinct jumped in quick. I stayed where I was and watched them. As I did, I saw Tiffany lean closer and they ... they kissed."

Violet shuddered, shaking herself. "I couldn't stand watching it. I jumped back into my car, quietly shut the door, covered my face, and slid down in my seat, praying they wouldn't notice me. Tiffany didn't know what car I drove, but Dennis did. Luckily, I had parked near the back of the lot, next to an old pickup truck. I did that on purpose, you see, to force myself to walk a little further if I was going to have a big Italian lunch. Anyway, another car pulled into the parking lot. I could hear it, and I don't know if that distracted them or not, but shortly after, they got into their cars and left. As soon as I got myself under control, I left as well." She gave me a sideways smile. "I had lost my appetite."

I didn't respond. My mind was racing. Tiffany and Dennis were at a restaurant together in the middle of the day? That seemed to contradict what Nina believed, for sure. Although it seemed clear that Nina still loved Dennis, so I wondered if maybe part of what was going on was that she didn't want to believe that Tiffany and Dennis were sleeping together while they were married, too.

"Were you the one who told Courtney you saw Tiffany and Dennis?"

Violet hung her head again.

"I was beside myself," she said. "I didn't know what to do. I kept racking my brain, trying to remember if I had seen any indication of an affair when I was their secretary, but nothing came to mind. I knew I had to find a way to tell Courtney, but how? She had already been feeling restless, like something was off with her marriage. I kept telling her not to worry. Dennis was a busy man, after all. And it was natural after the first couple of years for things to mellow out. Building a life with someone is a lot different than the early days of a relationship when you're falling in love. She listened to me, but I could tell she was still bothered.

"The next day, she called me in tears. She had found lipstick on his shirt. So, of course, I had to tell her the truth, that I had seen him with a woman, but at the last moment, I couldn't tell her it was Tiffany. I lied and said I couldn't see the woman's face. She was silent for a moment, and then she just fell apart. She couldn't stop crying. I rushed over there and comforted her as best I could. She kept saying she felt like something was off with the marriage … that she had just known it."

"Did you encourage her to talk to Dennis? Or maybe get couples' therapy?"

"Not then. She was too upset. I told her she should get herself under control before she talked to Dennis. She promised she would. After a few days, she told me she had thought about it a lot and wanted to save her marriage, so she was going to focus on that. I told her I thought that was the right move, because she still loved him. And then Courtney got pregnant, and I thought maybe it was all going to work out. Dennis really seemed to be excited to be a father, and I hoped that meant he would also step up and take his marriage seriously. Then this happened."

It didn't sound to me like Violet had encouraged Courtney to deal with her relationship in a healthy, adult way. Inwardly, I sighed. No wonder Courtney had never spoken to Dennis about her suspicions.

"So, you don't think Dennis was seeing Tiffany anymore?"

Violet pressed her lips together in a flat line. "I don't know," she said. "Courtney didn't like talking about it. I hoped he wasn't, but I wasn't sure."

"You never saw anything else, though."

"No."

There was something about how stiffly she held herself, and how she continued to avert my eyes, that made me think she was holding something back. But what?

I decided to switch tactics. "So why did you tell me to talk to Tiffany?"

Her posture relaxed. This was something she was comfortable talking about. "Because I'm sure she's involved somehow. I just know it. But the police aren't looking at her."

"You think she poisoned Dennis? Her lover?"

"I didn't say that," Violet said. "I mean, it's possible. I'm not putting it past her. What I said was, 'I'm sure she's involved.'"

"Involved how?"

"Well, what if Glenn found out about the two of them?" she asked. "Glenn and Dennis have been friends for years. What a terrible betrayal it would be to find out his best friend and wife were sleeping together."

"So you think Glenn did it?"

"I think he's got more of a motive than my daughter," she said, her eyes full of steel and determination. "And I don't trust Tiffany at all. I think it's quite possible she threw Dennis under the bus to save her own marriage. Made him look worse. I could see Glenn wanting revenge."

Violet had a good point, although it made me wonder even more about Glenn. It sure seemed like no one liked him. Nina clearly didn't care for him, his own wife seemed to prefer Dennis, and now, Violet.

Although maybe that wasn't true. Maybe I was letting what Nina said earlier color my perception. Maybe I needed to talk to someone who had firsthand interactions with Glenn.

"When you worked for Glenn and Dennis, what was Glenn like?"

She looked a little surprised at the change of subject. "He was a good boss," she said. "He wasn't really friendly or anything. But he was fair. If you showed up and did your work efficiently, everything was fine."

"How was it between Dennis and Glenn?"

"Well, Dennis was definitely the charmer. He had the most clients and was the face of the company. Glenn was more behind the scenes. He was focused on the reports and whatnot. They seemed to make a good team—each had his own strengths and weaknesses, and they balanced each other out."

"Do you think it's possible Dennis would ever steal from the business?"

"Heaven's no." Violet shook her head furiously. "I can't see Dennis stealing from anyone. Although," her expression turned thoughtful. "I couldn't see him cheating on anyone, either. Regardless," she gave herself a little shake. "I don't see how he could. He had very little to do with the books and accounting. That was all Glenn."

That was the same thing Nina had said.

"What about Maple Leaf Grove? Do you think Dennis had anything to do with that?"

I was expecting the same answer as when I asked about Dennis stealing, but to my surprise, Violet hesitated. "Well, usually, Dennis was the one who brought the investment ideas to the table," she said slowly.

I sat up a little straighter.

"He was usually pretty good at finding the solid ones," she continued. "Not that all of them worked out, of course. He definitely had a few that didn't. But still, it would surprise me if he had anything to do with such a big miss. Not to mention that I can't imagine him hurting his clients like that."

"What about Glenn? Do you think the idea came from him?"

She frowned. "He was the numbers guy, although he would occasionally bring an idea to the office. Dennis would usually shoot it down, though." She half-smiled at the memory. "The rest of the staff would always stay away if that happened, because Glenn would invariably be grumpy. And a grumpy Glenn was not one anyone wanted to be around, especially if you had to report to him. I think he secretly wished he had Dennis's magic touch, when it came to investments."

I pushed the desk calendar closer to her. "What about these notes? Do any of them mean anything to you?"

She picked it up and turned it so she could read it. "There were a few Jims, at least while I was there. Not sure which one he was referring to. Hans … that has to be Hans Christof."

Something in my head clicked. That was the name of the client who called Glenn the day I was there. "When I was meeting with Glenn, the secretary interrupted to let us know that Hans was on the phone. He was clearly upset."

"That's not entirely surprising." She handed the calendar back to me. "Hans was extremely detail-oriented, especially when it came to finances. He always knew how much he had in the bank, to the last penny. When F & H would send reports, he would go through them with a fine-toothed comb, and if he found any irregularities, he would call the office."

Was it possible that Hans was the one who discovered someone stealing from F & H?

She pursed her lips. "It is strange, though."

"What is?"

"Well, for Dennis to call him."

"Why, if Hans was a client?"

Violet shook her head. "That's the thing. He wasn't Dennis's client. He was Glenn's."

Chapter 16

Officer Brandon Wyle folded his arms across his broad chest and leaned back in his chair. "I thought you were here to tell me what you learned from Nina?"

"I am," I said impatiently. "This is part of it."

"What do allegations that Dennis stole from F & H have to do with Nina? Do you have some proof she was part of it?"

"Of course not. But Nina doesn't think Dennis was the one doing the stealing. And she isn't the only one."

Wyle lifted an eyebrow. "Who does she think is stealing, then?"

"Glenn."

"*Glenn*?" Wyle didn't look impressed. "If Glenn was stealing, why would he bring it up to us in the first place? Wouldn't he prefer not to draw attention to the stealing?"

"Not if someone found out." I pulled the folded calendar out of my purse and laid it on the table. "Look. See the note about Hans?"

"Where did you get this?"

"From Dennis's home office." I leaned over to point at the note. "Right there. That's Hans Christof, a long-term F & H client."

Wyle peered at it. "So?"

"So, Hans wasn't Dennis's client. He was Glenn's. And on the day that I was meeting with Glenn, his secretary came in to say that Hans was on the phone. She made it seem like he was upset."

Wyle glanced up at me. "None of that means anything. Hans could have been upset at any number of things. Including Dennis being murdered."

"Well, he wouldn't have been upset about Dennis being murdered when Dennis called him," I said. "Look, apparently Hans was very a detail-oriented client. He went over his reports very closely, and if he found any errors, he would call them out. What if he found some sort of irregularity, and when he brought it to F & H, Dennis began to realize something was wrong?"

Wyle dug under one of his towering piles of paper and pulled out a notebook and pen. "So, you think Glenn killed Dennis because he was going to find out Glenn was stealing from the company?"

"It makes sense, if you think about it," I said. "Glenn actually had a lot of reasons to want to kill Dennis. Between the affair with Tiffany and trying to cover up the stealing, he appears to be a more likely suspect than Courtney."

Wyle was busy writing notes. "IF Glenn was stealing. There's no evidence of that."

"That's why I was thinking you could call Hans and ask him."

Wyle glanced up at me. "You didn't talk to him?"

"Well, I tried," I said. "He didn't answer his phone. But I think it might be better coming from you anyway. If he is one of those who dots the I's and crosses the T's, he would probably feel more comfortable talking to someone official."

"I'll give him a call," Wyle said. "So, Nina thought Glenn was stealing?"

"Nina thought it was far more likely Glenn was stealing than Dennis," I said. "She also thought that the whole Maple Leaf Grove fiasco was more likely Glenn's fault then Dennis's, which, again, with Dennis gone, he does make a much better scapegoat. In all fairness, though, I feel like I should add that it's possible she's biased."

"Why? Because they were married? I would think that would make her more biased *against* Dennis."

"True, but in this case, I think she's still in love with him."

Wyle made another note in his notebook. "Anything else?"

I shifted uncomfortably in my seat. "Well ..."

Wyle gave me another look. "Charlie?"

"It's just ... Nina didn't think it likely that Dennis was having an affair with Tiffany."

Wyle stared at me for a moment, then put down his pen. "She didn't think it was likely that Dennis was having an affair at all, or that it was with Tiffany?"

"Both, actually. She thinks he's married to his work and can barely handle one relationship, much less something on the side. And, if he was going to cheat, Tiffany wouldn't be the one he'd choose."

Wyle pondered this. "What do you think?"

I sighed. "Quite honestly, I don't really know. Violet, Courtney's mother, is the one who saw them together. They were at Mario's in the middle of the day. Why would they be together like that if there wasn't something going on between them? Yet Nina was adamant. They all knew each other in college, and according to Nina, Tiffany had the hots for Dennis from the moment she laid eyes on him, but he didn't have the same feelings for her."

"Then why did she marry Glenn?"

"Nina didn't know for sure, but she guessed it was to stay close to Dennis. Nina made Tiffany out to be a bit of an obsessive stalker."

Wyle grew very still. "Obsessive enough to have killed Dennis?"

"Wouldn't she have more likely killed Courtney, in that case?"

"You'd be surprised," Wyle said drily. "It's not like obsessive people are particularly stable, and sometimes they decide if they can't have the object of their obsession, no one can."

I thought about it. "With Courtney being so pregnant, that does change things. Courtney would always be part of his life, even if they eventually divorced. Unlike Nina. So, Tiffany would have been less threatened by Nina than Courtney."

"It's also possible Dennis ended it," Wyle said. "The baby will arrive soon. Maybe he told Tiffany that it was over. And she, realizing that she was never going to get Dennis, became so furious that she killed him."

"She also does know her herbs," I said. "And she has re-lationships with businesses that sell herbs, so she could have purchased Monkshood."

Wyle gave me a look. "I guess I shouldn't be surprised you also know Monkshood can be purchased."

"I should say not," I said archly. "Making teas IS what I do."

"So you keep telling me," Wyle said. He jotted down anoth-er few notes. "Anything else?"

"Other than I hope you're no longer laser-focused on Court-ney?" I asked. "I think it's pretty clear by now that there are other suspects."

"If I tell you we're following up on other leads, will you stay out of it?"

"Probably," I said.

Wyle rolled his eyes.

"Okay then," I said, gathering my coat and preparing to leave. "I will leave you to your investigations."

Wyle sat back. "You do know that what you found out could still implicate Courtney, don't you?"

I paused and gave him a hard look. "In what way?"

Wyle tapped his pen on his desk. "Well, you still have Dennis cheating on Courtney. What if Dennis didn't end things with Tiffany, but he did with Courtney?"

I stilled. "What makes you think that happened?"

"Oh come on, Charlie," Wyle said. "You're not going to tell me you didn't know about Luke Zellner."

I closed my eyes.

Wyle nodded. "That's what I thought."

"How did you find out?" I asked.

"I should be asking YOU that."

"He came to see me," I said. "He's the one who told me about Maple Leaf Grove and that maybe one of Dennis's clients took revenge."

Wyle made some notes. "Did you know one of Luke's many jobs is gardening and yard work? Apparently, he's pretty good about it. One of his clients," at this, Wyle made a show of flip-ping back through his pages. "Ah, yes. A Mrs. Little. She loves her flowers. Has a huge flower garden that Luke helps her with every summer. Want to guess what's in that garden?"

I sat back down in my chair. "Monkshood."

Wyle nodded.

"How did you even figure this out?" I asked. "It's not like Monkshood is growing right now."

He flashed a grin at me. "Superior detective work."

I rolled my eyes.

"Actually, you helped with that," he conceded. "Your comment about how people grew it because it has beautiful flowers stuck with me, and I made a few calls to local nurseries. I got a list of avid flower-growers, including Mrs. Little, and went around to ask them about their gardens. Imagine my surprise when I discovered that Luke was her helper."

"As you pointed out, that's hardly proof of Luke putting the Monkshood in Dennis's brandy," I said. "Lots of people have Monkshood in their gardens."

"That's true, but not all of them know how poisonous it is. Mrs. Little did. She knows her flowers. And she made sure to tell Luke."

"That's still not proof," I said. "And, even so, it seems to implicate Luke more than Courtney."

"They could have done it together," he said.

"None of this gets Glenn off the hook," I countered. "If he's stealing from the company, or he's the one to blame for Maple Leaf, that gave him a powerful motive to get rid of Dennis."

"Or, Courtney could be trying to avoid financial issues," he said. "If F & H is going down because of Glenn's actions, Dennis would have been taken down with it. But with Dennis gone, if it can be proven it was all Glenn, then she'll likely be financially set. That could be another reason why Luke is trying to point the finger at Glenn."

I wasn't at all happy with the direction Wyle was going. "I don't know," I said. "Luke didn't strike me as a killer."

Wyle raised an eyebrow. "Oh? Are you familiar with many killers?"

"That's beside the point," I countered.

"I disagree," Wyle said. "I think that *is* the point."

"Actually, the point is, are you going to look at anyone other than Courtney?"

"Everyone is a suspect," he said.

"That's not an answer."

"We haven't eliminated anyone, if that's what you're asking," he said. "We're keeping our options open."

Clearly, that was all I was going to get out of Wyle. I stood up again to leave. "Oh, real quick ... how did you find out about Luke?"

Wyle flashed that grin again. "Actually, I wasn't sure. We knew Courtney and Luke were friends, but we didn't know there was anything else going on. So, thank you for confirming that."

Mentally, I kicked myself. First the gardening, and now the affair. Some private detective I was turning out to be.

As dignified as I could manage it, I turned on my heel and left the room.

"Thanks again, Charlie," Wyle called out, a hint of laughter in his voice. I ignored him.

* * *

I pulled open the door of Fit for Life. I knew I was taking a chance, but I felt like I had no choice.

While I had hoped Wyle would investigate Glenn and his financial dealings, I couldn't be sure. I also couldn't be sure he wouldn't try and turn the whole thing around on Courtney.

I needed something else. Some other proof that would point to someone else.

And all my instincts were screaming that Tiffany held the key.

I knew she was hiding something. That was clear. The question was, what?

Jillian was standing by the front desk again. "Hello and welcome!" she said, her voice cheery. "Are you a member?"

"Actually, I'm here to see Tiffany," I said. "I'm the one selling teas. I met with her a couple of weeks ago about it." Inwardly, I held my breath. Based on what I had seen of their relationship, I didn't think Tiffany would have confided to Jillian that I was really poking around for Courtney's sake, but I couldn't be sure.

Jillian studied me for a second before her face cleared. "Of course. I remember you now." Her face puckered in a frown. "I don't know if she's available or not."

"That's okay," I said, as I strode forward. "It won't take long. I'll just see if I can find her myself."

I walked over to Tiffany's office. The door was open a crack, but not quite enough for me to see if she was inside. I gently pushed it open a tiny bit further.

There she was, sitting at her desk, staring off into space. "I thought I told you to always knock, Jillian," she said, without looking.

I pushed it open a little further while simultaneously knocking.

She rolled her eyes and looked over at me. They widened as soon as she recognized me. "You have some nerve showing your face here," she said firmly.

I held my hands out. "Do you have a few minutes? I know I have no right to ask, but it's important."

Tiffany pressed her lips together so tightly, they turned white. She really didn't look well. Her face was plastered with makeup, even more thickly than the last time I saw her, but it still didn't hide how pale and greenish she looked, or the dark circles under her eyes.

"Glenn told me you were trouble," she said. "You were using me to get to him."

"Please, Tiffany," I said. "It will only take a moment. And if you don't want to see me again, you won't have to."

She looked away, visibly fighting with herself. I held my breath again. If she threw me out without speaking to me, I wasn't sure what I was going to do. I just had to hope I had read the situation between her and Glenn correctly.

"Fine," she spat. "You have five minutes. No more."

"Thank you," I said, easing my way into her office. I closed the door behind me and weaved my way through the piles of paper before seating myself in the chair in front of her.

She stared at me, her green eyes no longer intense, but dull and listless instead. "Well, what is it?"

"What do you know about the financial situation at F & H?"

Her expression turned wary. "What do you mean?"

"Has Glenn talked to you about what's going on?"

She dropped her gaze to her desk. "You mean that Dennis was stealing from the business?"

"Yes. Except ... what if it wasn't Dennis?"

Her face snapped up. "What are you talking about?"

"What if it was Glenn?"

A mixture of emotions played out on her face. "Glenn?"

I nodded, watching her carefully.

"That doesn't make any sense," she said. "Glenn would never do that."

"And Dennis would?"

"Dennis was desperate."

"Desperate? How so?"

She looked away. "Because of Maple Leaf."

I leaned forward slightly. "Did Glenn tell you that Dennis was desperate?"

"He didn't want to," Tiffany said, biting her lip. "He said that he felt terrible about what Dennis was going through. But unfortunately, Dennis's choices really hurt us. He said he didn't blame Dennis, because he was sure Dennis wasn't intending to cause us harm. He was just trying to take care of his family, but as the saying goes ... 'The road to hell is paved with good intentions.'"

"Dennis didn't actually lose any money with Maple Leaf."

Tiffany looked confused. "Of course he did. Everyone did."

I shook my head. "No. That's why some of their clients thought Dennis knew it was a bad investment ... because he purposefully didn't put much money into it."

Tiffany was shaking her head. "But that can't be. You must be mistaken. I mean, yes, someone at F & H messed up on the due diligence, it's true. But both Dennis and Glenn were fooled, and they both lost money. Dennis, unfortunately, made another bad choice to steal from the business, but that has nothing to do with the clients. That just affects us. I know the clients are upset, but it was because it was a bad investment, and as it was Dennis's idea, of course they blame him."

"No, that's really not true," I said quietly. "I can give you a list of clients who are furious at Dennis because he *didn't* invest very much of his own money. It has nothing to do with whose idea it was."

The color was starting to drain from Tiffany's face. "That can't be," she whispered.

The more I watched her, the sorrier I felt for her, and the more terrible I felt about what I was doing. It was like I was torturing her. But if she didn't tell me what she knew, Courtney would be the one who would suffer. And I couldn't have that.

"Here's what I think happened," I said. "I think Glenn was always a little jealous of Dennis. Dennis was the star of the business. He was the one who was great at sales, but even more than that, he also had a knack for finding the hot investments. I think Glenn wanted a little of that star power for himself. So, he went out and found Maple Leaf Grove. Dennis wasn't so sure about it, but Glenn was able to persuade him to go along with it. I'm not sure how—hopefully, he didn't go as far as to doctor any analyses, but who knows? Dennis was never completely convinced, which is why he didn't invest much of his own money, but also didn't stand in the way of Glenn presenting it to his clients. It's possible Dennis even told a few of his clients about it.

"When the whole thing crashed, that's when Glenn became desperate. He was probably invested heavily in the project, right?"

Tiffany was staring at the DON'T QUIT poster. "Nearly all we had," she said quietly. "He said he knew it would be tight for us for a few years, but it would be worth it. Once it paid off, we wouldn't have to worry about money anymore."

She looked so forlorn, I wanted to reach out and squeeze her hand. Instead, I took a deep breath and continued. "So, that's when he probably decided to steal from the business," I said. "And he probably did it for the same reasons he told you Dennis did it. For his family. For you. But unfortunately for him, he was found out. My guess is, he was taking money from the client accounts—not much, just a little bit from all of them—but some of the clients discovered it and told Dennis about it. Glenn had to do something, and my guess is he thought the best way to make it all go away was to get rid of Dennis. Then he could blame Dennis for the theft as well as the Maple Leaf mess, and start to rebuild the business and his finances from there."

Tiffany shook her head. "You're wrong," she said. "Glenn would never do any of that. It had to be Dennis."

"Tiffany, think," I said. "Dennis didn't have access to the accounting and the books the way Glenn did. Do you really think Dennis could have stolen from the business without Glenn knowing about it?"

She kept shaking her head. "I don't believe it," she said. "I've known Glenn for years. You've barely met him. He's a good man. He would never do anything like that."

"But Tiffany ..."

"You need to go now," she said flatly. "Your five minutes is up."

I wanted to protest, but her face had completely shut down. It was clear she was done listening.

I stood to leave. "Think long and hard about what you're doing, Tiffany," I said quietly. "There is a pregnant woman who is in real danger of going to jail over something she didn't do. Not only will her life be ruined, but so will her unborn child's. Will you be able to look at yourself in the mirror if you allow it?"

"If you don't leave now, I'm going to call the cops," she said, picking up her phone. "You have five seconds to get out of my office."

I picked my way toward the door, accepting defeat. My only hope was that my words had hit a weak spot, and that they'd keep poking at her until she did something about it.

Chapter 17

I was sound asleep when the loud jangle of the phone jarred me awake.

Disoriented, I flung an arm out, whacking Midnight, who was peacefully sleeping on the pillow. He let out an annoyed hiss, which made me think there was someone in the room with me ... until I realized it was the phone ringing.

I rolled over and stared bleary-eyed at the clock radio. It was nearly one in the morning. Terrified it was my sister Annabelle with some sort of devastating family news, I snatched up the phone.

"Hello?"

Silence.

"Hello?" I said again as I started to question myself. Had the phone even been ringing, or was it something else? No—there was no dial tone, so someone was obviously on the other line. "Hello?"

Was this some sort of prank? I was starting to get annoyed and was taking a deep breath to give whoever was on the other end of the line an earful when I heard it—the muffled sound of crying.

"Who is this?" I asked, keeping my voice as gentle as possible. "Courtney, is that you?" Oh no ... had she been arrested? Was there a problem with the baby? Thoughts swirled through my head.

I was about to tell Courtney to hang on, I would be there in a jiffy, when a shaky voice answered. "Not ... Courtney."

I couldn't recognize it, as it was too thick with tears. Pat, maybe? I didn't think so, but I couldn't tell. "I'm here," I said. "Let me know what you need."

"I ... I did it."

I sat straight up in bed, the last vestiges of sleep disappearing from my mind. "What did you do?"

"Glenn. I did it."

Suddenly, the pieces clicked together. "Tiffany?"

"After I found it, I called the cops."

"Wait, found what? Tiffany, what's going on? Where's Glenn?"

"Not ... not here."

"Then where?"

"At the station."

My eyes widened. Fully awake, I threw the covers off the bed. "I'll be right over."

* * *

It took me longer than I wanted, mostly because I had to look up Tiffany's address in the phonebook and then find it on a map. Tiffany was clearly not in any state to give me directions. I threw on the same pair of jeans and sweater I had worn earlier, grabbed the map, my keys, and a bag of lavender chamomile tea, and headed out.

Tiffany and Glenn lived in a large house in a quiet cul-de-sac. Even in the dark, I could tell it was larger and fancier than Dennis's home. I couldn't help but wonder again what Glenn really thought of Dennis. Were they really friends, as Dennis seemed to believe? Or had Glenn spent years quietly seething, feeling like a second-class citizen? After all, everyone loved Dennis, including, it seemed, his own wife. I almost felt sorry for him, having to hide his true feelings from everyone. Yet no matter how deep he buried them, they would reveal themselves in tiny ways ... as in the size of his house.

Then again, thinking about the damage he had apparently done to so many lives, I didn't feel quite so sorry.

Tiffany opened the door as I approached the porch. She was dressed in a bright-yellow tracksuit that was stained across the front, and her face was red and blotchy from tears. She was not a pretty crier.

She didn't say anything, just left the door open and walked away, weaving slightly. I wondered if she had been drinking.

I followed her into the house, closing the door behind me and hanging up my coat. The lights were off, and she barely responded when I called out, so it took a bit of stumbling around before I finally found her in the kitchen.

She was sitting at the table, a half-empty bottle of vodka in front of her alongside a glass. "Want some?" she asked, lifting the bottle toward me.

I shook my head, even though she wasn't looking at me. "I brought some tea," I said. "Would it be okay if I made a pot?"

"Suit yourself," she answered, taking a swig straight from the bottle.

"Can I turn on a light?" Even though my eyes were adjusting to the dimness, having the light on in an unfamiliar home would make things easier. It also might help me get Tiffany sobered up.

Tiffany shrugged, which I took as a "yes." I found the lightswitch and flipped it on. Tiffany shied away from the glare, putting both her hands up to cover her face while making a little "oof" noise. I didn't respond, instead heading further into the kitchen.

I couldn't find a teapot, so I prepared two mugs and brought them over to the table, placing one in front of Tiffany. Dully, she stared at me, but didn't move.

"So, what happened?" I asked, sitting down across from her.

Tiffany's throat contracted as she swallowed a couple of times, preparing to speak. "I kept thinking about what you said," she explained quietly, her voice still thick with tears and vodka. "Glenn, he ... I had my suspicions something was wrong. For a while now. Months. I felt like he hadn't been telling me the whole truth. I brushed it off, though. When the news broke on Maple Leaf ..." she shook her head. "It was awful. I thought Glenn was going to have a heart attack. He was completely out of control, drinking and pacing. Frankly, it terrified me. Glenn doesn't lose control. He just doesn't, but that night ..." She paused and chewed on her lip.

"Well, after that night, he was still really stressed, but he seemed better. More like Glenn. So, I wrote off those uneasy feelings I'd had as Glenn just being stressed and trying to fix things. He assured me he had a plan. He was going to find a way to replace our savings. We might have to tighten our belts for a little while, but he was going to take care of it. And I believed him. I'm such an idiot." At that, she reached for the bottle to take another drink.

"You love him," I said. "Of course you want to believe the best about him. There's nothing wrong, shameful, or stupid about that."

She let out a bark of laughter. "That's what makes everything even worse. I *don't* love him. I never have." She bowed her head, but not before I saw the sheen of tears in her eyes again.

"Why did you marry him if you didn't love him?"

"Because, again, I'm an idiot," she said. She blew the air out of her cheeks and raised her head to meet my eyes. "You probably already knew that, anyway. I don't know why I bother to hide it. Why I bother to hide anything. I'm such a fool." Her voice was bitter.

"We all make mistakes," I said. "You're human."

She muttered something. "I guess it doesn't matter anymore. Nothing matters. It's not like I'll ever be with him now, anyway."

"You're talking about Dennis."

Her lips curled into a cynical, self-loathing smile. "See? I knew you knew."

I reached for my tea and took a sip, hoping it would encourage Tiffany to do the same. "So, what happened?"

She didn't say anything for a moment, just kept staring at something off in the distance. "I fell in love with Dennis the moment I laid eyes on him." She said, her voice warm with the memory. "We were all in college. I was dating Glenn at the time, and it was fine. I wasn't in love with him or anything like that, but he was nice to me. Treated me well. Which I really liked, because before him, my boyfriend had been awful to me. Just terrible. So Glenn was a nice change. But when I met Dennis, everything shifted. I knew, in my heart, that he was my soulmate. But at the time, we were both with someone else.

"So, I waited, figuring he would eventually break up with Nina, and then I would break up with Glenn, and we would be together. He and Nina had such a volatile relationship; I assumed it was just a matter of time. As much as I could, I focused on being a good friend to Dennis, figuring that the more time I spent with him, the more likely it was that he would wake up and realize we were meant to be. But of course, that didn't happen. He got engaged to Nina.

"I was so depressed when that happened. I didn't know what to do. All I could think about was how much I had wasted my life. And for what? The love of my life was going to marry someone else.

"I spent the weekend hiding in my apartment, refusing to go out, binging on wine, ice cream, and bad television. By Monday, I had pulled myself together enough to go back to work, but I still couldn't stand to see anyone. For the next couple of weeks, all I did was go to work, come home, and spend my evenings eating way too much sugar and drinking way too much alcohol.

"In the middle of all of this, Glenn stopped by one night and asked me to marry him. I was completely and utterly shocked. He said he could tell I wasn't myself, and he thought it was because Dennis had asked Nina to marry him … he thought I was upset that he hadn't asked me yet! I was so flabbergasted, I ended up saying 'yes.' He was excited and wanted to stay and celebrate, but I managed to utter something about being sick and having a big day. I asked if we could celebrate that weekend. He agreed and left.

"I spent two days in a fog, wondering what I had just agreed to. I decided to tell Glenn I was sorry, but I couldn't marry him after all. Then, after I did that, I would pack up and move as far away as I could possibly get from this town. Maybe a fresh start was what I needed—somewhere with no Glenn or Dennis. Maybe I'd even eventually find someone new.

"But then Saturday night came, and Glenn showed up at my apartment. He was so happy, all dressed up and everything. He even had a ring with him. It felt like the words were stuck in my throat. He slid the ring onto my finger and whisked me off to a fancy restaurant. I remember sitting there at the table, watching Glenn eat his steak as I picked at my salmon, telling myself I had to do it. I had to tell him the truth. The longer I kept up the charade, the harder it was going to be on him. I wasn't even listening to him talk. I was so busy trying to steel myself to tell him the truth, and then I heard the words 'Dennis' and 'broken engagement.'

"Of course, that got my attention, and I asked him to repeat himself. What had happened was that Dennis and Nina had gotten into a huge fight and nearly broke off their engagement. Then, I remember Glenn shaking his head as he said, 'I don't know why Dennis puts up with it. All they do is fight. Doesn't he know he's setting himself up for a big divorce settlement?'

"And it was like lightning struck me. It wasn't over yet. Dennis still had Nina in his system, but once he was finally finished with her, I would be there for him, just as I had planned. Yes, it would be a little messier to divorce Glenn versus just breaking up with him, but so what? It would be worth it, if I could have Dennis in the long run. So I decided, at least in the short term, to keep the engagement going."

Tiffany paused to take another drink, her expression haunted and brooding.

"So, what happened when Dennis divorced Nina?" I asked. "Why didn't you leave Glenn then?"

She didn't answer for a moment, as she swallowed more vodka. Then, replacing the bottle to the table with a thud, she said, "He didn't want me."

My eyes widened, and I tried to hide my surprise. "You didn't have an affair with him?"

"We slept together a few times, if that's what you mean. While he was separated from Nina. But it was clear, even then, that he wasn't interested in a long-term relationship with me.

He kept saying he felt guilty cheating on his friend and business partner, but I knew the truth."

"But what about Courtney?"

She laughed, but it was an empty laugh, dark and void of humor. "Courtney. I had a bad feeling about her from the start. She was so different from Nina, just completely opposite, and I just knew ..." She shook her head. "I knew he wanted a family. He wanted kids and a wife who would stay home and take care of the family. I kept telling him if that's what he wanted, I could do it. I always wanted kids. Glenn never really did. I would have happily stayed home if it meant I could have Dennis and a family. But for some reason, Dennis didn't believe me. Or maybe he just didn't want to believe me. Every time it came up, he would just laugh and tell me I would last a year, maybe two, and then I would want to go back to work. He said there was nothing wrong with that, but he wanted something else. Anyway, Courtney just oozes stay-at-home mom energy. So, I tried to keep them from meeting. At the time, I was still trying to convince Dennis that I was the one for him. But Courtney didn't listen to me. The one time she decided not to listen. I was so angry with her, I nearly fired her on the spot. But I knew that wouldn't help me win back Dennis. So I kept my mouth shut. It didn't matter, though. None of it mattered. He fell in love with her, and that was it."

"So, the affair didn't continue after he married Courtney?"

Tiffany shook her head.

"But ... someone saw you two."

She jerked her head over to stare at me. "What are you talking about?"

She seemed genuinely bewildered. I was starting to wonder if Violet had been seeing things that day, although Courtney had also talked about Dennis having lipstick on his collar.

"You were at Mario's with him? And when you left, you kissed?"

Her expression was incredulous. "Someone saw *that*?"

I nodded.

"I guess they didn't see him pull away from me, and tell me it was over. He didn't have feelings for me like that. He said I should focus on my own marriage."

My eyes widened. "Ah, no. They definitely didn't see that."

"Figured."

"But why were you even at Mario's to begin with, if there wasn't anything going on?"

"A mistake," she spat. "A stupid mistake. I was meeting a friend there for lunch, but she never showed up. She got the day wrong, and Dennis had a business meeting cancel. The hostess had seated us near each other, and when we realized we were both going to sit alone, we decided to eat together. Dennis had ordered a bottle of wine, and silly me ... I had some."

She squeezed her eyes shut, like the memory was painful. "We had such a nice, relaxing lunch. He was funny and charming. I was sure it was a sign from the universe that we were going to be together. He had come to his senses and finally realized he was supposed to be with me."

She pressed her lips together. "I've done so many stupid things in my life, but this one takes the cake. After leaving the restaurant, I hugged and kissed him, sure we were about to rekindle our affair. After he got over the initial shock, though, he pushed me away. Told me it was over. It was never going to happen."

"I'm sorry," I said, even though I wasn't sure if it was the appropriate thing to say in the situation or not. Was I really sorry that she wasn't able to convince a man to cheat on his wife? No. But her grief and sadness were so real and so powerful, I felt like I had to say something. And I *was* sorry she had suffered so.

She shrugged. "Doesn't matter now. He's gone. Glenn is gone. It's all gone."

Her voice was hollow and empty, sending a chill up my spine. "You said Glenn was at the station. You mean the police station?"

She nodded. "I couldn't stop thinking about the last year. How stressed Glenn had been. How everything kept unraveling, even though he kept saying he had it all under control. And I kept thinking about what you said. Was it possible that Glenn, not Dennis, was the one to blame for all the financial issues?"

She paused and swallowed hard. "I couldn't stand it, so on Wednesday, I told Jillian I had to run an errand and to keep an eye on things. I went home. Glenn was at work, so it was a good time to go through his desk. It was ..." she closed her eyes. "It was worse than I thought. Credit cards are maxed. Bills are overdue. The more I dug, the sicker I got. But then, at the bottom of all the mess, I found some bank statements of Glenn's cousin, who died a couple of years ago. I didn't think anything of it at first—Glenn was the executor of his will, but as I was about to set them aside, something caused me to look a little closer. I saw that the account was opened a few months ago, in October. How did that happen, when his cousin is dead? And the account was set up at a bank in Riverview, but the address was a PO box in Redemption. His cousin lived in Milwaukee ... not that it even matters, considering he is dead. Dead people don't typically open up new bank accounts. I looked at the balance, and it was over *twenty thousand dollars*. I couldn't believe it. Did Glenn open an account with his cousin's name at a bank in a different town and put all this money in it? Why would he do that? Why wasn't he using the money to pay our bills?

"When he got home that night, we had a huge fight about it. He was furious that I had 'violated his trust' by digging around in his desk. He kept saying I needed to trust him, even though I had found a secret bank account! I started to think he was going to leave me and was hiding money, but he kept assuring me over and over that no, he loved me, and he was hiding the money for my own good. He kept repeating how I needed to trust him.

"Anyway, I couldn't stop thinking about that bank account and how he was depositing money regularly into it but not paying our bills. And then, I got to thinking, what if he WAS stealing money from the business, but he was trying to cover his tracks? No one would be looking for an account under his cousin's name. Was that what he was doing?

"Then, I started to think about Dennis's death, and the fact that it was supposedly Dennis's cousin who sent him the poisoned bottle. And how the poison was actually an herb. So, I called my herbalists to see if any of them had any orders for Monkshood sent to Redemption."

My uneasy feeling increased. "And did they?"

She nodded, her eyes filling up with tears. "Yes."

I sucked in my breath. "Did they tell you who ordered it?"

She turned her head to look at me. "Me."

"You?" My mouth dropped open in astonishment. "How is that possible?"

"I have an account, and it was charged to that."

"But ... how?"

She shook her head. "I don't know. I talked to the owner, but the order was placed over a month ago. As far as anyone is concerned, I am the one who ordered it."

I frowned. "But that couldn't have been Glenn, then. Glenn doesn't sound anything like you."

"I don't know if they wrote down the name of who ordered it, or if it's all just under my account," Tiffany said. "Jillian orders things for me all the time, but when I get a bill, there's nothing on it as to who ordered what ... just a list of dates and items in the shipment."

"But how would Glenn have gotten that information without you knowing?" I asked. "And wouldn't the order have come to Fit for Life? You would have seen the box."

She sighed. "Again, the record-keeping isn't great. I asked them where they shipped it, but they don't have any kind of real paper trail. It's entirely possible that whoever called it in simply requested it be sent to a PO box. It wasn't just Monkshood in the order, either. There were other things, too. Essential oils, homemade soaps, and candles. My guess is whoever put the order in told them it was supposed to be a surprise."

"Some surprise ... one you even paid for," I mused.

Her smile was twisted. "Well, we are married, so would it really matter anyhow? Quite honestly, I would never have known if I hadn't called. Glenn does my books. I don't even look at the bills they send. I just bring them home, hand them to Glenn, and he pays for them. I never would have been the wiser, otherwise."

The longer I listened, the more I had to hand it to Glenn. He had thought of nearly everything. If he had just handled stealing from the business a little better, he probably would have gotten away with it all, and Courtney would be sitting in the police station rather than him.

"I take it you told the cops all this," I said.

She nodded. "Glenn kept telling me it was all a mistake. He didn't do it. He didn't even know what Monkshood was." Her gaze slid off me, staring at nothing, her face numb with grief and pain. "But after all the lies, how can I possibly believe him anymore?"

"You did the right thing," I said.

Her lips curled in disgust. "Not really," she said. "When it comes right down to it, I was more than willing to let Courtney go to jail to save my marriage. Well, not my marriage per se, but my lifestyle. Deep down, I knew there was something dreadfully wrong. There were all these little things I kept ignoring, but once I had the proof in front of me, I realized I couldn't turn a blind eye anymore. It's not just how stressed he was last fall. He wasn't even that upset when we got the news that Dennis was murdered. He just went back to work like nothing had happened. And there was the day I found one of my herb reference books on my nightstand, even though I was sure I hadn't put it there. I even asked Glenn about it, but he said it was me, of course. I read a lot of magazines and books, and every time I see a new herb, I look it up, but I don't remember doing that. I just brushed it off, sure he was right … figured I had just forgotten I'd moved it. I do that a lot, as well … move things around and forget where I put them. But deep down, I knew there was something else going on. And now, I have to live with the fact that I was willing to let an innocent person go to jail—an innocent pregnant woman—because I didn't want to be inconvenienced."

I had no answer. There was nothing I could think of that didn't sound like worthless, empty platitudes. Instead, I did the one thing I had wanted do since I walked into her house. I pulled my chair closer to Tiffany's and put my arms around her. She was stiff as a board at first, but after a few minutes, she melted into me, laying her head against my chest and bawling like a baby.

Chapter 18

"So it was Glenn after all," Pat said.

"It seems so," I replied, tucking the phone between my neck and ear as I got the kettle boiling. I was exhausted. After Tiffany had her cry, which took a while, she let me lead her to the bedroom, docile and wrung out, and tuck her into bed. She was asleep before I even left the room.

Unfortunately for me, sleep eluded me. Locking Tiffany's door behind me, I drove home and climbed back into my own bed, alongside Midnight who was still curled up on a pillow. But all I could do was stare at the ceiling, puzzling over what Tiffany had told me.

Something wasn't right. I just couldn't put my finger on it.

"Well, he certainly is the most obvious suspect," Pat said. "Wasn't it Agatha Christie who said the obvious suspect is usually the one who did it?"

"Like anything Agatha Christie wrote was obvious," I muttered. "But yes, it does appear like Glenn had the most to gain. It makes the most sense."

"I guess we were wrong about poison being a woman's weapon," Pat mused. "That's really the only thing that doesn't completely fit."

I dragged a kitchen chair closer to the phone, so I didn't have to stretch out the cord so much, and sat down heavily, tea in hand. "I know. It's still sort of gnawing at me."

"But it's not like it could be anyone else," Pat continued. "I mean, who else would have known about Tiffany's herb distributor, and that she had an account there? It has to be Glenn."

"Yeah, it does seem likely," I said, wishing my head wasn't so foggy from lack of sleep. Something still wasn't adding up. All these details that only a handful of people would know. Dennis's favorite brandy. His relationship to his cousin. An out-of-town herb distributor who sold Monkshood.

Who would have known all those things?

"You don't sound convinced," Pat said.

"It's probably just because I'm exhausted," I said. "I probably just need to catch up on my sleep."

"I'm sure that's it," Pat said, although her tone sounded like she believed it about as much as I did.

***

"Charlie," Violet said, a huge smile on her face as she opened the door to her apartment. "Come in! It's so nice to see you."

"Thank you," I said, stepping inside and removing my coat. "Do you have a few moments?"

"Of course, of course," she said, bustling toward the kitchen. "I always have time for the woman who saved my daughter from jail. I'll go make some tea."

I hung my coat up and followed her into the kitchen. Her apartment was small but neat as a pin. The kitchen was cheery with accents of reds, yellows, oranges, and lots of roosters.

"Come sit," she said, holding a couple of bright-orange mugs with yellow flowers and placing them on the kitchen table. I sat as she brought out a tin of shortbread cookies. "I just love these," she said. "Have a few, so I don't eat all of them."

Obediently, I chose one, although I didn't take a bite. She didn't notice as she put a couple on her plate. "So, what can I do for you?" she asked. Then, her eyes went wide. "Oh! Did you want some money? I know you said you didn't when you first started helping us, but if you've changed your mind ..."

I waved my hand. "No, I'm fine. That's not why I'm here. I actually had a few more questions."

"Fire away," she said.

I paused, giving myself a moment to organize my thoughts. "Did you ever ask Dennis about what you saw?"

Violet looked at me in confusion, her smile faltering. "Saw?"

"Yes. The day you saw him and Tiffany at Mario's."

"What does that matter now?"

I smiled at her reassuringly. "Indulge me."

Her expression became wary. "Well, no. What would be the point? He would just lie." Her tone was bitter.

I nodded. "Yes, that does seem likely. Although, when I asked Tiffany about it two nights ago, she denied their having an affair while he was married to Courtney."

Her mouth flattened. "Well, of course she would."

"Really?" Now it was my turn to look confused. "Why would she lie now?"

"Well, she's married," Violet said, as if it were obvious. "She doesn't want her husband to find out."

"Her husband is charged with killing her lover," I said. "Do you think it matters now if he knows about the affair?"

She flapped her hands. "Well, it still makes her look bad, right? I mean, who wants to admit she had an affair?"

I picked up the mug to take a sip and tried not to make a face. Ugh. Store-bought. "That's true. I'm sure it would be difficult to admit to having an affair."

She sat back, her expression relaxing.

"Except," I continued pleasantly, watching the muscles in her face tense up again. "She DID admit to having an affair with Dennis."

"I thought you just said she didn't?"

"While he was married to Courtney, Tiffany wasn't," I said. "Nor while he was married to Nina, his first wife. But when his first marriage was ending and before he met Courtney, she told me they slept together a few times. It didn't last long, she said. Even if he hadn't met Courtney, it wasn't going anywhere, but once he met Courtney, that was definitely the end."

"She's lying," Violet said. The cookie she was holding in her hand snapped apart, scattering crumbs everywhere. "I saw them. Why would they be at Mario's together if they weren't having an affair? I saw them kiss!"

"She doesn't deny that," I said. "She explained that it was one of those weird coincidences. He had a business meeting cancel at the last minute, and she was having lunch with a friend, but the friend didn't show up. So, they had lunch together. They were friends, in a way, so it made sense. Dennis had ordered a bottle of wine already for his business lunch, and Tiffany ended up drinking too much and hugged and kissed him outside the restaurant. She claimed he pushed her away, but probably not before she got lipstick on his collar."

I paused. Violet's face was getting whiter and whiter. "You said you got back in your car and ducked down so they wouldn't catch you. Isn't in possible that you didn't see Dennis push her away?"

Violet shook her head, her face nearly frozen. "No," she whispered. "It's not possible. They were having an affair. *I saw it*. I saw it."

"My guess is you knew about Tiffany's herbal distributor from when Courtney worked there," I said cautiously. "She probably mentioned something to you. Since Tiffany has Jillian call her order in, I'm guessing Courtney called sometimes, too, and told you about it so that's how you knew. You may not have known specifically about Monkshood, but I bet you did know some herbs and flowers could be toxic. You were an avid gardener, after all. It wouldn't have been difficult to research. And it goes without saying that you would have known about the brandy and Dennis's cousin."

Violet sucked in her breath and turned away. "Who else knows?" she asked quietly, her voice defeated.

I crossed my fingers, praying I had made the right decision. "No one. For now. I was hoping you would come clean on your own. You don't want to let an innocent man go to jail for something you did."

"He's not innocent," she said. "He stole from people."

"And he'll be punished for stealing," I said. "But he shouldn't be punished for what he *didn't* do."

Violet was silent for a long time—so long, I was a little afraid she was going to tell me she didn't care. If she didn't confess, I had a feeling that would be the end. I suspected there would be no evidence against her ... nothing that couldn't also be used against Glenn.

"He wasn't supposed to die," she said finally, her voice cracking.

"What are you talking about? You put poison in his brandy."

"I put Monkshood in his brandy," she corrected.

"Which is a poison."

"At too high of a dose," she said. "At lower doses, it's used for pain relief. How else could I have bought it from an herb distributor?"

"That's true. It is used for pain relief. Is that what you were trying to do? Give Dennis something for pain? Was Dennis suffering?"

She shook her head. "I wasn't trying to use it medicinally. I wanted to make him sick."

"But not die."

"No."

"I don't understand."

She sighed, a long one, full of despair. She looked like she had aged about ten years since she'd answered the door. "My only daughter was about to give birth to my first grandchild, and she was in the pit of despair. She was sure her husband had fallen out of love with her, and nothing she was doing was changing that. She had convinced herself that once the baby was a little older and could be left with someone so she could go back to work, he would leave her.

"I begged her to sit down and have a heart-to-heart with Dennis, but she refused. She was sure that would just give him the opening he needed to ask her for a divorce. She thought the only thing saving her was that he didn't want to tell her while she was pregnant.

"I had to do something. The last thing I wanted was to see my daughter go through the struggles I went through when my husband walked out. Courtney was old enough to not require a sitter, so at least I didn't have to worry about that expense. But to watch her go through that heartache with a baby? I couldn't do it.

"For weeks, I racked my brain, trying to figure out how to make Dennis fall in love with her again. Then one night, I was flipping around the channels, and there was one of those made-for-TV movies on, where the husband is sick and ends up falling in love with the live-in nurse. And that's when it hit me. What if Dennis got sick ... really sick? Courtney of course would drop everything to nurse him back to health. And while she did that, she could make him fall in love with her again.

"It seemed perfect. Not only would Dennis be home, under Courtney's loving care, but he also wouldn't be seeing Tiffany at all. Out of sight, out of mind. It seemed like the answer to my prayers."

"If that's the case, why didn't you just slip something into a drink while you were there one night?" I asked. "Or, if you didn't want to be there, into one of the open bottles of brandy in his office?"

"Timing," she said. "I didn't want him to get sick after the baby was born. She couldn't play nurse to him then, because she would have the baby to worry about. Someone else would have to be in the house to help her, and even if that were me, I didn't want anything to get in the way of them falling in love again. All they were doing in December was going to parties. Party after party. There was no quiet evening when I could be sure he would drink the Monkshood.

"Giving it to him as a present seemed like the best option. I figured he would have a drink shortly after he opened the gift. And once he got sick, I could make sure no one else had any by 'accidentally' knocking the bottle over. And if it came up later, we could just chalk it up to a bad batch of brandy. It happens. But, instead, he drank too much and died before Courtney could get him to the hospital."

I chewed on my lip as I studied her. Was it possible? I didn't know how much Monkshood was in the bottle, but Wyle made it seem like there was quite a bit, and it didn't take much to be toxic. Was it really an innocent accident, as she said? That her intention really was just to make him sick, and she didn't realize she put in too much?

But then I remembered how she bought the Monkshood. Using Tiffany's account. Would someone who was only attempting to make someone sick cover her tracks so well?

Or, did she know exactly what she was doing all along?

"Why didn't you tell the police immediately after it happened?" I asked. "Why did you go through the whole charade of hiring me and having me look into it?"

She snapped her face around to look at me. "Because someone needed to look into Tiffany and Glenn," she cried. "They were guilty."

"Not of murder."

"No. But I knew something was wrong. That whole Maple Leaf Grove mess. Something was fishy with it. And Tiffany, well ..." her voice trailed off as if the sudden burst of anger had simply fizzled out.

"You really need to tell the police," I said quietly. "And Courtney, as well."

She sighed again, her skin grey. "I know," she said quietly. "I actually didn't think I would get away with it. I was shocked when they arrested Glenn. I told myself he deserved it. He was an awful boss, you know. I know I said before he was fine, but that wasn't the whole truth. Dennis was always nice to me, but Glenn treated everyone who worked for him like they were beneath him. It was nice to see him arrested, knowing he was getting a taste of his own medicine."

While I believed that Glenn was an awful boss, I wasn't sure I believed she would have eventually turned herself in.

"You're doing the right thing," I said.

She glanced at me, her eyes so much like Courtney's, it made my throat tighten. Courtney was about to give birth, and now, she'd have to navigate motherhood without her husband *or* her mother.

Violet gave me a sad smile. "I hope you're right."

Chapter 19

I stepped up onto the stoop, sucked in a deep breath of the frosty cold air, and rang the doorbell.

I had no idea how Courtney would react to seeing me. Because of me, she had lost her mother. Her husband was gone, too, and now, she was going to be truly alone with her new baby.

I listened to the soft footfalls as someone approached the door. Then, there was a long pause. I wondered if she was debating whether or not to open the door to me. Would it make sense to knock again, or just leave? As I considered my options, I heard the click of the deadbolt being pulled back, and the door opened.

I wasn't sure what I expected—her face red and puffy with tears again? Instead, it was composed and expressionless.

"Charlie," she said, her voice flat. "I wasn't expecting you."

I tried to smile as I held up a covered pan. "I hope it's not a bad time. I brought you some lasagna and tea."

She stared at me, her eyes as empty as glass, before turning around and walking away. For a moment, I could only stare at her retreating back, wondering what I should do, but as she left the door wide open, I took it as an invitation to enter. I stepped inside, closing the door behind me and pulling off my coat.

I found her in the kitchen, sitting at the table, a cup of tea in front of her. She didn't look at me as I put the lasagna in the fridge and the tea on the counter, nor did she offer me any sort of refreshment.

"I suppose I should thank you," she said, her voice hollow.

Cautiously I walked over to the table and slid into the seat across from her. "I'm not here for that."

"But still," she said. "You did get to the bottom of what happened. And now I know the truth."

Now that I was closer, I saw that I was wrong in thinking her face was expressionless. It was more like she was numb ... so shell-shocked from everything that had happened to her in the past few weeks that she had completely shut down emotionally.

"I'm sorry it was your mother."

She shrugged. "So am I."

I chewed on my lip. "Do you know what's happening with her?"

"It looks like there will be some sort of plea deal," she said. "I guess the prosecution doesn't want to throw the book at a soon-to-be-grandma who was only trying to help her daughter rekindle her marriage."

So, it appeared Violet had found a good enough lawyer to have convinced the legal system it was all a mistake. I wondered how the lawyer explained away using Tiffany's account. Or, maybe they decided Violet wasn't much of a public risk and wanted to just move on.

"That's good," I said. "Hopefully, she won't get as much jail time."

Courtney shrugged. "Maybe. Although I'm not sure how much I want to see her."

I blinked in surprise. "You don't want to see her?"

Courtney raised her face, fixing those strange, unsettling eyes on mine. "She killed my husband. The father of my baby."

"She was trying to help."

"She told me he was having an affair."

"She was mistaken," I said, wondering how I had found myself in a situation where I was defending Violet. "And, to be fair, what she saw was easy to misinterpret."

"That 'mistake' means my child will grow up without a father."

I couldn't argue with that.

"This is all my fault," Courtney said quietly.

I did a double take, wondering if I heard her correctly. "Wait. How is this *your* fault? You didn't poison anyone."

Her mouth was twisted. "I should have talked to Dennis," she said. "You were right. That's what most people would have done. Just asked their husband if they were having an affair. But not me. I bury my head in the sand, and look what happened. If I had had been braver, if I hadn't been so afraid he was going to leave me like my father left me, I could have told him what my mother saw. We could have talked about it … gotten to the bottom of it. Instead, I cheated on my husband and worked myself into such a state, my mother thought it was a good idea to poison my husband to bring us back together."

I was taken aback at the harshness in her tone. Her mouth pressed together so tightly, her lips had turned white. The numbness had slipped from her face like a mask, revealing the self-hatred beneath.

I took a deep breath, knowing I had to say something, but feeling like I had to tread very carefully. "While it's true you could have handled things better, this is still not your fault. Your mother is a grown-up who made her own decisions. Your husband made his own decisions. A marriage has two sides."

She stared at me, her face aghast. "You're blaming Dennis? He's dead!"

"This isn't about blame," I said. "It's about learning from your mistakes. It's about making better choices. And," I took another breath. "It's about forgiveness.'

She looked away. "I don't know if I can ever forgive my mother."

I let that slide. "What about yourself?"

Her face seemed to collapse on itself, like something inside her was cracking. "How can I? Dennis is dead. My mother is in jail. Look at the mess that's left."

"But that's what life is," I said. "It's messy. It's hard. It's uncomfortable. You're going to make mistakes. People around you are going to make mistakes. You're human. And if you don't learn to forgive, you're going to make life that much more difficult for yourself."

She was silent as she thought about what I said. "I don't know if I can."

"I didn't say you have to do it now," I said. "It takes time. And healing. And maybe you never will completely. But you can try. And that's what matters in the end."

She continued to sit there, pondering my words. Her face was thinner, I noticed. The skin stretched across her cheekbones. It made her look older.

Older and battle worn.

"Tiffany called me," she said, abruptly changing the subject.

I raised my eyebrows. "Really?"

Courtney nodded. "To apologize."

"Wow. That's a surprise."

Courtney's lips curled up in a tiny smile. "Yeah, it was a shock. But it was good. We had a good talk."

"Good," I said. I wondered if Courtney now knew the truth about Tiffany and Dennis, but I decided if she didn't bring it up, I didn't need to.

Courtney's smile became a little shy as she rubbed her belly. "She offered me my job back."

"Really?"

"Not right away, of course. I mean, it's more than just being pregnant. I need a little time. I forgive her, but … well. I need time. Besides, Tiffany said she has to build things back up. It's all a mess now, as you can imagine. But yeah." Her smile widened. "Even said I could bring the baby, and maybe we could offer childcare."

"Oh, that sounds like a smart idea."

"Yeah. She had talked about it before, offering something to make it easier for moms to work out, but she never was able to get it going. But, with my little one, maybe we can offer a whole new service."

"That's great news," I said. "I'm really happy for you. Maybe this will be the start of a whole new chapter for you."

Courtney nodded again, finally meeting my eyes. The hurt and grief were still there, but there was something else now, as well. Something that looked a little like hope. "Maybe," she agreed.

Author's Note

Hi there!

I hope you enjoyed *The Murder Before Christmas* as much as I enjoyed writing it. If you did, I would really appreciate it if you'd leave me a review and rating.

I'm busy working on the next Charlie Kingsley mystery, *Ice-Cold Murder*. It's available for preorder right now and will be released January 25, 2022.

In the meantime, if you want more Charlie, I'd love to invite you to get started with my award-winning *Secrets of Redemption* series. It's a little different from this series as it's more of a psychological suspense mystery, but keep reading for an excerpt from the first book, *It Began With a Lie*.

You can also grab a free novella called *The Secret Diary of Helen Blackstone*, which shares more of the history of Charlie's house on my website at MPWNovels.com. I've got lots of other fun things there to check out as well, including more on all my books, short stories, a book club, and more. (Even some recipes!).

For now, turn the page for a sneak peek at It *Began With a Lie*.

It Began With a Lie - Chapter 1

"You're right. It's perfect for us. I'm so glad we're here," I said, lying through my carefully pasted-on smile.

I tried to make my voice bright and cheery, but it sounded brittle and forced, even to me. I sucked in my breath and widened my smile, though my teeth were so clenched, my jaw hurt.

Stefan smiled back—actually, his mouth smiled but his dark-brown eyes, framed with those long, thick lashes any woman would envy, looked flat … distracted. He hugged me with one arm. "I told you everything would be okay," he whispered into my hair. His scent was even more musky than usual, probably from two straight days of driving and lack of shower.

I hugged him back, reminding myself to relax. *Yes, everything is going to be okay. Remember, this move represents a fresh start for us—time for us to reconnect and get our marriage back on track. It's not going to happen overnight.*

His iPhone buzzed. He didn't look at me as he dropped his arm and pulled it out of his pocket, his attention already elsewhere. "Sorry babe, gotta take this." He turned his back to me as he answered the call, walking away quickly. His dark hair, streaked with silver that added a quiet, distinguished air to his All-American good looks was longer than normal, curling around his collar. He definitely needed a haircut, but of course, we couldn't afford his normal stylist, and not just anyone was qualified to touch his hair.

I wrapped my arms around myself, goosebumps forming on my skin as a sudden breeze, especially cool for mid-May, brushed past me—the cold all the more shocking in the absence of Stefan's warm body.

He has to work, I reminded myself. *Remember why we're here.*

I remembered, all right. How could I forget?

I rubbed my hands up and down my arms as I took a deep breath, and finally focused on the house.

It was just as I remembered from my childhood—white with black shutters, outlined by bushy green shrubs, framed by tall, gently-swaying pine trees and the red porch with the swinging chair. It sat all by its lonesome in the middle of a never-developed cul-de-sac, the only "neighbors" being an overgrown forest on one side, and a marshy field on the other.

Okay, maybe it wasn't *exactly* the way I remembered it. The bushes actually looked pretty straggly. The lawn was overgrown, full of dandelions going to seed, and the porch could definitely use a new paint job.

I sighed. If the outside looked like this, what on earth waited for me on the inside?

Inside.

I swallowed back the bile that rose in the back of my throat. It slid to my stomach, turning into a cold, slimy lump.

The house of my childhood.

The house of my nightmares.

Oh God, I so didn't want to be here.

Stefan was still on the phone, facing away from me. I stared longingly at his back. *Turn around*, I silently begged. *Turn around and smile at me. A real smile. Like how you used to before we were married. Tell me it's going to be okay. You don't have to leave tonight like you thought. You realize how cruel it would be to leave me alone in this house the first night we're here, and you don't want to do that to me. Please, tell me. Or, better yet, tell me we're packing up and going back to New York. Say this was all a mistake; the firm is doing fine. Or, if you can't say that, say we'll figure it out. We'll make it work. We don't need to live here after all. Please, Stefan. Please don't leave me alone here.*

He half-turned, caught my eye, and made a gesture that indicated he was going to be awhile.

And I should start unpacking.

I closed my eyes. Depression settled around me like an old, familiar shawl. I could feel the beginning of a headache stab my temples.

Great. Just what I needed to complete this nightmare—a monster headache.

I turned to the car and saw Chrissy still in the backseat—headset on, bobbing to music only she could hear. Her long, dark hair—so dark it often looked black—spread out like a shiny cloak, the ends on one side dyed an electric blue.

Oh, yeah. That's right. I wouldn't be alone in the house after all.

Chrissy closed her eyes and turned her head away from me.

It just kept getting better and better.

I knocked on the window. She ignored me. I knocked again. She continued to ignore me.

For a moment, I imagined yanking the door open, snatching the headset off and telling her to—no, *insisting* that—she get her butt out of the car and help me unpack. I pictured her dark brown eyes, so much like Stefan's, widening, her pink lip-glossed mouth forming a perfect O, so shocked that she doesn't talk back, but instead meekly does what she's told.

More pain stabbed my temples. I closed my eyes and kept knocking on the window.

It's not her fault, I told myself for maybe the 200th time. *How would you act if you were sixteen years old and your mother abandoned you, dumped you at your father's, so she'd be free to travel across Europe with her boy toy?*

I squelched the little voice that reminded me I wasn't a whole heck of a lot older than said boy toy, and started pounding on the window. Stefan kept telling me she was warming up to me—I personally hadn't seen much evidence of that.

Chrissy finally turned her head and looked at me. "What?" she mouthed, disgust radiating off her, her eyes narrowing like an angry cat.

I motioned to the trunk. "I need your help."

Her lip curled as her head fell back on to the seat. She closed her eyes.

I had just been dismissed.

Great. Just great.

I looked around for Stefan—if he were standing with me, she would be out of the car and helping—a fake, sweet smile on her face, but he had moved to the corner of the street, still on the phone. I popped the trunk and headed over to him. Maybe I could finally get him to see reason—that it really was a dreadful idea to leave the two of us alone in Redemption, Wisconsin, while he commuted back and forth to New York to rescue his failing law firm. "See," I could say, "She doesn't listen to me. She doesn't respect me. She needs her father. I need you, too. She's going to run wild with you gone and I won't be able to deal with her."

Stefan hung up as I approached. "The movers should be here soon. You probably should start unpacking." Although his tone was mild, I could still hear the underlying faint chords of reproach—what's going on with you? Why haven't you started yet? Do I need to do everything around here?

"Yes, I was going to," I said, hating my defensive tone, but unable to stop it. "But there's a problem I think you need to deal with."

His eyes narrowed—clearly, he was losing his patience with me. "What?"

I opened my mouth to tell him about Chrissy, just as her voice floated toward us, "Can I get some help over here?"

I slowly turned around, gritting my teeth, trying not to show it. Chrissy stood by the trunk, arms loaded with boxes, an expectant look on her face. The pain darting through my head intensified.

"Rebecca, are you coming?" Stefan asked as he headed over to his charming daughter, waiting for him with a smug expression on her face, like a cat who ate the canary. I took a deep breath and trudged over, the sick knot in the pit of my stomach growing and tightening.

What on earth was I going to do with her while Stefan was gone?

Chrissy threw me a triumphant smile as she followed her father to the house. I resisted the urge to stick my tongue out at her, as I heaved a couple of boxes out of the trunk.

Really, all the crap with Chrissy was the least of my worries. It was more of a distraction, than anything.

The real problem was the house.

The house.

Oh God.

I turned to stare at it. It didn't look menacing or evil. It looked like a normal, everyday house.

Well, a normal, everyday house with peeling paint, a broken gutter and a few missing roof shingles.

Great. That probably meant we needed a new roof. New roofs were expensive. People who had to rescue failing law firms tended to not have money for things like new roofs. Even new roofs for houses that were going to be fixed up and eventually sold, ideally for a big, fat profit.

Would there be *any* good news today?

Again, I realized I was distracting myself. New roofs and paint jobs—those were trivial.

The real problem was *inside* the house.

Where all my nightmares took place.

Where my breakdown happened.

Where I almost died.

I swallowed hard. The sun went behind a cloud and, all of a sudden, the house was plunged into darkness. It loomed in front me, huge and monstrous, the windows dark, bottomless eyes staring at me ... the door a mouth with sharp teeth ...

"Rebecca! Are you coming?"

Stefan broke the spell. I blinked my eyes and tried to get myself together.

I was being silly. It was just a house, not a monster. How could a house even BE a monster? Only people could be mon-sters, which would mean my aunt, who had owned the house, was the monster.

And my aunt was dead now. Ding, dong, the witch is dead. Or, in this case, the monster.

Which meant there was nothing to fear in the house any-more. Which was exactly what Stefan kept telling me back in New York, over and over.

"Don't you think it's time you put all this childhood non-sense behind you?" he asked. "Look, I get it. Your aunt must have done something so dreadful that you've blocked it out, but she's dead. She can't hurt you anymore. And it couldn't have worked out any more perfectly for us—we have both a place to live rent-free right now, while I get things turned around. And, once we sell it, we can use the money to move back here and get a fresh start."

He was right, of course. But, still, I couldn't drop it.

"Why did she even will the house to me in the first place?" I persisted. "Why didn't she will it to CB? He was there a lot more than I was."

Stefan shrugged. "Maybe it was her way of apologizing to you all these years later. She was trying to make it up to you. Or maybe she changed—people said she was sick at the end. But, why does it matter why she willed it to you? The point is she did, and we really need it. Not to mention this could be a great way for you to finally get over whatever happened to you years ago."

Maybe. Back in New York, it had seemed so reasonable. So logical. Maybe the move wouldn't be a problem after all.

But, standing in the front yard with my arms filled with box-es, every cell in my body screamed that it was a really awful idea.

"Hey," Stefan whispered in my ear, his five o'clock shadow scratching my cheek. I jumped, so transfixed by the house that I hadn't even realized he had returned to me. "Look, I'm sorry. I should have known this would be rough for you. Come on, I'll walk in with you."

He rubbed my arm and smiled at me—a real smile. I could feel my insides start to thaw as all those old, exciting, passionate feelings reminiscent of when we first started dating swarmed over me. I remembered how he would shower me with red roses and whisk me off to romantic dinners that led to steaming, hot sex. He made me feel like a princess in a fairy tale. I still couldn't fathom how he ended up with me.

I met his eyes, and for the first time in what seemed like a long time, I felt the beginnings of a real smile on my lips. *See, he does care, even if he doesn't always show it. This is why the move was the perfect thing for our marriage; all we needed was to get away from the stress of New York, so we could rekindle things.* I nodded and started walking with him toward the house. Over her shoulder, Chrissy shot me a dirty look.

The closer we got to the house, the more I focused on my breathing. *It's going to be okay, I repeated to myself. It's just a house. A house can't hurt anyone. It's all going to be okay.*

An owl hooted, and I jumped. Why was an owl hooting in the daytime? Didn't that mean someone was going to die? Isn't that what the old stories and folklore taught? My entire body stiffened—all I wanted to do was run the other way. Stefan hugged me closer, gently massaging my arm, and urged me forward.

"It's going to be okay," he murmured into my hair. I closed my eyes for a moment, willing myself to believe it.

We stepped onto the porch, Chrissy impatiently waiting for Stefan to unlock the door. He put the boxes on the ground to fumble for his keys as I tried hard not to hyperventilate.

It's just a house. A house can't hurt anyone.

After an eternity that simultaneously wasn't nearly long enough, he located the keys and wrenched the door open, swearing under his breath.

His words barely registered. I found myself compelled forward, drawn in like those pathetic moths to the killing flame.

I could almost hear my aunt excitedly calling, "Becca? Is that you? Wait until you see this," as I stepped across the threshold into the house.

It was exactly like I remembered.

Well, maybe not exactly—it was filthy and dusty, full of cobwebs and brittle, dead bugs lying upside down on the floor with their legs sticking up. But I remembered it all—from the overstuffed floral sofa where I spent hours reading, to the end table covered with knick-knacks and frilly doilies, to the paintings lining the walls. I found myself wanting to hurry into the kitchen, where surely Aunt Charlie would have a cup of tea waiting for me. It didn't feel scary at all. It felt warm and comforting.

Like coming home.

How could this be?

Stefan was still muttering under his breath. "I can't believe all this crap. We're going to have put our stuff in storage for months while we go through it all. Christ, like we need another bill to worry about." He sighed, pulled his cell phone out, and started punching numbers.

"Dad, what do you mean our stuff is going into storage?" Chrissy said, clearly alarmed.

Stefan waved his arms. "Honey, look around you. Where are we going to put it? We have to put our things into storage until we get all this out of here."

"But Dad," Chrissy protested. I stopped listening. I walked slowly around, watching my aunt dashing down the stairs, her smock stained, arms filled with herbs and flowers, some even sticking out of her frizzy brown hair, muttering about the latest concoction she was crafting for one of the neighbors whose back was acting up again …

"Earth to Rebecca. Rebecca. Are you okay?" I suddenly realized Stefan was talking to me, and I pulled myself out of my memories.

"Sorry, it just …" my voice trailed off.

He came closer. "Are you okay? Are you remembering?"

There she was again, the ghost of Aunt Charlie, explaining yet again to the odd, overly-made-up, hair-over-teased, forty-something woman from the next town that no, she didn't do love potions. It was dangerous magic to mess around with either love or money, but if she wanted help with her thyroid that was clearly not working the way it should be, that was definitely in my aunt's wheelhouse.

I shook my head. "No, not really. It's just … weird."

I wanted him to dig deeper, ask me questions, invite me to talk about the memories flooding through me. I wanted him to look at me while I spoke, *really* look at me, the way he did before we were married.

Where had it all gone wrong? And how could he leave me alone in a lonely, isolated and desolate house a thousand miles away from New York? Sure, Chrissy would be there, but the jury was still out as to whether she made it better or worse. The memories pushed up against me, smothering me. I *needed* to talk about them, before they completely overwhelmed and suffocated me. And he knew it—he knew how much I needed to talk things through to keep the anxiety and panic at bay. He wouldn't let me down, not now, when I really needed him.

Would he?

It Began With a Lie - Chapter 2

The empty coffee pot mocked me.

It sat on the table, all smug and shiny, its cord wrapped tightly around it.

I had been so excited after unearthing it that morning—yes! Coffee! God knew I needed it.

The night before had been horrible, starting with the fights. I ended up in the living room, where I spent the night on the couch, a cold washcloth draped over my face in a feeble attempt to relieve the mother of all headaches.

Several times, I'd have just dozed off when the sound of Chrissy's footsteps would jerk me awake, as she paced up and down the upstairs hallway. I couldn't fathom what was keeping her up, so finally, after the fourth or fifth time of being woken up, I went upstairs to check on her. She must have heard me on the stairs, because all I saw was of the trail of her white nightgown as she disappeared into her room. I stood there for a moment, wondering if I should go talk to her, but the stabbing pain in my head drove me back downstairs to the safety of the couch and washcloth. I just couldn't face another argument then, in the middle of the night.

She must have decided to stay in her room after that, because I finally drifted off, only waking when the sun shone through the dirty living room window, illuminating all the dust motes floating in the air.

Coffee was exactly what I needed. Except … I had no beans to put in the coffeemaker. Not that it mattered, I realized after digging through the third box in frustration. I didn't have any cream or sugar either.

Well, at least my headache was gone, although what was left was a weird, hollow, slightly-drugged feeling. Still, I'd take that over the headache any day.

I sighed and rubbed my face. The whole move wasn't starting off very well. In fact, everything seemed to be going from bad to worse, including the fight with Stefan.

"Do you really need to leave?" I asked him again as I followed him to the door. He had just said goodbye to Chrissy, who had immediately disappeared upstairs, leaving us alone. I could see the taxi he had called sitting in the driveway and my heart sank. A part of me had hoped to talk him out of going, but with the taxi already there the possibility seemed even more remote.

He sighed. I could tell he was losing patience. "We've been through this. You know I have to."

"But you just got here! Surely you can take a few days—a week maybe—off to help us unpack and get settled."

He picked up his briefcase. "You know I can't. Not now."

"But when? You promised you would set it up so that you could work from here most of the time. Why can't you start that now?" I could tell his patience was just about gone, but I couldn't stop myself.

He opened the door. A fresh, cool breeze rushed in, a sharp contrast to the musty, stale house. "And I will. But it's too soon. There are still a few things I need to get cleaned up before I can do that. You know that. We talked about this."

He stepped outside and went to kiss me, but I turned my face away. "Are you going to see *her*?"

That stopped him. I could see his eyes narrow and his mouth tighten. I hadn't meant to say it; it just slipped out.

He paused and took a breath. "I know this whole situation has been tough on you, so I'm going to forget you said that. I'll call you."

Except he didn't. Not a single peep in the more than twelve hours since he had walked out the door. And every time I thought of it, I felt sick with shame.

I didn't *really* think he was cheating on me. I mean, there was something about Sabrina and her brittle, cool, blonde, perfect elegance that I didn't trust, but that wasn't on Stefan. I had no reason not to trust him. Just because my first husband cheated on me didn't mean Stefan would. And just because Sabrina looked at Stefan like he was a steak dinner, and she was starving, didn't mean it was reciprocated.

Worse, I knew I was making a bigger mess out of it every time I brought it up. The more I accused him, the more likely he would finally say, "Screw it, if I'm constantly accused of being a cheater, I might as well at least get something out of it." Even knowing all of that, I somehow couldn't stop myself.

Deep down, I knew I was driving him away. And I hated that part of myself. But still nothing changed.

To make matters worse, it didn't take long after Stefan left before things blew up with Chrissy. I asked her to help me start organizing the kitchen, and she responded with an outburst about how much she hated the move. She hated me, too—her life was ruined, and it was all my fault. She stormed off, slammed the door to her room, and that's how I ended up on the couch, my head pounding, wishing I was just about anywhere else.

Standing in the kitchen with the weak sunlight peeking through the dirty windows, the empty coffee maker taunting me, I gave in to my feelings of overwhelm. How on earth was I ever going to get the house organized? And the yard? And my aunt's massive garden? All the while researching what it would take to sell the house for top dollar, and dealing with Chrissy? My heart sank at that thought, although I wasn't completely sure which thought triggered it. Maybe it was all of them.

And if that wasn't difficult enough, I also had to deal with being in my aunt's home. Her presence *was everywhere*. I felt like an intruder. How could I do all of this, feeling her around me? How could I be in her home, when she wasn't? It wasn't my house. It was Aunt Charlie's. And I wasn't even sure I WANTED it to feel like my home.

Because if it did, then I would probably remember everything.

Including what happened that night.

The night I almost died.

God, I felt sick.

I needed coffee. And food.

Maybe I should take Chrissy out for breakfast as a peace of-fering. We could get out of the house, which would be good for me at least, and then go grocery shopping before coming home to tackle the cleaning and organizing.

I wanted to start in the kitchen. It was Aunt Charlie's favorite room in the house, and I knew it would have broken her heart to see how neglected and dingy it had become. When my aunt was alive, it was the center of the home—a light, cheery place with a bright-red tea kettle constantly simmering away on low heat on the stove. Oh, how Aunt Charlie loved her tea—that's why the kettle always had hot water in it—she'd say you just never knew when a cup would be needed. She was a strong believer that tea cured just about everything, just so long as you had the right blend. And, surprise, surprise, you could pretty much always find the right blend outside in her massive garden, which I had no doubt was completely overgrown now. I didn't have the heart to go look.

I could almost see her, standing in that very kitchen, prepar-ing me a cup. "Headache again, Becca?" she would murmur as she measured and poured and steeped. The warm fragrance would fill the homey kitchen as she pushed the hot cup in front of me, the taste strong, flavorful, and sweet, with just a hint of bitterness. And, lo and behold, not too long after drinking it, I would find my headache draining away.

I wondered if I would still find her tea blends in the kitchen. Maybe I could find that headache tea. And maybe, if I was even luckier, I would find a blend that would cure everything that ailed me that morning.

With some surprise, I realized just how much love encom-passed that memory. Nothing scary. Nothing that could possibly foretell the horror of what happened that dreadful night.

Could my aunt actually be the monster?

My mother certainly thought so. She forbade any contact, any mentioning of my aunt even, refusing to allow her to see me once I woke up in intensive care following the stomach pump.

She refused her again when I was transferred to a psych unit, after becoming hysterical when I was asked what had happened that night.

My mother blamed my aunt.

And, I, in my weakened, anxious, panicked state, was relieved to follow her lead. Actually, I was more than relieved; I was happy, too.

But sitting in that kitchen right then, I felt only love and comfort, and I began to question my choices.

My mother had been completely against us moving back here, even temporarily. At the time, listening to her arguments, I had chalked it up to her being overly protective. Now, I wondered. Was that it? Or was something deeper going on?

Chrissy chose that moment to stroll into the kitchen, her hair sticking up on one side. She was wearing her blue and red plaid sleep shorts and red tee shirt—the blue plaid almost an exact match to the blue highlight in her hair. Staring at her, something stirred deep inside me—a distinct feeling of wrongness ... of something being off—but when I reached for it, I came up empty.

She leaned against the counter and started checking her iPhone. "How sweet, you're being domestic."

I shook my head—that off feeling still nagged at me, but I just couldn't place it. I really needed coffee. Coffee would make everything better.

She tapped at her iPhone, not looking up. "Anything to eat in this God-awful place?"

I sighed. Maybe I should be looking for a tea that would cure Chrissy.

Acknowledgements

It's a team effort to birth a book, and I'd like to take a moment to thank everyone who helped, especially my wonderful editor, Megan Yakovich, who is always so patient with me, Rea Carr for her expert proofing support, and my husband Paul, for his love and support during this sometimes-painful birthing process.

Any mistakes are mine and mine alone.

About Michele

When Michele was 3 years old, she taught herself to read because she wanted to write stories so badly.

As you can imagine, writing has been a driving passion throughout her life.

* She's an award-winning, bestselling fiction author, writing a range of mystery novels, from psychological suspense to cozies.

* She's a bestselling nonfiction author, creating the popular "Love-Based Business" series of books.

* She's also a professional copywriter, blogger and journalist.

She holds a double major in English and Communications from the University of Wisconsin-Madison. Currently she lives in the mountains of Prescott, Arizona with her husband Paul and southern squirrel hunter Cassie.